by C. & S.L. RY. between

MORDEN

LON. GENERAL O'BUS to & from
) or SUTTON STATION No. (2)

UNTIL

SEASON TICKET

London Electric Ry.
Issued subject to the Co's
Bye laws, Regulations and
advertised conditions.
Available day of issue only.

Lon.Elec.Ry. (SBE
Issued subject to the Co.'s
Bye-Laws, Regulations and
advertised conditions
Available day of issue only

000
Wood Lane
(Shepherds Bush)C.L.Ry.
(1) TO
GOODGE STREET
Via Tottenham Court Road
Not transferable
(SBE) 1s. Day Child 1s. day Child

Goodge Street
(1) TO
WOOD LANE
(Shepherds Bush) C.L.Ry
Via Tottenham Court Road
Including Entrance to
SHEPHERDS BUSH
EXHIBITION
Fare 9d
000

B
London Passenger Transport Board
Available day of
issue only.
Available day of
issue only.
Valid for Bus Journey
Southfields

Stn. Kensington
TO

10000

SOUTHFIELDS
Via Earls Court
or ALL ENGLAND
TENNIS GROUND

TO
TENNISGROUND

3rd.ClassFare 8
To be cancelled on Bo
South Kens.(M.1

3rd. CLASS (SINGLE
To be surrendered at
Southfields Stat
For conditions see back

SHOPPING.

ON TICKET FOR
ES ONLY.

ny Station between
E and LIVERPOOL
er 10 a.m. during
ber, 1912.
ly Representative of

Travelcard
ZONES
1 2 3a
OUTER

D1493486

Photocard No.

£7.40

C

Weekly ⊖ 103969

£11. 2s. 0d. R

GREAT MISSENDEN

and BAKER ST. or MARYLEBONE

UNTIL

GM

via HARROW

NOT TRANSFERABLE · FOR CONDITIONS SEE BACK

Holder's Name

London Electric Railway.
Issued subject to the Companies' Bye-laws, Regulations
and advertised Conditions.

3 09154

BRENT
TO

COLINDALE
HAMPSTEAD
or intermediate

2d THIRD CLASS FARE 2d
Available day of issue only.

3 09154

3/6 AVAILABLE BETWEEN 3/6

BANK
AND
47
CLAPHAM COMMON

UNTIL Saturday 2 2 NOV 1930

Signature
This ticket is not valid unless it is signed by holder in ink or indelible pencil

No. CC. 3629

THIRD CLASS.

LONDON TRANSPORT 1

LAST DAY OF STEAM SHUTTLE
OPERATION
11th SEPTEMBER, 1960

Chesham
to
CHALFONT & LATIMER

2nd Cl. Fare 10d
For conditions see over

0156

METROPOLITAN LINE

SPECIAL TRAIN

BAKER ST. - AMERSHAM

15 JUNE 1962

160

LONDON TRANSPORT in conjunction
with The LOCAL AUTHORITY

Admit one Person for Shelter
(if available) at
COLLIERS WOOD Station

Persons permitted to use this
Station as, or as a means of access to, an
Air Raid Shelter do so at their own risk
in all respects.
FOR FURTHER CONDITIONS SEE BACK

100

37546

CENTRAL LONDON RAILWAY

Bk. 2d 13.
(1)
SINGLE JOURNEY
to or from any Station.

London Transport
Issued subject to the Bye-
laws, Regulations and
Conditions of the L.T.
Executive.
2nd June 1953
Available by any
Train from
Westminster
TO
HIGH ST (KENS)
Fare 10d
Not Transferable

London Transport
2nd June 1953
Available only by
SPECIAL TRAIN
at 8.45 a.m.
from
High St. (Kens)
TO
WESTMINSTER
Fare 10d
Not Transferable

0546

0546

1ST
HARROW
ON THE HILL
&
BAKER
STREET

oyster™

Issued subject to conditions — see over

⊖

VE Commemorative Travelcard

104531

V

Valid Saturday 6 May to Monday 8 May 1995
Adult Zones 1, 2, 3 & 4 £6.60
No photocard required

Y TICKET BETWEEN 7/3

Y HILL
2
GARDEN
TSBRIDGE
6 MAR 1940
in ink or indelible pencil above

SU 2224

3

UNDERGROUND

CITY & SOUTH LONDON RAILWAY

Mr

is entitled to travel between

BANK
and
CLAPHAM ROAD
CANCELLED
AVAILABLE UNTIL

4 MAR. 15

NOT TRANSFERABLE.

RATE £0 11s. 3D.

REDUCED RATE TICKET
ISSUED TO PASSENGER UNDER 18

No. 461 SEASON TICKET

UNDERGROUND

UNDERGROUND

HOW THE TUBE SHAPED LONDON

DAVID BOWNES
OLIVER GREEN
SAM MULLINS

ALLEN LANE
an imprint of
PENGUIN BOOKS
www.penguin.com

ALLEN LANE

Published by the Penguin Group
Penguin Books Ltd, 80 Strand, London WC2R 0RL, England
Penguin Group (USA) Inc., 375 Hudson Street, New York, New York 10014, USA
Penguin Group (Canada), 90 Eglinton Avenue East, Suite 700, Toronto, Ontario,
Canada M4P 2Y3 (a division of Pearson Canada Inc.)
Penguin Ireland, 25 St Stephen's Green, Dublin 2, Ireland (a division of Penguin Books Ltd)
Penguin Group (Australia), 250 Camberwell Road, Camberwell, Victoria 3124,
Australia (a division of Pearson Australia Group Pty Ltd)
Penguin Books India Pvt Ltd, 11 Community Centre,
Panchsheel Park, New Delhi – 110 017, India
Penguin Group (NZ), 67 Apollo Drive, Rosedale, Auckland 0632, New Zealand
(a division of Pearson New Zealand Ltd)
Penguin Books (South Africa) (Pty) Ltd, 24 Sturdee Avenue,
Rosebank 2196, South Africa

Penguin Books Ltd, Registered Offices: 80 Strand, London WC2R 0RL, England

www.penguin.com

First published 2012
1

Copyright © London Transport Museum, 2012

The moral right of the authors has been asserted

Typeset by Estuary English
Colour Reproduction by Tag: response
Printed in China

ISBN: 978-1-846-14462-2

CONTENTS

FOREWORD

Peter Hendy CBE,
Commissioner, Transport for London

The Underground described in this story is a vital part of the history of London itself. Over its first 150 years it has become a barometer of the economic health and vigour of one of the world's great cities, and today it is impossible to imagine one without the other. London and its Underground are indivisible.

Looking back from 2012 as head of Transport for London, I am acutely aware that today's citizens, commuters and visitors owe a huge debt to the visionaries, engineers and administrators of the past who created the astonishing system that keeps the city on the move.

Not long ago I was at 55 Broadway, the ancestral head office of London Transport and still the home of London Underground. I was addressing a meeting in the former chairman's office under the imperious gaze of Lord Ashfield, who created London Transport eighty years ago. From above the fireplace his imposing portrait looks down on his successors. For me he seems to have a particularly questioning look. What would he make of the state of transport in London today, compared with the great era when he was chairman of the new authority from 1933?

In 2012 he would still see in TfL the benefits of a unified transport body, something he always argued was essential for London. Today TfL covers a smaller area than his enormous empire stretching from Hitchin to Horsham, but it has wider responsibilities than London Transport, with better integration of services across the whole spectrum of travel.

The arteries of the Underground, Overground, DLR and bus routes provide the essential framework, supplemented by taxis, Tramlink and riverboats. TfL also has overarching responsibility for main roads, traffic management, cycling and walking, which covers practically everything that moves in the city.

Surely Ashfield would be impressed by the simplicity of the Oyster card and the online Journey Planner in revolutionising the customer's experience of this complex urban network. He would recognise the powerful brand, design and marketing as well as the systems that determine now, as they did then, how London develops, and the opportunities and constraints that go with them.

I have no doubt that eighty years ago the 'golden age' of London Transport was achieved through Ashfield's own exceptional political acumen coupled with the administrative ability of his brilliant chief executive, Frank Pick. But Ashfield would also confirm that success depends on the contribution of skilled and dedicated teams and individuals in every area of an organisation. TfL has fewer staff today but is responsible for far more journeys than London Transport in its heyday.

The remarkable recent changes in investment levels and revenue funding for London's transport are the result of having a strong elected Mayor with access to Government not available to a conventional public appointee. Since 2000 both London Mayors have taken the view that they should use transport as a primary tool for London's economic, social and environmental development.

The results are exciting and have brought world-wide interest in London's achievements. Wherever you look – and it is my job to look beyond the Underground across the whole of TfL – our service has great demands placed upon it and is constantly improving. London remains the engine of national economic growth, enabled by a second golden age in transport, even in the midst of recession. I believe we can look Ashfield and the other giants of this story in the eye and be confident that we have carried forward their impressive legacy.

INTRODUCTION

London and its transport are synonymous. The Underground roundel and the Tube map signify London. It's difficult to imagine London today without the Underground. Practically everybody uses it: Londoners, commuters, tourists, visitors, students, shoppers, clubbers, sports fans, theatre-goers, art lovers, young and old, for work or leisure. The Underground carries more people today than at any time in its 150-year history. Londoners since the mid-nineteenth century have been moved, and the identity of their city defined, by the growth of the transport system. The extent of the capital and the size of its population have repeatedly threatened to bring it to a standstill, only for it to be rescued by transport innovation. Today 1.2 billion journeys a year, four million a day, are made on the Underground alone. The Underground network is the beating heart of London: occasionally sclerotic, under constant repair, delivered daily by an operational miracle, subject to perennial and sceptical scrutiny, always close to the top of the Mayor's agenda. Mobility is a defining characteristic of a city; that is the point of the concentration of work and leisure which makes urban life so persuasive. The Underground and London's buses have provided the mobility which makes the city work and which are essential to its future sustainability.

A city of eight million-plus people and one as old and complex as London is a sophisticated organism. The triumph of the Underground is more than the movement of its citizens. The pervasive and essential nature of mass transport forms an integral part of the urban environment of London; through the blood-red tiling of Leslie Green's Edwardian stations, in his platform tile patterns and in the modernist station designs of Charles Holden for the Northern and Piccadilly lines. The Johnston typeface is London's alphabet, cutting cleanly through the visual clutter of the city's streets, while the Underground

U is the Underground,
pride of the nation,
The triumph of science
and civilisation.

1. Brixton station in 2008. Opened in 1971 and refurbished from 2001.

2. 'U is the Underground'. A page from a children's alphabet by Charles Pears, published by the Underground in 1915.

roundel stands out as a clear marker for stations and bus stops and symbolizes the brand, the civic values, of this public service. The Underground map is a visual representation of the layout of the city, a simplification of an otherwise extensive and complex city landscape. Visitors praise the Tube because the system and its map make it simple to move around the centre, while Londoners themselves understand its limitations and the large areas of London which it does not cover. It has become the mental map of the capital for both visitor and resident.

The world's first underground railway was proposed as a means of connecting the mainline railway stations, then restricted to the edges of the capital, with the City. In the 1850s London was grinding to a halt under the weight of horse-drawn wheeled traffic and pedestrians. In 1846 a regular traveller from Brighton found it quicker to walk from the railway terminus at London Bridge to his office in Trafalgar Square than to go by omnibus or cab. Eight years later the chairman of the London, Brighton and South Coast Railway confirmed this; he never took a cab if he was anywhere east of Temple Bar because he could not calculate to a quarter of an hour the time it would take to cross London Bridge.[1] Later in the century, the deep Tube was needed as a lasting solution to London's worsening traffic problems. London grew quickly as the focal point of the governance and trade of the British Empire, which embraced nearly a quarter of the world's population. Greater London's population grew from around one million in 1800 to over seven million by 1914 and to a peak in 1939 of 8.6 million. With a population of 8.3 million today, London is the prime economic mover at the heart of the UK's south-east region of up to 18 million people.

In the late Victorian period London's suburban railways and the surface extensions to the original underground lines both stimulated and defined the outward expansion of the urban area. By the turn of the century, the cutting-edge application of tunnelling, lift and electric traction technologies made it possible to create the world's first electric-powered deep tube railway and keep the centre of the capital moving beneath its busy streets. As London spread outwards between the wars, the growing Underground became the principal transport mode connecting the new suburbs with the shopper's West End and the banker's City.

Post-war planning policy promoted the extension of London's influence beyond the newly created Green Belt and sought to move homes and businesses out of the capital. The years of austerity after the war saw the Underground nationalized and neglected in favour of investment in the national rail network, health, education and social services. From the 1960s it became clear that the rise of the car had the potential to destroy the city, and a renewed commitment to mass transport led to new lines being built across the central zone to increase the capacity of the Tube system. From the mid-1980s, the population of central London began to grow again, as city living became once more desirable and fashionable, and as the rise of the City after the Big Bang fuelled inner-city regeneration.

3

4

3. Arnos Grove station opened in 1932, one of Holden's finest designs for the Underground.

4. Today, Arnos Grove station is a listed building, but still a working station like any other on the network.

Transport is symbiotic with the city, and the state of the Underground is a barometer for the health of London. The dirty, run-down, litter- and graffiti-strewn Tube of the 1980s said much about the state of the city at the time. At key periods in London's history, the Underground led the way. The heart of the network was created during the Edwardian era, through the innovation of deep tube lines and the application of corporate branding to what had been planned as a series of individual lines. Between the wars, under Ashfield and Pick, the Underground was the world's premier metro and a remarkable patron of the arts and architecture. In the 1990s, the Jubilee line extension echoed the interwar design tradition and was the essential enabler of Canary Wharf and London's current pre-eminence in global financial services.

The Underground also mirrors the place of London in relation to the rest of the UK. It is the only city with a substantial underground network. In the aftermath of the Second World War, government sought to disperse people and jobs away from London. With the post-war recession, the Underground was starved of investment and, despite the isolated triumphs of the Victoria line, half a Jubilee line and extensions to Heathrow, the system and London itself went into slow decline. The municipal socialism of the Livingstone years at the GLC saw a vision for transport in London proposed for the first time which was much closer to continental models, where transport was not just a cost on the city but a

5

6

key enabler of civilized life. Despite Frank Pick's high-minded view of the civilizing influence of the Underground, it has only recently attracted significant public funding. It was entirely privately funded until the 1930s with no municipal contribution from the London County Council and very little government funding after nationalization in 1948. After the transfer to the GLC in 1970, capital and revenue subsidy was limited, and the Underground remained largely funded by passenger revenues.

The early 1980s were a watershed for thinking on civic investment in London. The private car was no longer the saviour of the city; indeed it was its potential nemesis. Plans for more tarmac and the concrete motorway box were replaced by a more integrated and holistic approach to this complex and multi-layered city, for which Tube and bus were of renewed significance. 'Fares Fair' left the legacy of a ticketing system which was simple, easy to access with a fixed daily cost; in 1984 the Travelcard promoted the use of public transport and led eventually to the liberating facility of the Oyster card.

When the city is under the greatest stress, the true worth of its transport becomes clear. During the dark days of 1940–41, with London under attack every night for months, the deep Tube stations provided safe shelters for beleaguered citizens.

5. Metropolitan Railway ticket, 1868. Written on the reverse: 'Spent the whole day at 34 Albion Rd ... after exploring the new Ry, the fares along which are MONSTROUS'.

6. The Oyster smartcard was introduced in London in 2003. Over seven million cards were regularly in use in 2012.

Although Tube shelters provided in reality only a small proportion of refuges from the bombs, the camaraderie of this era has formed a significant part of Londoners' self-image. The running of the first buses, trams and trains across a battered and burned city in the morning after a raid was a matter of pride to London Transport staff and a hugely symbolic act for Londoners. With the capital under the most severe attack, transport was a symbol of normality, of the day-to-day. In July 2005, when once more under attack, this time from terrorists, the city's mobility was suddenly interrupted, and the resumption of transport services later the same day was of huge significance and positively palliative after such a terrible shock. London's public transport, with the Tube at its core, has proved to be a key factor in the capital's remarkable resilience.

Since the Second World War, most decisions about major public transport projects in London have been characterized by delay and uncertainty. Whatever the rational planning background, the social or regenerative benefits anticipated or the congestion to be relieved, because of the scale of costs and longevity of transport infrastructure the decision will be politically motivated. Michael Robbins, a senior figure in London Transport as the Managing Director for Railways (and also the organization's historian), saw a familiar pattern when writing in 1974: 'The story of the development of the Victoria line ... shows characteristic features of public handling of investment projects in mid-twentieth century Britain: general acceptance of the intention as desirable; delay for argument on constantly changing bases; final approval under temporary pressures which were largely irrelevant to the arguments.' Christian Wolmar has suggested adding 'constant rows over financing and cost overruns during construction'. This pattern was to be seen for the Fleet/Jubilee line and later for the Jubilee line extension. Public transport investment has a scale of expenditure and a horizon for the payback of political, social or economic benefits so long after the next local or national election that major projects from the Victoria line to Crossrail have been proposed, debated,

7 8

7. Damage caused by a V1 bomb attack on the Circle line near South Kensington, August 1944. The Underground kept running throughout the Second World War.

8. The aftermath of one of the suicide attacks on the Underground on 7 July 2005. A bomb exploded on one of these Circle line trains near Edgware Road.

buffeted, stopped and restarted; regardless of social cost benefit, there is no avoiding the reality that transport is a major political issue.

The post-war decline up to 1987 amounted to a failure in corporate management but also to a failure in political management of the Underground. The Tube is too crucial to London to be seen as a problem of cost, but that was how the Department for Transport viewed it in the 1970s and 80s. National government tended to regard transport in London as expensive and demanding relative to its political importance. Since 2000, transport has been the London Mayor's largest single responsibility. It takes up most of the budget, it is business critical for London; and its problems will always be on the front page. The transport strategy for the Olympic site in Stratford was a crucial element in securing the 2012 Olympics. For an elected politician, transport has huge vote-losing potential. It can no longer be ignored or left solely to transport managers. It's too important to the south-east region, which generates a third of the UK's wealth. Critically, unlike his post-war predecessors, the Mayor does not have to go cap in hand to the Secretary of State for Transport as he has the backing of London's powerful business interests and his office is of such stature that he can deal directly with the Prime Minister.

Political influence on funding the Tube has tightened steadily since the Second World War. It has proved far more attractive for ministers to announce shiny new lines and stations rather than an investment in repair and renewal of existing lines. While the major works programmes of the 1930s had balanced new lines and maintaining the existing system, the Victoria and Jubilee lines were approved only after long struggles in the politically charged era of the 1960s and 70s, at the expense of the rest of the network. Ultimately the Public Private Partnership (PPP) from 2003 concentrated purely on

renewal of the existing infrastructure. Endless changes in the governance of the Underground between local and national control consumed energy and promoted short-term solutions. It is only with the consistent importance of transport to an elected mayor that consensus on a long-term view has been finally achieved. Tony Travers of the London School of Economics is clear that 'there has been the largest, most consistent investment in the Tube that's ever been achieved and that has been maintained even in the current financial climate. It's inevitably to do with the lobbying power of the Mayor'.[2]

It is unlikely that another small-diameter Tube line will be built beneath London. The 1906

9. Piccadilly Circus station, at its opening in 1906.   10. The same view at Piccadilly Circus station almost a century later, 2001.

tiled stations with their three-car trains are today packed to capacity with an intense day-long service in full-length seven- or eight-car trains. The Tube's restricted loading gauge – at its maximum the tunnels are 12 feet (3.66 metres) in diameter – is unlikely to provide the carrying capacity needed in the future. The development of the Overground and the inevitable and necessary integration between suburban rail in London and the Underground are filling in key gaps in the mass transit network in east and south London and providing orbital links to reduce the pressure on the central area. The Overground is on the Underground map, and passengers regard it as an addition to the Tube network. Crossrail is being built on a mainline railway scale with a tunnel diameter of 6.2 metres while Crossrail 2, the former Hackney–Chelsea line, could also be built to the same scale. Crossrail will be an integrated part of the Underground rail system as the Overground has rapidly become since the transfer to Transport for London (TfL) in 2007. Any future small Tube railways are likely to be limited additions such as the proposed Northern line branch to Battersea rather than whole new lines. Transport is now recognized as being too important to the vitality and viability of the capital for anything other than a long-term view of station and line capacity to be taken.

Farringdon, the original City terminus of the world's first underground railway, where the celebratory opening banquet was held on 9 January 1863, will become a major transport hub in the near future. There is already interchange between the Underground and north–south cross-London Thameslink services here. By 2018 a much enlarged and modernized transport complex, including a brand new Crossrail station below the Underground and Thameslink, will be used by up to 140 trains an hour and 150,000 passengers a day. Part of the original station structure from the 1860s and the 1920s

II. The first permanent station buildings at Farringdon, opened in 1868.

booking hall will remain, carefully renovated as listed buildings for continued future use. This busy urban interchange will see the integration of London Underground's oldest tangible heritage with Crossrail, Europe's biggest current infrastructure project. Thus one of the network's first stations will regain its original primacy. Across the network, the historic infrastructure gives it character and is pressed by today's heavy use in a way its original proponents could never have envisaged.

In an age when the pace of change and economic recession have placed many of our great institutions under pressure to maintain popularity and relevance, the London Underground, suggests one contemporary commentator, 'is more expansive and confident now than at any time in memory'.[3] And yet Londoners' relationship with their Tube remains paradoxical. The Underground has a 'reputation for having a bad reputation', suggested one TfL customer research specialist recently in seeking to unpick this conundrum, yet those same people when asked generally express high satisfaction with their last journey and more Londoners than ever believe the Tube to be 'on the up'. 'Few, if any, brands have an image that is more at odds with the organization's actual service performance.' Brand associations with the Underground are almost wholly independent of the actual journey experience.

Negative associations with being underground go back to the earliest days of the Metropolitan and have persisted into the twenty-first century, despite the fact that much

12. Artist's impression of Crossrail station at Farringdon, due to open in 2018.

of the outer network is above ground. Alongside rational complaints about reliability and ageing infrastructure, it is suggested, are long-term more emotional and deep-rooted feelings about the alien and claustrophobic environment of the Tube; 'dirty', 'depressing', 'dingy', 'dangerous' and 'dark' are the words commonly used to express those fears, which are at odds with today's clean, bright and secure system. At the heart of this appears to be the primal fear of being underground. The 7/7 bombings were greeted by a universal sense of outrage by and through the media but the 'intrinsically alien nature of the underground environment ... made the carnage even more horrific and frightening'. The bus network, despite being slower and with lower perceptions of safety and security, scores higher for Londoners simply because it is above ground and without the apparently deep ethnographic connotations of travelling underground.[4]

Rolling back the years of under-investment since the start of the PPP in 2003 have accustomed Londoners to prolonged weekend closures of parts of the system. But the Underground and its passengers are starting to see the benefits of that long-term sustained investment – more and longer trains, state-of-the-art signalling, major stations rebuilt, real-time information, better communication with customers – as well as the additional capacity of the Overground, the facility of Oyster 'through' ticketing on the

13. Earl's Court District Railway station, 1896.

national rail network and the promise of Crossrail. Against the background of 3.5 million journeys a day and up to 4.1 million on the busiest days – more than double that of 1982 – this is a remarkable achievement, the equal of London Transport's golden age of the 1930s.

The story of London's Underground over the last 150 years that is told in this book reflects the wider social and economic history of the great metropolis. It is a tale of trains and technology from the age of steam to the convenience of the smartphone, but it is also much more than this. It is a narrative of money, politics and urban geography. The story involves managers, technicians, planners, engineers, architects and designers, transport staff and their passengers. The focus shifts in different periods of our timespan from alleviating the problems of the crowded city centre to the creation of the suburbs, from issues of urban regeneration in Docklands and east London to the challenge of upgrading the oldest metro in the world to be fit for purpose in the twenty-first century. The Underground has played a key role in both shaping and serving London and the changing needs of its citizens. It remains the lifeblood of the city today and will become ever more important to London's future sustainability.

A note on the authors

All three authors have played a part in London Transport Museum's development and aspiration since 1980 to become the world's leading museum of urban transport, preserving and presenting collections of major historic importance, and the tangible material and knowledge which informs this narrative. As it is not a straightforward single narrative, we have taken a slightly different approach as authors where this seemed appropriate, rather than trying to create a seamless chronological sequence. David Bownes contributed chapters 1 and 4, Oliver Green chapters 2 and 3, and Sam Mullins chapters 5 and 6. However, we take collective responsibility as authors for the whole book, including any errors that may have crept in. Opinions expressed are our own, except where attributed to others, and do not necessarily reflect the official view of Transport for London or London Underground.

14. Earl's Court District line station, c.1990.

CHAPTER I

THE VICTORIAN UNDERGROUND

Shortly after 1.00 p.m. on 9 January 1863 the inaugural train of the world's first underground railway pulled out of Paddington station in west London, to begin a 3½-mile journey under the capital's streets and into the history books. The ground-breaking line had been built and financed by a private company, the Metropolitan Railway, to link the mainline stations at Paddington, Euston and King's Cross with the business district of central London. Much of the operational equipment and infrastructure, however, would have seemed very familiar to observers. The train itself consisted of an ordinary-looking steam locomotive and several conventional carriages, while the wide-vaulted roof covering the twin tracks had the appearance of a traditional railway tunnel – quite unlike the deep-level tubes which later generations would associate with the 'underground'. It wasn't even very deep underground, with just a flight of steps leading from the street to the platform. Yet there was something truly novel and exciting about this new form of travel which led hundreds of cheering well-wishers to gather for the departure of the first train. The *Daily News* probably came closest to summing up the sense of fascination felt by many at the time: 'For the first time in the history of the world men can ride in pleasant carriages, and with considerable comfort, lower down than gas pipes and water pipes . . . lower than the graveyards.'[1]

It was a novelty that thousands of Londoners were eager to experience for themselves, although they had to wait another twenty-four hours before the line was open to the general public. Instead, the first passengers were all VIPs (and mainly men), drawn from the business people and engineers who had built the railway, together with the landowners, MPs and civic dignitaries whose continued support they relied on. At each station along the way, the train stopped for the guests to inspect the work and to admire what one newspaper called 'the most stupendous engineering undertaking yet achieved in the railway world'.[2] No detail of ventilation shafts or gas lighting was too minor to escape lengthy explanation. A gruelling two and a half hours later, rather than the eighteen minutes scheduled for normal service, the exhausted travellers reached the temporary Farringdon Street terminus.

I. One of the first underground trains approaching
Baker Street station, 1863.

There they were greeted with an even more frantic display of popular enthusiasm before being whisked off for a sumptuous banquet held within the station itself and accompanied by 'enlivening airs' performed by the band of the City of London Police. Amongst the 700 assembled diners were the Lord Mayor of London and various members of the government, although notable by his absence was the Prime Minister, Lord Palmerston, who had replied that at seventy-nine he would prefer to stay above the ground for a few more years.

OPENING OF THE METROPOLITAN RAILWAY: BANQUET AT THE FARRINGDON-STREET STATION.—SEE SUPPLEMENT, PAGE 74.

As the last dishes were cleared away the inevitable speeches began, faithfully reported in the daily papers that week alongside stories from the American Civil War and rebellion in Poland. But such international concerns were a long way from the minds of the assembled dignitaries in London as they enjoyed the free cigars and brandy laid on by their host, the Metropolitan Railway. Their focus, not surprisingly, was on the profits the new venture would bring and its benefit to London's economy. A series of triumphant speakers, each heralded by a trumpet call, praised the ingenuity of the railway company and the wisdom of its financial backers in bringing about such a miracle of public transport. City Fathers were praised, too, for their enlightened support, although there was never much doubt that the day belonged to the men of commerce rather than the politicians.

2. The luxurious banquet laid on for the Metropolitan Railway's backers and supporters at Farringdon Street station, 9 January 1863. According to contemporary accounts the walls and ceiling were lined with red-and-white cloth, decorated with 'banners of all the nations' (*Illustrated London News*, 17 January 1863).

The launch had been a great success, and the guests were doubtless entitled to their moment of self-congratulation. But in its celebration of private capital and business interests the banquet was more than just a tipsy junket for stakeholders. It was an affirmation of the aims of the underground pioneers that set the tone for the development of London's Underground for the rest of the nineteenth century and beyond.

The birth of the underground

The origins of the world's first underground railway lay in the search for a solution to London's traffic problem. By the mid-nineteenth century, London was the largest and most prosperous city in the world. Its success, based on Britain's rapidly growing empire, led to an unprecedented explosion in the city's population, from just under one million in 1800, to over 2.5 million by the time of the Great Exhibition in 1851. Each day an estimated quarter of a million people journeyed to work in the financial and administrative heart of the capital, known as the City.

London had become a modern metropolis, with institutions and ambitions to match. Yet it lacked an urban transport system to support development. Railways, which began to appear from the 1830s, were initially banished from the city centre, while the narrow, congested, streets retained a medieval appearance, filled to capacity with slow-moving horse-drawn traffic. Cabs and horse buses (first introduced in 1829) provided the only public transport, for those who could afford the fares, but with traffic at a near standstill many preferred to walk. This in turn meant that most Londoners had to live near to their place of employment, with an inevitable rise in property values, and slum housing for the worst off. Something had to be done.

There had, in fact, been some efforts to improve the situation before the 1850s, most notably the construction of 'New Road' (now the Marylebone and Euston Roads) in 1756 to connect the growing villages of Paddington and

3. Gustave Doré's famous depiction of congestion at Ludgate Circus, in the heart of the City, 1872. Published almost ten years after the underground was opened to supposedly alleviate such scenes, it serves as a reminder that there has never been an easy solution to London's traffic problems. Among the maelstrom of vehicles are horse buses, Hackney cabs, horse-drawn wagons and a flock of sheep being driven to market – a familiar sight until railways took over the transportation of livestock.

Islington with the City, and the creation of Regent Street (1825) to alleviate congestion around Charing Cross and the western end of the Strand. In the absence of a single London-wide planning authority to coordinate improvement, though, such initiatives were bound to be inconsistently pursued. The notoriously congested streets leading into the City from the north (along the course of the old Fleet River) remained scandalously unimproved. Robert Stephenson, the famous railway engineer, had considered extending the London and Birmingham Railway from its terminus at Euston (opened in 1837) along this route to Waterloo Bridge but was deterred by the high costs. Similar proposals followed, prompted by the success of London's first suburban railway to Greenwich (1836-7) which had shown the potential of such routes to make money, yet these too failed to get past the planning stage.

They did, however, attract the attention of the City of London Solicitor Charles Pearson, a social reformer who was to play an important role in the Undergound's birth. Pearson believed that railways held the key to transforming the city as part of a wider programme of road building and slum clearance, including the provision of cheap rail tickets to enable the displaced poor to live in healthier surroundings outside London. In 1845 he brought these ideas together in a pamphlet to show how a street-level railway, drawn by atmospheric power and encased in glazed arches, would transform the Fleet

valley and improve connections between the City and the mainline railways converging on north London. When this failed to get the necessary support, Pearson turned his attention to the potential of a semi-underground railway following a similar route from a new central London station at Farringdon to a connection near the recently opened King's Cross railway station. From here further connections could potentially be made with the mainline stations at Euston and Paddington, although Pearson's scheme did not make clear how this would be achieved.

Meanwhile, the so-called Railway Mania of the 1840s had resulted in an avalanche of competing schemes to criss-cross London with new routes, prompting parliament to take a strategic view despite its laissez-faire instincts. The result was the Royal Commission on Metropolitan Railway Termini (1846), which ruled that stations should be sited on the edge of the city, and railways banned from crossing the central area. This decision, prompted by a desire to preserve the integrity of the city centre, virtually ensured that some sort of sub-surface railway would be needed to link the termini together. As one recent historian of the Underground has commented, 'Pearson was promoting an idea whose time had come'.[3]

Even so, Pearson's commitment to expensive road-building and slum-clearance projects as part of the overall vision ensured the collapse of his next attempt in 1851, which failed to interest either the banks or the mainline railway companies. Clearly, philanthropic outcomes alone were

4. Charles Pearson (1793–1862). Of all the promoters, financiers, businessmen and idealists associated with the early underground, Pearson had the vision and tenacity to bring the dream to reality. A social reformer, campaigner, and briefly MP for Lambeth, he used his position as City Solicitor to push schemes aimed at improving the lot of ordinary Londoners by tackling the capital's growing traffic problem.

not going to sway the businessmen whose support mattered most. Undaunted, Pearson and his supporters regrouped as the City Terminus Company to press on with the scheme, albeit in a modified form.

Their efforts gained unexpected support from a new, and more commercially motivated, venture known at first as the Bayswater, Paddington & Holborn Bridge Railway. This company developed Pearson's aims to their obvious conclusion by proposing to extend his route from Holborn northward to link Paddington, King's Cross and Euston stations with the City. Unlike the City Terminus project, this scheme did not involve demolishing houses or costly road-building. Instead, the railway would be built under the existing New Road. Pearson's friend John Hargreaves Stevens was appointed surveyor, with John (later Sir John) Fowler as engineer. In many ways, this line was the true originator of the underground and received the Royal Assent in 1853 as the North Metropolitan Railway.

Pearson's more altruistic plan fared less well and was gradually absorbed into the larger ambitions of the North Metropolitan. His dream of a central London terminus was dropped, although his original proposal for a railway along the Fleet valley to Farringdon was retained, albeit largely underground. Further modifications to the North Metropolitan's approved plans included a direct connection with the Great Western Railway at Paddington, bringing the total estimated costs to £1 million. After much legal wrangling, the modifications were approved by parliament in 1854 and, with a few changes to the route over the ensuing four years, became the Metropolitan Railway – the world's first underground.

Even so, it took a huge leap of faith to persuade financiers to support an underground railway – a radical, and not at first obvious, solution to the capital's transport problems. Indeed, in the mid-1850s a number of rival, and equally original, alternatives were put forward in response to a government inquiry. These included a 12-mile railway built above ground and encased in an iron and glass arcade incorporating houses and shops. The 'Grand Girdle Railway and Boulevard under Glass', as it was inelegantly known, was the brainchild of Sir Joseph Paxton, who had previously designed the Crystal Palace. Like Pearson's original scheme, it was designed to run on 'atmospheric power', with trains pulled silently, and smokelessly, by pneumatic pumps. A similar atmospheric railway, the Crystal Way,

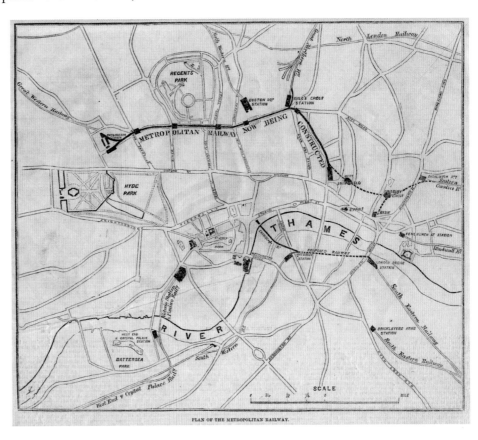

PLAN OF THE METROPOLITAN RAILWAY.

5. The route of the Metropolitan Railway as finally agreed, linking Paddington, Euston and King's Cross stations with the City. Published in the *Illustrated London News* 7 April, 1860.

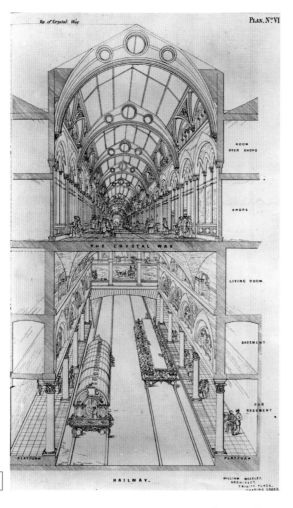

was put forward by William Moseley, with the railway running at basement level beneath a multi-storey arcade of shops and walkways.

Ultimately, these schemes were rejected as being too expensive and too intrusive. Underground railways, on the other hand, had the advantage of not incurring the exorbitant cost of purchasing and demolishing properties along the route, providing they followed the paths of existing roads. There were other risks, though, for potential investors to worry about. How would the underground be built? Tunnels and railway cuttings were all very well in the countryside, but could they support the huge weight of overhead city traffic? And what about subsidence to neighbouring buildings, resulting in massive compensation claims, to say nothing of the technical problems of operating steam locomotives underground?

John Fowler and his colleagues at the Metropolitan proved more than a match for the critics, bringing forth a welter of expert opinion to support their cause, although Fowler later admitted that many of the practical difficulties of construction and operation were only solved through hands-on experimentation, rather than detailed pre-planning. Of particular weight in swaying the parliamentary doubters was the evidence of Isambard

6. William Moseley's unsuccessful plan for a multi-storey 'Crystal Way', between St Paul's and Oxford Circus (1855).

7. Sir Joseph Paxton's proposed Grand Girdle Railway (1855). The 12-mile circular railway broadly anticipated the route taken by the Circle Line thirty years later.

Kingdom Brunel, the greatest and most famous engineer of his time, who had told the 1854 inquiry that 'it would be perfectly easy to work this line with an ordinary locomotive, without any peculiar artificial means of ventilation', adding dismissively that he thought 'the impression had been exploded long since that railway tunnels require much ventilation.'[4]

Raising the money was to prove trickier, though, a task made worse by an uncertain money market throughout the late 1850s and the reluctance of the mainline companies to invest. In 1858 the Metropolitan was almost wound up in despair, spending £1,000 of shareholder money on advertising in a last-ditch attempt to attract funding. Pearson's continued support for the project now proved critical. He used his role as City of London Solicitor to persuade the Corporation to invest in the underground, arguing that business in the City was being damaged by the congested roads and workers forced to live in squalid conditions because they had to walk to work. Whatever the motivation of his partners might have been, Pearson remained resolutely committed to the philanthropic aims of his original vision, telling a meeting of Metropolitan shareholders in 1858 that 'no English railway scheme could hope to attain support unless it could be shown to be useful to the public', cannily adding that it should also be profitable for the investors.[5]

Pearson's tireless efforts, which included writing a pamphlet encouraging Londoners to become shareholders in the venture, paid off. With the City's financial backing, and support from both the Great Western and Great Northern railways, enough capital was at last forthcoming to enable construction to begin in 1860.

The first underground railway

The crucial job of chief engineer was given to John Fowler, who remained with the project from his appointment in 1853 through to the official opening ten years later. Another long-standing supporter of the scheme, John Parson, was put in charge of building operations, with the construction contracts split between John Jay and Smith & Knight. The entire 3½ mile route would be built in covered cuttings, except for a 700-yard conventional tunnel under the hill of Mount Pleasant in Clerkenwell, using mixed-gauge track to accommodate the differing widths of Great Western and Great Northern trains.

The main section, from Paddington to King's Cross, ran directly under the New Road and consequently didn't require the demolition of any buildings. This wasn't the case though, for the second part, which veered south at King's Cross down

8

8. John Fowler (1817–98). Fowler's career began in Yorkshire and Lincolnshire during the 1840s. He became chief engineer for both the Metropolitan and District underground railways and was later responsible for many railway schemes at home and abroad, including the Forth Railway Bridge in Scotland (1890). He was knighted in 1885.

the crowded Fleet valley to Farringdon. As the law required railway companies to buy any property they passed under, the Metropolitan was obliged to purchase, and then demolish, many homes that lay in its path. The enormous costs were to some extent ameliorated by a deal brokered by Pearson with the City Corporation, which had sold the railway a prime parcel of land at Farringdon for a knock-down rate. Other land deals went better than expected, with the Company surveyor able to report that purchases were nearly complete and within budget by February 1860.[6]

The official number of people displaced was put at 307 – a remarkably low figure, especially when compared with the destruction wrought by the entry of the mainline railways into north London a few years before. One contemporary source claimed that the true figure was much higher, with as many as a 1,000 homes destroyed in the Fleet valley alone and 12,000 made homeless.[7] Certainly, the demolition of overcrowded slum properties, one of Pearson's original goals, would have disproportionately affected the poorest-off, who may have been evicted, and therefore not counted, long before work began. Eager to avoid bad publicity and conscious of Pearson's mission to rehouse the poor, the Metropolitan bought property in nearby St Bartholomew's for that purpose. But it was a cynical move, and within two years the tenants had been evicted and the houses converted into warehouses.

Construction was planned to take just two years, with the line opening in time for the International Exhibition of 1862. Yet there were many technical difficulties to overcome. The basic 'cut and cover' approach was straightforward enough, employing existing technology to build the railway within an excavated cutting. The innovation lay in covering the cutting with a tunnel roof and laying the road back over the top. Of more concern was what lay under the path of the railway, graphically expressed by John Hollingshead, who published an eyewitness account of the underground's construction in 1862:

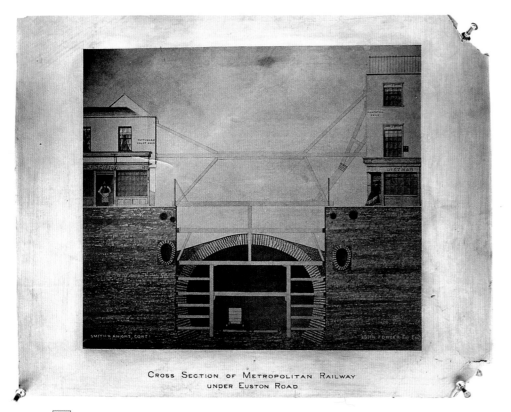

CROSS SECTION OF METROPOLITAN RAILWAY
UNDER EUSTON ROAD

9

The process of tunnelling under the London streets is very different from a like process in the open country... the bed of a London thoroughfare may be compared to the human body - for it is full of veins and arteries which it is death to cut. There are water-mains, with their connecting pipes; the main or branch sewers, with their connecting drains; the gas mains, with their connecting pipes... and very often the tubes containing long lines of telegraph wires. [8]

9. A surveyor's drawing, made for the contractors Smith & Knight, showing a cross-section of the tunnel under the Euston Road, built using the 'cut and cover' method' (c.1861). Also depicted are the enormous beams needed to support adjoining buildings during construction.

There was also the notoriously foul Fleet River, long since consigned to an underground sewer, which had to be crossed three times, as well as questions regarding the appropriateness of the infrastructure for an urban environment. 'Learned engineers,' recalled the writer and campaigner Henry Mayhew in 1865, 'were not wanting to foretell how the projected tunnel must necessarily fall in from the mere weight of the traffic in the streets above, and how the adjacent houses would not only be shaken to their foundations by the vibrations of the engines, but the families residing in them would be one and all poisoned by the sulphurous exhalations from the fuel with which the boilers were heated.'[9]

A more immediate cause of distress for local residents was the unprecedented disruption once building work got started. Streets were blocked off and traffic diverted to make way for an army of labourers, equipped with vast wooden engines to haul up spoil from the hand-dug cuttings. Many houses along the route had to be shored up with huge beams during the construction phase, and access generally was severely hampered by all sorts of building debris. The *Daily News* in June 1862 observed:

The title of Underground Railway, which has been given to this enterprise by popular consent, would seem to imply a certain mole like secrecy of construction in its works. Those who have had the misfortune to live, or whose business has called them frequently along the line of its operation, know too well that this is a great mistake. No railway works were ever more painfully plain and above board. For the best part of three years a great public thoroughfare has been turned into a builders' yard.[10]

Not surprisingly, newspapers were full of complaints from angry householders and local business people, especially when inevitable delays dragged the work out for months longer than expected. Major Wilkinson, who lived on the Euston Road, spoke for many of his well-to-do neighbours when he railed against the 'monstrous tyranny and oppression which parliament was continually permitting speculating companies to assume over public rights'.[11] Others took their complaints to court, resulting in years of litigation for the Metropolitan Railway, fighting often outrageous compensation claims for lost business or damage to

10. 'The Metropolitan Railway Machine for Hoisting Up Earth From Below – Sketched in The Euston Road', *Illustrated London News*, 19 October 1861. The hand-dug spoil was carted away to tips on the outskirts of London.

25

property. The owner of an artificial flower factory in Charterhouse Square, for example, claimed £18,000 in lost revenue. The jury awarded him £2,250.[12]

Local residents were almost equally perturbed by the presence of the weather-beaten 'gravel coloured men' who built the underground.[13] Known as 'navvies', after the original navigators who dug the canals a generation earlier, they were drawn from across the nation, with a notable contingent from Ireland and the Scottish Highlands. Working in shifts, day and night, navvies had a well-earned reputation for hard living and were frequently in trouble with the police for drunken behaviour – none of which endeared them to the local population.[14]

Considering the extent of the work, there were relatively few accidents on site, although newspapers carried lurid descriptions of even the most minor mishaps.[15] To reassure the public, the Metropolitan regularly invited journalists and illustrators to inspect progress, sometimes laying on carefully stage-managed trips on the unfinished line in open contractors' wagons. One of the first, in November 1861, was devised to showcase Fowler's prototype low-emission steam locomotive, specially designed for the confined conditions underground. Although not a mechanical engineer, Fowler had readily taken on the challenge of underground traction after rejecting earlier proposals to haul the trains by cable. Instead, he developed a so-called 'smokeless' locomotive which operated normally in the open cuttings but used preheated firebricks to maintain steam power when in the tunnels. To further reduce emissions, the design also included a rudimentary condensing system whereby steam was piped to a cold water tank under the boiler. Built by Robert Stephenson & Co at a cost of £4,518 (twice the price of a conventional engine), the locomotive was favourably reviewed, mainly because the unfortunate pressmen had to

11. One of a series of remarkable photographs taken during 1860–62 to record the construction of the underground. This carefully posed image shows a group of surveyors with navvies below and in the background, during cut and cover excavation on the Marylebone Road. Mains pipes are visible on the right of the picture, as are the hoardings put up in front of residents' gardens.

12. A celebratory dinner at Gower Street station for the men who built the underground, August 1862. The keynote speech was given by the Metropolitan Railway Secretary, Mr Henchman, aptly named given the sometimes robust nature of the company's business dealing. (The Penny Illustrated Paper, 16 August 1862)

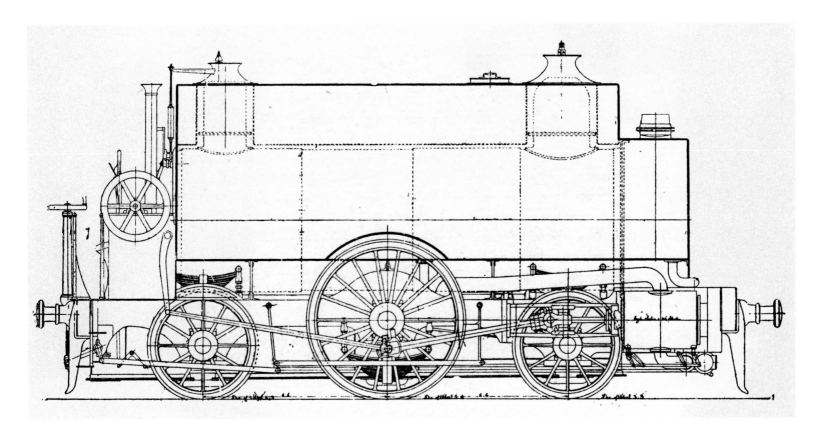

endure a second trip behind an unmodified contractor's engine 'vomiting all the smoke and steam it produced'.[16] The assembled guests were then taken to the nearby Great Northern Hotel at King's Cross 'where an excellent repast was prepared'. Well fed and watered, the press overlooked the obvious trick that had been played on them. Even so, the prototype locomotive was not a practical success, and never entered service.

By far the worst accident to befall the railway during the construction phase occurred in June 1862, when the Fleet sewer burst. Despite a two-day struggle to prevent flooding, a large section of the line was deluged, and all hopes of opening that year dashed. The Metropolitan's publicity machine was soon in action, assuring the media that such a calamity could not happen again. More trips along the line were organized in August to demonstrate how quickly the problem had been rectified. On one of these, over 500 VIP passengers were conveyed from Farringdon Street to Paddington in a mixture of open wagons and carriages, pulled by a new type of condensing locomotive designed by Daniel Gooch of the Great Western Railway. At Edgware Road station the guests were entertained to 'yet another very substantial luncheon', which seems to have helped journalists overcome their initial doubts. The *Daily News* was moved to dismiss criticism that travellers would find conditions underground intolerable by reminding readers that rail passengers daily used the 3-mile Box tunnel (near Bath) without complaint.[17] The *Illustrated London News* went further, claiming the underground tunnels were 'so well lighted and ventilated' that 'instead of being close, dark, damp and offensive,

13. A contemporary drawing of the broad gauge 'smokeless' locomotive built by Robert Stephenson & Co for the Metropolitan Railway in 1861. Following short distance trials on both the Great Western mainline and parts of the underground , the engine was abandoned as unreliable and advertised for sale in 1865 "either entire or in parts". The locomotive was later christened 'Fowler's Ghost' by the *Railway Magazine*, due to the designer's reluctance to discuss his expensive failure.

14

are wide, spacious, clean and luminous, and more like a well-kept street at night, than a subterranean passage through the very heart of the metropolis'.[18]

After more trial runs to satisfy the Board of Trade's inspectors, the railway was finally ready to open in January 1863 – almost a year late. An inaugural service for key stakeholders and VIPs travelled the length of the line on the 9th, with large crowds helping to create a sense of genuine anticipation for the public opening on the next day. Absent from all of the excitement was Charles Pearson, the man whose tireless efforts had done so much to create the railway in the first place. In a cruel twist of fate, Pearson had died during the previous September, only a few months before his vision was realized.

The much anticipated public opening was an immense success, with almost 40,000 passengers undertaking the eighteen-minute journey on the first day alone. Extra trains had to be laid on to supplement the 120 scheduled in each direction, with passengers travelling in three different classes, paying three pence, four pence and six pence for a single journey, and five pence, six pence and nine pence return. One early passenger, Sir William Hardman, recorded his experiences of a trip down 'the Drain' (as it was already being called) a couple of weeks later:

> We experienced no disagreeable odour, beyond the smell common to tunnels. The carriages (broad gauge) hold ten persons, with divided seats, and are lighted by gas (two lights): they are also so lofty that a six footer may stand erect with his hat on.[19]

The first underground stations, however, gave little outward indication of the pioneering urban railway that lay within. At street level, passengers entered through

15

14. A famous, but slightly mysterious, photograph of one of the pre-opening 'trial trips' showing the Chancellor of the Exchequer (later Prime Minister) William Gladstone, seated next to John Fowler (wearing the white top hat) in an open contractor's wagon at Edgware Road station. This image was first published by the Metropolitan Railway and dated to 24 May 1862, but no trips were reported on or around that date. Inexplicably, Gladstone, clearly the most important celebrity here, is not listed among the guests of any of the trips reported to have taken place between 1861 and 1863.

15. The original crest of the Metropolitan Railway, combining the arms of the City of London with a depiction of underground trains entering and emerging from tunnels. The legend 'We work for all' reflects the philanthropic motives of Charles Pearson and his supporters.

modest single-storey buildings finished in white Suffolk brick and decorated in the conservative Italianate style popular at the time. A short flight of stairs led to the platforms, which, in most cases, were built in open cuttings with high glazed canopies to disperse locomotive fumes and illuminated by gas lighting suspended from the ceilings in huge glass globes – a marked improvement on the oil lamps used by mainline railways.

The station designs received mixed reviews at the time, although most contemporary accounts were united in their admiration of the lighting and ventilation solutions employed at Gower Street and Baker Street – the only truly underground stations on the line – where tiled shafts, capped with thick sheets of glass, ran from the sides of the platform to the surface level above.[20] 'Independently of their value as economisers of light and air', wrote a typical piece in the *Standard*, 'these gleaming light shafts, with their pure white lining shimmering through the steamy darkness, have a very good artistic effect'.[21] They weren't very practical, though,

16

17

16. A Metropolitan train in the tunnel near Paddington, 1863. This shows the original broad gauge locomotive and coaches provided by the Great Western Railway.

17. Poster timetable from the public opening of the Metropolitan Railway, 10 January 1863. There is a lengthy 'church break' in the train service on Sunday mornings.

STEAM UNDERGROUND

The search for a reliable, low-emission, alternative to the first underground locomotives led to one of the most successful tank engine designs in British railway history – the condensing locomotives, built by the Manchester firm of Beyer, Peacock and Co. from 1864 and used on the underground until the end of steam operation in 1905.

The basic specification was drawn up by the Metropolitan's chief engineer, John Fowler, but it was Robert Harvey Burnett and others at Beyer, Peacock who developed the design based on similar tank engines supplied by the company for overseas railways. The key feature was the condensing equipment, which prevented most of the steam from escaping into the tunnel by directing it from the cylinders into the water tanks via two large pipes. Here the steam was condensed on the surface of the water, although success depended on the diligence of the driver, who needed to regularly refill the water to keep it cool.

The engines were visually striking, resplendent in olive-green livery with burnished copper chimney tops and polished brass steam domes above the boiler. The

absence of a cab, deemed an unnecessary expense for the enclosed conditions underground, gave the engines an antique appearance in an age when locomotive crews could reasonably expect protection from the smoke and dirt. The first eighteen, delivered in the summer of 1864, carried names derived from classical mythology, including Pluto – the god of the Underworld. More followed between 1866 and 1870, designated 'A Class' by the Metropolitan Railway, who used them for all passenger services on the underground, including those of the District Railway which unhesitatingly purchased identical locos when it started operating its own trains after 1871. A second, slightly heavier, version known as the 'B Class' began to appear on both the Met and District from 1879. In total, 120 of these highly successful locomotives were built, providing the basis for motive power on all cut and cover lines until the advent of electrification in the 1900s.

But they were not without problems. At 45 tons each, they were

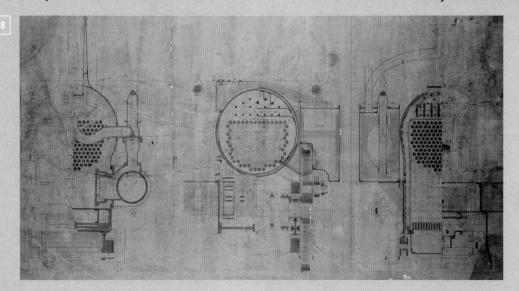

18. General arrangement drawing of Beyer, Peacock 4-4-0T engine, as supplied to the Metropolitan Railway, c.1864. The condensing pipes, leading to the side water tanks, are marked 'A'.

19. A chromolithograph from the 1870s showing the locomotive sidings at Mansion House, with the underground station in the distance. The railwayman on the far left is loading coal from baskets on to the engine.

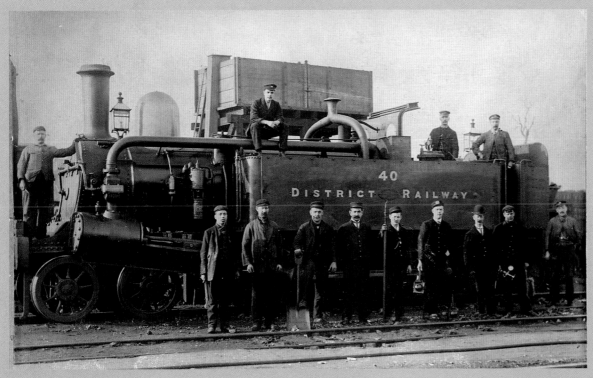

heavy for their purpose and prone to failures caused by continuous working and frequent stopping and starting at stations. They were also hard locomotives to work. Coal (manhandled underground in wicker baskets) had to be topped up regularly, and the water in the engine's tanks (heated to boiling point by the condensed steam) emptied and refilled. Neither did the condensing gear fully alleviate the problems of smoke in the tunnels, which remained a constant source of passenger complaint.

Some idea of the working conditions endured on the footplate can be imagined from the recollections of George Spiller, a fireman, or 'stoker', on the District Railway in the 1900s:

> We worked ten hour days, eight times round the Circle. In the summer you could hardly breathe going through the tunnels, it was so hot. It was enough to boil you on the footplate. I'd shovel about [one ton] of coal in a day's work: it was a dirty, hot, sweaty job. And there was no cover outside ... we had to put up with rain and wind and snow. [23]

Following electrification, most of the 4-4-0Ts (some now over forty years old) were either scrapped or sold on to provincial railways and collieries.[24] A few remained in service on the Underground into the 1930s, mainly for shunting work or hauling passenger trains on the Metropolitan's remote Brill Branch in rural Buckinghamshire. One of these, No. 23, was saved for preservation and is now displayed at London Transport Museum in Covent Garden.

20. Despite tough working conditions, high pay and status made driving trains an enviable job. The hierarchy of depot life is clearly shown in this photograph from about 1902, where the drivers and firemen pose on top of their engine with a group of maintenance staff and shunters standing below.

21. The sole survivor of its class, Metropolitan Railway No. 23, built in 1866. The engine is seen here restored to its 1903 appearance. From about 1885, all Met locomotives were painted in this maroon livery.

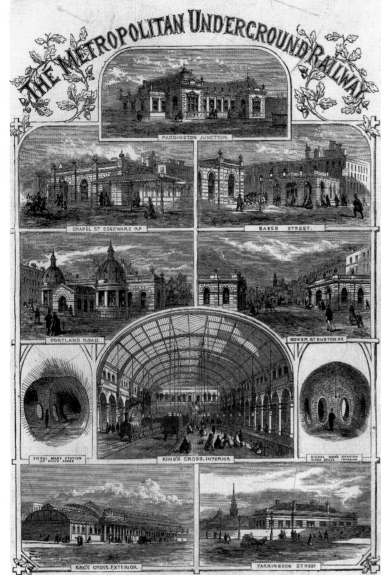

THE METROPOLITAN UNDERGROUND RAILWAY

PADDINGTON JUNCTION.

CHAPEL ST. EDGEWARE RD.

BAKER STREET.

PORTLAND ROAD.

GOWER ST EUSTON RD.

SIGNAL MAN'S STATION AT KING'S CROSS

KING'S CROSS. INTERIOR.

SIGNAL MAN'S STATION KING'S CROSS. INTERIOR.

KING'S CROSS. EXTERIOR.

FARRINGDON STREET.

 22

 23

and within a few months the glass caps had been removed to improve ventilation.

And therein lay a serious problem. There was simply no getting away from the fact that steam trains create a smoky atmosphere, no matter what precautions are put in place. On the opening day itself a porter was hospitalized suffering from 'vitiated atmosphere' and several passengers removed from the tunnels in an 'insensible state' after inhaling locomotive fumes.[22] It was a bad omen for the future.

Underground journeys

The new underground offered passengers a far more extensive range of destinations than the short 3½-mile route alone suggested. Connections with the Great Western at Paddington and the Great Northern at King's Cross provided a direct link between the emerging railway suburbs and the City exploited by regular 'through' trains operated by the mainline railways. Freight, too, was carried over the Metropolitan to warehouses near Farringdon, with an underground spur opened to serve Smithfield meat market in 1868. This close relationship with the mainline railways was a valuable source of revenue for the Metropolitan and became a defining factor in the growth of the underground network over the next twenty years.

At first, the Great Western provided all passenger services on behalf of the Metropolitan. The agreement was soon rescinded though, following an acrimonious dispute over train frequency, which led the Metropolitan to purchase its own rolling

22. A deceptively spacious view of King's Cross underground station in the 1860s. Illustrations from this time invariably depict middle-class passengers using the underground, despite the disproportionately high number of workmen's fares and third-class tickets sold by the Metropolitan.

23. A contemporary illustration from the *Illustrated London News*, 27 December 1862, of the original seven Metropolitan Railway underground stations, including the interior of King's Cross. Construction was overseen by John Fowler and the resident engineer, Thomas Marr Johnson.

stock. Mayhew thought the new carriages 'extremely handsome and roomy vehicles', while the *Morning Post* cooed over the cushioned luxury of first-class seating, 'as soft and yielding as the most coveted drawing-room couch'.[25] More generally, the trains were regarded as being well lit, comfortable and frequent, contributing to an increase in passenger numbers and a healthy profit for the first year of operation (1864).

Fares were relatively high, however, for low earners, some of whom may have been displaced by the demolition of slum housing during the railway's construction. In 1861, parliament stipulated that any future expansion of the underground through working-class districts should be offset by the provision of cheap trains for working men – one of Pearson's original aims. In response, the Metropolitan became the first railway in Britain to offer discounted workmen's tickets in 1864, valid for travel before 6.00 a.m. At just three pence (later reduced to two) for a return journey, workmen's trains were very popular and helped establish the Underground as a mode of transport for all Londoners. Indeed, in the early years, 70 per cent of Metropolitan passengers travelled third class, compared with 20 per cent in second and just 10 per cent in first.

Plans to extend the underground had been approved by parliament even before the public opening in 1863. An overground extension to Hammersmith opened in June 1864, operated jointly by the Metropolitan and Great Western, despite their recent antagonism. By now, over 353 trains were scheduled to depart from Farringdon every weekday, including through services to Windsor, Hatfield and Hitchin. A year later, the Metropolitan reached Moorgate, closer to the heart of the City.

Meanwhile, the steady increase in suburban rail traffic had resulted in an ambitious scheme to double the track between King's Cross and Moorgate, including a connection at Farringdon with the London Chatham and Dover Railway, which crossed the Thames from south London at Blackfriars. Opened in 1868, the 'city widened lines', and the link through Ludgate Hill with main lines from south of the river, provided passengers with an almost limitless variety of potential

24. An early-morning workman's train at Moorgate station in the mid-1860s. Henry Mayhew described a similar underground scene in 1865, where he found the platform 'all of a bustle with men, a large number of whom had bass baskets in their hand or tin flagons or basins done up in red handkerchiefs. Some few carried large saws under their arms, and beneath the overcoat of others one could just see a little bit of the flannel jacket worn by carpenters, whilst some were habited in the grey and clay stained fustian peculiar to ground labourers.'

25. Nineteenth-century building sites were dangerous places to work. Accidents were commonplace, and no overall figure survives for the number of workmen killed or injured building the underground. This dramatic illustration from the *Penny Illustrated News*, 16 September 1865, shows the moment three navvies fell from the scaffolding during construction of Aldersgate station (now Barbican) on the Farringdon to Moorgate extension.

destinations. These were increased a few months later by a connecting curve under St Pancras station with the Midland Railway's newly built main line from the north. This new north–south London railway proved almost equally important for goods traffic seeking a direct way through the capital and provided a useful source of revenue for the rest of the Metropolitan's existence. Goods services continued on this line until the 1960s, but through passenger services ended during the First World War. They were reinstated with electrification in the 1980s as the first stage of the Thameslink project, which has developed cross-London mainline through services on this line from Bedford to Brighton. Farringdon, the Metropolitan's original terminus, will become one of the busiest hub stations in central London when Crossrail opens in 2018.

Back in the nineteenth century not everyone approved of these new travelling possibilities. 'Hurry people through London, or make them travel habitually underground, and what is to become of the shops?' opined a letter writer to the *Morning Post*.[26] Others worried that London would be 'burrowed through and through like a rabbit-warren' unless government took a strategic lead.[27] Such fears were not without foundation, as the early success of the Underground had helped spur a flurry of proposals for railway building within central London. As in the 1840s and 50s, a key aim of the promoters was to provide City and now West End access for new mainline stations – this time coming into London, and over the Thames, from the south at Victoria, Charing Cross and Cannon Street. Parliament intervened to find a solution, recommending in 1864 the construction of a circular underground railway to link the mainline termini, north and south, with the City.

A new company, the Metropolitan District Railway (usually shortened to 'District'), was formed to build the southern part of the circuit, while the Metropolitan undertook to extend its line west to South Kensington and east to Tower Hill, where the railways would join. From the start, the two companies were intended to work very closely together, leading to eventual amalgamation. John Fowler was appointed engineer for the new works, and the Metropolitan agreed to operate all train services on the District. But disagreements, fuelled by personal rivalries at senior management level, frustrated harmonious working. The 'inner circle', as the railway was called at the time, took twenty years to complete, and it was to be a further

26

26. Work in progress on the Metropolitan's western extension at Praed Street (Paddington), c.1866. The navvies appear to be taking a break next to one of the primitive-looking steam cranes, known as 'engines'.

fifty years before the two companies were brought under the same management.

Money, not surprisingly, was at the root of the problem. The up to now profitable Metropolitan was expected to raise £1.9 million, with the District finding the remaining £3.6 million. The District, however, ran into financial problems even before the first part of its line opened in 1868, while Metropolitan dividends fell sharply under the burden of raising the extra cash. The situation was not helped by the banking crisis of the mid-1860s, which damaged investment opportunities, nor by the spiralling costs of construction, exacerbated by the route passing through some of the most valuable real estate in Britain. The Metropolitan extensions through residential Bayswater were especially costly, as was the District's building programme from South Kensington to Westminster.

By 1866 over 2,000 navvies were employed by the District alone, assisted by 200 horses and fifty-eight steam cranes. Huge temporary kilns at Earl's Court baked the 140 million bricks needed for the cuttings and tunnels. Even so, progress was hampered by vested interests imposing often unreasonable demands (for example, Lord Harrington banned ventilation

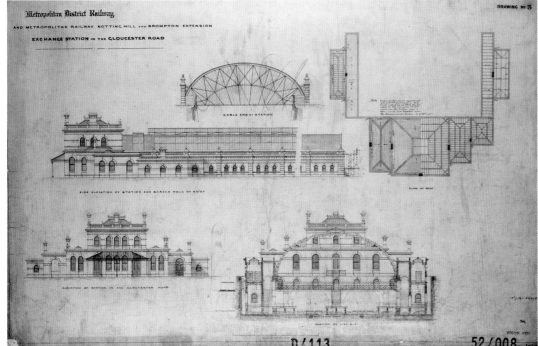

27. Cut without the cover. Large sections of the new extension were built in open cuttings with brick retaining walls, as shown here at Bayswater, c.1867. In this instance, a house has been demolished where the railway passes under the road. The Metropolitan were obliged to build a dummy façade to preserve the continuity of the street, which can still be seen at 23/24 Leinster Gardens.

28. Gloucester Road station plan, c.1868, showing the main building astride the platforms, which were protected from the elements by an extended glazed train shed.

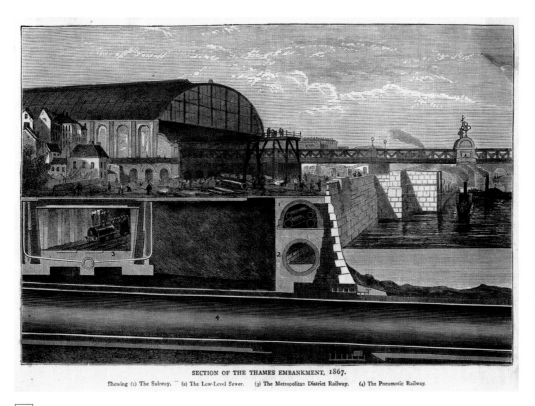

SECTION OF THE THAMES EMBANKMENT, 1867.
Showing (1) The Subway. (2) The Low-Level Sewer. (3) The Metropolitan District Railway. (4) The Pneumatic Railway.

29

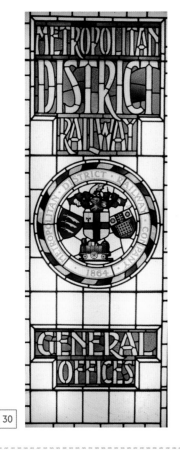

30

shafts on his Kensington estates) and by engineering difficulties, which included channelling the River Westbourne in a pipe over the platform at Sloane Square. Consequently, just the first stretch of the District, from Westminster to Kensington, took three years to complete at a cost of £3 million – a ruinous amount for the cash-strapped railway.

Things weren't going much better for the Metropolitan, which opened the first part of its western extension to Gloucester Road in October 1868. Most of the extension was built in open cutting, to disperse locomotive smoke, rather than being truly underground. Nevertheless, within a few months the two railways were connected in west London. Services were initially provided by the Metropolitan, until inevitable bickering over costs led the District to buy its own trains direct from the Metropolitan's suppliers.

Further east, the District was experiencing great difficulty raising the capital to extend its line to the City. From Westminster Bridge to Temple Gardens, railway construction should have combined with the Metropolitan Board of Works' ambitious Thames Embankment – a new roadway incorporating the underground and main sewers, designed by Sir Joseph Bazalgette. But work on the District was fitful and uncertain. By the time the District had raised enough money to complete the job in 1869, the Embankment was already finished and had to be partly ripped up to accommodate the railway.

With funds finally in place, work continued swiftly to Blackfriars (opened 1870) and Mansion House (1871) under the direction of Benjamin Baker, a close associate of John Fowler. Through trains began running all the way from Mansion House to Moorgate, via Kensington. Now, surely, was the time for the Metropolitan and District to put aside their differences and amalgamate.

However, the direction of the railways was in the hands of two men whose fierce personal rivalry was to shape the development of the Victorian underground and make cooperation impossible. James Staats Forbes had been appointed managing director of the District in 1870 with a remit to save the company from financial ruin. He had previously worked with Brunel on the Great Western and saved the London Chatham and Dover Railway (LCDR) from bankruptcy, first as general manager and later as director – a position he was to hold for

29. Cross-section of Joseph Bazalgette's Victoria Embankment, during construction in 1867. The District Railway was accommodated beneath the new road, with separate tunnels for public utilities and sewerage. The tunnel at the base of the illustration was intended to house a proposed pneumatic railway from Whitehall to Waterloo, which was never completed. In the background are the Hungerford Bridge and Charing Cross railway station.

30. Stained-glass window from the headquarters of the Metropolitan District Railway, incorporating the company crest, c.1880.

forty years. Within two years of joining the District, he had ousted the chairman (the Earl of Devon) and taken charge of the company's woeful finances.

A similar financial crisis had precipitated a shareholder revolt at the Metropolitan, leading to the appointment of Sir Edward Watkin as chairman in 1872. Watkin was one of the most experienced, and at times belligerent, railwaymen of his age, with controlling interests in several railways at home and overseas.[28] He was also the chairman of the South Eastern Railway – the arch rival of the LCDR and true source of the personal rivalry with Forbes. On taking charge of the Metropolitan he was quick to expose the shortcomings and financial irregularities of his predecessors, discovering that a quarter of shareholder dividends had been paid out of capital. He was particularly scathing in his attack on John Fowler, who had done very well for himself, earning over £330,000. 'No engineer in the world was so highly paid,' Watkin fumed in a letter to Fowler, 'taking it any way you like – time, speciality, risk, quantity, value or all combined, you have set an example of charges which seems to me to have largely aided in the demoralization of professional men or all sorts who have lived upon the suffering shareholders for the past ten years.' [29]

Watkin was instrumental in raising a further £250,000 needed to extend the Metropolitan from Moorgate to Liverpool Street – the new terminus of the Great Eastern Railway, reached in 1875. A year later, the Metropolitan extended further east, to Aldgate, but by now Watkin was more interested in the potential of the Underground to connect with other railways under his control than any desire to complete the Circle. The District, too, under the direction of Forbes, was looking to extend its lines west, rather than east, to tap the lucrative suburban market. Neither company had fared well from inner-city expansion, partly because of the enormous costs, and partly because fewer passengers than expected were changing from the new south London termini on to the underground. As a result, work on the Inner Circle ground to a halt.

Although unsuccessful in monetary terms, the enlarged underground opened up a wealth of opportunities for the adventurous Victorian passenger. Most of the main lines were now connected with the Metropolitan and Distinct in one way or another. Suburban 'feeder lines', such as the Metropolitan branch from Baker Street to Swiss Cottage (opened 1868), also encouraged a new breed of commuter. By the mid-1870s, an estimated 60 million passengers a year were travelling

31

31. A composite illustration of the newly opened Aldgate terminus, in the *Illustrated London News*, 2 December 1876, showing the street-level station and impressive canopied platforms, built in an open cutting.

underground. Many were making short trips around town, much like the Underground is used today, rather than between mainline termini as originally envisaged by promoters and parliament alike. According to the number of angry letters published in local newspapers, the trains themselves were often overcrowded, even outside peak hours. One writer found it 'simply abominable' that his ticket didn't necessarily entitle him to a seat.[30] First-class passengers complained about the apparently common practice of third-class travellers entering whichever carriage they fancied. 'I may be doing her an injustice,' mused one to the *Pall Mall Gazette* in 1877, 'but I think the Irish lady without a bonnet and with an infant in arms in my carriage was not a first-class passenger.'[31]

Part of the underground's success, in passenger terms, was due to its excellent safety record. In the first twenty years of operation, there were no serious mishaps, thanks in part to the use of modern interlocking signals. Nor were there any explosions caused by the build-up of mysterious underground gases, predicted as being 'imminent' by some journalists in the 1860s.[32]

Air quality, however, continued to cause concern, although it is doubtful whether conditions were as bad as some contemporaries made out, as so many were prepared to use the system. Locomotive drivers also became more skilled at managing emissions from their engines as time went on and faced stiff fines for creating undue amounts of smoke in the tunnels.[33] Even so, the Metropolitan faced a public relations disaster in 1867 when three people died on separate occasions, allegedly as a result of inhaling 'choke damp' (the name given to the sulphurous fumes emitted by the locomotives). At the resulting inquests, the Metropolitan produced expert witnesses to successfully prove that the deaths were from natural causes, rather than anything untoward in the underground atmosphere. To prove the point Myles Fenton, the general manager, presented statistical evidence to show how staff sickness rates were lower on the underground than for other railways, but conceded that ventilation could be improved.[34] The whole affair, however, clearly unnerved the company's directors who went on a charm offensive with the press, eliciting the support of a variety of paid experts along the way. One of these, Dr Letherby, described by the Metropolitan Railway as an 'eminent analytical chemist', assured readers that the pungent smell of the underground was caused not by locomotive smoke but by the friction of wooden brake blocks used on the carriages. In a comic misuse of science for public relations ends, the doctor went on to explain that the 'the partial combustion of the wood produces a pyroligeneous carbo-hydrogen, which may provoke coughing and sneezing but is not at all dangerous to health'.[35]

The Times sided with the Metropolitan, agreeing that reports about unpleasant air were exaggerated. This view was shared by the London Correspondent for the *New York Times* (1869), who told American readers he had 'never experienced anything but the most trifling consciousness of a change of atmosphere' when travelling underground.[36] However, improvements were made in the early 1870s, with the installation of ventilation shafts and 'blow holes' along the worst-affected section from King's Cross to Edgware Road.

This didn't stop the complaints, however. In 1879, *The Times* published a letter suggesting that illness caused by the sulphurous conditions was all too common:

> I was travelling on [the Metropolitan] with my wife between Edgware-road and King's-cross. The condition of the atmosphere was so poisonous that, although a mining engineer, I almost suffocated, and was obliged to be assisted out of the train at an intermediate station. On reaching the open air I requested to be taken to alchemists close at hand, and to him I explained as well as I could that I desired to have some restorative. Without a moment's hesitation he said 'oh, I see – Metropolitan Railway', and at once poured out a wine glassful of what I conclude he designates 'Metropolitan Mixture'. Although very unwell, I was amused at the promptness with which he acted, and was induced to ask him whether he often had such cases, to which he rejoined, 'Why bless you, Sir, we have often 20 cases a day.' [37]

The *Pall Mall Gazette*, a newspaper seldom favourably disposed to the underground's cause, facetiously advised readers to take a trip on the railway to experience 'the full portentousness of our Metropolitan inferno'. So foul is the air, we are assured, and so barbarous the treatment of passengers by station staff that within a short time 'you are as indifferent to [the possibility of] a collision as a seasick voyager is to shipwreck'. Looking forward to the future, the *Gazette* drew this conclusion:

> Some of these days, when the circle is quite finished, we shall, no doubt, turn it to its natural use, as a place of punishment. Prisoners will be condemned to so many continuous 'round trips' as they are now to so many weeks in jail or so many lashes. [37]

32. In this comic Christmas card from the 1880s a young man with a cigar attempts to enter a non-smoking compartment of an undergound carriage, to the disapproval of the gentleman in the brown coat. A rather tedious verse (printed on the back) relates the ensuing argument and victory of the smoker. It also refers to the newspaper boy selling copies of *Punch, Fun, Judy, Graphic* and 'London Noos' to the City commuters.

Whether the atmosphere was oppressive or not, nothing was allowed to interfere with a Victorian gentleman's right to smoke wherever he pleased. The Metropolitan had initially banned smoking in carriages and vainly tried to prosecute offenders. The injunction was widely flouted, and, following a campaign led by the MP H. B. Sheridan, the Metropolitan was forced to overturn this 'intolerable [and] positively ridiculous' ban in 1874. [39]

For observers in other parts of Britain, the convenience of underground travel had come at a heavy cost. It wasn't just the unpleasant air, as bad as that might be, but rather the whole notion of underground travel which threatened to ruin health and home, as a journalist on the *Newcastle Courant* explained in 1882:

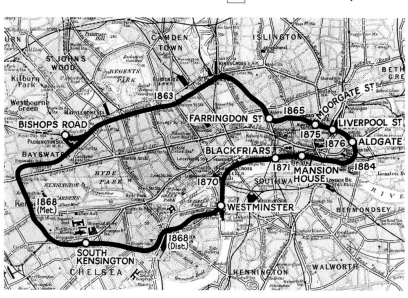

[Londoners] must bear as philosophically as they can the rush, hurry and scurry, the possibility of paralysis, nay, even of madness itself, which doctors cynically tell us is super induced by much underground railway travelling, the noise and smoke, the darkness, and the stifling sulphurous atmosphere, as well as the destruction of the dwellings in which they happen to live. These drawbacks may be placed as a set off to the daily and hourly convenience and the unquestionable benefits conferred by the underground. [40]

This dual fascination with the benefits and drawbacks of subterranean railways became a common theme in books and articles about modern London as the underground entered its third decade. Passenger numbers, however, continued to grow. Far from been a dangerous novelty, as some regional newspapers liked to suggest, the underground had become part of everyday life.

Completing the circle

With so many passengers using the underground, the impetus to complete the Inner Circle was irresistible. But even if they had been on friendlier terms, the impecunious Metropolitan and District railways were in no position to construct the final, expensive, link between Aldgate and Mansion House. Things got so bad that frustrated financiers set up a rival company to finish the job, resulting in a parliamentary inquiry to determine the best way forward. Its decision placed the onus of responsibility on the two underground companies, with financial support from the Commission of Sewers and the Metropolitan Board of Works. With funding in place, the first section from Aldgate to Trinity Square opened in 1882. The extension included a spur to Whitechapel and a connection with the East London Railway, which ran south to New Cross. This important cross-London route was to play a significant role in Watkin's ambitions for the Metropolitan and was probably the deciding factor in encouraging his involvement with the scheme.

33. A map of the Inner Circle, with the completion dates of the various sections from 1863 to 1884.

34. Underground tickets from the 1890s. To assist passengers in travelling round the Circle by the shortest route, tickets and platforms were marked 'I' for the inner track and 'O' for the outer.

The last 2¼ miles, between Tower Hill and Mansion House, finally opened to the public in October 1884 at a staggering cost of £2.5 million. The entire 15-mile circular route took about seventy minutes. Most Metropolitan trains ran clockwise round the outer track, with those of the District operating in the opposite direction on the inside track. There were now over 800 scheduled trains using all, or part, of the Inner Circle every day.

Instead of ending the rivalry between Forbes and Watkin, the completion of the circle fuelled an outbreak of renewed, and sustained, hostility. Interminable court battles over running costs soured relations, while both companies promoted their branch traffic at the expense of circle-line services. Passengers experienced intolerable delays, made worse by the increasingly desperate methods employed by the Metropolitan and District railways to steal customers from each other. At some stations where both companies had booking offices unwary passengers were sold tickets for the longest possible route by unscrupulous staff. Misleading poster campaigns added to the confusion by denigrating rival services, rather than clarifying travel information.

Efforts to regulate fares in the interests of passengers fell on deaf ears, and the matter was only resolved through costly arbitration, much to the disgust of the *Railway News*:

> It is little short of a public scandal that squabbles of this sort should continue. A minor matter of fixing fares, which two railway managers might agree upon in half-an-hour's conversation, has been dragged through Parliament, and into an arbitration, and can only be settled – if it be now finally disposed of – by an appeal to the Law Courts. A heavy responsibility rests somewhere for the litigious spirit which gives rise these endless discussions and enormous legal and other expenses. [41]

At times, the rivalry reached absurd levels. Following a dispute over the use of a siding at South Kensington, the District chained one of its locomotives to the spot

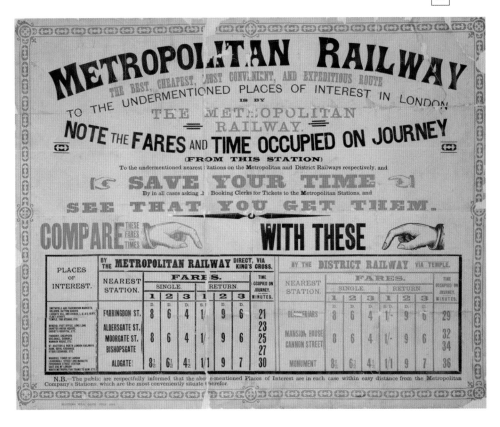

35. A typical Metropolitan Railway poster from 1886, suggesting that passengers can save time and money by using their trains, rather than those of the District Railway.

36. The principal villains of the piece: Edward Watkin (1819–1901) and James Staats Forbes (1823–1904), as drawn by the cartoonist Spy. Beloved by their shareholders for taking an aggressively competitive approach to business, Watkin and Forbes ensured that relations between the Metropolitan and District railways would remain strained well into the twentieth century.

to deny the Metropolitan access, resulting in a farcical tug of war when the latter sent three of its engines to (unsuccessfully) tow the other away.

Financially the completion of the circle was a failure. Passenger numbers continued to grow, reaching 115 million by the mid-1880s, but this wasn't enough to offset the very high construction costs. Both companies suffered, but the burden fell heaviest on the already impoverished District. In 1886, Forbes confessed to shareholders that the venture had been 'almost disastrous'. The social reformer and artist William Morris agreed for different reasons, arguing that the commercially motivated directors had misused their monopoly to force Londoners on to 'the beastly sewers through which run stink-traps under the name of carriages'.[42] In the long term, though, the circle transformed the way Londoners used the underground. From now on more and more passengers made journeys which began and ended at underground stations, rather than merely travelling between mainline stations.

The subterranean world

By the time the circle was completed, the underground was already a well-established part of the capital's transport infrastructure. It was also deeply embedded in the popular consciousness of the age. Periodicals and newspapers fed a seemingly insatiable appetite for every detail of the railway's development, with regular articles appearing in the *Illustrated London News*, the *Graphic* and the *Penny Illustrated*, among many others. Even *The Lady* felt obliged to keep its readers informed about the miracle of underground travel.[43] Meanwhile, a growing body of fictional literature set against the backdrop of the underground, together with sensational press reporting of real-life incidents, ensured that the railway entered the Victorian imagination as a place of mystery and intrigue.

For some, the sulphurous atmosphere and subterranean nature of the underground conjured up images of the demonic underworld. 'I had my first experience of Hades to-day', wrote the author and journalist R. D. Blumenthal about a trip on the Metropolitan in 1887, 'and if the real thing is to be like that I shall never again do anything wrong.'[44] In the same year, David Ker, a journalist with the *New York Times*, told American readers that to travel

37. The ubiquitous railway news stall was a convenient dispenser of literature about the underground, as well as being the place to buy the day's paper. *Punch* magazine, though, was not impressed with the quality of all the items on sale: 'I bought from the stall at Victoria / A horrible sixpenny story, a / Book of a kind / It pained me to find / For sale at our English emporia' ('Blackfriars to Sloane Square', *Punch*, c.1895). Photo: Victoria underground station, 23 November 1896.

38. Charing Cross underground station (now Embankment) photographed in 1894. The scene is an almost exact depiction of the one described by Angus Evan Abbott in *The Spawn of Fortune* (1896).

on the Inner Circle was to enter a noxious 'realm of darkness, mystery and tunnels' in a strained allusion to the Circles of Hell.[45] Certainly the murky underground environment lent itself to melodramatic treatment. In Angus Evan Abbott's *The Spawn of Fortune* (1896) Charing Cross underground station is transformed by the arrival of a satanic steam locomotive:

> A few waiting passengers sauntered up and down the platform. Smoke hung about in fantastic blue whiffs, writhing and twisting and swirling lazily towards the roof, and the gas burned yellow in the glass globes that hung from above the doorway... [then] two yellow eyes trembled and blinked in the darkness, and the next instance a Richmond train came wheezing, rocking, screeching, and grinding out of the blackness, and stopped with a jerk at the platform.[46]

The underground's remarkable safety record gave few opportunities for criticism, but this didn't stop the press from reporting every minor mishap with dramatic relish. The first accidents occurred within a couple of months of the railway opening in 1863. On two separate occasions, slow-moving trains collided at Farringdon Street station as a result of signalling errors. Despite reports that the incidents had been of 'an alarming' and 'violent' character, the worst injury discovered by journalists was a fractured nose sustained by a first-class passenger.[47] Considerably more interest was aroused by a bizarre accident in 1866, when three passengers were killed after a girder fell on their carriage at Aldersgate station. The accident, which was the result of negligence in securing one of the huge iron beams used in the construction of the adjacent Smithfield meat market, created a media sensation. Newspapers from Cornwall to Glasgow related every detail of the tragedy and consequent inquest.[48] The public's understandable fear of being

SERIOUS COLLISIONS ON THE METROPOLITAN RAILWAY.

39

39. A dramatic newspaper depiction of what was actually a minor collision near Portland Road underground station. *Illustrated Police News*, 6 February 1869.

trapped in an underground disaster was again exploited in 1869 when a passenger train ran into stationary carriages near Portland Road. It was described, erroneously, as being a 'serious collision'; the *Illustrated Police News* carried graphic portrayals of terrified passengers caught up in an inferno. In fact, no one was seriously hurt. A similarly minor event on the District Railway in 1873 was reported under the heading 'The dangers of underground railway travelling'. In this instance, poor working practices were blamed, and the District instructed to settle claims from thirty-two passengers – mostly for crushed hats and umbrellas.[49]

The most serious accident on the Victorian underground involved a head-on collision near Earl's Court in August 1885. An engine driver and fireman were killed, although no passengers were badly hurt. The incident was given the usual dramatic treatment by the *Illustrated London News* and widely reported throughout Britain.[50] It didn't, however, undermine passenger confidence, as numbers using the underground continued to grow. Similarly, a spate of terrorist attacks in the 1880s and 90s had little effect in disrupting travelling behaviour. The first were committed by Fenian bombers who sought to pressure the British government into meeting their demands for Irish Home Rule by bringing terror to the rush-hour commute. The worst incident, between Paddington and Edgware Road in October 1883, injured sixty-two passengers. Subsequent attacks at Charing Cross (also October 1883) and King's Cross (1885) only caused superficial damage to railway infrastructure. A fourth bomb, allegedly planted by anarchists to create alarm in the run-up to the Queen's Diamond Jubilee, exploded at Aldersgate station in April 1897, killing one passenger and severely injuring several others, one of whom later died in hospital.

More mundane cases of criminal activity on the underground were no more or less common than for other nineteenth-century railways. Yet the subterranean location appears to have infused alleged incidents (whether real or not) with a fascinating potency for Victorian audiences. Reports of 'mysterious deaths' in dark tunnels and empty carriages occasionally made national news. When a drunken passenger fell to her death under a train in 1864, for example, it was initially reported that she'd been pushed by

SUICIDE ON THE METROPOLITAN RAILWAY

40. A bizarre souvenir made from the wreckage of a first-class carriage destroyed in the Aldersgate bombing on 26 April 1897. No information survives as to why, or for whom, this inkstand was made, but it appears to have been professionally put together at the Metropolitan Railway's workshops.

41. 'Suicide on the Metropolitan Railway' (*Illustrated Police News*, 31 October 1868).

an unknown assailant lurking in the shadows.[51] The first recorded case of an underground shooting was similarly less sensational than early reports of a failed murder attempt suggested. The unlikely story involved an eighteen-year-old clerk, Sidney Morris, who accidentally shot a London merchant, Sigesmund Schweinburg, in the confines of their shared carriage. At the trial, Morris claimed that he carried a loaded revolver with him at all times for 'protection' and that he had unwittingly pulled the trigger on the day in question when taking the firearm out of his pocket for inspection. This version of events was accepted at face value, and Morris acquitted.[52]

In 1880, however, a real robbery and assault in a first-class carriage provoked considerable public interest. The story had all the hallmarks of the 'penny dreadful' thrillers sold at railway book stalls. The attacker knew his victim to be carrying a large sum in cash and waited until the carriage had emptied before launching an assault in the tunnel. After failing to subdue his victim with chloroform, the assailant used 'a loaded stick' to beat him into submission. The attack ended at Aldersgate, where the would-be murderer was apprehended trying to escape.[53] In the same year, the body of a middle-aged man was recovered from the tunnels near Temple station. Despite forensic evidence that he'd been assaulted with 'both a blunt and a sharp instrument', the subsequent inquest was unable to reach a conclusive verdict as to how and where he met his death.[54]

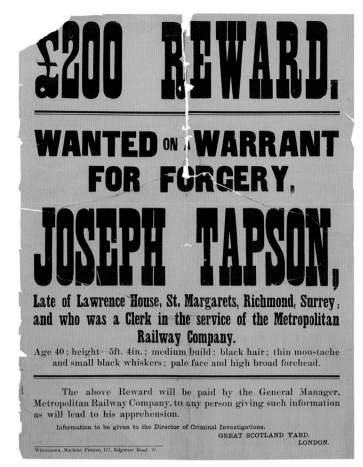

Underground suicides provided an almost equally rich source of human interest stories for vicarious journalists. From the 1860s onwards, lurid tales of 'decapitations' and 'dreadfully mutilated' bodies appeared with depressing regularity.[55] 'There seems to be an epidemic of Suicide... in London,' wrote the *Penny Illustrated Paper* in 1887, before describing in gory detail the 'romantic suicide' of a young man who had first tried to shoot his sweetheart at Charing Cross Underground station before turning the gun on himself.[56] The newspaper even included a drawing of the man's head exploding in a puff of smoke, in case the reader had trouble picturing the scene. On another occasion, the 'extraordinary suicide' of a 45-year-old man at Edgware Road was pictorially rendered by the *Illustrated Police News* for the enlightenment of its readership.[57]

Occasionally, the underground itself became the subject of a serious crime, as when Joseph Tapson, a clerk on the Metropolitan Railway, embezzled over £9,000 from company funds in 1880. After a substantial reward was offered for his arrest, he was eventually tracked down to Philadelphia and later sentenced to five years' hard labour.

How far fiction writers were influenced by press reporting is a moot point, but several clearly took their inspiration from the dramatic potential of the Underground. One of the first was Dion Boucicault, whose 1868 play *After Dark: A Drama of London Life*

42. A poster offering a huge reward (equivalent to two years' pay for a skilled worker) for the capture of the embezzler Joseph Tapson (1880).

43. Sheet music from Dion Boucicault's 1868 play *After Dark: A Drama of London Life*. The stage production included realistic locomotive sounds and lighting to represent a train approaching at speed.

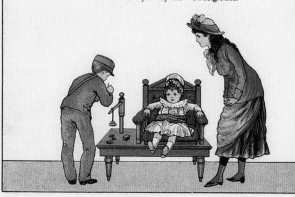

The Underground Railway

WHO is this in the Weighing Chair?
Why, little Dot, I do declare!
Three stone five! "So much as that?"
Calls out Miss Dot; "then I *must* be fat!"

On this and the opposite page you see
Dot's mother, and brother, and sisters three.
They wait for an underground train to come
And carry them swiftly back to their home.

Wonderful trains! From morn till night,
Clattering through tunnels without daylight,
Hither and thither they run, up and down,
Beneath the streets of London Town.

Many prefer these trains instead
Of the cabs and "Busses" overhead,
For they run much faster than horses can.
Miss Dot's papa is a busy man,

And goes to the City every day
By the "Underground,"—the quickest way:
And One Hundred Millions of people, 'tis found,
Are carried each year by the "Underground."

28

29

44

ran for nearly a year in the West End. A key moment in the plot sees the hero, Captain Chumley, tied to the tracks of the Metropolitan Railway, only to be saved at the last minute from certain death – a device which was to be used over and again by early filmmakers. David Welsh, the historian of underground literature, has identified several similar occasions when the underground played host to murder mysteries, including C. J. Cutcliffe Hyne's *The Tragedy of a Third Smoker* (1898), set on the Hammersmith & City Railway, and Baroness Orczy's short story *The Mysterious Death on the Underground Railway* (1901).[58] Another short story, *A Mystery on the Underground* by John Oxenham (1897), which features an ex-railway employee turned serial killer, was deemed so realistic that it provoked a complaint from the District Railway when it was serialized in *To-Day* magazine. Ironically, it was the author's use of fictionalized newspaper reports to describe the killings which aroused official censure.[59]

Perhaps surprisingly, the greatest fictional detective of all, Sherlock Holmes, rarely used the underground, even though his lodgings at 221b Baker Street would have been convenient for the Metropolitan Railway. The only story to feature the underground extensively is the

44. *London Town*, by Thomas Crane and Ellen Houghton, published by Marcus Ward and Company, 1883.

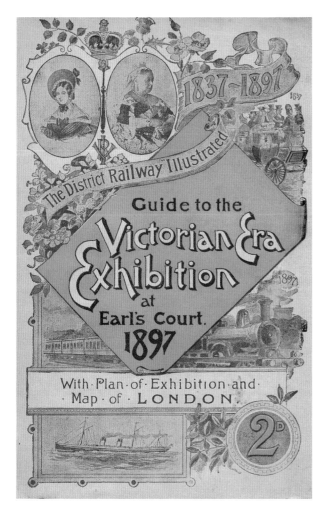

Adventure of the Bruce-Partington Plans, written in 1908 but set in 1895.[60] In a plot which has a passing resemblance to the real-life discovery of a dead body on the District Railway in 1880, a murdered civil servant is found on the tracks at Aldgate. At first it is uncertain where, or how, he was killed, but Holmes soon discovers that the murder took place in a house overlooking the railway at Gloucester Road, from where the body was dumped on the roof of a passing train, later falling off on the curve at Aldgate.

Nursery rhymes and songs also played a part in establishing the underground in the public mind. *London Town* (1883), a children's book by Thomas Crane and Ellen Houghton, features an illustrated poem about a well-to-do family returning from a trip into town by underground (a mode, we are told, that their father uses every day to reach his City office). For those of a musical inclination, you could buy the sheet music for the *Metropolitan Railway Quadrille*, composed by Paul Sommer (1878), to play at home. Alternatively, you could visit one of the capital's many music halls to hear the latest, and less genteel, take on the perils of underground travel.[61]

Literary and artistic depictions aside, for most Londoners and visitors to the capital

45. District Railway guide book to the Victorian Era Exhibition at Earl's Court – one of many held there between 1887 and 1913.

46. The Ferris wheel at Earl's Court, with the underground station visible in the foreground (commercial postcard, c.1902). Over 2.5 million visitors paid to ride on this forerunner of the modern London Eye during its twelve-year life.

the underground was simply the most efficient way of getting about town. The essential *Baedeker Handbook* for London had this advice:

> At first, in order to make himself acquainted with the Metropolis, the stranger will naturally prefer to make use of omnibuses and cabs, but when his early curiosity is satisfied he will probably often avail himself of the easy, rapid and economical mode of travelling afforded by the Underground Railway.[62]

Not that using the underground was always easy for out-of-towners. The best direction of travel on the Circle, for example, was not always clarified by the rival railway companies themselves. Station names, painted on benches, walls and the globes of gas lights, were often indistinguishable from the mass of commercial advertising which covered the dimly lit platform walls, evocatively described in this account of a journey taken by a farmer's wife visiting London for the coronation of Edward VII (1902):

> Time sped on, and, with it, the Circle train, past Bishopsgate, Farringdon Street, and King's Cross, with its maze of metropolitan underground lines; through dismal tunnels, black with smoke; through brick-lined cuttings, foul with sooty deposit; past stations, each one hung, by way of adornment, with the same monotonous, highly coloured 'works of art', drawing attention to Colman's Mustard, Reckitts's Blue, Nestle's Milk, Bovril, Oxo, Lemco, Globe Polish, Ogden's Cigarettes, Bird's Custard and Stephen's Inks.[63]

Inevitably, she misses her stop. In fact, this was such a common problem that platform staff were instructed to call out the station name as the train arrived. According to a contemporary guide, however, mispronunciation only added to the confusion, leaving bewildered visitors to make what they could of 'Emma Smith' (Hammersmith), 'Bish-er-git' (Bishopsgate) and other misleading announcements.[64] For regular travellers knowing how to use the system became something of a badge of honour, much as it still is today. *Punch*, in particular, delighted in apocryphal tales of rustics endlessly travelling round the circle in search of their destination, while the London correspondent of the *New York Times* thought that only 'careless, stupid, or inexperienced traveller[s] are apt to get badly "mixed" with the variety of trains and platforms'.[65]

In addition to everyday traffic, the underground benefited from a London-wide increase in leisure travel during the last quarter of the nineteenth century. Passenger journeys of all types, whether by underground, tram or horse bus, rose by nearly 300 per cent. This figure is far higher than the comparable rise in population (50 per cent) and is only partially explained by broader social trends, such as improvements in pay, shorter working hours and paid holidays. Instead, it would appear that the underground, in conjunction with other modes of transport, was helping to stimulate greater use of public transport.[66]

The District Railway became especially adept at developing traffic to places of interest along its route. In 1885, the company built a pedestrian subway to link South Kensington station with the popular temporary exhibition grounds and museums on Exhibition Road. A year later, a new exhibition venue opened at Earl's Court on a redundant site owned and served by the District. Over the next twenty years, Earl's Court together with nearby Olympia (also on the District line) became one of the most visited tourist destinations in London. Millions flocked to see the exhibitions, circuses and, from 1895, the spectacular 300-foot Ferris wheel.

In general, the underground was well placed to capitalize on the popularity of more established forms of entertainment. Theatres and music halls, for example, enjoyed massive success in the 1880s and 90s, with an estimated 45,000 attending performances every night. Most were in easy reach of the underground. One, Turnham's Music Hall, even changed its name to the Metropolitan to cash in on the success of the nearby line at Edgware Road. Similarly, the convenience of underground stations for the large West End stores, including Harrods (South Kensington) and Whiteleys (Bayswater), assisted a boom in shopping as a leisure pursuit for the better off. Always keen to encourage middle-class passengers, the Metropolitan briefly introduced Ladies Only carriages on its first- and second-class services in 1875. The designation was soon withdrawn, however, as most female passengers apparently preferred to travel in mixed carriages. [67] Even so, more women were travelling by underground than ever before, often alone, as several contemporary illustrations show. This would suggest that the underground was perceived to be a safe and respectable mode of transport, despite occasional lurid newspaper reports of single women accosted in deserted railway carriages. [68]

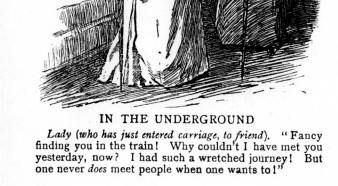

IN THE UNDERGROUND

Lady (who has just entered carriage, to friend). " Fancy finding you in the train! Why couldn't I have met you yesterday, now? I had such a wretched journey! But one never *does* meet people when one wants to!"

47

The extra revenue generated by off-peak leisure travel was certainly welcomed by the cash-strapped underground companies. But there was a more lucrative, and frequent, traveller on the subterranean railway – the suburban commuter. To secure this valuable business, the underground first had to break out of central London into the emerging suburbs beyond.

The push north and west

The underground had been conceived as a means of whisking people from the mainline railway stations to the City. From the outset, though, the Metropolitan and District railways recognized the financial potential of carrying passengers direct from their homes in the suburbs to the city centre. In this respect the underground had an enormous advantage over its mainline competitors, which were excluded from central London. There were other factors, too, which made suburban expansion very attractive to the underground companies. From the 1860s, railway development had shown

47. A late nineteenth-century cartoon from the pages of *Punch* magazine. One of the ladies may have had a 'wretched journey' the day before, but the illustration serves to show that underground travel was considered safe, and respectable, for middle-class women.

how new lines could both tap existing residential markets and help create new ones in previously rural areas.[69] Suburban railways were also comparatively cheap to build, as they ran above ground with no need for expensive tunnelling or compensation payments to the owners of adjoining properties. Moreover, given the ongoing feud between Watkin and Forbes, and the vast cost of completing the troublesome circle, it made sense for the two companies to pursue independent sources of revenue further afield.

The Metropolitan's suburban ambitions had started off modestly enough in the 1860s, with two jointly owned branch lines to Hammersmith, in west London, and Swiss Cottage to the north. The latter, which joined the underground at Baker Street station, served an existing residential area that included St John's Wood, while the line to Hammersmith helped develop an up-and-coming suburb for City clerks. There had been plans to extend the northern branch to Hampstead, but financial uncertainty delayed construction. All this was to change in the 1870s, when the Metropolitan became embroiled in Watkin's grandiose, and inconsistent, schemes to create a national rail network connecting the various companies under his control.[70]

The Swiss Cottage branch now assumed a key significance in Watkin's overall strategy, as its extension offered a way into London for his northern interests, with Baker Street transformed into a mainline terminus. It would be mistaken, though, to imagine Watkin pursuing a single grand vision with the approval of the Metropolitan

48. The underground goes overground. A train for Harrow hauled by 'A Class' locomotive No. 14 pulls out of Kingsbury and Neasden station in the 1890s. The open fields would soon be transformed by industrial and housing developments.

directors. In fact, he took an opportunistic and secretive approach to empire building, lending his support to a range of projects when it suited him – not all of which came to fruition. One of his many proposals, for example, was for a railway linking Manchester with Paris, via the underground and a prototype Channel tunnel. On other occasions Watkin pushed the Metropolitan further north than it would otherwise have contemplated, to fulfil often short-lived objectives.[71]

The result of Watkin's scheming saw the Metropolitan extending far out beyond its underground origins, into rural Middlesex, Hertfordshire and Buckinghamshire. In 1879, the railway reached West Hampstead, Kilburn and Willesden Green. A year later, it was at Harrow, with extensions to Pinner, Rickmansworth and Chesham following in the 1880s. By 1892, Metropolitan trains were serving Aylesbury, and a few years later the railway reached its northernmost limit at the remote Verney Junction station – 50 miles from Baker Street. As an indication of the extent to which the Metropolitan had become enmeshed in Watkin's plans, the new extension also included an infrequently used branch line to the remote village of Brill in Buckinghamshire, which Watkin briefly imagined could be used as a springboard for further expansion.

Ultimately, Watkin's plans to create a new main line to Baker Street came to nothing. Instead, the Metropolitan was left with a conventional overground railway, requiring new locomotives, goods vehicles and carriages, although long-suffering passengers often had to put up with retired underground stock. The 'Main Line', as it was rather grandly called, also bequeathed the Metropolitan considerable quantities of surplus land, bought during the construction phase. At Neasden, this enabled the company to build an engineering works and depot, complete with housing for railway employees. It also opened up the prospect of developing commuter traffic on the stretches closest to London.

Strictly speaking, railway companies were obliged to sell off unwanted land after ten years, to prevent abuse of the compulsory purchase powers granted to them by parliament. The Metropolitan, however, managed to obtain unique, and legally dubious, privileges which allowed it to develop land for non-railway operating purposes. From the 1880s onwards, a sub-committee of directors managed small-scale property developments on behalf of the Metropolitan at sites adjacent to the railway, firstly at Willesden Green, and later at Harrow and Pinner. The new housing was mostly aimed at City men, many

49

49. The cover of a Metropolitan Railway timetable advertising the new extension to Northwood and Rickmansworth, 1887.

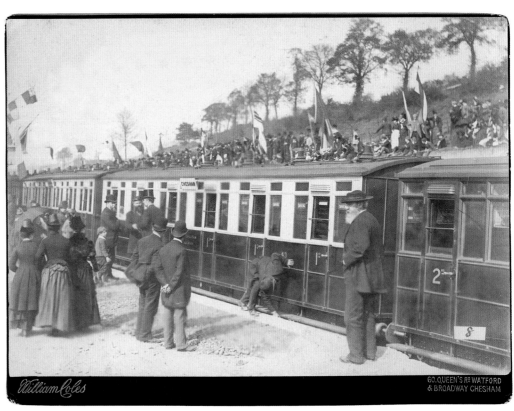

of whom became valuable first-class season ticket holders, lured to the suburbs by the Metropolitan's frequent and direct train service. These humble beginnings laid the foundations for the extensive, and very successful, railway-led suburban development of the early twentieth century known as 'Metro-land'.

Where the railway passed through Wembley Park, Watkin and his associates took a very different approach to developing traffic. Inspired by the success of Earl's Court, Watkin set up an independent company to buy the park and turn it into a rail-fed leisure attraction, dominated by a vast steel tower incorporating restaurants, theatres, exhibitions and even Turkish baths. The first level of the tower (to have been the tallest in Europe) opened in 1896, but public interest waned and the money ran out. Nicknamed 'Watkin's Folly', the incomplete tower was demolished in 1907 – six years after Watkin's death. The site was later redeveloped in the 1920s as the location of the world-famous Wembley stadium.

Although the Metropolitan was to become the suburban rail developer par excellence in the 1920s, the District arguably did more to stimulate development during the nineteenth century. Unencumbered by any mainline pretensions, its westward expansion was motivated solely by the intention to stimulate commuter traffic in an area scattered with prosperous villages eager to be connected with the underground.

The District's first extension from Earl's Court to Hammersmith in 1874 was a controversial move, considering the growing suburb was already served by the Great

50. Metropolitan Railway 'E Class' locomotive No. 1 (1898), with a rake of restored Metropolitan carriages from the 1890s, photographed on the Bluebell Railway, East Sussex in 2007. The Metropolitan purchased a number of locomotives specifically to work the 'Main Line', together with smaller tank engines for depot shunting. No. 1 is the only survivor from this period and is now owned by the Buckinghamshire Railway Centre, based at the former Metropolitan Railway Quainton Road station.

51. The official opening-day train to Chesham, 15 May 1889. The carriages were originally designed for the underground in the 1860s and could prove uncomfortable for longer 'Main Line' journeys. The white-painted panelling denoted first-class accommodation.

The Lake, Wembley Park.   J. W. H. Steel, Wembley.

Western and Metropolitan Joint Railway. The move did nothing to sweeten relations between the warring Forbes and Watkin, but it was a smart decision nonetheless, as it provided a staging post for further extensions westwards to Richmond (1877), Ealing (1879) and Hounslow (1883). To the south, the railway branched out from West Brompton to Putney in 1880 with the initial goal of encouraging leisure traffic centred on the River Thames – the annual Oxford and Cambridge boat race being a particularly big draw for tourists. A few years later, the branch was extended in partnership with the London and South Western Railway to its present-day terminus in suburban Wimbledon.

The District's new lines were geographically much closer to the centre of town than those of the Metropolitan, making it far easier to stimulate speculative housing development along the route, such as the Bedford Park estate begun at Turnham Green in the 1870s. Consequently, the District didn't need to hang on to its surplus lands or try to ape mainline railways by providing goods services.

For both companies, suburban development fed traffic on to the underground sections of their railways and provided much-needed regular income from daily commuters. Even so, some services remained poorly used, and it wasn't until the massive growth of suburban London in the inter-war period that the lines built by the Metropolitan and District railways reached their full potential.

52. The undergound's ability to take commuters direct from their homes to the city centre was an important factor in the success of nineteenth-century suburban development – and a vital source of revenue for the railway companies, reflected in the prominence given to suburban advertising at undergound stations. (Victoria undergound station, c.1895.)

53. Wembley Park in the early years of the twentieth century. Watkin had wanted Gustave Eiffel to build the tower (seen here in its final unfinished state) higher than his Parisian masterpiece. But the Frenchman declined the job.

54. The Avenue, Bedford Park, 1882. The estate, situated next to Turnham Green station, was an early example of a progressive garden suburb, with large architect-designed homes by the fashionable Richard Norman Shaw intended to create a healthy and 'artistic' living environment for middle-class residents, with convenient rail access to town.

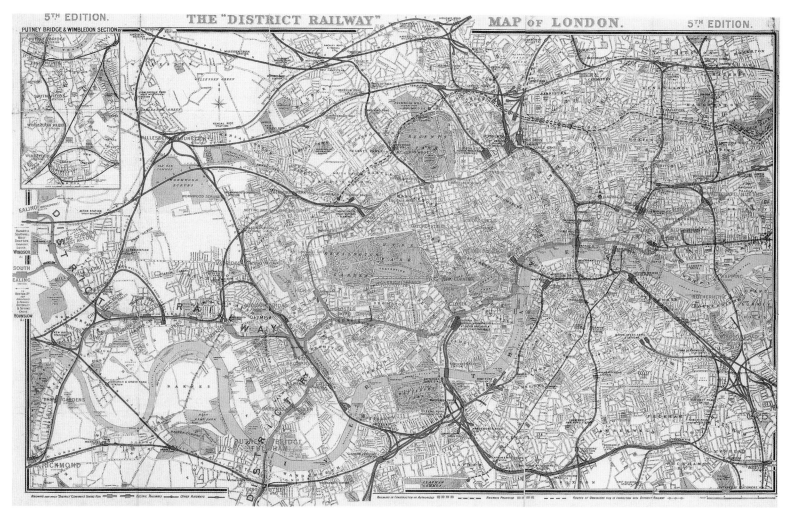

55

The end of steam

Away from the green fields and burgeoning suburbs of the extension lines, the Metropolitan and District railways were coming under increasing pressure to do something about the smoky atmosphere of the underground tunnels. Complaints about poor ventilation continued throughout the 1880s and 90s, and passenger numbers actually declined in the summer months as many preferred the slower, but open-air, option of travelling by horse bus. The underground also suffered by comparison with the newly opened City and South London Railway (1890) – the world's first deep-level electrically powered 'Tube' railway. Commuters using this route from Stockwell to the City enjoyed a clean, fast, service which made the Underground look archaic. The *Yorkshire Herald* was one of many newspapers to draw the inevitable conclusion that the days of steam were numbered:

> Those who have travelled by the Metropolitan Railway, and have felt, after coming out of the sulphurous atmosphere of the subterranean passage, as if they had been

55. The District Railway Map of London, c.1892, showing the Circle line and District suburban extensions to Ealing, Richmond and Putney in red.

chewing Lucifer matches, will rejoice to hear that some day yet the underground will be worked by electricity.[72]

But, as in the 1860s and 70s, opinion remained divided about just how bad conditions underground really were. In 1893, an intrepid journalist with the *English Illustrated Magazine* was given a footplate ride round the circle to experience conditions at first hand. Pulling out of St James's Park station, he thought 'the sensation altogether was much like the inhalation of gas preparatory to having a tooth drawn'.[73] Once the journey was underway, though, he was surprised to find 'the air far purer than I had expected, and the bad air so much complained of by the "sewer rats" – as those who habitually use the circle are called in "the City" – is due in a great measure to their almost universal habit of keeping all the windows and ventilators closed.' His sentiments were shared by the underground directors, but even they couldn't ignore the more typical, and numerous, criticisms raised by the 'sewer rats' themselves. Nor could they dismiss the official concerns of the Board of Trade, which had identified poor visibility as a contributory factor in several of the recent underground collisions. On one occasion, the tunnels were described as being 'so thick from smoke and steam that [the signalman] could not see a train as it was passing alongside his box'.[74]

The persistent complaints eventually led to a special Board of Trade inquiry in 1897, which was to have a decisive impact in hastening the end of steam operation on the underground. The investigation focused on the enclosed tunnel section between Edgware Road and King's Cross, used by 523 passenger and fourteen goods trains every day. Air samples showed that ventilation needed to be improved, although the report acknowledged the Metropolitan's efforts in this direction over the previous thirty years, including the use of 'best Welsh smokeless coal' for its engines. The company replied, rather unconvincingly, that, far from being a cause of illness, fume-filled stations like Portland Road were 'actually used as sanatoriums for men who had been afflicted with asthma and bronchial complaints', and that only minor changes would be needed to alleviate some of the worse problems. The inquiry was unimpressed and recommended that 'by far the most satisfactory mode of dealing with the ventilation of the Metropolitan tunnels would be the adoption of electric traction'.[75] As an interim measure, permission was given for further openings to be made at stations, on the understanding that the underground would eventually be electrified.

There was a problem, though. Neither railway could readily afford to electrify, while continuing rivalry meant that they couldn't even

56

56. 'Notice to Quit'. The fairy Electra is shown banishing the 'steam locomotive underground demon' following the opening of the electrified Central London Railway in June 1900 (*Punch*, 4 July 1900).

agree on which method to use. The Metropolitan favoured the Hungarian system of overhead power equipment, which had the attraction of being relatively cheap to install but was completely untried in the UK. The District, on the other hand, preferred the conductor rail system, similar to that in use on the City and South London Railway. Following independent trials on quiet parts of their network, both companies eventually agreed to cooperate in the experimental electrification of a short section of track between High Street Kensington and Earl's Court, using a four-rail (i.e. twin conductor rail) direct current system. Passengers used the line from May 1900, but the purpose-built six-car electric trains were not a great success, and the service was withdrawn in November. The experiment had failed, also, to resolve the issue of power supply, with the Metropolitan more adamant than ever in its commitment to overhead cabling.

In the meantime a new electric Tube, the Central London Railway, had cut through the heart of the capital from Shepherd's Bush to the Bank. From the start, the underground began haemorrhaging passengers to this cheaper and cleaner rival. To make matters worse, the price of high-quality coal, needed to limit pollution in the tunnels, had rocketed. Wholesale electrification couldn't be delayed any longer, and outstanding differences of approach needed to be quickly resolved.

The catalyst for change was the American financier and urban transit mogul Charles Tyson Yerkes, whose colourful business practices and takeover of the District Railway in 1901 are more fully discussed in chapter 2. Yerkes had no time for the bickering over power supply, confident instead that the only practical method was the direct current conductor rail system already proven on American metro systems. His persistence ensured that the matter went to the Board of Trade for arbitration, which ruled in favour of the District Railway.

With the matter settled, the underground railways set about creating the infrastructure necessary to support electrification. Separate power stations were built by the Metropolitan at Neasden (1904) and by the District at Lots Road in Chelsea (1905). As always, lack of coordination between the rival companies caused delays, with both pursuing independent trials and even using different equipment. On the District, the recently built branch line to South Harrow proved ideal for testing the new American-style electrical multiple-unit trains ordered by the company's engineer, James Chapman, and for training drivers (or 'motormen', as they were known after American practice). The first public service of electric trains began here in 1903 between Mill Hill Park (now Acton Town) and South Ealing, using a temporary generating station at Alperton. In a rare display of cooperation, prototype Metropolitan electrics were also allowed to draw power from this source and began experimental running from Rayners Lane to South Harrow in 1904. A few months later, on 1 January 1905, the Metropolitan introduced its first multiple-unit electric trains into regular service from Baker Street to Uxbridge, via Harrow.

Meanwhile, the electrification of the Inner Circle was also progressing remarkably quickly, with teams of up to 1,000 men working overnight to lay the new conductor

rails. The first timetabled passenger trains began in the summer of 1905, and once the inevitable teething difficulties had been ironed out a full service was introduced by the end of the year. The transition to electricity reached the jointly owned Hammersmith & City line in 1906, with the remainder of the District Railway following suit soon after. With a much larger overground network to consider, the Metropolitan initially extended electrification only as far north as Harrow, where steam locomotives took over for the remainder of the journey. Other railway companies using the underground sections of the Metropolitan gradually phased out steam-hauled passenger operation altogether, with Great Western through services being the last to go in September 1907. Occasional steam-hauled freight trains continued to use parts of the underground into the 1960s, with the Metropolitan (by then part of London Transport) retaining a few steam locomotives for engineers' trains until 1971.

For passengers, however, steam on the underground was now a thing of the past, consigned to the memory of the Victorian era. Yet the delayed transition to electricity didn't bring about an immediate transformation of the underground's finances, despite the efforts of the Metropolitan and District to introduce new trains and spruce up their stations. Neither did it end congestion on the streets, which, if anything, was getting worse as the new century dawned. The initiative had passed from the underground to the Tube, and the solution, so it appeared, lay in tunnelling deeper under London.

57. The trial run of the new electric stock on the Metropolitan line between Baker Street and Uxbridge, 13 December 1904. The 7½-mile branch line from Harrow to Uxbridge had opened to the public just five months earlier as a conventional steam-hauled railway.

58. The final version of the Metropolitan Railway crest introduced in 1904. The clenched fist and sparks at the top represent the power of electricity. Below are the arms of the City of London and the three counties served by the railway: Middlesex, Buckinghamshire and Hertfordshire. This crest was photographed on the side panel of restored coach No. 400, part of the London Transport Museum collection.

CENTRAL LONDON (TUBE) RAILWAY.

TAKING THE TICKET AT BANK STATION.

No worry about price
2ᴰ any distance

DISPOSING OF THE TICKET.

All tickets dropped into this box
No worry about losing them

SAFE & COMMODIOUS LIFTS.

TAKE THE TWOPENNY TUBE

No Worry about accidents

AND AVOID ALL ANXIETY

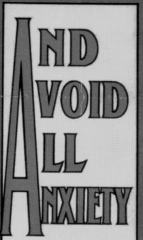

SHEPHERD'S BUSH. HOLLAND PARK. NOTTING HILL GATE. QUEEN'S Rᴰ. LANCASTER GATE. MARBLE ARCH. BOND Sᵀ. OXFORD CIRCUS. TOTTENHAM COURT Rᴰ. BRITISH MUSEUM. CHANCERY LANE. POST OFFICE. THE BANK.

CENTRAL LONDON RAILWAY.

ENTERING THE TRAIN.

Trains every few minutes
No worry about catching them.

LEAVING THE STATION AT SHEPHERD'S BUSH.

The whole distance covered so quickly
That there's nothing to worry about.

CHAPTER 2

DOWN THE TUBE

Buried on an inside page of the *Pall Mall Gazette* for 6 March 1890 was a short account of a highly significant but barely publicized event in London. 'Underground railway travelling, even at the unprecedented depth of sixty feet, is not so objectionable as may be supposed by people whose experience has been gained on the sulphurous Metropolitan lines,' it began.

> The experimental run in the subway from the City to the Elephant & Castle, which the directors made yesterday, demonstrated that a perfectly pure current of air can be maintained at that abnormal depth by the use of electric traction, and moreover that a very rapid means of suburban conveyance will shortly be established ... subways of the Southwark class are sure to grow into favour in overcrowded cities, possessing as they do notable advantages as compared with either existing underground or overground railroads.[1]

Nine months later the 'subway', renamed the City & South London Railway (C&SLR), was opened to the public, and Londoners could try out this revolutionary development for themselves. Unlike the original underground lines, which were essentially conventional steam railways laid in covered cuttings just below ground level, this was a major engineering and technological breakthrough. A railway running in deep tunnels under the city using electric trains was more than a simple novelty. The *Gazette* journalist who reported on the trial run clearly sensed that he had witnessed something important. His journey was a glimpse into the future of rapid transit in London, and the railway's completion was the first step in the creation of a completely new urban travelling environment that would soon become familiar to Londoners. Deep tunnels, passenger lifts and electric power were successfully combined for the first time anywhere in the world. These were the modest but pioneering beginnings of what was to grow into the London Tube.

---

1. 'Take the Twopenny Tube and avoid all anxiety'. A poster designed to make tube travel look safe and simple, c.1905. This is when the Tube became a proper name for the first time.

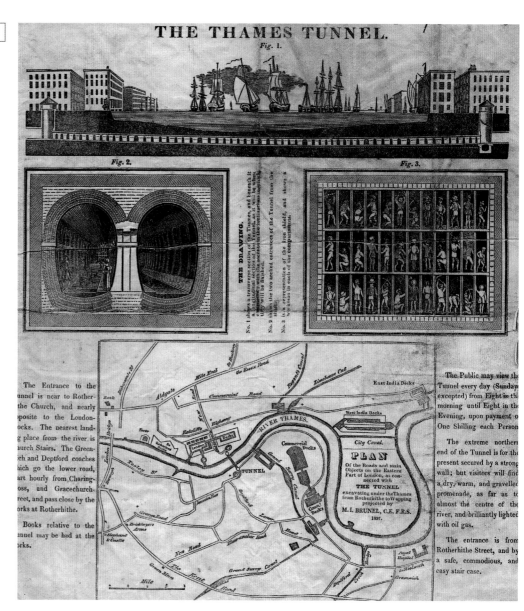

Under the river

Attempts at deep-level tunnelling under London in fact predate the cut-and-cover construction of the Metropolitan Railway by more than fifty years. As early as 1807 the inventive Cornish engineer Richard Trevithick, who was about to demonstrate a steam railway locomotive on a circular track in London, started work on a tunnel under the Thames. With the pilot driftway almost complete, the river broke in, and Trevithick had to abandon the project when his financial backers withdrew. Like so many of his schemes, including the development of railway engines, it led nowhere.[2]

Eleven years later, in 1818, Marc Isambard Brunel patented a method of tunnelling through soft ground such as London clay using a protective shield. He was apparently inspired by the burrowing method of the tiny but destructive shipworm *teredo navalis*,

2. Cross-section and map of the Thames Tunnel as completed in 1843. Figure 3 shows a cross-section of Brunel's tunnelling shield with miners working in individual protective frames.

3 and 4. A Thames Tunnel medallion and peep show sold as souvenirs in the 1840s to help fund the loss-making project.

which he had studied while working at Chatham Dockyard.[3] The technique of the shipworm was first applied by Brunel himself in 1825 when work began on the first successful tunnel under the Thames, close to Trevithick's failed scheme, between Rotherhithe and Wapping. Brunel planned it as a road crossing to link the growing docks on either side of the river at a time when there was no bridge over the Thames downstream from London Bridge, and no railway had even been proposed for central London, let alone built.

The principle of shield tunnelling was sound, but the practice was far from straightforward. In particular, the risk of getting too close to the uneven bed of the river was ever-present. Construction of the Thames Tunnel was plagued by setbacks and serious accidents which included fatalities when the river broke into the excavations at least five times. Seven workmen were killed, and Brunel's son Isambard, the resident engineer at the start of the project, was himself swept away and nearly drowned. Investors lost confidence in the scheme, the money ran out, and work was suspended for more than seven years, by which time the tunnel had become widely lampooned as 'The Great Bore'.

It was eventually completed and fully opened in 1843, eighteen years after digging started, but with no funds to build the spiral road ramps at each end, it could be used only by pedestrians, who paid a penny toll. The tunnel attracted enormous public interest, Queen Victoria and Prince Albert visited, and it became for a while one of the sights of London. Despite this, the company never paid a dividend and was unable even to pay the interest on its government loan. Impressive though it was as a structure, the tunnel was a financial disaster. As historian Charles E. Lee neatly summarized the position by the 1850s, 'it was obvious that the value of the tunnel as a tourist attraction could never make the undertaking a commercial success'.[4]

A House of Lords committee considering the rash of new railway schemes proposed for London in the early 1860s, just as the Metropolitan Railway opened, recommended that the Thames Tunnel should be adapted to serve as a rail link route between north and south London lines. In 1865 the East London Railway Company (ELR) was set up to do just that. Brunel's famous tunnel was sold to the railway company, and four years later steam-hauled passenger trains were running through it. After some complicated additional tunnelling under the London

5

5. A train emerging from the northern end of the Thames Tunnel after its conversion to rail operation, 1869. Brunel's twin tunnel is still used by the East London line today, now part of the London Overground network.

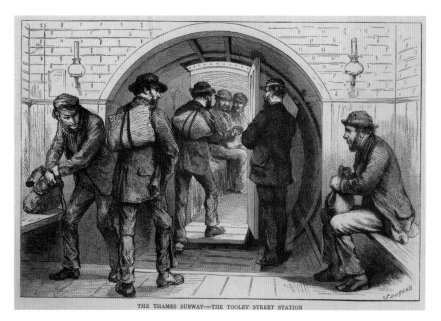

THE THAMES SUBWAY—THE TOOLEY STREET STATION

Docks the East London line was extended northwards to link up with the new Great Eastern Railway terminus at Liverpool Street in 1876 and connecting main lines south of the river at New Cross.

The East London line has had a complicated history since the late Victorian period, when it was run as a joint operation by several railway companies. Eventually in 1913 it was taken over by the Metropolitan Railway and electrified, becoming effectively part of the London underground system.[5]

The Tower Subway

In 1869, just as the East London Railway was being laid through the Thames Tunnel, a second tunnel was constructed under the river close to the Tower of London. It was built by Peter William Barlow, a railway engineer whose newly devised tunnelling method enabled him to construct the Tower Subway in just five months. When building Lambeth Suspension Bridge ten years earlier, Barlow had used cast-iron cylinders sunk vertically into the riverbed to create the bridge piers. He realized that this technique could be adapted to drive a subway horizontally under the river, and patented an excavating shield to do this in 1864.

Barlow's shield was cylindrical rather than rectangular, and instead of brick the tunnel was lined with curved cast-iron segments. His subway was a modest undertaking compared to the Thames Tunnel, with an internal diameter of just 2.3 metres, but Barlow's tunnelling method was a huge advance on Brunel's long and tortuous process. His Tower Subway was effectively the first tube tunnel.

The tunnelling shield worked like a giant apple corer. At the cutting end one or two miners worked inside a protective chamber, excavating the clay from the tunnel face. The shield was then forced forward into the space that had been cut, and the tunnel was lined with cast-iron rings made by bolting together curved segments. As the work progressed this created a cylindrical, self-supporting tube tunnel. A quick-setting lime grout was pumped into the gap left all round the tunnel rings by the skin of the shield to prevent the soil from settling and causing subsidence at ground level.

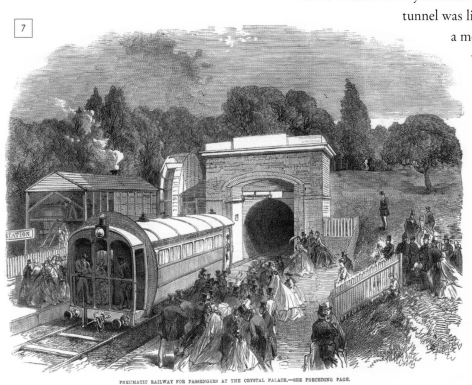

PNEUMATIC RAILWAY FOR PASSENGERS AT THE CRYSTAL PALACE.—SEE PRECEDING PAGE.

6. The Tooley Street 'station' at the south bank end of the Tower Subway when it opened in 1870. This illustration from The *Graphic* is unusual in showing working men rather than middle-class passengers using the river crossing. The passenger car, shown in the background, was soon removed and the first tube tunnel became a pedestrian subway.

7. The pneumatic underground railway demonstrated by Thomas Rammell at Sydenham in 1864. From the *Illustrated London News*, which described its complex working arrangements in great detail. It looked promising, but all pneumatic systems turned out to be a technological dead end.

Barlow's construction method was a triumph, and the principle is still applied today with modern equipment. Unfortunately his mechanical methods of transporting passengers down to, up from and through the subway were a disaster. There was a lift at each end of the tube tunnel, and a single, small cable-hauled railcar was used to take a dozen passengers through the subway at a time. All this mechanical equipment was powered by stationary steam engines, which proved very unreliable. Only three months after the official opening on 2 August 1870, the Tower Subway Company went bankrupt, and both the lifts and cable car were taken out. The world's first tube railway was reduced to being a cramped and inconvenient pedestrian tunnel at the bottom of a deep spiral staircase. Nevertheless, more than one million people paid the toll to walk through the subway every year until 1894, when Tower Bridge opened nearby as a free river crossing, and the subway was closed to the public. It was then adapted to carry hydraulic power and water mains under the river. All that can be seen today at ground level is the original entrance kiosk close to the Tower of London.[6]

Leaving steam behind

The first tube railway had failed because the transit system was unsatisfactory. Barlow's tunnelling method was sound, but there could be no real future for Tubes as a transport mode until some satisfactory alternative to the air-polluting steam locomotive was found for underground travel. Pneumatic power, with trains driven underground by air pressure, had looked promising when a short experimental line was built in the grounds of the rebuilt Crystal Palace at Sydenham in 1864. Thomas Rammell, the engineer who patented this pneumatic system, began work the following year on the Waterloo & Whitehall Railway, which would have used this technology to carry passengers under the Thames. The project ran out of money in the financial crisis of 1866 and was abandoned long before the tunnel was complete.

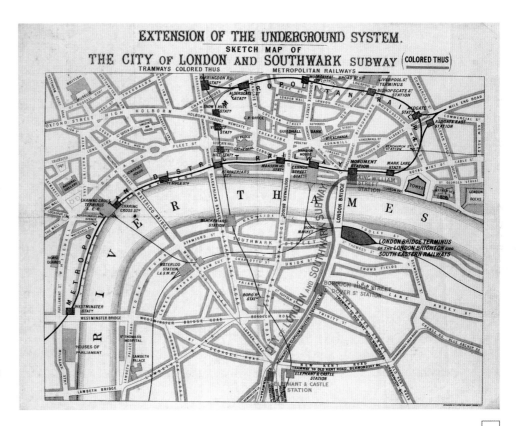

A short pneumatic underground railway on a much smaller scale was built by Rammell for the Post Office to carry mailbags between Euston station and the nearest sorting office, about 500 metres away. The London Pneumatic Despatch Company railway began operating in February 1863, just one month after the Metropolitan Railway was opened for passenger traffic nearby. When the line was extended in 1865

8. Map of the proposed City of London & Southwark Subway, 1884. By the time construction began two years later there were plans to double the length of the line to a southern terminus at Stockwell.

9. Modern cutaway showing how construction of the
City & South London began in 1886. A vertical shaft
was sunk from Old Swan Pier, near London Bridge, to
below the riverbed. Tunnels were then driven out in
both directions using Greathead shields. This view is
looking west towards Cannon Street railway bridge,
completed twenty years earlier.

to the main General Post Office near St Paul's, the Duke of Buckingham opened it by riding through the tunnel in one of the little open mail cars. He told the *Illustrated London News* that 'The sensation of starting, and still more of arriving, was not agreeable ... but once fairly within the tube, these sensations were got rid of, or left behind.'[7] The Duke was probably the first person to record his experience of such a primitive form of tube travel, but of course this original Post Office line was never intended for passenger use.[8]

The next passenger tube railway project planned for London was not authorized by parliament until 1884, the year the original underground lines round central London were finally linked up to complete the Inner Circle. The cut and cover method used to build the last section of the Circle line had become almost prohibitively expensive, and the continued use of steam trains offered no hope of improving the sulphurous atmosphere on the existing underground.

The City of London & Southwark Subway Company was set up with James Henry Greathead as engineer-in-chief. South African-born Greathead was a former pupil of Barlow and had been his contractor for the Tower Subway, largely because Barlow could find nobody else willing or able to do it. Greathead planned to use the same shield tunnelling method to build the next tube railway, but on a larger scale with twin tunnels just over 3 metres in diameter, and his name has been given to the soft-ground tunnelling shields used in London ever since.

The original planned route of the subway, from the Elephant & Castle, under the river to the City near the Monument, was only 2.4 km (1.5 miles) long. As a business proposition it did not look particularly promising as it seemed unlikely to lure City clerks from their horse buses to complete a daily journey to the Bank with a short trip deep underground. Greathead found clever solutions to the engineering difficulties of building his tube, but seemed less adept at route planning and assessing the passenger market for the subway. Whether there was a demonstrable demand or need for a new tube railway here remains unclear. Greathead may have seen it primarily as an engineering challenge and experiment.[9]

It seems to have been Charles Grey Mott, a businessman with railway experience who was made company chairman in 1886 just as construction started, who became the principal advocate and developer of the project. Mott got some influential supporters on board, including the ageing John Fowler and his partner Benjamin Baker, who were well paid as respected consulting engineers to talk the subway up, particularly with the parliamentary committees that had to approve the new railway. Work was already well under way at this stage to build the Forth Bridge in Scotland, for which both engineers were honoured on its completion.

Powers were quickly secured to more than double the length of the tube tunnels under south London with an initial extension to Stockwell. No part of the railway was opened until the full length, now just over 4.6 km (3 miles) underground and therefore a similar distance to the original Metropolitan line, was complete and ready for operation

10

in 1890. At this point the expanded subway project was renamed with the more appropriate and grandiose title of the City & South London Railway.

Construction of the subway began in May 1886, when a shaft was sunk from Old Swan Pier, off the north bank of the Thames near London Bridge, to a point well below the riverbed. Tunnels were driven out in each direction under the river using Greathead's improved tunnelling shields, which were lowered down the shaft and assembled at the bottom. One running tunnel was built above the other at this point. Starting construction in mid-river may seem perverse, but it allowed the contractors to remove all spoil from the tunnels by barge and meant that there was no need to acquire an expensive construction site in central London.

Powering the line

It was essential to find a suitably reliable and pollution-free form of power to use in the subway. The original plan was to use cable haulage, but with a more sophisticated system than the simple to-and-fro winding arrangement that had failed to work reliably in the Tower Subway. During the 1870s, Londoner Andrew Smith Hallidie had developed his patent gripper cable system for street railways in the USA, first on the steep hills of San Francisco and later in other American cities including Chicago, New York and Washington. It was the first viable alternative to the horse tram for use on urban streets.[10]

The first Hallidie cable system in Europe was opened up Highgate Hill in north London in 1884, largely as a demonstration. Cable haulage had never been used underground, but it would have looked potentially suitable as a non-polluting form of motive power when Greathead's subway was first proposed. When Mott arrived he was concerned about the limitations of the cable system that had been agreed, but it was only when the installation company suddenly went bankrupt in January 1888 that alternatives could be considered.

At this stage, with the tunnelling well advanced, electric traction was the only real option for the subway, but it was quite a leap in the dark. An electric locomotive had first been demonstrated by Werner von Siemens at a Berlin trade fair as recently as 1879, and the first public electric railway in England had been opened on the seafront at Brighton by Magnus Volk, another German engineer, four years later. By 1887 a number of short electric tramways were operating in Britain, Germany and the United States, but all of them were still experimental and none of them ran underground.

10. Building a tube tunnel in the 1880s. In the background miners are excavating the London clay inside a Greathead shield, and the spoil is being removed by the navvies on the left. The man on the right is pumping a quick-setting lime grout into the gap left by the shield between the tunnel rings and the surrounding soil.

In January 1889 the Salford engineering company Mather & Platt, which had the licence to build American Edison electric dynamos in Britain, won the contract to design and equip the world's first underground electric railway. Nine months later the first trial run took place in the subway tunnels, and before the end of the following year a full public service was in operation. This was a technological breakthrough achieved at astonishing speed, largely due to the pioneering work of two brilliant, but now almost forgotten, electrical engineer brothers from Manchester who had both worked for Siemens.

Edward Hopkinson designed and supervised the construction of the little electric locomotives. These were built in Gorton, Manchester, by Beyer, Peacock, suppliers of the original Metropolitan Railway steam locomotives, and fitted with Hopkinson's electric motors by Mather & Platt just a few streets away. Edward's elder brother, John, oversaw the installation and testing of the electrical generation and supply equipment, including the fitting out of a power station for the tube railway in Stockwell.[11]

A novel experience

Everything about the City & South London Railway was different from conventional railway travel and practice. All those who used it when the railway opened in 1890 found the new tube a completely novel experience in every way from the moment they arrived at a station.

Firstly, the City terminus at King William Street was entered at street level through an existing office building, an original example of a 'hole-in-the-wall' station entrance. The other five stations south of the river, all ornate little red-brick buildings on street corners, were each dominated by a large dome. This standard design by architect T. Phillips Figgis was highly distinctive, although the striking domes were largely decorative rather than a practical necessity.[12] The only one of these original tube station buildings to survive is at Kennington and is now listed.

II

Secondly, there was originally a standard flat-rate fare of 2d on the C&SLR, and no tickets were issued. Passengers paid a booking clerk, who let them through a turnstile. They were then taken down to platform level in a large but slow hydraulic lift, one of a pair at each station that could each hold about fifty people. Passenger lifts were still unusual at this time and found mainly in large hotels, where they carried guests to upper floors but never deep underground.

On the C&SLR the passenger lifts descended about 17 metres to the station tunnel, where there was a single

II. Stockwell station, the terminus of the first electric tube line, decorated for the official inauguration by the Prince of Wales, 4 November 1890. His carriage awaits. The station was later rebuilt, and Kennington is now the only surviving City & South London station in close to original condition with a dome.

island platform between two tracks, a layout that survives on the London Underground only at Clapham Common. This bleak space originally had only gas lamps as at first the power station could barely generate enough electricity for the trains, let alone lighting. There was separate hydraulic machinery at the depot to deliver water under pressure to work the large passenger lifts. Electric lifts came later.

Each train consisted of a small electric locomotive and three passenger 'cars', as carriages became known on the tube. There was no class distinction, another novelty, and the cars had only small opaque windows, presumably because it was thought there was nothing to see in the tunnels. There were comfortable cushioned bench seats and dim electric lighting inside at a time when most railway carriages had gas or oil lamps. Gatemen riding on the entrance platforms between the cars had to call out the station names and open the sliding end doors and lattice gates for passengers at each stop. The claustrophobic carriages were soon known as 'padded cells' for obvious reasons, and after many complaints the next deliveries of coaches were supplied with full-size windows. Despite the poor ventilation, there was one smoking car in each train, from which ladies were excluded.

A full journey from Stockwell to the City took about eighteen minutes, twice the average speed of the Inner Circle steam trains, and considerably faster than the horse-drawn trams and omnibuses on the streets above, though this did not include the time spent travelling up and down in the lifts. At the official inauguration the Prince of Wales spoke of his hope that 'the first electric railway in England will do much to relieve the congestion of traffic which exists in the City. Business men who have great distances to come will by this means find an easy way of leaving the City, and of enjoying the fresh

12. Invitation for the opening of the City & South London, 4 November 1890. The public had to wait another six weeks for access to the new line.

13. Platform view of Stockwell tube station, 1890, a pretty bleak and uninviting environment.

air of the country. The railway will also be a material boon to the working man who is obliged to work all day in a not always pleasant atmosphere for it will enable him to get a little fresh air.'[13]

The Prince's observations were a little off beam, as by this time Stockwell was a built-up inner suburb some distance from the country air. His hope that the line might reduce London's traffic congestion was also over optimistic, but he was not alone in this. The railway opened to the public on 18 December 1890, nearly six weeks after the Prince's official visit, and 10,000 people took a trip on that first day. Soon there were 15,000 people using the line every working day, and the overcrowding in rush hour led

to the introduction of graduated fares and season tickets. *Punch* quickly christened it the 'sardine box railway', and there was much comment in the press about the lack of class distinction. The *Railway Times* observed airily that 'we have scarcely yet been educated up to that condition of social equality when lords and ladies will be content to ride side by side with Billingsgate "fish fags" and Smithfield butchers'.[14] Nevertheless, the important precedent of single-class travel for all on London's tube railways was set and remained. By contrast, the Paris Metro opened ten years later with separate first-class compartments and maintained this distinction on its trains until the 1980s.

Despite its popularity, the City & South London had many problems and failings. As Mott admitted to a parliamentary committee in 1891, 'We were the experimenters, and made the City & South London line a little too small.'[15] The electric locomotives were often unable to cope with heavily laden trains, causing breakdowns and delays. There was not enough power supplied from Stockwell to keep a full service running, and a fourth generator set of steam engine and dynamo had to be installed in 1892. The underground layout of the stations and tunnels had been designed with cable traction in mind, and it was not ideal for electric working.

Yet the novelty of it all was such that, in response to public demand, the company built a viewing gallery at the power station and began charging visitors eager to see the generators in action. The wonder of electricity had a magical appeal at the turn of the century which was widely exploited in theatrical productions and the new popular

14. Stockwell power station c.1892. Leather belts coupled steam engines (on the right) to electric generators (left). The original power output proved inadequate to run a full train service, and an extra generator soon had to be installed.

15. The restored CSLR 'padded cell' car which has been on display in the London Transport Museum since 1980.

literature of science fiction. One early visitor to Stockwell was H. G. Wells, who was inspired by what he saw to write a rather grisly short story called 'The Lord of the Dynamos', published in a popular newspaper in 1894.[16]

After the pilot

Interest in and excitement about the potential of electric transport below ground did not lead to any immediate followers of the first electric tube. The City & South London only carried about half as many passengers in its first year as the Metropolitan had done over a similar original mileage. The directors had already secured parliamentary powers to extend southwards to Clapham even before the original section was opened. In 1893 a northern extension to the Angel was authorized, which diverted the line in new, larger tunnels, cutting out altogether the original cramped City terminus at King William Street[17] with its tight curve and sharp gradient. This meant further costly tunnelling and more rolling stock for the extended service, but would shareholders ever see a return on their investment?

The problem that has bedevilled underground railway construction ever since the nineteenth century was already apparent: they do not make a profit. The City & South London, despite its difficulties, was a triumph of engineering enterprise, but it could

16

16. In the depths of the Drain. One of the original American-built electric motor cars of the Waterloo & City Line, opened in 1898.

not achieve financial rewards for its investors. It paid no dividend for the first year and even after seven years was paying only 2 per cent. Revenue from fares was never going to be sufficient, and never has been, to cover the inevitably heavy capital costs of building an underground railway. Its social benefits may be considerable, but as an investment opportunity it never does stand up well.[18]

Between 1891 and 1893, five more new tube railways under London were authorized by parliament, but only one of them, the Waterloo & City, was built and opened before the turn of the century.[19] A parliamentary committee which considered four of them in 1892 recommended that in future tube tunnels should have a minimum diameter of 3.5 metres (11.5 feet), larger than the City & South London's original tunnels but still too small to take mainline trains. Inevitably, few new tube projects with larger tunnels were proposed after this because of the greater cost.[20] In the long run this has created a problem for London by limiting capacity and making it impossible to run standard mainline-size trains on the deep tube system.

Another significant recommendation with long-term consequences was that railway companies should no longer be obliged to purchase any properties they passed under on an approved new tube route. A 'wayleave' (permission to tunnel under someone's land) was considered sufficient, and for lines running below public streets this would now be granted free of charge. The result was that new lines were usually routed directly below main roads wherever possible to keep costs down. In London, where few streets are straight, this led to some sharp curves being created in tunnels that follow the street layout above rather than the most direct line between two points. The most obvious example of this is the sharp double curve of the Bakerloo line between Piccadilly and Oxford Circus, where the tunnels follow the line of Regent Street above.

The second tube line to be built was the Waterloo & City Railway, the only one for which capital was raised without difficulty. This is because it had the full backing of the London & South Western Railway (LSWR), the sole mainline company whose London terminus was neither within easy walking distance of the City nor linked to it by the Circle line of the steam underground. A short, direct tube link under the river from Waterloo to the Bank was the obvious answer. It was built in just over four years and opened by the Duke of Cambridge in 1898.

As no British manufacturer could meet the required delivery dates, the original rolling stock was imported from the US manufacturers Jackson & Sharp and fitted with Siemens motors and electrical equipment when they arrived in Britain. The Waterloo & City is unique in being the only passenger underground railway in London to have remained independent of the others.

Because it was a one-stop shuttle service, the line was soon generally referred to by City commuters as 'the Drain', an unofficial name it has retained ever since. The Drain was operated for nine years by the London & South Western in return for 55 per cent of the revenue income. In 1907 the mainline railway formally took over the tube company, becoming part of the Southern Railway in 1923 and British Railways (BR) after nationalization in 1948. Eventually, the Waterloo & City was transferred from BR to London Underground management in 1994, but it remains physically separate to both the overground and tube networks, with no rail connection to either.

The big tube

The Great Northern Railway was the main line that reached London on the east coast route to King's Cross in 1850. Like all the mainline companies, it wanted direct access to the City. The Great Northern was unable to do this with a surface railway, which would have been expensive and disruptive, requiring extensive property demolition.

As the Great Northern developed its suburban network in north London, there were problems running services through King's Cross, where mainline and local trains converged in the tunnels just outside the terminus. Local trains could join the Metropolitan Railway's City Widened Lines from here to Moorgate from the late 1860s, but it was a slow journey. By the 1890s the commuter trains from north London suburbs like Barnet, Enfield and Muswell Hill were facing serious delays in the bottleneck of the King's Cross tunnels.

Greathead, having just completed the first electric tube railway in south London, proposed something similar to the Great Northern in 1891 as a solution to its congestion problems. The plan was to route the steam-hauled suburban trains off the main line at Finsbury Park and, after a switch to electric traction, to run them underground in new tube tunnels from Drayton Park to Moorgate. It was therefore the only new tube line planned with large-diameter 4.9 metre (16 feet) tunnels that could accommodate standard-size overground trains.

Construction of the Great Northern & City was authorized by parliament in 1892, but no further progress was made because the GNR would not commit any funds to the project. Eventually the money was raised elsewhere, including a substantial sum from the contractors, S. Pearson & Sons. Work began in 1898, and the main tube section was completed by 1902.

Meanwhile the Great Northern had lost all interest in the project and refused to build the link to the main line, insisting that the tube had to terminate under Finsbury Park overground station. Through-working by Great Northern suburban trains was then impossible, and the whole point of the new tube was scuppered. Pearson agreed a three-year contract to operate the 5.6 km (3½ mile) line they had built themselves from 1904.

17

17. Promotional postcard for the Great Northern & City Railway c.1904, a dull and uninspired piece of advertising which reflects the line's low status and lack of funds. It was never well used, until the long-planned link with the main line was finally achieved in the 1970s.

With no connection to the Great Northern main line except its name, the Great Northern & City became a sort of orphan of the tube system. It used its own unique current-collection system from two outer conductor rails and large American-style multiple unit trains similar to the original Metropolitan electric trains introduced at this time. A short-lived power station was built at Poole Street, Islington, which was closed down ten years later when the line was acquired by the Metropolitan Railway and supplied by its own generating station at Neasden. The Poole Street power house then became a film studio for Gainsborough Pictures and was used by Alfred Hitchcock to shoot part of his penultimate British thriller, *The Lady Vanishes*, in 1938.

Until 1907, the Great Northern & City carried an average of 16 million passengers a year, but with competition from new electric tramways this dropped to 12 million in 1908. The original prospectus for the company had estimated 23 million, but without the mainline link this was completely unrealistic. Eventually, something close to the original plan was completed, but decades later. As part of British Rail's suburban electrification programme the link to the main line at Finsbury Park was finally built in the 1970s. The whole line was transferred to BR, and since 1976 Great Northern electric trains on outer suburban services have been running through to Moorgate. The big tube had eventually made it, but not as part of the London Underground network.[21]

The Twopenny tube

The next London tube to open was a considerably more ambitious project than the other lines started in the late 1890s. It also cost nearly five times as much as the original City & South London. This was the Central London Railway (CLR), planned to run from Shepherd's Bush to the Bank via Oxford Circus, with a projected extension to Liverpool Street. The CLR was authorized by parliament in 1892, despite strong objections from both the Metropolitan and District Railways, who correctly saw it as a threat to their traffic on the Inner Circle. Watkin, speaking for the Metropolitan, even made the desperate claim that there was no future in electric traction and that steam was still 'the only efficient form of locomotive power'.

Enough investors remained convinced that another London tube railway might be made profitable, even though the City & South London's returns already suggested otherwise. The projected route of the Central London certainly showed more thoughtful planning. It would be the first railway to penetrate the West End, linking affluent residential areas of west London directly with the City. The long, straight route below Bayswater Road, Oxford Street, High Holborn and Cheapside was already London's main east-west traffic artery. It was served by 239 omnibuses, which carried nearly 6 million passengers between Bayswater and the City in the second half of 1889.[22] This was a far more promising business market for a tube line than the C&SLR's route to the City from Stockwell via Elephant & Castle.

Many of the leading members of the Central London syndicate were prominent

18

German and American bankers such as Ernest Cassel, Henry Oppenheim and Darius Ogden Mills. Cassell, who originally came from Frankfurt, was a close friend of the Prince of Wales. With considerable influence in European financial circles, he was credited at the time with being the principal capital fundraiser for the project.[23] The Rothschilds also gave their financial backing. Cassell and his associates set up a separate company to build the line, which also took up all unsold shares in the project. This was the first of the complex financial arrangements through syndicates and holding companies by which most of the individual tube schemes were funded at the turn of the century.

Construction began in 1896 with the formidable trio of Fowler, Greathead and Baker as engineers. Of these three only the youngest, Sir Benjamin Baker, lived to see the railway completed. Wherever possible, the line was built directly below the streets to secure the free wayleave, which meant that where the road narrowed it was necessary for one line to run above the other rather than in parallel tunnels at the same depth.[24]

18. Building the Central London Railway at Tottenham Court Road, 1897. The men are working within the protection of a Greathead shield.

Another feature of the line was the provision of a rising gradient at the approach to each station platform to assist braking and a sharper falling gradient just beyond the platform to aid acceleration.

The station platforms were deeper than on the City & South London, but reached by fast electric lifts and lit by powerful arc lamps, which reflected brightly off the white tiled walls. All these were improvements on the first tube's cramped, basic and underpowered facilities. Greathead shields were used to dig the tunnels, and for some of the work an early mechanical excavator was introduced which enabled faster digging, though it was not very reliable. The Central London also learned from the City & South London's mistakes, which included using arched brick support instead of tubular cast-iron segments to line the larger station tunnels, and proved a false economy. Unlike the self-supporting tubes, these masonry structures had settled and caused subsidence and cracking of buildings on the surface. Greathead was only too well aware of potential litigation from nearby property holders who might bring a genuine or bogus claim against the railway for damages.

C. L. R. TWOPENNY TUBE. — A TRAIN AT SHEPHERD'S BUSH STATION.

19

One of the surprising 'large-scale' choices for the line was the decision to use big, heavy locomotives. Something more powerful than the City & South London's primitive little engines was clearly necessary to work longer trains, but the choice of cumbersome American-built 'camel-back' electric locomotives was a serious mistake. Their great weight and poor suspension soon led to complaints about vibration and a risk of property damage claims, much as the City & South London had experienced. Within three years the locomotives had to be replaced by lighter and more flexible multiple-unit trains, another American innovation which should have been adopted in the first place.

The multiple-unit system was devised in the USA by Frank Sprague, who first applied it when electrifying the South Side Elevated in Chicago in 1898.[25] Motors and control equipment on this system were fitted to some of the passenger cars in a train, linked by a low-voltage control circuit. This allowed operation from one controller in the cab of the leading car. With a cab at both ends of the train, it can be driven in either direction like a tram. This made locomotives redundant, an important step forward for rapid transit

20

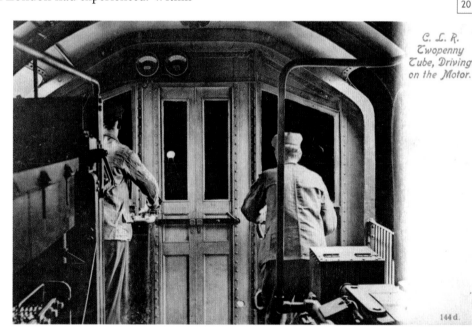

C. L. R. Twopenny Tube, Driving on the Motor.

144 d.

19. Postcard view of Shepherd's Bush station platform with an original 'camel-back' locomotive, c.1901. These original engines were replaced in 1903 because they were too heavy and risked causing subsidence along the line.

20. An unusual postcard view of the cab interior of a Central London Railway motor car, c.1903.

21

and underground railways because there was no longer the rigmarole of running a locomotive round a train at the terminus before making a return journey. The driver of a multiple-unit train simply walks to the cab at the other end to make the return journey in reverse, and the whole operation is speeded up and simplified.

In 1903 the Central London became the first railway in Britain to be worked entirely by multiple-unit trains. These were also the first to be equipped with a 'dead man's handle' safety system in each cab, another American invention which stopped the train by automatically applying the brakes if the driver collapsed and released his grip on the controls.

Sprague's multiple-unit system was adopted for all other London Tube lines and for the larger electric trains introduced on the Metropolitan and District Railways when these were electrified in 1905. Power-supply and current-collection arrangements, which varied between the early electric lines, were gradually standardized. Today there are still variations in the types of train used on different London Underground lines, but they are all multiple-units.

When the Central London Railway was ceremonially opened in June 1900, the Prince of Wales again did the honours. The line was opened to the public in July and immediately seemed to catch the imagination of both the

21. CLR managers pose at Wood Lane depot with one of their smart new multiple unit trains which replaced locomotives in 1903. Electric locomotives were still used for shunting in the yards, where for safety reasons there were no conductor rails and the power was drawn from overhead wires, seen here above the train.

22. A postcard of 'el tubo' sent home by an admiring visitor from Buenos Aires in 1904. Tube travel offered a much faster journey across central London than the old horse buses shown here.

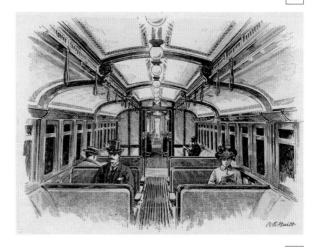

popular press and Londoners to a much greater degree than the City & South London had a decade earlier. It was certainly much more impressive. As the railway author O. S. Nock put it many years later, 'Where the City & South London displayed remarkable ostentation above ground and the most dismal cramped conditions on the railway itself, the Central London did almost exactly the reverse. The surface buildings were simple and business-like, but underground there was plenty of space and light.'[26]

Everyone seemed to particularly like the trains, perhaps because they were such a swanky contrast to the cramped old City & South London stock. Alfred Harmsworth's new popular newspaper, the *Daily Mail*, was particularly gushing in its reports on the new line, praising the 'palatial, luxuriously upholstered passenger cars' of the 'long, brilliantly lighted train'.[27] Even the Board of Trade Inspector, Colonel Yorke, commented in his official report that the trains were 'very commodious and comfortable . . . smooth running, quiet and well lighted'.[28] *The Times* referred to the 'American fashion' of the open saloon cars, which certainly followed the design style of US passenger cars, although the coaches were in fact built in Manchester.

It was the *Mail* that first came up with the catchy name 'Twopenny Tube' just five days after the public opening. The press nickname was quickly adopted by the railway itself for advertising and publicity and was soon widely used in songs, games, toys and plays, an instant part of popular culture. Even Gilbert and Sullivan changed the lyrics to their 1900 revival of *Patience* from a man travelling on a threepenny bus to 'the very delectable, highly respectable, Twopenny Tube young man'. It was an expression everyone immediately understood.

Within weeks 100,000 people were travelling on the Twopenny Tube every day. By the end of 1900 almost 15 million had been carried across London. The following twelve months saw 41 million passengers taking the Tube, eight times as many as had used the City & South London in its first year, and ordinary shareholders got their first dividend of 2.5 per cent. The Tube had definitely arrived, with a capital 'T'.

The combination of City commuter traffic and leisure travel, particularly among middle-class women, who found it convenient for the West End theatres and shops, gave the Twopenny Tube a wide customer base. The line gave a new boost to shops that were well established in Oxford Street and Regent Street such as Liberty's and D. H. Evans. More

23 and 24. Passengers in a spacious, single-class Twopenny Tube car and outside the new station at Oxford Circus. An appealing vision of luxury travel to the West End for all in the new century.

significantly, it brought custom to the flourishing new Oxford Street department stores like Peter Robinson, Bourne & Hollingsworth and Selfridges. American retailer Gordon Selfridge, who opened his giant Oxford Street emporium in 1909, recognized the promotional benefits of the Tube and lobbied the railway (unsuccessfully) to get Bond Street, the nearest station, renamed Selfridges.

The Twopenny Tube was always on the lookout for marketing opportunities itself, and introduced cheap off-peak shopping tickets in 1912. By this time competition from new motor buses had forced the railway to abandon its flat fare, but the name stuck. Other new 'add-on' services such as a 'Lightning Parcels Express' were also introduced to promote the line as it faced competition from other new Tube railways and the electrified Inner Circle.

Short extensions at both ends tapped into new traffic. A loop line from Shepherd's Bush to Wood Lane served the White City exhibition grounds, with a new station opened for the Franco-British Exhibition and the London Olympics in 1908, then used for a series of popular annual displays. At the eastern end a short extension from Bank to Liverpool Street in 1912 gave the line direct access to what had become the busiest mainline terminus in London. But these boosts were

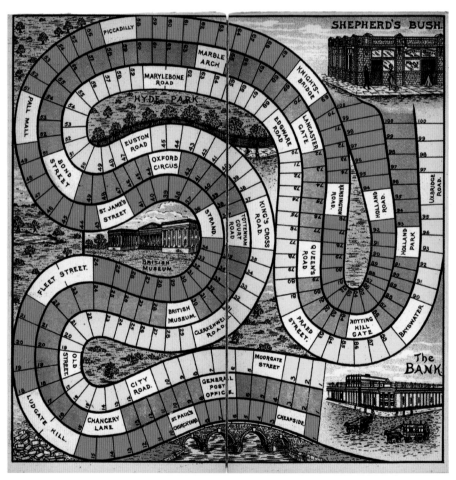

25, 26 and 27. Toy train, songsheet and board game inspired by the instant popularity of the Tuppenny Tube.

not sufficient to keep the Central thriving as an independent railway. A year later, in 1913, both the City & South London and the Central were forced to merge with the Underground Group.

Edwardian electric

In January 1901, seven months after opening the Central London Railway, the Prince of Wales succeeded his mother, Queen Victoria, to the throne. As King Edward VII he never travelled by Tube again, but the ten years of his reign witnessed dramatic developments in London's underground railways. Greater London's population had now risen to some 6.5 million; it was still the largest city in the world. The process of suburban expansion, encouraged in particular by the electric underground, electric trams and later feeder motor buses, got well under way. Once the feverish activity of the Edwardian period was over, it would be fifty years before another underground line was built below central London.

Edwardian London quickly became a grand imperial metropolis. This was also an era when new transport developments were based not only on new technology but on new money, where complex international syndicates led by bankers and financiers set the pace rather than the old Victorian railway barons, who had either died or been ousted by new people who took a different attitude to infrastructure projects. Greathead, Fowler, Baker, Watkin and Forbes were all key figures of the previous generation who died or retired between 1891 and 1901.

The question now was not how to develop the electric underground. Most of the technical issues were solved, often thanks to American electrical engineers like Sprague

28 and 29. A Twopenny Tube ticket, c.1900. The flat fare was abandoned in 1907, when motor bus competition forced the railway to introduce graduated fares, but the name stuck. The circular ladies' season ticket for Xmas shopping was a special promotion in 1912.

30. The Central London Railway was smoke-free, but even the line's general manager admitted that it had a 'peculiar smell' which couldn't be explained and was difficult to shift. They tried using powerful fans to improve air circulation and in 1911 started pumping in filtered and 'ozonized' air which was supposed to smell like the sea, as this poster of Neptune suggests. It was not very effective.

31. Delivery boy for the 'Lightning Parcels Express' service introduced by the Central London Railway in 1912. It was an interesting idea to get extra income for the line, but the company soon confined operations to its core business of carrying passengers.

and Edison, who were generally more entrepreneurial and successful than their British counterparts.[29] But finding the funding for expensive capital projects like new Tubes was not easy. Parliament still saw railways as private enterprise and wanted to keep a light touch on regulation without any state financial involvement. The London County Council planned a major investment in an electric tram network, opening its first route in 1903 from Westminster Bridge to Tooting, where it served a large new council housing estate.

The LCC saw the provision of cheap public transport as part of its progressive drive to improve living and working conditions in London, but not with buses or Tubes. Electric trams were its chosen agents of social transport policy in the metropolis. Every local authority had the power to take over private horse tramways and modernize them. Many did so all over the country at this time, creating large municipal systems in nearly every urban area in the 1900s, including great city networks like Birmingham, Glasgow and Manchester.

Local authorities were less interested in, and could not have afforded, municipal control or funding for new Tube railways under their city centres. The LCC built one shallow subway to take its electric trams under the new Kingsway and below Aldwych to the Embankment, but this was the only underground transport infrastructure that the council paid for.[30] Outside London Tube schemes were proposed for both Brighton and Manchester, but in the UK Glasgow was the only city to successfully complete an

32

32. Poster advertising the Glasgow Subway, opened in 1896. This was the only complete underground railway opened in the UK outside London.

underground railway project in the 1890s. The Glasgow District Subway, a sort of mini circle line of 10.5 km (6.5 miles), was opened in 1896. It started life as a private company using a cable haulage system, but by the 1920s had to be rescued financially by Glasgow Corporation, who took over its management and operation, eventually electrifying the subway in 1935.[31]

A Royal Commission on London's traffic sat in 1903 to consider the best way forward for transport in the great metropolis. It took pages of evidence from experts, and the not so expert, and compiled maps and statistics, but when it reported two years later had come to no firm conclusions about how new systems including electric trams and Tubes should be managed and developed. A Royal Commission can make recommendations, but has no power to implement them. It was clear that London's traffic would not be controlled or funded by a single private or municipal authority, but the Commission was confident that things would somehow work out: 'Private enterprise can, we hope, be relied on to provide as many railways as are required, provided that such railways are made and worked, as in our judgement they should be, on a commercial basis.' The city's mixed economy would continue, regulation should have a light touch, and transport planning was not yet ready for coordination.[32] This was very different from the strong municipal involvement in metro development in Paris, Berlin and New York, which all opened new electric rapid transit underground lines at the turn of the century.

The American titan

The answer to some of London's Underground funding problems in the Edwardian years was to come from a rather dubious, not to say dishonest, American source. The completion of the District's electrification and three more approved Tube projects that were struggling to raise capital took place in an atmosphere of fraud and trickery in the early 1900s. The man who achieved the transformation, though he died before these modern electric marvels were complete, was the wealthy entrepreneur and businessman Charles Tyson Yerkes. This larger-than-life character, who could have modelled himself on Anthony Trollope's fictional anti-hero the devious railway financier Augustus Melmotte,[33] once described his business method as simply to 'buy up old junk, fix it up a little, and unload it upon other fellows'.[34]

Yet even before Yerkes arrived from Chicago at the turn of the century on his mission to electrify London's transit, a serious fraud involving the finances of the company set up to back the Baker Street & Waterloo Railway, authorized in 1893, was unravelling. The new Tube company was struggling to raise capital. Whitaker Wright was an English millionaire who had made a fortune from mining interests in

33. Charles Tyson Yerkes (1837–1905), entrepreneur, swindler and saviour of the London Underground, at his desk, c.1902.

WORLD METRO TRANSIT

No other major world city copied London in the nineteenth century by building an urban underground railway to deal with its traffic congestion. Paris, which had pioneered the use of omnibuses and cabs as new modes of public transport in the 1820s, was replanned on a grand scale by Baron Haussmann for Napoleon III in the 1850s, with wide boulevards cutting through the narrow streets. It did not need an underground railway at this stage. New York, laid out on a strict grid pattern where London looks almost random, had introduced both omnibuses and the first horse tram lines in the 1830s, but little consideration was given to rapid transit by rail in the city until the 1860s.

The first proposal for a subway in New York was made by Hugh B. Willson, a Michigan railroad man who was present at the opening of London's Metropolitan Railway in January 1863. On his return to the US, Willson set up an American Metropolitan Railway Company to build a similar steam-powered cut-and-cover line in Manhattan, but his proposal was thrown out by the New York State Legislature. An amended scheme was approved at a second attempt but vetoed by the Governor after strong opposition and lobbying by the existing street railway companies.

A cable-powered elevated railway was first demonstrated in New York by Charles T. Harvey in 1868, but the cable system did not work well, and under new ownership the line switched to steam operation in 1871. Meanwhile the first experimental passenger subway in the city had been built under a short section of Broadway by Alfred Ely Beach, an inventor and publisher of *Scientific American* magazine. Beach built an underground 'pneumatic dispatch' line with a railcar which was blown forward and sucked backwards by a large fan, a system similar to Rammell's experiments in London. He opened his demonstration line to the public in 1870 but failed to get financial backing or the city's permission to build a longer,

34. An elevated section of the Berlin U-Bahn, with a train on a trial run just before the public opening of the system in 1902.

35. City Hall, the most elaborately tiled original station platform on the New York Subway, shown on a coloured postcard of 1904. This line is no longer part of the working system but has been preserved, and public visits are occasionally arranged by the New York Transit Museum.

1758   *PARIS. — Une Station du Métropolitain. — LL.*

permanent underground line. Instead, a network of elevated lines known as 'els' were constructed in Manhattan in the 1870s, using conventional steam locomotives to power the trains. [35]

No further passenger subways were built in New York or anywhere else until after the City & South London Railway had pioneered the use of electric power underground in 1890. The first electric subway to open in mainland Europe was in Budapest, Hungary, where a short passenger line running just below one of the city's main streets was completed in 1896. More substantial metros opened in quick succession in major cities at the turn of the century, nearly all of them running partly underground and using electric multiple unit trains.

New metro rapid transit lines were built in a succession of cities from the turn of the century. Urban railways opened in Vienna (1898), Paris (1900), Boston (1901), Berlin (1902), New York (1904), Philadelphia (1908), Hamburg (1912), Buenos Aires (1913), Madrid (1917) and Tokyo (1927). Only Vienna operated its new system with conventional steam trains, because it was entirely overground. In the UK, the Liverpool Overhead Railway, opened in 1893, was a pioneer urban electric passenger line serving the city's docks and the first elevated electric railway in the world. It was closed down and demolished in 1956. [36] Chicago, by contrast, has kept its distinctive turn-of-the-century elevated transit system in the city centre 'loop' and only put two of its elevated lines below ground in subways from the 1940s onwards. [37]

36. An early postcard of the Paris Metro, first opened in time for the great International Exhibition of 1900.

the USA. He approached the Tube company on behalf of the London & Globe Finance Corporation, in which he owned almost one-third of the shares, and offered to invest £700,000 in the new railway.

This allowed construction of the Bakerloo line to begin in 1898, but within eighteen months Wright's dodgy finance company had failed when he tried to manipulate the market. Work on the Tube was stopped as contractors waited to be paid, and Wright fled the country bankrupt. Eventually arrested in New York, he was brought back to London and convicted in 1904 of defrauding investors to the value of £5 million. Sentenced to 'the severest punishment which the Act permits ... penal servitude for seven years',[38] Wright left the courtroom proclaiming his innocence. A few minutes later, he collapsed dead, having swallowed a cyanide capsule. When police searched his body they found a loaded revolver in his pocket, which he had evidently concealed throughout the trial as a back-up for his planned suicide.

By the time Wright's case came to trial, Charles Yerkes was well on the way to fulfilling his ambitious moneymaking plans for developing rapid transit lines in London. Having been virtually driven out of Chicago for bribery and corruption in his manipulation of the city's street railway contracts, Yerkes came to London to try his luck. As described in chapter 1, he began by acquiring a controlling interest in the District Railway in March 1901, expertly using the power of the wealthy American financial syndicates he represented. James Staat Forbes, who had been the railway's managing director for twenty-nine years, was persuaded to retire, and the old steam underground company was taken down a new modernizing track into the twentieth century.

In July, Yerkes and his associates formed the Metropolitan District Electric Traction Company to build a power station and electrify the railway. At this stage the Yerkes group already had plans to build additional Tube lines and to acquire electric tramways. A vast riverside generating station was therefore planned which could supply a number of separate electric railways and tramways across London.

It was through Yerkes, and the wealthy American financial syndicates he represented, that nearly all the capital for further Tube construction in the early 1900s was found, but his influence in London was first felt in the battle over the rival electrification proposals for the steam underground. He turned down the untried Hungarian Ganz overhead system in favour of the direct-current conductor-rail system that had been tried and tested on his lines in Chicago. The Metropolitan challenged his decision and appealed

37. Cover of a Metropolitan Railway timetable for 1913, showing electric trains underground in the City and in open country near Harrow.

to the Board of Trade, which referred the matter to arbitration. A tribunal sat for twelve days in 1901 and eventually agreed with Yerkes. The Met was forced to accept the verdict, as electrifying the jointly operated Inner Circle on two different systems was clearly unworkable.

Rejecting a takeover bid by Yerkes in his hour of triumph, the Met proceeded with electrification on a 600V DC system similar to the District. It was an essential and long-overdue modernization, though initially the Met seemed to have little idea how to plan its future development beyond the huge initial capital commitment to electrification.

By the autumn of 1905 the District's smart new electric trains, painted maroon with gold lettering, were running right through central London as far as East Ham in one direction and over the railway's various western branches to Wimbledon, Richmond, Hounslow, Ealing and South Harrow in the other. Suddenly the railway's long-held reputation for slowness, dirt and unreliability in the final years of steam was swept away. Londoners discovered rapid transit in comfortable and capacious open saloon cars that could swallow large crowds, though they also had to learn a new etiquette of sliding doors and 'straphanging', as the Americans called it, during rush hours.

Yerkes lived just long enough to see his Chicago-style commuting up and running in London. 'Londoners are the worst people to get a move on I ever knew,' he declared in one of his last interviews. 'To see them board and get off a train one thinks they had a hundred years to do it in; still, they are doing better, and in the end I shall work them down to an

38. Poster featuring the District Railway's smart new American-style electric trains, c.1905.

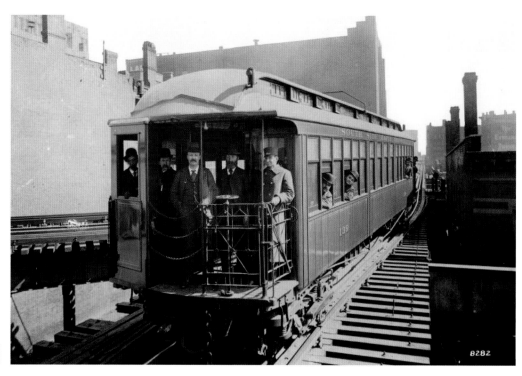

allowance of thirty seconds.'[39] Yerkes was still talking confidently of the impact his plans would have on metropolitan travel: 'When my scheme is complete, the Londoner will be able to get from one end of the city to the other or all round it for twopence.' He would not live to see his 'scheme' finished and died just a few weeks later on 29 December 1905 at the Waldorf Astoria Hotel in New York.

In London, the late traction magnate was widely hailed in press obituaries as a public benefactor. 'Rapid transit was the ideal he worked for,' commented the *Westminster Gazette*, 'and he became a street railway king in this respect not only in American cities but in London as well. We owe much to the man who revolutionised our old-fashioned methods of going to and fro.'[40]

The Yerkes Tubes

Of the Tube railways promoted and approved after the opening of the City & South London, only three more reached fruition in the Edwardian decade after 1905. These three, now the Bakerloo, Piccadilly and Northern lines, were all projects taken over by the Yerkes group. After their completion in 1906/7, no further Tube railways were built under central London for sixty years, and a period of consolidation began.

The final Tube boom was over just six years after

39. The inspiration for London. A driving car on the newly electrified elevated tracks in Chicago, 1898. Frank Sprague, inventor of the multiple-unit control system, is standing second left.

40. Strap-hangers. One of a series of comic cards set on the District Railway featuring the American habits and expressions of the electric Underground, where all carriages and coaches now became cars.

it began. Within days of securing control of the District Railway in 1901, Yerkes' financial syndicate began negotiations to take over the stalled Baker Street & Waterloo project. He had already, in 1900, bought the powers to construct the Charing Cross, Euston & Hampstead Railway, authorized in 1893 but unable to raise capital funding. The third Tube line built by the Yerkes group was the Piccadilly, created through the amalgamation of two separate railway projects in 1901.

In 1902 Yerkes reconstituted his Metropolitan District Electric Traction Company as the Underground Electric Railways of London Ltd (UERL), a holding company for all his theoretically separate transport interests, with himself as chairman. The UERL proceeded to successfully scupper all rival attempts to build new Tube railways in London. Yerkes even managed to beat off John Pierpont Morgan, the wealthiest of all the American industrial 'robber barons' of the day, who was backing an alternative proposal for what became the Piccadilly line. Morgan was no slouch at dodgy dealing himself, but Yerkes won this particular battle.[41] It is a complex tale of business intrigue, certain details of which are still shrouded in mystery. Suffice to say that

AN UNDERGROUND IMPROMPTU. THE TUBE STEP. [41]

[42]

although 1902 was another boom year for Tube proposals, with nearly thirty bills coming before parliament, only the UERL-backed schemes were eventually both authorized and constructed. Within five years these new Tube lines were all in operation.

The common management of the three UERL Tubes led to a general standardization in the design of stations, rolling stock, signalling and other equipment. All three routes were intended to open up access to the West End rather than the City, following the success of the Twopenny Tube, and close attention was paid to the appearance of the stations both above and below ground. Instead of the rather low-key surface buildings of the Central, with their nondescript terracotta

41. The Edwardians found endless humour in the new, enforced proximity of the sexes and social classes in crowded open-saloon Tube cars. This *Punch* cartoon of 1909 is a typical observation.

42. Overhauling the motor bogies of electric cars at Mill Hill Park (now Ealing Common), the main depot for the District Railway, c.1910.

entrances, the UERL stations were given a distinctive common identity by architect Leslie W. Green. The surface buildings, housing the booking hall and lifts, were of load-bearing steel-frame construction to take the weight of the lift motors on a mezzanine floor and allow the addition of lettable office storeys in the air space above. This was very much in the progressive spirit of Chicago, where steel-frame office building had pioneered early skyscraper construction at the end of the nineteenth century.

One hundred and forty identical electric lifts were installed at the UERL stations, the largest single lift contract in the country. All of them were supplied by the Otis Elevator Company, another example of the group's close American connections. Some of these elevators remained in service for eighty years before being replaced, and at Aldwych station, closed in 1994, both the original lift cars are still in place, though not operational. At another Piccadilly line station, Holloway Road, a spare lift shaft was used in 1906 to try out an alternative to the lift that proved a little ahead of its time. American inventor Jesse Reno was given the opportunity to demonstrate his patent spiral escalator in the shaft. Only one photograph survives of Reno's rather terrifying-looking machine, which was apparently never put into public service.[42]

Reno sold out to Otis, and five years later the first straight, angled escalator was successfully installed between the District and Piccadilly lines at Earl's Court station.[43] It was quickly established that 'moving staircases', as they were originally called, are a much more efficient means of moving large numbers of people vertically, and escalators were fitted in preference to lifts at all new deep-level stations after 1911.[44]

Both the colour light automatic signalling system and all other electrical equipment on the UERL Tubes emulated American precedents adopted by Chapman on the District.[45] The rolling stock also followed American practice with Sprague/Thomson-Houston multiple-unit control equipment. The trains were all to the same general design, with fireproof all-steel bodies, though built by different manufacturers in the USA, France and Hungary as well as Britain because no one company could fulfil the large order on time. Multi-national manufacture for export is nothing new. The American-built cars were shipped to Britain in knocked-down form and assembled at Trafford Park, Manchester.[46]

The UERL trains were similar to the Twopenny Tube's cars, though rather more austere inside. Entry and exit was via end platforms protected by lattice metal gates. These were operated by a gateman who stood on the gangway between each car.

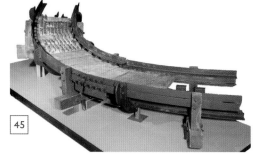

43. One of the new platform nameboards introduced by the UERL from 1908 which later developed into the company's roundel symbol.

44. The only known photograph of the Reno spiral escalator installed at Holloway Road station in 1906 but never put into service.

45. Some of the remains of the spiral escalator, discovered at the bottom of a lift shaft in the 1990s, have been reassembled at the London Transport Museum Depot.

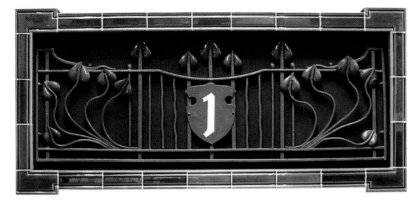

Passengers sat on hard rattan-covered seats in open saloons with no class divisions, so everyone had the same travelling experience. Unlike the Twopenny Tube's original flat fare, which it was soon forced to abandon, all three of the UERL lines (and the District, which the company also controlled) had a graduated fare structure. Numbers grew steadily on the UERL Tubes, but remained well below the company's optimistic estimates before opening. In 1908, the first full year of operation for all three, the Hampstead Tube carried 25 million passengers, the Bakerloo 28 million and the Piccadilly 34.5 million.

Growing the business

Londoners quickly took to the Tubes for both daily commuting and leisure travel, but passenger numbers were nowhere near enough to produce the good return for investors that the persuasive Yerkes had promised. The American directors of the UERL went headhunting on their side of the Atlantic and appointed a new general manager for the London project in 1907. This was Albert Stanley, the future Lord Ashfield, who arrived from New Jersey with a temporary contract and a brief to sort out the UERL's desperate financial situation. Within five years this remarkable transport manager, English born but American trained, completely turned the company's fortunes round. The organization that Yerkes had left facing potential bankruptcy became the flourishing core of London's newly modernized public transport network. Rather than returning to America after making a few adjustments to the company, Stanley became the key figure in London's transport development for the next forty years, and was commemorated after his death as the creator of London Transport.[47]

Stanley's early career in the US had been as a tramway manager in Detroit. He had no experience of urban railway operation, but an astute understanding of what was needed to run a successful city transport undertaking. Instead of cutting back to stave off financial collapse, Stanley built new alliances and

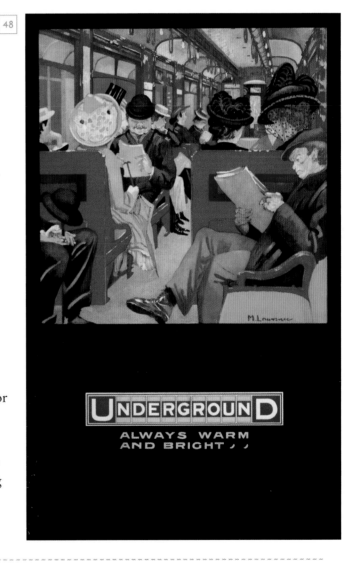

46. Art nouveau-style lift shaft ventilation grille originally used at all of Leslie Green's UERL stations.

47. Watercolour of Oxford Circus station by architect Leslie Green, exhibited at the Royal Academy in 1905. More than forty stations were built for the UERL Tubes in 1906-7 to this standard design, with distinctive ox-blood glazed brick exteriors on steel frames.

48. A colourful view of comfortable travel on the District in a poster by Marc Laurence, 1912.

THE POWER HOUSE

Lots Road, Chelsea, was quite literally the power source for all Yerkes' transit schemes and was the largest electrical generating station in Europe when it was built in 1902–5. The design of Lots Road and the electrification of the District and three new Tubes was carried out under the direction of James Russell Chapman, an American electrical engineer who was one of the chief officers in the Yerkes syndicate. Yerkes himself had little knowledge of the new technology, but he was good at hiring the best people to carry out the work for him. Chapman was one of the leading experts in the field, having successfully electrified more than 400 miles of street railway in Chicago for Yerkes since 1895. He was put in charge of all of Yerkes' electrical engineering work in London, working with a small, tightly knit team of American assistants, who not surprisingly followed the latest US practice very closely. [48]

Yerkes' plans to build an enormous power station on the Thames at Chelsea met with strong but ultimately futile opposition. One of the principal objectors was the flamboyant American-born artist James McNeill Whistler, who lived in a house overlooking the river on Cheyne Walk and had painted this stretch of the Thames many times since the 1860s. Whistler, now old and frail, died in 1903 before the completion of Lots Road changed the river view at Chelsea forever.

Yerkes only just saw his great power station finished and operational, as he died at the end of 1905. Five years later, with no hint of irony, the UERL commissioned a poster of Lots Road by the lithographer Thomas Robert Way in moody Whistlerian style. It was Way's father who had encouraged Whistler to take up lithography many years earlier, so here was the next artistic generation presenting a view of the new electric London in the style of one of the former avant garde.

Lots Road generated the power for most of London's Underground for a century. The site had been chosen

49. 'The Moving Spirit of London'. Underground poster of Lots Road in the style of Whistler by T. R. Way, gently informing Londoners of the power station's impressive statistics, 1910.

MPTON RY.-POWER HOUSE, CHELSEA.

On top of a Chimney Shaft.
The Largest Stacks of the World.
(275 feet high with an internal diameter of 19 feet.) Built by the Alphons Custodis Chimney Construction Co., Westminster, at the New Chelsea Power House for the Underground Electric Railways Co., of London Ltd.

because coal barges could be unloaded in a specially constructed tidal basin at Chelsea Creek, and the adjacent West London railway also allowed easy coal supply by rail. The power station burned 500 tons of coal a day, needed to run the eight turbo-generators which supplied current at 11,000V AC, reduced at sub-stations to the Underground's operating current of 550–600V DC. The generating capacity was improved over the years, allowing the much smaller original power stations of the City & South London and Central London [49] lines to be closed down.

In the 1960s Lots Road was converted to gas turbine operation and eventually it was closed down at the start of the twenty-first century, when London Underground's power supply was transferred to the national grid. It was then redundant, but like London's Battersea and Bankside power stations it had become a listed building looking for a new use. Lots Road will not become an art gallery like Tate Modern at Bankside but it will eventually be adapted for residential use with new apartments, preserving the original control room, which still has the air of a science fiction film set. Even in converted form, the 'Chelsea monster' that shocked the Edwardians will remain a monument to early electric power in London and the vision of the American traction king who built it.

52

50. Postcard of the completed UERL power house at Lots Road, Chelsea c.1905, the largest generating station in Europe.

51. The seat of power. Panels from the Lots Road control room, now in the London Transport Museum.

52. Novelty postcard showing surveyors on top of a newly completed Lots Road chimney stack high above Chelsea Creek, 1904.

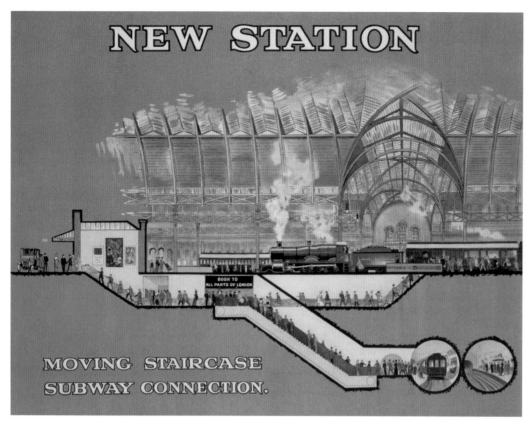

NEW STATION

MOVING STAIRCASE
SUBWAY CONNECTION.

UNDERGROUND

THE GHOSTLY DRIVER
WHO SECURES YOUR SAFETY WHEN TRAVELLING BY UNDERGROUND
READ ALL ABOUT HIM AND THE MANY OTHER WONDERS OF
LONDON'S TRAFFIC IN THE STRIKING ARTICLE WHICH APPEARS

IN THE JUNE NUMBER OF
PEARSON'S MAGAZINE
NOW ON SALE. PRICE 6ᴰ

53 54

negotiated mergers with smooth talk and good public relations. It was clear to him that the smaller underground and tram companies could not survive as independent operators, and that partnership agreements and amalgamations were the way forward.

The UERL had already acquired one tramway operator, the London United, in Yerkes' time. By 1912 it controlled another, the Metropolitan Electric, and was about to take over the London General Omnibus Company (LGOC), which ran most of the capital's newly mechanized bus services. The expanding UERL empire, commonly referred to at this time as the London Traffic Combine, was able to use its bus and tram services as feeders rather than competitors to the Underground. A year later the Combine swallowed up two of the three remaining small independent Tube railways, the City & South London and the Central London. The third, the Great Northern & City, was acquired by the Metropolitan, which remained the only underground railway outside the Combine's control. An offer of amalgamation was made by the UERL in 1913 but firmly rejected by the Met.

Under the confident leadership of Robert Hope Selbie,[50] who became its General Manager in 1908, the Metropolitan was recovering some of the forward-thinking lost to Yerkes in the battle over electrification a few years earlier. Selbie saw no reason to fall on his sword and join Stanley's Combine like the smaller Tube companies. Instead, he celebrated the Met's Jubilee as the original underground railway with a special

55

53. Detail from a poster by Charles Pears announcing the opening of the new Bakerloo Tube station at Paddington, 1913. By this date all new deep-level stations had 'moving staircases' (escalators) instead of lifts.

54. 'The Ghostly Driver'. Poster advertising *Pearson's Magazine*, June 1912, featuring the 'dead man's handle' safety mechanism fitted to all electric Underground trains and obligingly publicized by the popular press.

55. Albert Stanley (1874–1948), creator of London Transport. This photograph was taken in 1910 when he became Managing Director of the Underground Group. Knighted in 1914 for services to transport, he was made Lord Ashfield in 1920 after serving in the wartime government of Lloyd George. He became the first Chairman of London Transport in 1933.

publication in January 1913[51] and continued to plan for an independent future while cooperating with the UERL to a limited degree in joint marketing initiatives.

By 1914 most Londoners' travel habits had changed considerably since the start of the new century. Nearly twice as many rides per head of population were being taken on public transport as were recorded in 1901.[52] There was an immense growth in demand for transport, partly fuelled by what was suddenly available that was both cheap and convenient for users. The electric underground lines had started this trend, then been joined by electric tramways from 1901 and finally reliable motor buses from about 1908. For Londoners it must have seemed like a new golden age of transport opportunity where easy travel was available for all at very low cost. For investors it was less opportune, as the financial returns on all these projects, and particularly the underground railways, was generally minimal. If it had not been for fraudsters like Yerkes, the system we now rely on might never have been built.

There was a certain brashness and populism about the American style of the UERL which clearly grated with some British commentators used to the more conservative approach of the established Victorian railway companies. When the first of the Yerkes Tubes, the Baker Street & Waterloo Railway, opened in March 1906 the shorter name 'Bakerloo' was suggested soon afterwards by the diarist of the *Evening News*. A few months later it was officially adopted by the company, much to the disgust of the *Railway Magazine*. 'Some latitude is allowable, perhaps, in the use of nicknames, but for a railway itself to adopt its gutter title is not what we expect from a railway company. English railway officers have more dignity than to act in this manner.'[53]

Few people in Britain shared or believed in the American vision of electric railway and 'street car' suburbs that Yerkes brought to London at the turn of the century. Even the US-born journalist Ralph Blumenfeld, later to become editor of the *Daily Express*, was sceptical after interviewing Yerkes in 1900 on an early visit to London, while crossing the city in a Hansom cab. 'Although he is a very shrewd man,' Blumenfeld wrote in his diary at the time, 'he is a good deal of a dreamer.'[54]

Yet less than a decade after Yerkes' death, his plans for a suburban town built around the projected Hampstead Tube terminus at Golders Green came to fruition. This was the only point where one of Yerkes' Tube lines came to the surface in open country, just beyond the built-up area. The site for the station and depot were carefully chosen with future development in mind. When they opened in 1907 beside a country crossroads there was little to be seen over the fields except the new London crematorium tower looming on the horizon. But a few years later a thriving new community had grown up at Golders Green complete with shopping parades, churches, a landscaped park, cinema and the grand Hippodrome theatre. By 1914 over 3,600 new homes had been built within easy walking distance of the station, and Hampstead Garden Suburb had been established nearby.

Golders Green was the pioneer Underground suburb, only 5 miles or twenty minutes' travel time by Tube from the West End. Some 1.5 million passengers used the new station

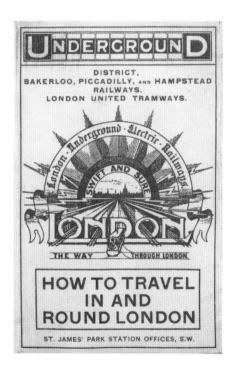

56 UERL publicity brochure, 1908, featuring the new UNDERGROUND lettering introduced for corporate marketing and the first logo for the group, featuring railways, trams and electrical symbols. It was soon replaced by the simpler roundel logo.

in its first full year of traffic, rising to more than 10 million by 1914.[55] When H. G. Wells looked even further ahead that same year, predicting that before long season ticket holders would have a 100-mile radius of central London for daily travel by high-speed train, the concept no longer seemed like science fiction.[56]

An unavoidable consequence of this new rapid transit by Tube was that speed did not always mean comfort, and almost inevitably planned improvements could become problems rather than benefits. An official UERL internal Traffic Notice as early as January 1908 reminded all staff that:

> on no account must over-crowding of trains be allowed. It must be remembered that over-crowding may constitute a serious public danger, and should a train be full, Station Masters, Inspectors, Conductors and Gatemen and all concerned must politely request intending passengers to wait for the next train, which will arrive within three minutes. Under no circumstances must passengers be allowed to ride on the car platforms.[57]

Compare this official instruction with O. S. Nock's story of a friend's experience in the early years of the Hampstead Tube. Rush-hour overcrowding was not unusual, and clearly passengers were sometimes forced to ride squeezed together on the open gated

57. The first free Underground map, issued in 1908. This was a joint marketing exercise featuring all the underground lines even though they were still run competitively by separate private companies at this stage.

platforms. On one particularly busy evening Nock's friend got off a packed train at Golders Green, walked the quarter mile or so to his home and took off his overcoat to find the diamond grill pattern of the Tube car gates still clearly imprinted on the back of the coat as he hung it up.[58] This sort of contrast between the rules and the reality of Tube travel has, of course, continued to this day.

Pick of the posters

Sir Albert Stanley was always disarmingly frank about the inevitable discomfort of peak hours on the Underground. As he remarked as early as 1915, 'Overcrowding, in the sense of people standing in the cars, must be regarded as a permanent feature of the rush periods of urban traffic operation.'[59] He saw no reason to apologize for what has now been a fact of London life for over a century. But even before the First World War, the less attractive aspects of the passenger experience and lingering opposition to the UERL's American origins were being very effectively countered in the company's publicity. Stanley had given this responsibility to Frank Pick, who was to become an almost legendary figure at the Underground for his exceptional design management and administrative skills.

Pick had joined the UERL in 1906, just one year before Stanley's arrival. He had started his transport career in York with the North Eastern Railway (NER), becoming personal assistant to the company's progressive General Manager, Sir George Gibb. When Gibb was headhunted to run the UERL, he invited Pick to join him. Initially, Pick found his role in London frustrating because it was ill defined, and he was outspoken in his criticism of the way the Underground was managed and promoted.

58. A postcard of Golders Green issued in 1912 showing the transformation from country crossroads to suburban centre in just eight years. This view is looking north up the Finchley Road towards the new Tube station.

59. 'London's Latest Suburbs'. Cover of a commercial guidebook to homes on the Hampstead Tube, 1910.

60. Frank Pick (1878–1941) was made Commercial Manager of the Underground Group in 1912. He rose to become Managing Director in the 1920s and the first Chief Executive of London Transport in 1933.

When Stanley joined the company and set about reorganizing the management and operation, he recognized Pick's potential and in 1908 put him in charge of publicity, traffic promotion and development. Stanley had an astute American appreciation of the value of marketing and public relations in business, concepts rarely taken seriously in the traditional world of British railway management. Pick was soon able to combine Gibb's meticulous use of statistical analysis in forward planning, which he had applied rigorously at the NER, with Stanley's broader ambition and opportunism for the Underground.

Stanley succeeded Gibb as UERL Managing Director in 1910. Two years later, when Stanley engineered the takeover of the LGOC buses and the independent Tube companies, Pick was made commercial manager of the much-enlarged UERL Combine. This led him to develop and promote the buses and Underground as integrated and coordinated services. His chosen instrument to publicize this was the pictorial poster, which he had been using with growing acclaim since 1908.

Although he was later hailed as a 'modern Medici' and commercial patron of the arts, Pick's early use of pictorial posters was driven entirely by the UERL's immediate business objectives set by Stanley. The Underground desperately needed more passengers in order to stay afloat. As Christian Barman comments in his biography, 'Pick had no intention of turning the Underground into a picture gallery . . . it was necessary that each poster should earn its keep in a commercial sense; its job was to make people want to get around, to travel to places that were easy to get to by Underground, by bus, by tram'.[60]

From his first 'fumbling experiments' of 1908 onwards, Pick tried out new approaches to every aspect of poster publicity – subject, artist, production, display, target market and variety – until he 'arrived at some notion of what poster advertising ought to be. Everyone seemed to be quite pleased with what I did, and I got a reputation that really sprang out of nothing.'[61] Pick's false modesty disguised the striking innovation and creativity in his poster commissioning, which quickly moved beyond the rather staid and banal approach to the medium adopted by other railway companies and most commercial advertisers.

Pick had no previous experience in this area, but quickly immersed himself in the world of applied art, getting to

61. 'Too much of a good thing'. Poster by John Henry Lloyd, 1910, featuring five other posters recently issued in Pick's growing publicity drive.

ODBEFHIJKLMN PQURSTVWCG QU WA &YXZJ

Notes of details (in case of
some being overlooked or
in case of slight inaccuracies)
Note : the 2nd QU to be cut together on one body,

height of letters = 1
width of stem = ⅐ th.
(the curves of (B) are)
slightly less than ⅐ th.)

OQCGS&, are a little taller than I and project
slightly above & below top & foot lines.
J projects slightly below foot line
K, top arm K'& W, centre W, fall slightly below top line

WITH CARE. INK NOT waterproof.

Revised 4 – 12 March
passed H W S J W &I drawn
New N X K K S B added Zth

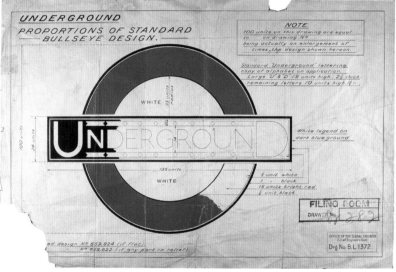

62

63

know printers, lithographers and craftsmen as well as artists and teachers at leading London art schools. Although he had not studied art or design history in any detail, and approached it from the perspective of a business manager wanting to make the best use of applied art, Pick's emerging philosophy was not far removed from the more progressive elements of the arts and crafts movement. He shared many of the moral concerns of John Ruskin and William Morris about the social and practical value to society of applied art and design. Pick admired traditional standards of hand craftsmanship, but he was equally aware of the needs of a large modern commercial organization like the Underground, for which mass production and automation were industry requirements.

There was an inbuilt contradiction here which Pick never quite managed to resolve in the progressive but conservative design management culture he fostered at the Underground. The approach he represented was the philosophy of the Design and Industries Association (DIA), of which he became a founder member in 1915. The DIA's slogan and mantra at the time was 'fitness for purpose', but its curious cultural blend of a pre-industrial past with a technological future has been aptly labelled recently as 'medieval modernism'.[62]

Perhaps the most important and lasting innovation that Pick oversaw in his early years at the Underground was the introduction of a clear new display typeface, which

62. Edward Johnston's hand-drawn alphabet for the Underground submitted to Pick in 1916.

63. Johnston's instructions for the correct proportions of the redesigned Underground bullseye to incorporate the new typeface, c.1925.

97

was to become the cornerstone of the company's communication with its customers and passengers. Through Gerard Meynell, head of the Westminster Press, which printed many of the UERL's publicity posters, Pick was introduced to Edward Johnston, an accomplished calligrapher who taught at London's Central School of Arts and Crafts.[63]

Pick wanted the Underground to have a design with, as he put it, 'the bold simplicity of the authentic lettering of the finest periods' and yet 'belonging unmistakably to the twentieth century'.[64] Johnston had a conservative craftsman's hatred of modern industry and mechanical reproduction, but was eventually persuaded in 1913 to take on the commission. He met Pick's requirements by turning to classical Roman capitals for his inspiration and proportions. Once these had been established the Underground face, he claimed, 'designed itself', though getting to this stage took him nearly three years.

The drawings he finally presented to Pick in 1916 showed a sans serif alphabet based on squares and circles, Johnston's O being a perfect circle and his capital M a square with the diagonal strokes meeting precisely in the centre of the letter. The Johnston letterface was a copyright design for the exclusive use of the Underground Group, one of the earliest expressions of corporate identity in this country.[65]

Johnston's lettering was used at first only as a display face on posters and signs, but he was soon asked to redesign the Underground's bar and circle symbol to incorporate it, and to produce a condensed version for use on bus destination boards. His meticulous Underground Sans is still used today in a modified form adapted for computer typesetting and a range of fonts. New Johnston remains crisp and distinctive, particularly in combination with the roundel logo, and is still both classic and modern just as it was in the original hand-drawn display lettering introduced nearly a century ago.

The First World War

At the end of 1913 both the Underground Group and the Metropolitan Railway were planning for growth, not retrenchment. After the massive capital expenditure on electrification and new tube tunnelling in the 1900s, their priority as private companies was to expand their passenger market and improve revenue income. This in turn required some further investment to attract more traffic, particularly from the suburbs, but the prospects looked good and the business economy was booming. Financial returns for the underground railways were steadily improving. In the new year's honours list, the managing director of the Underground Group became Sir Albert Stanley, knighted in recognition of his services to London's passenger transport.

The outbreak of war in August 1914 threw all the improvement plans being pursued by Stanley, Pick and Selbie into disarray, though the real impact of a conflict on such an unprecedented scale was not predicted by anyone. Plans to expand Underground services into the suburbs had to be put on hold, apart from an extension to the Bakerloo line, which was opened beyond Paddington to Queen's Park in 1915. Here it came to the surface and joined the new overground electric suburban lines of the London &

64

64. A female lift attendant. One of a set of lithographs by A. S. Hartrick published by the Underground in 1919 to celebrate the contribution to war work made by its staff. The Dover Street sign refers to a London Tube station (later renamed Green Park) and the London street names often given to British trenches on the Western Front.

North Western Railway (LNWR). Eventually, two years later, Bakerloo line trains began operating over the full 20 miles from Elephant & Castle in south London to Watford Junction in Hertfordshire, the first Tube service far into London's countryside.

This single new development was rather overshadowed by the growing difficulties of wartime operation on the rest of the system. There was a large surge in London's population as workers were drawn to the capital by temporary but well-paid war industries such as munitions. Troops in transit or on leave and reductions in bus services also contributed to much heavier use of the Underground, but this was not the traffic increase the companies had planned for. The Underground carried nearly 70 per cent more passengers in 1918 than it had in 1914,[66] but costs went up, repairs and maintenance were reduced because of wartime economies and new trains were not available, leading to serious overcrowding and delays.

The biggest difficulty was the growing shortage of staff as men left the UERL and the Met for military service. By 1915 the railway companies had reluctantly begun to recruit women as temporary replacements for male staff. Women were soon being taken on as booking clerks, ticket collectors, porters, lift attendants, gatewomen, bill posters, painters and cleaners, all exclusively male jobs before the war. When the new Bakerloo line extension station at Maida Vale opened on 6 June 1915, it was entirely staffed by women. Train driving remained a 'reserved occupation' from which men were not released for military service, so there were no 'motorwomen', but in 1916 the Metropolitan took the unprecedented decision to recruit women as train guards. This was a skilled and responsible job as the guard had full responsibility for the safety of a train and its passengers. By the end of 1917 the Met had 522 women on its staff.[67]

London experienced its first air raids from 1915 onwards, carried out at first by Zeppelin airships and later by bomber aircraft. Initially the only air raid precautions taken by the underground railways were polite notices inside trains asking passengers to keep the blinds drawn at night on overground sections of the District line. No public shelters had been provided, and as the raids intensified people invaded the Tube in their thousands, correctly assuming that the deep-level stations would be the safest places to take cover.

An official report after the first night raid by German Gotha bombers in September 1917 described what happened when the anti-aircraft

65

65. Eva Carver became a Metropolitan Railway guard on the Hammersmith & City Line during the war. She was photographed in civvies at Hammersmith station and in uniform with lamp and flag at the nearby depot just as her war work ended in 1919.

DURING THE PRESENT CRISIS

PASSENGERS ARE RE-
QUESTED TO KEEP THE
BLINDS DRAWN at NIGHT

EAST OF BOW ROAD AND
WEST OF GLOUCESTER ROAD

guns in London suddenly opened fire: 'many people rushed for shelter. Those nearer the Tubes went to the stations in all stages of undress and were conveyed in the lifts to the underground platforms. There were hundreds of women and children and scores of men who made for these places of refuge.' Police reports estimated that 300,000 people were taking shelter in Tube stations.[68]

There was a sad little press report on 5 October which recorded the first death of a Tube shelterer:

At an inquest held by Dr Waldo in the City on Monday on the body of a Russian Jewess, living in Whitechapel, who was killed as the result of the crush at Liverpool Street Central London Railway station last Friday night, a special constable named Godwin said that there were 200 or 300 people of the poorer classes, mostly aliens, women and children. The police were unable to stem the torrent. The jury returned a verdict of accidental death, and expressed themselves satisfied that the police and officials did all that they could.[69]

In fact there had not been an air raid that night, and this unfortunate woman was the victim of a crowd panic.

Altogether, 670 people were killed and over 2,000 wounded in the 31 bombing raids on London in 1915-18. The effect on the transport network, and particularly on the Underground, was considerable disruption rather than physical damage, but the

66. There are no surviving photographs of Tube sheltering in the First World War, but artist Walter Bayes recorded the scene he witnessed at Elephant & Castle station in 1917 in a large oil painting he called *The Underworld*.

67. Air raid precautions on the District line, 1915.

WAR
TO ARMS CITIZENS
OF THE EMPIRE!!

WHY BOTHER ABOUT THE
GERMANS INVADING
THE COUNTRY?

INVADE IT YOURSELF
BY UNDERGROUND AND MOTOR-'BUS

EASTER · 1915

experience was an uncomfortable foretaste of the much more devastating attacks of the Blitz in 1940–41. With tragic irony, the heaviest death toll involving Tube shelterers in the Second World War was to be another, but far more serious, outcome of a crowd rushing for shelter underground after a false air raid alert.[70]

An ambivalent and slightly confusing attitude to the war was reflected in the Underground's poster advertising, which took on a propaganda rather than a publicity role. A powerful recruiting poster designed free by the popular artist Frank Brangwyn appeared on stations soon after war broke out in August 1914. Only nine months later, and with the conflict clearly not 'all over by Christmas', as many had assumed, a jaunty leisure poster appeared urging families to forget about the threat of a German invasion of the country and to 'invade it yourself by Underground and motor bus'.

68 and 69. Mixed messages? Frank Brangwyn's dramatic recruitment poster issued by the Underground in 1914 and the Warbis Brothers' jaunty publicity for country excursions produced a few months later for Easter 1915.

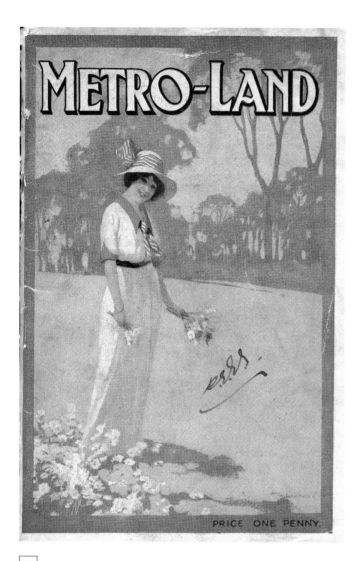

 70

The 'carry on as normal' approach to leisure travel was continued in the Underground's posters throughout 1916. UERL publicity still encouraged Londoners to get out of town and enjoy the countryside, but for leisure purposes rather than evacuation from an urban environment under aerial attack. There was clearly some uncertainty about how best to tread the line in wartime publicity between maintaining morale and smug complacency.

The Metropolitan took a similar approach to the UERL and virtually ignored the war in its publicity produced during the first eighteen months of the conflict. Early in 1915 the railway even launched a new illustrated guide called *Metro-land*, promoted as 'a comprehensive description of the country districts served by the Metropolitan Railway'.[71] It was aimed at walkers, excursionists, party organizers and house-hunters, but it seems an odd time to encourage these activities, especially moving house. Metro-land's time would come after the war, and Selbie was ready with ambitious plans for suburban development as soon as peace was declared.

Sir Albert Stanley was asked to serve as President of the Board of Trade in Lloyd George's wartime government and stepped down as the Underground's managing director to take on this role in 1916. On Stanley's recommendation, Frank Pick also left his post as the UERL's commercial officer in 1917 to manage the wartime crisis in domestic fuel supplies for the government's coal mines department. Both of them returned to the Underground at the end of the war, somewhat chastened by their experience of civil service procedures. Stanley was rewarded in the 1920 New Year's honours, becoming Lord Ashfield of Southwell, and in 1921 Pick was promoted to become the UERL's assistant managing director.

The UERL released just over 3,000 railway staff for war service, representing half the total workforce of the District Railway and the Tubes in 1914. The figure was far higher in the Combine's bus division, the LGOC, where nearly 10,000 men joined the armed forces, almost 60 per cent of the staff. Just over 1,100 Met men served in the forces, representing nearly 30 per cent of the pre-war staff total.

The 137 Metropolitan employees killed or missing are commemorated on a white marble memorial on the platform at Baker Street station. This was unveiled on Armistice Day, 1920 by the company chairman, Lord Aberconway.[72] The chairman had lost his own son in the war, the Hon. Francis McLaren MP, who had resigned his Metropolitan directorship in 1914 to join the Royal Flying Corps.

Despite the many personal tragedies of the conflict, and encouraged by a general belief that this had been a 'war to end all wars', the underground companies were well prepared for the peace in November 1918. Following a difficult year of recovery and readjustment from wartime privations during 1919, plans to assist with the provision

70. Early edition of the Metro-land booklet, 1916.

of 'homes fit for heroes' through the development of London's suburbs were central to the post-war recovery schemes announced in 1920. Underground railways were the key to moving Londoners out but also to enabling them to travel back into the city for business or pleasure.

The next two decades would see the fastest growth in residential housing that outer London had ever experienced, and a mass migration to the suburbs that was encouraged by new extensions to the network. Selbie shrewdly seized the commercial opportunities of the Metro-land dream and set about making the Metropolitan a thriving suburban commuter railway. At the Underground Ashfield and Pick planned their strategy on a much grander scale. They effectively reshaped the environment of Greater London both by transforming the heart of the city above and below ground and by linking the City and West End to new suburbs through the growing urban transport network.

71. Women bill stickers at Willesden Green station pasting up advertisements for Metro-land, 1916. It was a curious publicity campaign to launch in wartime.

72. Rededication of the restored Metropolitan war memorial at Baker Street station on Remembrance Day, 11 November 2010, exactly ninety years after it was first unveiled.

CHAPTER 3

THE UNDERGROUND GOES OVERGROUND

A new heart for London

Ashort ceremony that took place below the streets of central London just before Christmas in 1928 marked an important milestone for the Underground. On the morning of 10 December the Mayor of Westminster was formally invited by Lord Ashfield to open London's latest Underground marvel by throwing a switch in the new booking hall at Piccadilly Circus station. This lit up an elaborate Art Deco marble and glass lamp and started the escalators that were about to carry thousands of passengers down to the platforms below. The mayor was issued with a 2d ticket from one of the twenty-six coin-operated ticket machines, state-of-the-art travel aids never seen in conventional railway stations at that time. He stepped on to an escalator and descended under a giant painted map of the world, which homed in on London as its focal point, the busy hub of the British Empire.[1]

The Underground's showpiece development scheme was revealed at last. It was the culmination of four years' complex engineering work at the very heart of London, where the Bakerloo and Piccadilly lines intersect. Passenger numbers using Piccadilly Circus had risen from 1.5 million in 1907, after the first year's operation, to 18 million by 1922. The cramped original station could not cope with the crowds, and a major reconstruction scheme was carried out, entirely below ground and hidden from public view. Eleven fast escalators replaced the original lifts, running down from a spacious new circular entrance hall created directly underneath the famous road junction, and the statue of Eros was temporarily removed for its own protection while building work took place.

A large excavated space had been transformed by architect Charles Holden from a bleak engineers' hole in the ground into an attractive pedestrian concourse, which became one of the sights of London. Marble wall panels, bronze fittings, glass showcases and elegant lighting made it quite unlike a traditional railway station but a suitably opulent extension to the high-class shopping environment of Regent Street above. Overseas visitors were particularly impressed with this prime example of well-designed urban sophistication.

1. An impressive cutaway drawing of the reconstructed Piccadilly Circus station by D. Macpherson, 1928. This was widely used in the Underground's publicity for its grand new project.

2. The Mayor of Westminster (centre) opens the new Piccadilly Circus station in December 1928 by switching on a special Art Deco lamp, now in London Transport Museum's care. Lord Ashfield stands on his right.

The renowned Danish urban planner Steen Eiler Rasmussen called it 'an excellent illustration of what the Underground has done for modern civilisation'. He considered it one of the finest pieces of new architecture in London, better than anything above ground.[2] Visiting Soviet engineers preparing to build the Moscow Metro reported back to Krushchev, their project leader, who in turn persuaded Stalin, that they should use the London Underground as the model for their own system. Piccadilly was cited in particular, 'the best station in London, right in the heart of the most aristocratic section of the city ... built deep in the ground and it has escalators rather than elevators'.[3] In 1932 Moscow duly became the first of many world cities to use the London Underground for consultancy advice on new metro construction.

The Underground itself was not slow to promote its most impressive achievement to date, announcing it as a £500,000 modernization scheme which would allow up to 50 million passengers a year to use Piccadilly Circus station in comfort. Many more would be able to stroll through its attractive circulating area as a way of crossing the busy circus safely, avoiding both traffic and weather above while window shopping in showcases for the rebuilt Swan & Edgar department store upstairs. Everything about the experience was modern, electric and available to all. The Underground was literally reshaping the heart of the city with tremendous style, and it made sure that this was widely promoted through press articles and its own increasingly confident publicity.

Moving out

In the decade since the end of the 1914–18 war, the Underground had made remarkable progress, developing from a still-novel means of rapid transit under central London to being one of the main instruments of suburban growth. These were the years in which the Underground grew to become, in Frank Pick's phrase, 'the framework of the town', shaping and underpinning the daily life of what was still the world's greatest city, now spreading well beyond its traditional borders. The population of Middlesex, covering the suburban districts of north and west London, increased by 30 per cent in the 1920s, the fastest growth of any county in England and Wales. Much of this expansion was directly linked to the provision of new underground services.[4]

It was the dynamic combination of Ashfield's persuasive political skills and Pick's formidable management style that drove the Underground forward in this period. This was in the absence of any clear direction from the government, which was well aware of public concern about emerging problems with transport, particularly in London.

3. A publicity postcard for the glamorous new Piccadilly Circus station, c1930. The world clock map (top left) is still in place today.

Conductor. "OUTSIDE ONLY!"

J.H.DOWD.'19

4 5

Public ownership, even full nationalization, was rumoured as a possible solution, but ruled out as far too radical at a time when there were fears about the possible spread of communism across Europe in the aftermath of the revolution and civil war in Russia and the defeat of Germany.

A parliamentary select committee set up in 1919 to investigate congestion, overcrowding and fare increases in London reported that these problems had become 'a public scandal', but absolutely nothing happened. The government did create a Ministry of Transport and soon announced plans to build arterial roads and merge Britain's 120 independent railways into four large private companies. But the minister, Sir Eric Geddes, failed to come up with a scheme to unify London's public transport under common management, admitting rather pathetically to the House of Commons in 1921 that 'I deplore my inability to deal with it . . . I cannot see how to do it'.[5]

The apparently insoluble problem of coordinating London's public transport arose from the complicated mix of service modes and operating authorities. There were still two Underground railway operators, the UERL and the Metropolitan, which remained completely separate from the services of the overground suburban rail companies,[6] as well as various different providers of bus and tram services on the roads. These ranged from tiny independent bus companies with a couple of vehicles to the giant London County Council Tramways (LCCT) system. None of them could work efficiently or profitably as stand-alone operations. Despite the mergers that had taken place before the First World War, there were numerous conflicts and tensions between the remaining operators which needed resolution. Yet further coordination and agreement seemed a long way off.

4. A crowded Tube platform at Piccadilly Circus, 1922.

5. The problems of boarding a gate stock train in rush hour as depicted by J. H. Dowd in *Punch* magazine, 1919.

6

7

Ashfield's UERL, still an association of private companies, was the largest operator in London but did not control everything. It ran the District Railway and most of the deep Tube lines, but not the Metropolitan, which managed the Hammersmith & City, East London and Great Northern & City lines as well as its own main line. Operation of the Circle line, still known as the Inner Circle, was shared with the District. There was yet another suggestion in 1921 that the Met and UERL could be merged, but it came to nothing.

On the roads the UERL continued to run the main bus company, the LGOC, but did not have a monopoly and faced competition on busy routes from dozens of independent 'pirate' operators. The UERL also controlled three tram networks that ran outside the London County Council area but had no power over the LCC tram system or the various local authority-run tramways in east London.

By the 1920s it was no longer possible to plan or manage the future development of the Underground as if it was entirely separate from these other transport modes or the administration of London itself. Further coordination was necessary, but a decision on how this might be achieved was ducked by the government. Yet despite this messy and fragmented picture, the inter-war years saw unprecedented growth and improvement in London's public transport. Bus services flourished, even though bitter battles arose between the LGOC and the independent operators. For the underground railways this also turned out to be a golden age of development and achievement, led not by politicians or the government, but by the Underground's own far-sighted management.

Making the case for expansion

It was clear to Ashfield and Pick that the Underground could only move on by growth and modernization, but this required funding assistance in some form. There was an obvious need and public demand for new and improved transport services. However, even the fairly straightforward projection of Tube lines into the suburbs, where it could be done mainly on the surface without expensive tunnelling, was not necessarily a profitable option for a private company. The Bakerloo line extension of 1915–17 had disappointing traffic results, and a modest western extension of the Central line from Shepherd's Bush to Ealing Broadway, opened in 1920, also brought limited financial returns.

Neither of these initial extension projects was particularly expensive for the UERL, because construction costs on the overground

6. Lord Ashfield (right) and Frank Pick (left), c.1923, very different personalities but a powerful partnership for more than thirty years.

7. East Acton, on the newly opened Central line extension, 1920. This very basic wooden station was built to serve a growing council housing estate, visible under construction in the background.

sections were largely met in these cases by the mainline railway companies that shared the tracks.[7] Yet building costs had more than doubled during the war, and the heavy overall increase in passenger numbers did not provide sufficient income through fares to justify more capital investment. As Ashfield put it bluntly in a speech to UERL shareholders in 1924, 'The underground railways in London have never been, in their whole career, a financial success. In other words they have failed to earn anything approaching a reasonable return upon the capital invested in them.'[8]

This was perfectly true, but political and economic circumstances change, and Ashfield was able to find the further investment he needed without making unrealistic promises of future profits. Faced with a dramatic post-war rise in unemployment, the government had introduced a Trade Facilities Act in 1921 which offered Treasury guarantees against capital loans for new works that could provide jobs. Here was an unexpected opportunity, and Ashfield was ready to take immediate advantage of it. The UERL already had a series of planned and authorized, but unfunded, investment schemes to improve the Underground that had been drawn up before the war and put on hold. Now these could provide construction jobs[9] in London as well as substantial contracts with the steel industry and other major suppliers outside the capital.

A private enterprise could not have raised the sums required on the open market in the 1920s, but this indirect method of state support allowed major new works to go ahead which were in the public interest and could also stimulate the wider economy. It was the first recognition that, when infrastructure costs are taken into account, an underground railway cannot pay its way and some form of state subsidy is necessary. All subsequent capital projects on the London Underground have needed this, and the same is true for metro projects that have been developed all over the world.

In just four years, between 1922 and 1926, and at a speed which could probably not be matched in Britain today, London acquired a state-of-the-art spinal Tube line running right through the metropolis from Edgware in the north to Morden in the south. This involved enlarging, linking and extending two separate existing Tubes to create the Northern line. The modernized network divided below

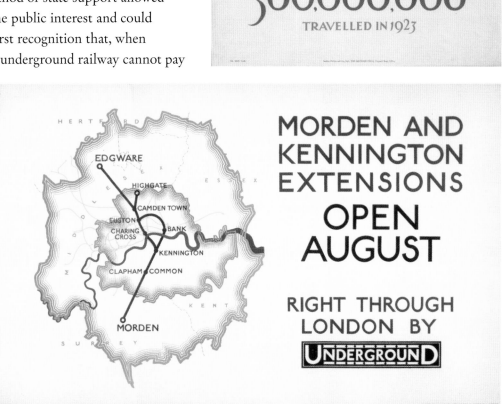

8. 'The Problem of the Underground'. A 1924 poster by Irene Fawkes, which sets out some of the UERL's statistics and seems to suggest that the 'problem' is mainly financial.

9. Tube car panel poster showing the part-new, part-modernized spinal Tube line serving both the City and West End with separate branches, completed in 1926. Eleven years later, in 1937, it eventually got its familiar title and became the Northern line.

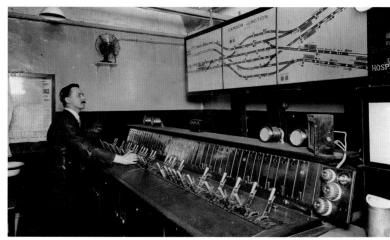

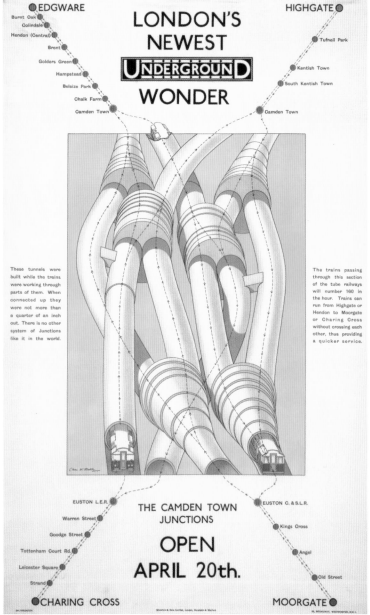

central London, with branches under both the City and West End, and served new districts on the surface, beyond the old built-up area, where suburban development was set to take off.[10]

The engineering complexity of this project, particularly in the central sections below ground, was, of course, invisible to passengers, but the Underground was becoming ever more sophisticated in its self-promotion. Pick ensured maximum publicity for the company's advanced technical prowess with photographs, posters and press articles showing features like the Camden Town underground junctions, the most intricate hub in the world but controlled by a safe and sophisticated signalling system.

In retrospect, the most surprising aspect of this astonishing three-part project is that it was not given a new name even when it was completed. The combined C&SLR and Hampstead Tubes remained officially known by separate titles as the City Railway and the Hampstead line. Some years later they were clumsily renamed the Edgware, Highgate & Morden line. The simpler abbreviation Northern line was finally adopted in 1937.

Homes fit for heroes

In the 1920s there was a construction boom in both social and private enterprise housing, particularly in the London suburbs. Building societies began offering low-interest mortgages, and for the first time many Londoners were able to buy their own house. Before the war even the middle classes in Britain had usually rented their homes, but there was now the opportunity for many more people to purchase an affordable, newly built property. In the days before mass car ownership, good public transport to work was an essential part of the package for anyone tempted to move out

10. 'London's Newest Underground Wonder'. A poster by Charles Baker with an impression of the complex new junction at Camden Town, 1924.

11. Signalman Alf Powell at the electric lever frame controlling the four-way junction at Camden, May 1924. The illuminated diagram shows the changing position of every train.

Within the poster image:

UNDERGROUND

EUSTON

THE CITY AND SOUTH LONDON RAILWAY

RE-OPENED 1924

at an extra cost of £3,000,000

THE CITY AND SOUTH LONDON RAILWAY

OPENED 1890

its total cost was £3,000,000

CLAPHAM

FROM EUSTON TO CLAPHAM COMMON
THE TRANSFORMATION
IS COMPLETE

12

to suburbia. A station nearby, or at least a bus service to the station, was vital and was usually the first essential feature of a new commuter suburb.

The policy of suburban expansion adopted by the Underground was a logical continuation of Yerkes' original vision for the Tube described in chapter 2, but with the much sounder financial base of government-backed capital. It also chimed well with the new political emphasis on better housing for a nation returning from war to peace and civilian life. Lloyd George's famous election slogan of 1918, 'Homes fit for heroes', was embodied in government legislation in 1919, which for the first time forced all local authorities to provide low rent council housing. There were also new subsidies available to help revive the building industry, which had virtually collapsed during the war.[11]

Lord Ashfield and Sir Philip Lloyd-Greame, his successor as president of the Board of Trade, jointly performed the ceremony of 'cutting the first sod' for the start of the Edgware extension on 12 June 1922. Golders Green, where construction work began, had already grown in the fifteen years since the Hampstead Tube's arrival, from a rural crossroads into a suburban township of 10,500 people. In fact it was so densely built up

12. Poster by R. T. Cooper celebrating the transformation of the old City Line, seen as a ghostly apparition on the right, after full reconstruction to take modern Tube trains, 1924.

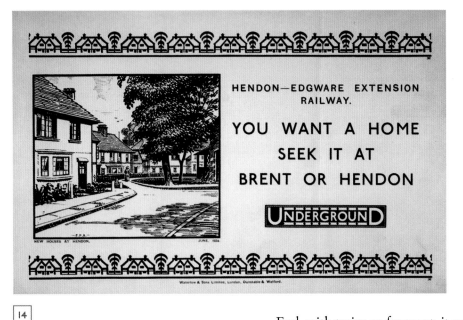

that some of the nearly new semi-detached houses had to be demolished to make way for the Tube line's overground progress.[12]

The extension was opened as far as Hendon in November 1923. Whole streets of new housing were already being laid out by private developers on the adjacent green fields and completed almost as fast as the railway. During 1923/4 more than 2,000 new houses and shops were built or approved in the Hendon area. The old village centre and parish church were about a mile away from the Tube, but the new station was named Hendon Central anyway, and the shopping parade that sprang up around its 'circus' design quickly created a new community focus.

The final section of the Tube extension opened to Edgware in August 1924. The change from rural isolation into outer-London suburbia was not as fast as the Underground's impact on Golders Green or Hendon, but it was equally dramatic. The village of Edgware had been a stopping point for changing horses eight miles out of London on Watling Street, one of the main roads to the north, since Roman times. Electric trams arrived in 1904 and motor buses in 1913. A meandering railway branch line from London had opened to Edgware as early as 1867, but all these transport links to the metropolis were slow and indirect. None of them stimulated development, and in 1921 the population of Edgware parish was still only 1,516.

The arrival of the Tube suddenly made Edgware a desirable place to live. It was an unspoilt rural area but now only thirty-five minutes from the City or West End, with trains so frequent, it was claimed, that passengers would not need to consult a timetable. Even so, speculative housing development on the green fields was slow to take off, and the Underground started an intensive campaign of press and poster advertising to promote Edgware's charms. Once development did take place there was less publicity emphasis on Edgware's quaint olde world village character and the attraction of living in the country, neither of which applied to the suburban township it soon became.[13]

When the new Tube terminus first opened in 1924 it was soon being used by 75,000 passengers a month. Five years later it was 233,000. The local population had more than

13. The station site at Brent, in the green fields of Hendon, September 1922. The station opened just over a year later as new housing appeared right across this country scene.

14. Panel poster used inside the new trains on the Hampstead Tube, 1924.

doubled by 1929, then doubled again in the next two years. New bus services to the station were carrying 6,000 passengers a day from nearby areas as newly built developer housing sprang up from Canons Park across to Mill Hill. It demonstrated the success of the UERL's policy of using LGOC buses as 'feeders' to the Underground, and the spread of the northern suburbs continued.[14]

Close to Burnt Oak , the next station down the line from Edgware, the London County Council (LCC) developed Watling, one of its largest out-of-town social housing estates. By 1930 more than 4,000 new homes had been completed and many of the residents were taking the Tube to work in central London every day at the cheap-rate workmen's fares available before 7.30 a.m.

The next stop towards London was Colindale, less well used on a daily basis but exceptionally busy on special occasions because

15. A striking 1923 poster by Fred Taylor that did not need any text to explain its message. Housing is following the Underground on the Hendon extension.

16. Aerial view of Edgware, 1926, two years after the Tube's arrival. The station is in the centre, with a new LGOC bus garage next door. A shopping parade has been built over the road, but the units are not yet occupied. Housing is going up beyond the trees.

it was close to Hendon aerodrome. Colindale station regularly dealt with the largest crowds on the line when the annual RAF Pageant attracted up to 80,000 visitors, at least half of them arriving by Tube.

The Underground used these events to test its ability to deal with exceptional traffic flow. Records taken at the 1927 pageant showed 28,000 people arriving at Colindale station in a two-hour period. Each train of the latest standard Tube stock used on the Edgware line, which had wide, air-operated sliding doors, carried 750 passengers and could be unloaded in just twenty seconds. This compared with seventy-five seconds, nearly four times as long, to unload one of the original Hampstead line trains with their manually operated platform gates at the end of each car.[15]

Within a decade of its first arrival in the open fields of Golders Green, the Underground had effectively created a huge swathe of suburbia which extended London outwards for a further five or six miles through Middlesex to the borders of Hertfordshire. Transport really was growing the town, and the Tube link effectively made all these districts part of Greater London.

South of the river

The extension of the Tube into south London in 1924–6, beyond the Clapham terminus it had reached in 1900, was a far more costly and complex project than the Edgware line. The railway north of Golders Green was entirely above ground apart from a short tunnel at Hendon. By contrast the entire 5-mile extension from Clapham Common to Morden had to be shield-driven in deep tunnels as it followed the main road through Balham, Tooting and Merton, which were already heavily built up on the surface.

17. 'Live in Edgware, work in London'. An Underground press advertisement promoting the new line, 1926.

18. A snapshot of middle-class life in a Tube suburb on a summer Saturday afternoon in 1926. Two men arriving at Edgware after a morning at the office, still the norm on a Saturday at this time, are heading for a game of cricket; a wife and son are meeting Daddy off the train; other commuters living further out will take the 142 bus home.

19 20

Tunnelling was complicated by the presence of water-bearing gravel beds below ground, which are much more difficult to work through than London clay. The stations were sited less than a mile apart at road junctions, all of which required demolition of existing buildings before the station entrances and escalator shafts could be started. The line only came to the surface at the first open ground, immediately before the Morden terminus, which was the sole greenfield site. Farmland just beyond the station was acquired to build a new depot for the trains.

Before these practical engineering issues could be addressed there was a major dispute between the Underground and the newly created Southern Railway (SR) about the route of the new line. The Southern objected to the UERL's original plan to take their Tube trains overground beyond Morden to Wimbledon and Sutton, well into the SR's suburban traffic area, which it was busy extending and electrifying. A compromise was eventually reached whereby the SR agreed to the Tube extension to Morden but no further.

The SR would have blocked any subsequent Tube construction south of the river which threatened to compete with their overground suburban lines. This is the main reason why no other Tube lines were built in south London for more than forty years. Eventually, the new Victoria line was projected under the Thames in 1971, but still only as far as Brixton.

19 and 20. Poster by Charles Burton for the RAF Hendon Display of 1930, and part of the huge crowd that attended the annual summer show, on their way home outside Colindale station.

By this time the SR and the Underground had both been nationalized and were no longer in competition as private companies.[16]

A new look

Pick's promotion to Assistant Managing Director of the UERL gave him scope to broaden his design interests and responsibilities beyond his well-received publicity posters to a much wider canvas embracing architecture and industrial design. He had come to believe that good design was the key to improving a successful and socially responsible business. Without Pick's passionate personal commitment to this idea, it is unlikely that the Underground would have developed into the remarkable and visually distinctive organization that it became in the 1920s. Ashfield was certainly less interested in this wider concern for design that Pick championed, but he recognized its benefits to the organization and gave Pick his full support.

Pick was not satisfied with the pleasant but rather bland neo-Georgian architectural style of the Edgware extension stations, which had been designed by the UERL's in-house architect. He was determined to give the Morden line a more progressive character. In 1925 Pick visited the major International Exhibition of Decorative Arts in Paris, where many examples of European modernism were on display, but was not persuaded to follow slavishly any particular decorative style he saw there.[17] In August he sent Stanley Heaps, the staff architect, a memo announcing that: 'I think as we are to venture upon a new style in architecture for our station fronts on the Morden extension, we are bound to secure independent advice. I therefore propose that the elevations and sketch plans of these be submitted to Mr Holden of Messrs. Adams, Holden and Pearson for his consideration.'[18]

Pick had known Charles Holden since 1915, when they had both been founder members of the Design and Industries Association (DIA). They found they had similar views on architecture and a shared interest in improving the standards of commercial art and design. Both of them strongly supported the DIA's crusading philosophy of 'fitness for purpose' in new work.

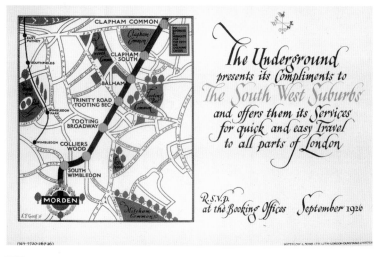

21

22

21. Survey and construction work at Tooting Broadway, 1926. The escalator shaft is on the left, with the curved foundation wall of the booking hall on the right. As with all the Morden extension stations except the terminus, the surrounding streets are already built up.

22. A public invitation to the opening of the Underground's first Tube extension into south-west London in September 1926, which was also its last move into Southern Electric territory.

Pick had offered Holden a small architectural test piece in 1924, when he had asked the architect to remodel the side entrance to Westminster station. A year later Holden's 'independent advice' referred to in Pick's memo to Heaps rapidly turned into a commission to design the street frontages of the seven new Morden line stations. By the end of 1925 Holden had come up with a deceptively simple 'folding screen' entrance façade. This design would give each station the same appearance but could be adapted from a flat front (Morden) to a curve (Tooting Broadway and South Wimbledon) or variations on a three-leaf angle (Clapham South, Balham and Tooting Bec), depending on the available space at each site. It was a subtle but very effective exercise in corporate identity, and just what Pick wanted.[19]

A scaled-down wood and plaster mock-up of the first station entrance (Clapham South) was built inside one of the old exhibition halls at Earl's Court. Pick was delighted with it and wrote excitedly to his DIA colleague Harry Peach:[20] 'We are going to build our stations upon the Morden extension to the most modern pattern . . . we are going to represent the DIA gone mad, and in order that I may go mad in good company I have got Holden to see that we do it properly.'[21]

Holden's revolutionary station entrance buildings, all seven of them listed structures today, were the main focus of attention when the Morden line opened in September 1926. The souvenir booklet handed out to the press (and probably written by Pick himself) describes the station design as being 'of no particular school: it neither apes the past nor underlines modernity by violating taste'.[22]

BRIGHTEST LONDON
IS BEST REACHED BY
UNDERGROUND

23

24

23. 'Brightest London', a poster by Horace Taylor with copy in Johnston's bold, legible lettering, 1924. This is typical of the Underground's stylish publicity at this time.

24. Reduced-size mock-up of Charles Holden's design for the entrance kiosk to Clapham South station, built inside an exhibition hall at Earl's Court in January 1926. The actual station, faced in Portland stone, opened just nine months later.

I entered the Tube Station and took my place
    in the queue.
I had the exact fare ready.
I passed across the lift.
I stood clear of the gates.
I bewared of pick-pockets.
I passed down to the other end of the platform.
I let them off the car first.
I stepped on quickly.
I passed right down inside.
I passed out quickly.
I stood on the right of the escalator.
I allowed others to pass.
I did not sit on the stairs.
I stepped off with the right foot.
I had my ticket ready.
I emerged by the "Exit only".
I walked smartly to the office.
Why?
Because I do it every day.
Why?
Because I'm, unfortunately, that sort of chap.

A FAIR AVERAGE CONDUCT
HELPS THE SERVICE.

25

25. 'A Fair Average Conduct Helps the Service'. The Underground's ideal passenger in a poster illustrated by Lunt Roberts, 1927. The stations are clearly based on Holden's latest designs for the Morden extension.

This rather downbeat description was at odds with their striking appearance at regular intervals along a typical inner suburban London high road dominated by Victorian and Edwardian houses and shopping parades. The white Portland stone of the station frontages was a dramatic contrast to the red brick of the older structures, and there were prominent Underground symbols over the entrance canopy and in the large glass windows. At night they were even more visible, with the coloured glass roundels backlit from inside, the stonework floodlit and, for a short time after opening, a searchlight beaming into the sky from the roof.

When new the stations must have seemed like alien spacecraft dotted along this drab and poorly lit south London street, but they seemed to be popular with critics and the travelling public alike. The *Architect's Journal* praised Holden for 'a design that solves its problem, creates a new type of building and improves the face of London'.[23] As Eitan Karol comments in his carefully researched biography of Holden, 'higher praise than this is hard for an architect to find'.[24]

The design of the Morden line stations was important because they had to fulfil a more complex role than the Edgware line structures, which initially sat alone like little houses on the Middlesex prairie. In built-up south London the new stations had to stand out like beacons to attract passengers from the existing street transport whilst also fitting in with, and contributing to, an improved urban environment.

For Frank Pick this was a major step forward in his wider vision where appropriately applied art and design could change and improve society. He saw this as the Underground actively taking its social duty as seriously as its commercial responsibilities. Historian Michael Saler has described Pick's growing ambition at this stage rather well: 'the Underground would be a model of aesthetic integration and communal service, a catalyst for a more harmonious London of the future'.[25]

At a more basic level, the Morden extension would provide a much improved public transport service all along the route.[26] It was clearly, following the Edgware experience, also going to have a considerable impact beyond the Tube terminus. When Morden station opened in 1926 there was still a working farm on the other side of the road in what was better described as a hamlet than a village. There were a few cottages, two or three larger houses and an inn, surrounded by open fields, except where the new Underground depot had been built.

A panoramic photograph taken ten years later from the roof of the new cinema opposite the station shows new suburban housing stretching into the distance covering all the open countryside. There are ten buses in the station forecourt, indicating the wider reach of the Tube through connecting services to more distant communities

like Worcester Park, Sutton, Carshalton and Cheam, which were all becoming outer London suburbs. By this time Morden was the most heavily used of all the suburban Tube stations. With growing complaints about overcrowding on peak services, the Underground once again stopped promoting the benefits of a suburban idyll at the end of the line in its posters and advertising. Expanding into the suburbs created problems and difficulties as well as benefits and opportunities.

Metro-land

The Metropolitan Railway, still fiercely independent of the Underground, took a rather different approach to development after the First World War. Robert Selbie, the general manager, had decided early on that concentrating on outer suburban services was a better strategy than investing in central London, where new transport provision was becoming almost saturated in the Edwardian years. He saw too many competing electric tram, Tube and motor bus services, all forced to offer cheap fares, but with little margin for profit.

The autocratic but far-sighted Selbie saw more potential in first-class and long-distance traffic development than in mass-market rapid transit under London. He did not ignore central London and the original urban sections of the Metropolitan, now at last all electrified. However, he set his sights on development up what was called the 'Extension line' from Baker Street into the country areas north-west of London to

26. Morden Underground station from the roof of the new cinema, a key feature of every inter-war suburb, in 1936. All the housing in the background had been built in the ten years since the arrival of the Tube in this once rural part of Surrey.

SPEND A DAY IN METRO-LAND

GORGEOUS AUTUMNAL SCENERY
CHARMING COUNTRY WALKS

GET A COPY OF METRO-LAND AT ANY BOOKING OFFICE OR BOOKSTALL
PRICE TWOPENCE

R·H·SELBIE GENERAL MANAGER
BAKER STREET STATION NW1

27

which the wealthier middle classes could be attracted. A sign of the new standards to which he aspired even before the war was the introduction of two luxury Pullman cars in 1910 named *Mayflower* and *Galatea*. These were used on some of the fast long-distance services to and from Buckinghamshire, providing drinks and light refreshments to first-class passengers paying a supplementary fare.

This was the opposite end of the scale from the classless, flat-fare Twopenny Tube, and naturally such luxuries were only taken up by a small proportion of the Metropolitan's clientele. The Pullman service was more of an image builder than a profit maker, but other more significant improvements that could be appreciated and experienced by all the railway's passengers were also started in this period. Selbie set up a publicity department in 1911, which produced postcards, brochures, country walks leaflets and even a film showing a journey down the line from Baker Street to Aylesbury.[27] These productions were aimed at holidaymakers and day trippers, but Selbie was convinced that the railway could also build up long-distance commuter traffic if it could offer demonstrably better and faster services. In his mind the former 'Extension line' out to the country from Baker Street was now the main line in more ways than one, and this was the focus of both the railway's promotion and its improvement.

A major investment in additional express tracks over the busy bottleneck section between Finchley Road and Wembley Park during 1913–15 was a crucial step forward. Complete reconstruction of Baker Street station, the hub of the Metropolitan, had begun in 1910 and was almost complete by 1914.

A new head office for the company was built over the back of the new station, one of the first designs by Charles W. Clark, the Met's recently appointed 'architectural assistant to the engineer'.[28] There were even ambitious plans to build a large hotel over the Baker Street station frontage on Marylebone Road, but initial work on this was stopped by war conditions in 1917.

Selbie's additional proposals to extend the electrification of the main line beyond Harrow to Rickmansworth, and to build a new electric branch to Watford, had to be postponed with the outbreak of war in 1914. Wartime economic conditions soon also curtailed Selbie's particularly favoured project, which was to develop housing estates on railway-owned land close to its suburban and country stations. The Met had started this

27. 'Spend a Day in Metro-land', a Metropolitan Railway poster by 'Shep', 1926. The Met's publicity was effective but never matched the style and quality of the Underground.

practice in a low-key way near Willesden Green back in the 1880s, followed by some housing at Wembley and Pinner in the early 1900s.

As described in chapter 2, Selbie was so anxious to promote more of the districts served by the railway as ideal to live in, rather than just visit, that he launched the first edition of the *Metro-land* guidebook in May 1915. Against expectation the war dragged on for three more years. Selbie stuck to his strategy, and the 1920 edition of the guide was still using much of the soothing copy from the first:

> The strain which the London business or professional man has to undergo amidst the turmoil and bustle of Town can only be counteracted by the quiet restfulness and comfort of a residence amidst pure air and surroundings, and whilst jaded vitality and taxed nerves are the natural penalties of modern conditions, Nature has, in the delightful districts abounding in Metro-land, placed a potential remedy at hand.[29]

The initial promotion may have been premature, but Selbie kept new season ticket holders in his sights. By the end of the war he had even devised his own plan to organize the direct development of Metro-land, which anticipated perfectly the post-war demand for new homes out of town.

In January 1919, just two months after the Armistice, Selbie announced the creation of a new property company, Metropolitan Railway Country Estates Ltd (MRCE). This was a mechanism for actively managing and developing the Met's 'surplus' land holdings, meaning property adjacent to the line acquired before it was built but often unused once the railway was complete. Legally, it was a separate company independent of the railway, but in practice the MRCE was under the control of the Metropolitan's directors.

Selbie, who was an MRCE director from the start, became a director of the Metropolitan Railway in 1922 while continuing to serve as its general manager. It was a cosy arrangement that gave the Metropolitan the unique opportunity among railway companies to become closely involved with quite extensive private property

28

28. An advertisement for the local Harrow Building Society from a Metropolitan Railway coach compartment, c.1930. The society offered low-cost mortgages to many first-time buyers in Metro-land.

29

29. A relief map of Metro-land first displayed at the British Empire Exhibition at Wembley, showing the location of golf courses marked with a red flag – a clear indicator of Selbie's target market of first-class season ticket holders.

development. 'Railway companies,' wrote Selbie smugly in 1921 'are trusted and not open to the suspicion that often attaches to the speculative builder and estate developer.'[30]

Between 1919 and 1933, the MRCE developed a string of housing estates near stations all down the line at Wembley Park, Northwick Park, Eastcote, Rayners Lane, Ruislip, Hillingdon, Pinner, Rickmansworth, Chorleywood and Amersham. In the early days, the estates company built some houses itself, but the usual pattern was to lay out an estate and then sell plots to individual purchasers wishing to have a house built to their own specifications. Later on, the design and construction was usually undertaken by other companies, who would offer the prospective purchaser a choice of house sizes and styles at a range of prices.

The annual *Metro-land* guide became the main advertising medium for these developments. The seductive dream of a new house on the edge of beautiful countryside but with every modern convenience, including a fast rail service to central London, was an appealing vision ninety years ago and remains so today. In true advertising tradition the Met's copywriters went way over the top in their purple prose, trying rather unconvincingly to blend notions of age-old rural tradition with civilized progress: 'This is a good parcel of English soil in which to build home and strike root, inhabited from of old ... the new settlement of Metro-land proceeds apace; the new colonists thrive amain.'[31]

The language must have sounded contrived even then,[32] although a quick glance at the ads and features in the weekly 'Homes and Property' supplement of the London *Evening Standard* will show that marketing methods have changed only superficially. Metro-land was one of the first and most successful examples in Britain[33] of a 'lifestyle' approach to property marketing that is now familiar to us all, and the attraction of a fast rail link to London is still paramount for today's suburban commuters.

Metro-land remains very popular as a place to live, particularly in the outer areas that are still countrified but now among the most affluent communities in the Home Counties. In a social survey by Oxford University in 2004, Chorleywood, with the lowest levels of deprivation in the country, was defined as the happiest place in England.[34]

A comparison of the census returns for 1921 and 1931 shows a population increase of nearly 11 per cent for Greater London as a whole, with a much higher rate of

30 and 31. Sheet music for 'My Little Metro-land Home', a vocal one-step published in 1920. The houses shown on the cover are in Pinner. The 'Live in Metro-land' message was even inscribed on the brass doorplates of Metropolitan Railway carriages in the 1920s.

32. The housing estate near Rayners Lane station on the Uxbridge branch was rebranded as Harrow Garden Village in 1929. It was soon one of the most successful new developments in Metro-land but very much a suburb rather than a village. By 1938 passenger numbers had outgrown the primitive railway facilities here, and a brand new station in London Transport's modern corporate style was provided.

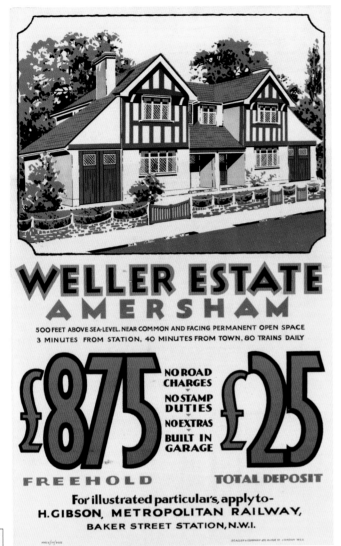

growth in the north-west suburbs between five and ten miles from the centre. The Metro-land districts of Harrow, Ruislip-Northwood, Uxbridge and Wembley all experienced increases of more than 50 per cent. In 1929, the Metropolitan Railway's commercial manager estimated that, between 1919 and 1928, some 12,000 houses had been built within half a mile of the stations between Willesden Green and Uxbridge, with a further 17,000 planned.

Only a small proportion of these had been built through the MRCE, but most of them contributed to the significant rise in ticket sales on the Met, particularly of seasons. Sample monthly season ticket issue figures from individual stations show that between 1921 and 1928 sales at Rickmansworth and Ruislip nearly doubled, for example. At Preston Road, Northwick Park and Wembley Park the rise was more than 700 per cent. The most spectacular growth of all was at Ickenham, where only fifty-nine monthly season tickets were sold in 1921, compared to 1,497 in 1928.[35]

Wonderful Wembley

The British Empire Exhibition of 1924/5 put Wembley permanently on the map and acted as a timely boost for Metro-land as a whole. It was not a project originally promoted by the Metropolitan Railway, but the fortuitous choice of Wembley Park as the site led to considerable benefits for the railway and the area. The exhibition was the largest in this country since the Great Exhibition of 1851 drew the crowds to the Crystal Palace in Hyde Park. Its purpose was to promote both the image and the economy of the British Empire or, in the words of the official guidebook, 'to display the natural resources of the Empire, and the activities, industrial and social, of their peoples'. The Metropolitan was the first to profit from the venture through the sale of 216 acres of Wembley Park to the exhibition company in January 1922, at last recouping some of Watkin's ill-fated investment of the 1890s described in chapter 1.

The first physical manifestation of the exhibition was erected, appropriately enough, on the site of Watkin's Folly, the unfinished tower which had been demolished in 1907. The new structure was a huge national sports arena, the largest of its kind in the world, built almost entirely with the newly refined technique of reinforced concrete. The Empire Stadium at Wembley could accommodate 125,000 spectators and was first used to stage the FA Cup Final in 1923.[36] The giant twin towers of the stadium came to symbolize Wembley as the national home of English football and stood for eighty years until the controversial but long-overdue redevelopment of the stadium in 2003. Match days are still the busiest occasions for Wembley Park station today.

The various ferro-concrete palaces and pavilions of the Empire Exhibition,

33. Poster advertising the Weller Estate at Amersham, 1930. This was the last and furthest flung of the MRCE housing developments, on the hill close to the railway station but more than a mile from old Amersham town centre in the valley below.

34. A Met parcel label from 1930. The company owned a fleet of delivery vans that brought parcels and other goods to your door in Metro-land.

and the adjacent amusements park,[37] were ready for a grand royal inauguration by King George V on St George's Day, 1924. The King's speech was relayed by the BBC to nearly seven million listeners, who for the first time heard a monarch's voice over the wireless. The exhibition organizers confidently predicted at least 25 million visitors to 'Wonderful Wembley'. In fact only 17.4 million people had passed through the turnstiles when the exhibition closed on 1 November. A second season in 1925 with various new exhibits was inevitably less popular, attracting 9.7 million customers.[38] The exhibition had its own special bus station and a new railway station on the LNER line from Marylebone, but a large proportion of the visitors would have arrived on the Metropolitan's trains at Wembley Park.

Comfortable modernity

Some of Selbie's shelved pre-war modernization plans were implemented in this period to help meet and further stimulate growing traffic demand. The extension of electric working on the Met main line beyond Harrow to Rickmansworth and the construction of a new branch to Watford were both completed in 1925. The Watford branch was built jointly with the LNER, taking advantage of the financial guarantees offered by the Trade Facilities Act that had also made the UERL's Tube extensions possible. Traffic was, and always has been, disappointing, largely because the terminus is in a residential area one mile from the centre of Watford. Only in this particular case were Selbie's predictions of a healthy commuter market from new suburbanites flawed.

The Met ordered a fleet of twenty powerful 1200hp electric locomotives from Metropolitan-Vickers to handle the improved services. These were to provide the main motive power for the long-distance services for nearly forty years, hauling trains as far as Rickmansworth (from 1925), where steam engines took over for the remainder of the journey to Aylesbury and Verney Junction. The 'Metro-Vicks' were the only electric locomotives used on mainline passenger services in the country at the time, and the railway proudly put one on display in the Palace of Engineering at the Wembley exhibition in 1925, its side panelling removed to show off the equipment inside. Nearby the LNER had displayed *Flying Scotsman*, one of its crack express passenger engines designed for the east coast main line, as a 1924 exhibit. Impressive as the great steam locomotive was, it essentially represented the newest refinement of old technology. With its latest electric engine the Met could promote itself at Wembley as the railway of the future.[39]

Yet the Met's modernity was not always fully apparent because of its generally conservative appearance. Quite deliberately, virtually everything about the railway had a

35. Cover of the 1924 edition of *Metro-land* featuring one of the giant concrete towers of the brand new Wembley Stadium, portrayed with foliage as though it had stood there since antiquity. Inside was a guide to the British Empire Exhibition alongside.

comforting, old-fashioned look even when it made use of up-to-date equipment. Selbie's Metropolitan remained visibly Edwardian in this respect, even by 1930, while Pick's Underground was increasingly setting the pace as a thoroughly advanced transport system that looked far more sleek and stylish.

The Metro-Vick locomotives have a rather heavy, utilitarian appearance that could not be described as elegant, and the new multiple-unit electric trains introduced by the Met at the end of the 1920s looked exactly the same as the traditional coaches pulled by steam locomotives on the main line. They still had comfortably furnished individual compartments and slam doors. This aesthetic was nothing like the smooth lines of the latest Underground trains, with their open saloons and sliding air doors controlled by the guard.

The Metropolitan continued to replicate, on a smaller scale, nearly all the features of a traditional mainline railway, with mixed goods trains and a parcels service offering home deliveries as well as

36. One of the Met's new electric locomotives displayed in the Palace of Engineering, its side panels removed when the Wembley exhibition reopened for a second season in 1925.

37. Steam locomotives continued to work all Met main line trains beyond Rickmansworth. This is an Aylesbury service near Chorleywood, c.1925, hauled by one of the Met's big 'H Class' express tank engines built in 1920. The Edwardian slam-door carriages with separate compartments were used for another thirty-five years, until electrification finally reached Amersham in 1961.

passenger operations. Lord Aberconway, the company chairman, often made a virtue of this anomaly for a mixed urban, suburban and country line, describing the Met with some pride as 'a trunk line in miniature'.[40] It still gave the Met an unusual split personality, and in the end it was impossible to sustain this as an independent operation.

Even the new Metro-land stations designed by Charles W. Clark, such as the branch termini at Watford and Stanmore, had the reassuring look of a miniature country house about them. They had every modern facility but solid, traditional styling. Meanwhile Clark was also responsible for Chiltern Court, the enormous block of flats built over Baker Street station in 1927–9. This had the slightly dated and overpowering feel of a grand Edwardian hotel, as it was originally intended to be, and boasted its own large restaurant. Writers H. G. Wells and Arnold Bennett were among the first tenants. Inevitably Metro-land claimed that it was the biggest and most luxurious apartment block in London, which 'opened a new chapter of advance in residential flat technique'.[41] A comparison with the new Underground group headquarters at St James's Park, designed by Charles Holden, which was built at the same time, demonstrates the widening aesthetic contrast between the UERL and the Met.

39

Projecting the Piccadilly

The extensions to the Hampstead and City lines in the 1920s originated from plans submitted by the Underground itself in the expectation of generating more traffic. They were not the result of outside pressure on the railway companies to provide

38. Chiltern Court, the largest apartment block in London, was opened over Baker Street station in 1929. It was designed by the Met's architect C. W. Clark and is seen here in a drawing from the original sales brochure.

39. Metro-Vick locomotive No. 12 *Sarah Siddons* built in 1922 and now the oldest working mainline electric locomotive in the country. It is seen on a special heritage train event at Amersham in 2008.

55 BROADWAY

NEW OFFICES IN BROADWAY FOR THE LONDON ELECTRIC RAILWAYS
ADAMS · HOLDEN & PEARSON · F.F.R.I.B.A. · ARCHITECTS · 8 KNIGHTSBRIDGE · HYDE PARK CORNER · S.W.1.

40

The rapid expansion of the Underground Group in the 1920s brought a need for a company headquarters building which could both accommodate the growing administrative staff and make a visual statement about the UERL's importance and progress. The success of the Morden extension stations brought this prestigious architectural commission to Charles Holden in 1926. Frank Pick, speaking at a DIA meeting that year, promised his audience that 'a new style of architectural decoration will arise' which would herald 'Modern London – modern not garbled classic or Renaissance'.[42]

Holden had already been asked to provide a sympathetic architectural treatment of the underground concourse at Piccadilly, which Pick was determined to make an inviting environment, unlike earlier booking halls at key central stations like Bank. Piccadilly was an entirely subterranean space but a very busy one. The new head office was all above ground, but had to be built on an awkward triangular site incorporating St James's Park station underneath it.

Holden saw this as a challenge and came up with an ingenious solution, a cross-shaped plan which allowed London's first American-style office skyscraper to rise up in steps above a sub-surface Underground station. He later told a meeting of civil engineers: 'I do not think I was ever more excited than when I realised the full possibilities of this cross-shaped plan – good light, short corridors, and a compact centre containing all services, complete with lifts and staircase communicating directly with all four wings.'[43]

Holden achieved simplicity and grandeur at 55 Broadway, as the building has always been known, without resorting to the usual application of assorted classical add-ons favoured

40. An impression of the Underground headquarters at 55 Broadway by Muirhead Bone, drawn when it was still being built. Holden's ingenious stepped cruciform design on this difficult triangular site was a radical contrast to Clark's contemporary Chiltern Court.

by most architects of office buildings at that time. The Underground headquarters was awarded the Royal Institute of British Architects (RIBA) London Architectural Medal for 1929, the year it was completed. At ten storeys it was the tallest office block in Westminster, modest by American standards but technically breaching the London County Council's building regulations. The top floor could not be used by staff until the LCC rules were amended.[44]

Broadway gained some brief public notoriety because of the sculptures decorating the façade. The eight on the upper storeys, representing the four winds, include artworks by Eric Gill and the first public sculpture by the young Henry Moore. These attracted little attention, partly because they are too high up to be seen clearly from the street. Two large sculptures representing *Day* and *Night* were carved in situ by Jacob Epstein at first-floor level. These avant garde figures were heavily criticized in the popular press as primitive, ugly and indecent. One was even attacked by vandals, who threw paint over it.

The controversy was such that Pick, feeling that he should back his architect's judgement on this despite his personal dislike for Epstein's work, tendered his resignation. It was not accepted. The sculptures stayed, although in a deliberately absurd gesture of compromise, Epstein dramatically chipped an inch off the penis of the naked young boy depicted in *Day*.[45]

55 Broadway and its sculptures no longer attract special attention, but its fine design remains a supreme example of how to integrate an underground station into an office development and give each equal prominence and dignity. The building, by then London Transport's head office, was listed in 1970 to give it protection. In 2011 English Heritage raised its listed status to grade I, recognizing Broadway's importance as one of the finest early twentieth-century buildings in London. It is still London Underground's headquarters.

41. Jacob Epstein with *Night*, one of his controversial sculptures carved in situ on the façade of 55 Broadway, 1929.

improved services for the public. But proposals to extend the Piccadilly line originated in just this way as a result of concern by the ratepayers of north-east London at the poor and overcrowded transport facilities in the districts of the capital north of Finsbury Park.

A constant barrage of public complaints from 1919 onwards eventually persuaded the Minister of Transport to set up the London and Home Counties Traffic Advisory Committee in 1925. One of the major problems on which the public inquiry concentrated was the severe rush-hour congestion and potentially dangerous daily crush at Finsbury Park caused by interchange between the mainline suburban railway, buses, trams and the two Tube lines, the Great Northern & City and the Piccadilly, which both terminated there.

Counsel for the local authorities spoke of 'pandemonium . . . something very like a free fight' in the evening rush hour at Finsbury Park. Newspaper accounts described how 'men and women fight like rugby players to reach their homes' and that 'clothes are torn, and fainting girls and women are so common as to pass almost without comment'.[46] It was clearly a desperate situation.

The solution recommended in the report was a northern extension of the Piccadilly line so that fewer passengers would have to break their journey at Finsbury Park, but as usual there was no suggestion as to how this might be financed. It was not a priority for the Underground, which was at this stage still working on the Morden extension. The mainline company operating through Finsbury Park was the LNER, which took over the GNR in 1923 and showed no more interest than its predecessors in its London suburban services.

As described in chapter 2, the GNR had prevented the Great Northern & City Tube from making a through link to its overground suburban lines here. Unlike the Southern, which was busily electrifying suburban lines south of the river, the LNER avoided committing to any modernization of its suburban lines in north London in the 1920s. It was not supportive of any underground extensions which might compete with its own overground steam services, but also claimed that it could not afford to electrify. The LNER concentrated instead on its freight services, in those days more profitable than commuters, and on promoting its glamorous long-distance mainline passenger trains.

The Underground duly prepared a Piccadilly extension scheme but took no action until a source of capital was available. This came suddenly in 1929, when the newly elected Labour government

42

42. Evening rush hour at Finsbury Park, with passengers leaving the Tube terminus crowding on to trams and buses to complete their journeys home to north London, 1930. Extending the Piccadilly line two years later solved this particular problem.

rushed through the Development (Loans, Guarantee and Grants) Act. Like the 1921 legislation that had enabled the Edgware and Morden extensions to go ahead, this was intended to assist new works that could relieve the growing levels of unemployment, soon to get worse after the Wall Street crash.

This time the government assistance was broader, with fifteen-year treasury guarantees offered on the interest incurred by capital loans. The theory was that by this time the extended line would be paying its way, with healthily rising passenger revenue from new season ticket holders in the suburbs, and the loans would be repaid.

43. 'New Works' poster, by Thomas Lightfoot, 1932. It captures perfectly the dynamic, progressive and ever-improving Underground image that Pick always tried to promote.

OPENING OF THE PICCADILLY LINE EXTENSION

FINSBURY PARK TO ARNOS GROVE

ARNOS GROVE

BOUNDS GREEN

WOOD GREEN

TURNPIKE LANE

MANOR HOUSE

FINSBURY PARK

PICCADILLY

UNDERGROUND

5 NEW STATIONS FOR NORTH LONDON 19TH • OPEN SEPTEMBER

CW BACON

44

In practice, of course, like nearly all major capital projects, this never happened.

Taking immediate advantage of the Act's generous provision, the Underground quickly put forward a £12.4 million development programme covering far more than a northern extension to the Piccadilly line. As well as the 7.5-mile projection of the Piccadilly line from Finsbury Park to Cockfosters, this included a 4.5-mile western extension overground alongside the District line, with four-tracking from Hammersmith to Northfields. New Piccadilly Tube trains would then run further west over the District line branches beyond Acton Town to Hounslow and, via South Harrow, to Uxbridge. Various major infrastructure improvements to the central area, including a new interchange station with the Central line at Holborn, were also proposed. The scale of the work was similar to the Northern line improvements of 1924-6.

Work began in 1930, and by 1932 the first part of the Piccadilly extensions at both the northern and western ends of the line were opened, with final completion in 1933. Again, the speed of construction was remarkable. North of Finsbury Park the line was built in twin-tube tunnels under the already built-up suburban districts of Turnpike Lane, Wood Green and Bounds Green, coming to the surface at Arnos Grove. The line then continued overground, mainly on embankments and viaducts, through open country to rural Cockfosters, with a short tunnel under Southgate, the only village in this peaceful part of Middlesex that was still ripe for development. The western extension from Hammersmith was all above ground and mainly involved widening part of the District line and rebuilding a number of stations. Depots for a new fleet of Piccadilly Tube trains were built at Cockfosters and Northfields.

In preparing its package of improvements to the Piccadilly, the Underground was not simply hoping to encourage more suburban development, and therefore traffic, from the outer extensions of the line. It was also trying to meet a growing market for easier and faster travel to London's West End. Throughout the Victorian period, and still to some extent in the early 1900s, the City had always been seen as the prime destination for new railway services in London. By the 1920s the West End offered a much wider range of attractions and reasons to travel than the business and financial services of the square mile. The impressive rebuilding of Piccadilly Circus station in 1924–8 as a new transport hub was the Underground's first major response to this, but it only highlighted the inadequate provision elsewhere in central London.

As a result the improvement scheme also included the reconstruction of various

44. Rolling out a new Tube. Poster by C. W. Bacon showing the route of the Piccadilly northern extension opened in 1932.

other busy central-area stations as well as the closure of inner Piccadilly line stations that were under-used.[47] These changes, together with the additional express tracks on the Hammersmith–Acton Town section, a feature copied from the New York Subway, all contributed to the transformation of the Piccadilly into a modern rapid transit line with faster services over a route that was more than double its original length.[48]

Much as the Underground prided itself at this time on planning for and providing what London needed, based on the best statistical analysis available, this was never a precise process. As J. P. Thomas, the Underground's General Manager, wrote in 1934 after the first year's operating experience of the fully extended Piccadilly line: 'an entirely new traffic appears to be created wherever a through West End service is introduced'.[49] However, trends were not easily predictable, and traffic figures did not automatically follow a steadily rising path, particularly in the uncertain economic climate of the 1930s.

A distinctive style

Frank Pick was as determined as ever that the new works on the Piccadilly line should follow the theory of continuous business improvement within the resources available, as well as the DIA's 'fitness for purpose' design principles that he championed. Charles Holden was retained as consulting architect to the Underground, and before work started on the new Piccadilly line stations he and Pick went on an architectural study tour of northern Europe together in 1930. They visited Germany, Scandinavia and Holland to take a close look at some of the recent commercial and civic architecture on the Continent that they particularly admired. This included the work of Erik Asplund in Stockholm and Willem Dudok in the Dutch city of Hilversum. Both these architects' design styles and lean combination of brick, concrete and metal-framed glass were particularly influential on Holden's next commissioned work for the Underground.

The prototype for the Piccadilly line stations was completed at Sudbury Town in the western suburbs in July 1931. It was the first of what Holden came to describe as his 'brick boxes with concrete lids'. If that sounds uninspiring, the reality is far from it. The box is double height, with four large windows arranged symmetrically above the entrance, rising to the name frieze below the cornice. The arrangement of the station was planned to stand out in the suburban landscape but also to promote the most efficient movement of people. A generously spaced

The West-End is awakening—
And once again there is everything for your pleasure

By UNDERGROUND

46

45. Underground poster by Ernest Dinkel promoting travel to the West End 'for your pleasure', 1931.

46. Sudbury Town station was the first of Holden's 'brick box with a concrete lid' designs, completed in 1931. Every new station for the Piccadilly extensions had similar features, but no two were identical.

ticket hall at the main entrance gives direct access to the London-bound platform, and a covered concrete bridge to the other.

Sudbury Town represented an even more extraordinary leap forward in station design in this country than the Morden line. Again, it was quite unlike anything on the mainline railways or on the Metropolitan. It also heralded a new era in Underground architecture. Holden's clean, simple and functional design blended traditional building forms and materials like brickwork with the modernity of concrete and careful attention to details like light fittings. Pick, who had taken a close interest in the station's evolution, was delighted with the result but dismayed to find discordant additions inside when he inspected the completed building:

> On the platforms I found that some seven or eight automatic machines have been dumped down and are now going to spoil the cleanness and clearness of the platforms. Somehow there seems to be a desire on the part of everyone to break up and destroy the tidiness and spaciousness of this station. The only way in which, in my opinion, the spaciousness can be filled properly is by passengers and not by a lot of impediments.[50]

Pick then asked the operating manager to provide Holden with a complete list of all fittings and equipment that would be needed in each new station, and Holden was given final responsibility for ensuring that all these items were incorporated in the design from the start. Holden either designed or selected everything from seats and ticket machines to clocks and litter bins and determined the final position of all these items.

47

THE LATEST IN RAILWAY STATION ARCHITECTURE
Come and see it

DIRECT FROM PICCADILLY

Manor House	16 mins.
Turnpike Lane	19 ,,
Wood Green	21 ,,
Bounds Green	23 ,,
Arnos Grove	25 ,,

It was total design with a vengeance, an integrated approach to planning and quality standards which is still rarely followed in public buildings and environments.

Holden found working with Pick challenging but inspirational: 'It was an exciting adventure all the time, sometimes a very strenuous one – it was certainly never allowed to be dull.'[51] Pick had set out clearly his intentions in commissioning new stations in a lecture to a group of architects in March 1930, just before the new Piccadilly line work began: 'The passenger must be made to feel as though he were a guest. The doors are to be set wide open, to be modest not vast ... the sense of orderliness must flow from some

47. 'The latest in Railway Architecture'. A panel poster advertising Holden's new Piccadilly line stations as an attraction in themselves, 1933

48. Night view of the new booking hall interior at Sudbury Town. Spacious, uncluttered and beautifully lit, this was a revolution in station design. It replaced the District Railway's cheap shack station building of 1903.

49. Arnos Grove, probably Holden's finest station design, 1932. The 'drum on a cube' main building echoed Asplund's City Library in Stockholm, which Pick and Holden had visited on their architectural study tour of northern Europe.

50. Cockfosters, the new northern terminus of the Piccadilly line, opened in August 1933. Holden's concrete and glass trainshed was a modern interpretation of the great Victorian arched iron structures like St Pancras.

51. At Southgate, the circular shape of the booking hall was matched by a traffic roundabout, a bus station and a curved parade of shops. Holden designed them all in the same flowing style, creating a new focal point for the village-turned-suburb.

THE BECK MAP

The classic diagrammatic Underground map designed by Harry Beck was first produced in 1933 and became an instant success with the travelling public. It is now rightly seen as a radical breakthrough in the design of communication graphics but often wrongly attributed to the culture of modernism that Pick had established at the Underground. Unlike Johnston's letterface and the redesign of the symbol, which had been directly commissioned by Pick himself, the new map was devised by Beck in his spare time and taken to the Underground's publicity department by him as a personal proposal. It was one individual's smart idea that met with little initial enthusiasm in the organization.

Henry C. Beck (1902–74) was a young engineering draughtsman who worked initially in the Underground's Signal Engineer's office from 1925. While temporarily laid off during the depression in 1931, he devised the first version of his map, apparently inspired by electrical circuit diagrams.

Every development and variation of the system map drawn up annually since 1908, when the first free maps were issued, was a geographical representation of the network. Beck realized that passengers do not need a geographically accurate map, but might prefer a simple diagram showing them the sequence of stations and where to change lines to reach their destination.[52] His line diagram abandoned geographical accuracy and all other features except the river. By expanding the central area of the city and shrinking the outer areas, he made the distances between stations equal. The whole network is shown as a series of colour-coded interconnecting vertical, horizontal and diagonal lines.

The result is a complete distortion of London, the River Thames and the Underground system, but as a

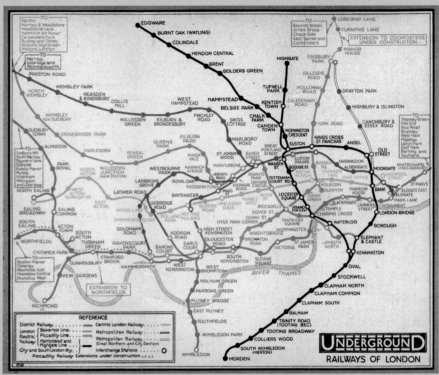

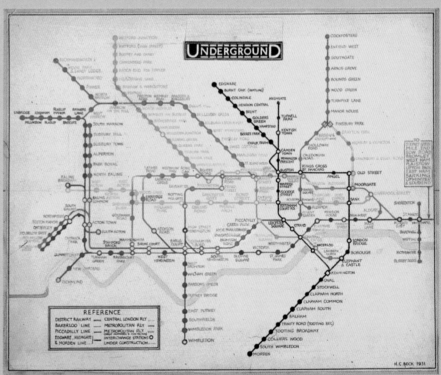

52. The 1931 edition of the official Underground pocket map, designed by F. H. Stingemore. Fitting the whole system on to it while keeping the map legible was becoming increasingly difficult.

53. Harry Beck's first presentation design, offered to the Underground in 1931 and initially rejected.

office until a final falling-out took place. The last map with his name on it was printed in 1959.[53]

Beck died in 1974, bitter to the end at what he felt had been his unreasonable treatment by London Transport, particularly in the 1960s, when he was neither involved in further changes nor acknowledged as the map's originator. Eventually, by the 1990s the significance of his enormous contribution to graphic design development through the map became widely recognized. His name reappeared under the large-format system maps on every London Underground station, and the map itself became an icon of modernism, endlessly copied, imitated and plagiarized in advertising and artworks.

The greatest tribute to Beck's map is not in the various imitations and copies elsewhere, but in its astonishing versatility and adaptability as a travel guide to London. This flexibility has allowed a multitude of extensions and additions to be fitted into its grid over the years, including London rail services that are not part of the Underground, such as the DLR and Overground lines.

Despite its denial of the city's true geography, the Tube map's alternative vision of the city has become a familiar feature of London life which few people would wish to see changed. In 2006 it came second in a BBC competition to find the public's favourite British design of the twentieth century.[54] When Beck's distorted and angular River Thames disappeared from the pocket map in 2009 there was uproar on the web and in the media. The Mayor was forced to step in and guarantee the river's reinstatement for the next edition. Popular opinion would make any more fundamental redesign of this particular London icon out of the question.

travel aid it is brilliantly simple, being very easy to read and use. Beck pestered the Underground for two years to get a trial printing, and eventually 750,000 copies were printed in January 1933 with a request for comments from passengers on the cover. Much to the Underground's surprise, the public reception was very enthusiastic.

Beck, by this time a member of staff again and working in the publicity office, was paid a derisory ten guineas (£10.50) for his initial design preparation but remained a contracted freelance for his map work. The public response to his innovative design led the Underground to make his diagram the standard system map. It has been used almost continuously since 1933, though with regular changes, both as a large poster map on stations and as a free-folding pocket map for travellers.

Beck had a difficult relationship with London Transport (LT) for the rest of his working life. He insisted on retaining control of the map and personally overseeing all changes himself for more than twenty-five years, even after he left LT employment in the late 1940s. His constant revisions and meticulous reworkings became almost an obsession, and inevitably there were constant clashes with the publicity

54. The first printed Beck pocket map, 1933. A polite message on the cover read: 'A new design for an old map. We should welcome your comments.' Passengers responded with enthusiasm.

unity that binds together all the various components that constitute the well-equipped station into the expression of a single idea.'[55]

Three years later, when he took members of the DIA on a tour of the completed Southgate extension, Holden suggested diffidently that the design of the new stations was simply a matter of keeping to the DIA's philosophy, which both he and Pick had always supported: 'There is no need to go out of one's way in the search for novelty: a proper sense of fitness for purpose will supply all the material for the adventure.'[56]

It was in this period that Pick and Holden refined the elements of what developed into an instantly recognizable Underground house style, soon to be extended to bus stops, shelters and garages to reflect the wider corporate identity of London Transport. The brick box at Sudbury Town established a kit of parts and materials that was reflected in new infrastructure all down the extended Piccadilly line both above and below ground, and in everything from passenger environments in stations to signal cabins, car depots and electricity sub-stations.

No two stations were identical, and Holden's strong overall design identity allowed for both consistency and variation at a wide range of locations. The 'brick box' could have a drum on top of it (Arnos Grove), become a low, circular structure (Southgate), have a tower to mark it out at a distance (Chiswick Park) or a concrete and glass trainshed to cover the platforms at the terminus (Cockfosters). All the stations are recognizably 'on the Tube' and instantly made any nearby mainline suburban stations, which all dated from before 1900, look old-fashioned and shabby.

Even the stations on the Metropolitan Railway's last extension, the branch from Wembley Park to Stanmore, which opened in December 1932 and was also built with a capital loan guaranteed by the treasury under the 1929 Act, were not in the same league. Holden's Piccadilly line stations, including his best individual buildings, probably Arnos Grove and Southgate, were hailed at the time as some of the finest new commercial architecture in Britain. Today they are nearly all listed buildings and have recently been refurbished, remaining as functional and fit for purpose as any of the Underground's travel environments.

The triumph of London Transport

As early as 1863, the year that the first underground railway had opened in London, a House of Lords Committee had suggested that a single transport authority was needed to coordinate and integrate transport services in the capital. Over the next fifty years many government bodies had reinforced that opinion, and yet by 1913 only a limited degree of amalgamation had taken place, with none of it driven by state intervention.

55

POWER

THE NERVE CENTRE OF LONDON'S

UNDERGROUND

55. 'Power', by Edward McKnight Kauffer, 1931. A dramatic modernist poster by the Underground's star designer, underlining the UERL's key role as the powerhouse and nerve centre of London.

1. The Purpose

The Board is a public authority appointed under Act of Parliament charged with responsibility for providing an adequate and properly co-ordinated system of passenger transport within the London Passenger Transport Area. It is required to take such steps as it considers necessary for avoiding wasteful, competitive services and for extending and improving London's passenger transport facilities, so as to meet the growing needs of the vast population working and dwelling within the area over which the Board's operations extend.

For all inquiries
LONDON PASSENGER TRANSPORT BOARD
55, Broadway, Westminster, S.W.1
Telephone: VICtoria 6800
Telegrams: Passengers Sowest London

This is No. 1 of a series of four announcements by the London Passenger Transport Board. Other announcements will be published at fortnightly intervals, as follows: 2. The Territory. 3. The Service. 4. The Staff.

2. The Territory

The area comprises 2,000 square miles, and the railway, tramway, omnibus and coach services which operate within its boundaries cater for a population of 9,000,000 people.

For all inquiries
LONDON PASSENGER TRANSPORT BOARD
55, Broadway, Westminster, S.W.1
Telephone: VICtoria 6800
Telegrams: Passengers Sowest London

This is No. 2 of a series of four announcements by the London Passenger Transport Board. Other announcements will be published at fortnightly intervals as follows: 3. The Service. 4. The Staff.

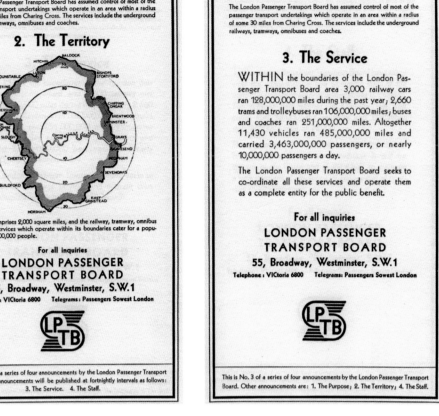

3. The Service

WITHIN the boundaries of the London Passenger Transport Board area 3,000 railway cars ran 128,000,000 miles during the past year; 2,660 trams and trolleybuses ran 106,000,000 miles; buses and coaches ran 251,000,000 miles. Altogether 11,430 vehicles ran 485,000,000 miles and carried 3,463,000,000 passengers, or nearly 10,000,000 passengers a day.

The London Passenger Transport Board seeks to co-ordinate all these services and operate them as a complete entity for the public benefit.

For all inquiries
LONDON PASSENGER TRANSPORT BOARD
55, Broadway, Westminster, S.W.1
Telephone: VICtoria 6800   Telegrams: Passengers Sowest London

This is No. 3 of a series of four announcements by the London Passenger Transport Board. Other announcements are: 1. The Purpose; 2. The Territory; 4. The Staff.

56

As we have seen, the Underground Group of companies was still the most powerful force in London's public transport in the 1920s, but not in overall control. The continuing conflict of interest between the various private and municipal transport operators, particularly on the roads, with so many separate bus and tram companies, made progress with coordination slow. Clearly the needs of the travelling public and London as a whole were still not being met, but, as we have seen, successive governments failed to take matters forward.

Eventually the two largest operators, the Underground Group and the LCC, agreed in 1928 to promote two separate Bills in parliament which would enable full coordination and joint management of their services, with a common fund of earnings. Ownership would remain separate. But while these bills were going through parliament there was a general election, in May 1929. The Labour Party, which opposed a scheme that seemed to favour the privately run UERL over the council operator, was now in control. Both coordination bills were quickly thrown out.[57]

However, a way forward now emerged largely through the unlikely cooperation of Lord Ashfield, the Underground Group chairman, and Herbert Morrison, the new Labour Minister of Transport. Morrison, the cockney socialist who had started his political career as a Labour member of the LCC, had long argued against what he saw

4. The Staff

THE London Passenger Transport Board have taken over the administrative and operating staffs of the various passenger transport undertaking in London. The railway staff number 14,300; the bus and coach staff 38,000; the tramway and trolleybus staff 19,600; a total of 71,900.

The employees of the Board have behind them a long experience and a great tradition. It will be the aim of the Board and of their staff to maintain a high standard of efficiency, of service and of courtesy to all passengers.

For all inquiries
LONDON PASSENGER TRANSPORT BOARD
55, Broadway, Westminster, S.W.1
Telephone: VICtoria 6800   Telegrams: Passengers Sowest London

A folder containing a series of four announcements by the London Passenger Transport Board may be obtained on application to the above address. The other subjects in the series are: 1. The Purpose; 2. The Territory; 3. The Service.

56. London Transport's four press advertisements announcing its purpose and role, July 1933. A new LPTB logo was used on these but quickly replaced with the familiar bar and circle.

as Ashfield's ambition to create a protected, private monopoly of public transport in London. 'Common theft' was Morrison's description of it, 'a capitalist counter-offensive against public property'.[58] Morrison wanted public ownership and control. Ashfield and Pick had consistently called for common management but did not want political interference.

In December 1929 Morrison announced his proposals for a comprehensive solution to the apparently insoluble 'London traffic problem'. At the time he seemed to be the only politician who fully understood the issues at stake and had the ability to negotiate and steer through a workable scheme that could satisfy nearly everyone. Above all, he had to get the cooperation and support of the two key players, Ashfield and Pick, that 'formidable pair' as he later described them. Despite their virtually opposite approach to his, he felt he could do business with them and come up with something the Underground Group would accept.

Morrison recommended the creation of a new transport board for London, to be run on similar lines to the recently established BBC and Central Electricity Board. It was to be self-supporting and unsubsidized, with a degree of public control but non-political management. The only major element of public transport in the capital excluded from the proposed authority was the overground suburban railway network. The four companies argued that their suburban lines could not be run separately from their main lines, but they did eventually agree to a fare-pooling scheme in London and a joint committee with the new authority to plan future developments.

No such compromise was offered to the independent bus operators or the Metropolitan Railway, who remained firmly opposed to the scheme. The sudden death of Selbie in 1930 removed the strongest advocate of an independent Met, but the case for continuing with the status quo was weak. Despite an active campaign against it, and the fall of the Labour government in 1931, when Morrison was removed from office, the legislation was eventually passed by parliament, and on 1 July 1933 the new authority came into being. Its full title was the London Passenger Transport Board (LPTB), soon generally known as London Transport, the name that began to appear in gold Johnston lettering on every bus, tram, trolleybus and Underground train in London from 1934.

Under the new Board, ultimate authority was removed from the local authorities that had run council tram services and from the shareholders of all the various London bus, tram and underground railway companies, from the pirates to the Combine. All shareholders received either cash payments or shares in the new undertaking. There was some public control over new developments, but real power rested with the Board, which in practice was dominated by the leading individuals and inherited philosophy of the Underground Group. Lord Ashfield became its first chairman and Frank Pick the vice-chairman and chief executive.

57. The familiar London Transport bar and circle, 1933.

The London Traffic Area for which the LPTB was responsible was much larger than the current boundaries of Greater London, which is roughly the M25 ring, or 15–20 miles from central London. From 1933 London Transport covered some 2,000 square miles within a 20–30 mile radius of Charing Cross, including a large area of London's countryside, which was served by green country buses and coaches. London Transport had to plan and provide road and rail services for a population then rapidly approaching 9.5 million people.

New Works Programme

Ashfield and Pick had always been clear that a metropolis of London's size and complexity needed a suitable mix of public transport provision in different areas: buses, trams, underground and overground railways. The problem they had faced throughout the 1920s had been the absence of coordination between these modes, caused largely by the range of ownership and management. This had made forward planning difficult if not impossible, because the UERL did not have complete control of any one area or mode of transport, although it had a partial involvement in all of them.

The creation of the LPTB changed this situation at a stroke, as it effectively gave the new organization a virtual monopoly, but it brought with it new obligations and expectations. As chairman and chief executive of a public corporation, Ashfield and Pick now had responsibilities which were no less demanding than those to the UERL's former private shareholders. London Transport was a public service authority on an unprecedented scale, with a formidable challenge ahead of it.

A continuing difficulty was how to break even financially. This inevitably meant a degree of cross-subsidy within the LPTB, between its road and rail services. Buses were still profitable, earning more from fares than they cost to run, but could not cope with London's travel needs on their own. The large tram network now carried fewer passengers than the buses and was losing money. Major renewals or complete replacement of the system were necessary.

58

58. Tram, bus and Underground services meet at Hammersmith, August 1934. All three transport modes had been run as part of one organization, the LPTB, for just one year. A few months later new trolleybuses began to replace trams in west London.

THE BEST TRAINS IN THE WORLD

London Transport's underground trains were unquestionably the best in the world in the 1930s. The UERL's philosophy of continuous improvement meant that engineering research and design development had become increasingly sophisticated since the creation of Acton railway works in 1921/2, built alongside the LGOC's Chiswick bus works, which was constructed at the same time. The growing complex at Acton housed the Underground's main overhaul and repair facilities, which were centralized and run on the latest factory 'flow-line' principles from 1928. The UERL's new rolling stock was not actually built at Acton, but all train design, development and experimental work took place there.[59]

William S. Graff Baker (1889–1952), who became chief mechanical engineer (railways) in 1935, had worked for the Underground since joining as a junior electrical fitter in 1910. He led the team that designed the advanced new Tube and sub-surface trains that entered service from 1937/8 as part of the LPTB's massive expansion and modernization programme.

The small diameter of London's deep-level tunnels limited the size of Tube trains, and Graff Baker's engineers experimented with new space-saving techniques. The control equipment which took up a quarter of each driving motor car behind the cab of the Standard Tube stock built from 1923 to 1934 was ingeniously redistributed and located below the floor of experimental cars built in 1935, giving more room for passenger seating.

The interior design and layout was improved, with new flexible grab handles for straphangers and deep-cushioned seating, now covered in woollen moquette specially commissioned from textile designers rather than the manufacturers' standard range. The new Tube cars still had varnished, slatted hardwood floors which, combined with the red and green panels and seating units, had a warm and inviting appearance. Everything was highly functional but looked surprisingly luxurious, right down to the Art

59

59. London Transport shows off its technical modernity in a poster by Laszlo Moholy-Nagy featuring the latest pneumatic doors on the new Tube trains, 1937.

Deco lampshades, which could have graced an expensive restaurant.

Trials with fully streamlined Tube cars showed that this fashionable 1930s bodystyling was of no benefit to low-speed trains in Tube tunnels. However, the smooth exterior finish of the new prototype cars, with uncluttered panels and flush-fitted windows, was adopted for mass production. This was a more attractive design and a practical benefit when trains were cleaned by running them through the new automatic washing machines. Passengers could open the pneumatic doors with push buttons. The driver could now talk directly to the guard at the back through a speaking tube. A new 'wedglock' automatic coupler made it easier and faster to lengthen or shorten trains as required.

All these improved features were incorporated in the production 1938 stock built for the LPTB in Birmingham,[60] which is now regarded as the classic London Tube train and a design benchmark. It did not have the glamour of the famous streamlined steam express trains of the period such as the Silver Jubilee and the Coronation Scot, but it was a technically far more advanced design and carried thousands of ordinary Londoners on their daily journey to work rather than a handful of wealthy first-class travellers.

Graff Baker took a similar view to Pick and Holden on the crucial importance of good, practical design engineering. He said he always asked five key questions of any new development in train design: Will it work? Is it as simple as possible? Could it easily be maintained in service? Can it be manufactured? Does it look well? 'Engineering design,' he claimed, 'is an art just as much as is the work of a painter or an architect.'[61] Some of his beautifully designed pieces of applied art were in service on the London Underground for fifty years, and a four-car set of 1938 stock has been restored to working order by London Transport Museum for occasional public outings on the system.[62]

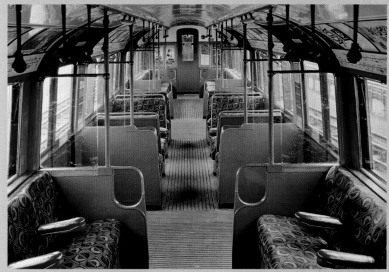

60. A brand new three-car 1938 Tube stock unit at Acton Town. These were probably the most advanced trains in the world at the time.

61. The comfortable interior of a 1938 stock car, still fit for purpose in the 1960s.

62. London Transport Museum's four-car unit of 1938 stock on a heritage run at Harrow-on-the-Hill, 2008.

63   64

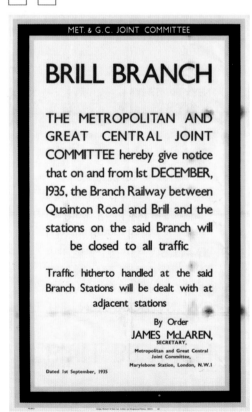

MET. & G.C. JOINT COMMITTEE

BRILL BRANCH

THE METROPOLITAN AND GREAT CENTRAL JOINT COMMITTEE hereby give notice that on and from Ist DECEMBER, 1935, the Branch Railway between Quainton Road and Brill and the stations on the said Branch will be closed to all traffic

Traffic hitherto handled at the said Branch Stations will be dealt with at adjacent stations

By Order
JAMES McLAREN,
SECRETARY,
Metropolitan and Great Central Joint Committee,
Marylebone Station, London, N.W.I

Dated Ist September, 1935

The Underground was the essential transport network underpinning London which required further investment, but it was also expensive to run. In 1933 the LPTB inherited an underground railway network covering 227 route miles[63] and carrying some 415 million passengers a year. Both needed to grow.[64] As Pick put it at a senior staff conference in 1937,

> The railways represent an inescapable basic service for London. Whether they are able to operate at an efficiency which makes them financially sound or not, they must be provided to support the mass of road transport that has been built up around them. They have every claim to a subsidy from road transport if that be the only basis upon which they can be enlarged and continued.[65]

London Transport's ambitious plans in the 1930s involved modernizing and developing services across the board. On the roads, it was decided that all new buses would have more efficient diesel instead of petrol engines. Trams would be replaced by electric trolleybuses, which were cheaper and more flexible to run because they did not require rails in the road. More than half of London's huge tram network was replaced in this way between 1935 and 1940.

On the Underground, the first in a series of new schemes was announced in November 1934, involving upgrades to the Metropolitan line. A new branch of the Bakerloo Tube would run below the Met between Baker Street and Finchley Road,

---

63 and 64. The Brill branch train at Quainton Road, Bucks, in 1934. This remote and little-used rural service inherited from the Met was closed by the LPTB a year later, but both the steam engine and the station shown here survive in preservation.

65 66

relieving overcrowding on this section. Bakerloo services would be projected overground alongside the Met to Wembley Park and take over the newly built branch to Stanmore.

As part of London Transport, the Met was no longer permitted the luxury of regarding itself as a mainline railway, and operations at the outer end of the line beyond the Chilterns in rural Bucks were soon cut back. The lightly used Brill branch, worked by sixty-year old steam locomotives[66] with a mixed goods and passenger train, was closed in 1935. Two years later the LNER took over the steam passenger workings beyond Rickmansworth, and London Transport transferred half of their old Metropolitan Railway steam engines to the mainline company.

The LNER also took over the remaining goods services on the Met, a final recognition that this was no longer part of the core business of a modern, urban passenger railway. The last symbols of Selbie's luxury mainline service, the two Met Pullman cars, were withdrawn at the outbreak of war.

London Transport's wider 1935–40 New Works Programme for the Underground was planned in partnership with the LNER and GWR, to further improve suburban services in north and west London. The Central line was to be extended in the west on new overground tracks from North Acton to Ruislip and Denham. An eastern extension would run in Tube tunnels from Liverpool Street to Stratford and join up with the LNER's overground branch lines into Essex. The existing steam suburban services from Liverpool Street to Epping, Ongar and the Fairlop loop would be taken over by electric Tube trains.

The Underground would also take over and electrify the LNER's

67

65. Tube passengers using the new escalators at Holborn station, rebuilt in 1933 as an interchange between the Central and Piccadilly lines. This allowed the original British Museum station near by to be closed. The stylish bronze uplighters are another Holden design.

66. Sign from Queensbury station, opened by the LPTB in 1934. Kingsbury, the next stop on the Stanmore branch, is the name of an ancient village near the railway, but 'Queensbury' was the adopted winner in a local competition to name the brand new suburban settlement created here on the former Stag Lane airfield in the 1930s.

67. The Met's two luxurious Pullman cars remained in service with the LPTB until war broke out. Affluent first-class passengers make themselves comfortable in *Mayflower* at Baker Street awaiting departure for the Chilterns, 1934.

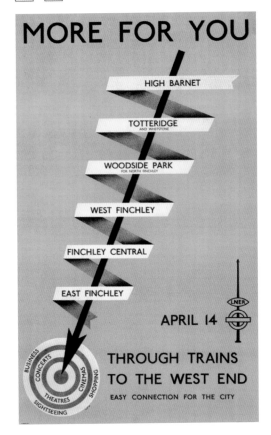

'Northern Heights' suburban branch lines with new links to the Northern line. An extension from the original 1907 Tube terminus at Highgate (Archway) would come to the surface at East Finchley and join the LNER line to High Barnet. Tube trains would also take over from steam on the overground sections, which would be electrified back to Finsbury Park. The Highgate to Alexandra Palace and Finchley Church End to Edgware sections would also become part of the Northern line, with a further extension beyond Edgware to Bushey Heath.

This was a massive series of capital projects, which included further modernization work on the Underground in central London, as well as other suburban improvements. London Transport's New Works Programme was to be financed by the now well-established mechanism of loans under government guarantee. No public money was granted, but Treasury agreement was given for a finance corporation to raise the £40 million required.

Work began on all three Tube lines involved in 1936 and proceeded rapidly. London Transport had inherited the UERL's skills and experience in managing large engineering projects. For Ashfield and Pick the greater worry was maintaining revenue funding and their obligation to cover the LPTB's running costs. The financial viability of both the Underground's existing operations and planned future development depended on the continued growth and expansion of London attracting yet more passengers on to the system. While operation was becoming ever more efficient, the most recent extensions of the Piccadilly line and the Stanmore branch were not providing as much extra traffic as had been hoped and planned for. New suburban housing followed both lines, but more slowly than at Hendon and Edgware.

Economies had to be found, and some of the development plans were scaled back. This was particularly painful for Pick, who still insisted on maintaining high standards and not cutting corners.[67] He now found that costs were being squeezed and financial savings were necessary. There is even a telling story of Holden complaining to Pick about the replacement of the escalator murals at Piccadilly Circus with a giant Ovaltine advertisement in the mid-1930s. Pick apparently replied that the advertisement was contributing some £2,000 a year to the Underground's revenue and that if Holden would contribute the same he would have it removed. Art and design were important to him, but they had to pay their way.[68]

68. Brochure for the new Laing estate at Enfield West (now Oakwood), 1936.

69. Poster by Beath announcing the start of the through Northern line service from High Barnet to the West End, 1940.

The progress of modernization and improvement in the first five years of the LPTB was remarkable, but by 1938 it was being slowed by economic uncertainty and the deteriorating international situation in Europe.[69] The outbreak of war in September 1939 stopped London's suburban sprawl in its tracks, and only the Bakerloo extension was almost ready. A new Tube service from Stanmore through to the West End opened in November.[70] Northern line Tube trains were running right up to High Barnet a few months later, from April 1940, but work on all the other extension projects was suspended for the duration of the war, some never to be completed.[71] The Battle of Britain was about to begin, and London Transport's boom years were suddenly over.

70

71

70. Architect's perspective of the new Park Royal station, Ealing, 1936. This was designed in the Holden style by Welch and Lander, architects of the houses, flats and shops on the adjacent Hanger Hill estate.

71. East Finchley was the only former LNER station on the High Barnet branch to be completely reconstructed in LPTB style to a Holden design and opened for Tube services in 1940. Eric Aumonier's Art Deco archer is still speeding Northern line trains towards central London today.

CHAPTER 4

FROM WAR TO AUSTERITY

On the morning of 1 September 1939 Frank Pick's chauffeur-driven Daimler pulled up outside Enfield West station on the Piccadilly line,[1] where hundreds of children were being evacuated by Tube from inner London. Typically, Pick had arrived without warning to silently observe the effectiveness of the detailed evacuation plans he'd spent months preparing with colleagues on behalf of the government.[2] Now, with the formal declaration of war with Germany only hours away, it was down to London Transport to move children and expectant mothers from those areas perceived to be at the greatest risk of imminent air attack. It was an anxious time for all concerned.

Station staff, police and volunteer helpers, many with children of their own to worry about, did their best to cope with the extraordinary situation, calmly processing each trainload of new arrivals. Older children, carrying battered suitcases labelled with their names and addresses, clutched younger siblings. Mothers carried infants. On the forecourt, London Transport buses stood in readiness to ferry the bewildered evacuees to nearby New Barnet station on the main line, from where they would continue their journey to new homes and families far away from the endangered capital.

The same scene was being played out at Underground stations across London. Within a couple of days, London Transport had successfully evacuated nearly 600,000 vulnerable Londoners. Pick could return to his office satisfied that this unprecedented movement of civilians had been achieved without mishap.

In the decades since the war, the Underground's much-publicized role as a communal shelter during the Blitz has overshadowed LT's wider contribution to the war effort. Yet it was the Board's ability to pull off spectacular feats of organization (such as the evacuation) and to carry on running a near-normal service during the most difficult situations imaginable that was its real triumph.[3] It was also to be its downfall. Exhausted by six years of emergency operation and in desperate need of inward investment, London Transport was to fare badly in the period of post-war austerity, which in turn heralded a new era of decline for what had been the greatest urban transit system in the world.

----

1. School children being evacuated under the watchful eye of a female police officer at Ealing Broadway station, September 1939.

Preparing for war

London Transport was far more prepared for war in 1939 than the Underground had been in 1914. Back then, war had seemed a distant reality, only gradually impacting on the travelling public through fuel shortages, the belated employment of women and, eventually, sporadic air attacks. By the late 1930s, few were in any doubt that war with Nazi Germany would have a much more immediate impact on the 'Home Front'. Many shared the government's pessimistic assessment that London would be disabled within days of sustained bombing raids, with civilian casualties totalling tens of thousands. As

early as 1932 the Conservative Prime Minister, Stanley Baldwin, had warned the British people that 'the bomber will always get through', irrespective of air defence systems - a prophecy apparently realized in 1937 when German planes obliterated Guernica during the Spanish Civil War. The feeling of national anxiety was reflected in a spate of novels and films graphically depicting the result of aerial bombardment on urban populations, most notably in *The Shape of Things to Come* (H. G. Wells, 1933), which was transferred to the big screen by Alexander Korda in 1936. Underlying all these fears was the very real prospect that the enemy would use poison gas to bring the city to a standstill.

In consultation with the government, London Transport responded by setting up its own Air Raid Precautions (ARP) committee in 1937. By now the Board's integrated network of Underground trains, buses,

2. Brompton Road station on the Piccadilly line, closed in 1934, was converted to provide an underground Operations Room for London's anti-aircraft control.

3. London Transport ARP training certificate, awarded to Station Foreman J. E. Powell, July 1938.

coaches, trams and trolleybuses was carrying an astounding 3.8 billion passengers a year. Protecting the system from the threat of aerial attack was, therefore, more than a matter of local convenience for commuters, it was essential for the effective operation of London. The point was made clear in the preamble of London Transport's first ARP Notice (September 1938), which instructed staff that 'during war every effort must be made to provide on the Board's Railways as normal a service as possible'.[4]

Preparations were quickly put in hand. Selected staff received training in all branches of Civil Defence, including anti-gas measures, first aid and firefighting, with over 6,000 qualified by 1940, rising to 20,000 by the end of the war. More than a million pounds was

spent on comprehensive defensive works, ranging from staff shelters and first aid posts at larger depots to the strengthening of vulnerable bridges and the installation of blast walls at station entrances. This figure also included vast quantities of repair materials wisely stockpiled by the Purchasing Department for future use, together with a mind-boggling array of protective clothing, water pumps, sandbags and other necessary items. Meanwhile, all new stations under construction were fitted with anti-gas precautions as standard, and provision made for the Underground to obtain electricity from the national grid in the event of its own power stations at Lots Road and Neasden being knocked out by enemy action.[5] Brompton Road station on the Piccadilly line, which had been closed to passengers since 1934, was sold to the government in November 1938 for military use. Part of it was then converted to house the main 'ops room' for London's anti-aircraft control, which was based here throughout the war.[6]

Frank Pick, frustrated by the slow pace of government-led ARP activity, took personal charge of the Board's planning.[7] Under his leadership detailed schemes were drawn up for the evacuation of civilians and the decentralization of offices and stores to locations outside London. Some disused stations and tunnels were converted into bomb-proof offices for military and government use. One of these, at

4. Staff at Acton Works practising their firefighting drill, September 1939.

5. A Permanent Way gang practising repair work in their cumbersome anti-gas suits, Neasden, February 1940. Gas attack remained a constant fear throughout the war, with notices reminding passengers to carry their masks at all times pasted in vehicles and at stations. Mercifully, the threat never materialized.

Down Street, was later used by the War Cabinet in 1940–41 and still retains evidence of its secretive wartime past in the form of stencilled notices on the walls and a dingy bathroom and bedroom installed for Churchill's personal use.

The Munich Crisis of September 1938, when war seemed just days away, revealed how much there was still to do. Pick badgered the then Minister of Transport, E. L. Burgin, with his concerns about the potentially devastating effect of high-explosive bombs on Tube tunnels running under the Thames, some of which were only 10 feet below the river bed.[8] A breach in any one of these would have rapidly flooded most of the Tube network from Tooting in the south to King's Cross in the north, and taken months to repair. The government agreed and authorized Pick's recommendation to install concrete plugs at critical points, even though this led to the temporary suspension of cross-river services. Surprisingly, Pick took a more relaxed view of the dangers faced

6

from flooding on the sub-surface District Railway between Westminster and Blackfriars which, he wrote, was separated from the river by 'no more than the Thames Embankment wall'. Here he felt that the suspension of services during a raid would be sufficient precaution as the ingress of water would depend on tidal levels, adding chillingly that 'there will be some risk of people being caught between those points if the warning is not simple'.[9]

As the immediate crisis passed, the concrete plugs were removed, and a more permanent solution found in the form of huge electrically operated iron floodgates, which took just thirty seconds to close during an air raid. Twenty-five were eventually installed in the tunnels at a cost of £¾ million, although by the time war was declared on 3 September 1939 only the gates on the Bakerloo had been completed. The remainder were all in place by October 1940, just after the Blitz had started, and were monitored from a central control room at Leicester Square. In the end, only a disused and sealed loop tunnel from the Strand to Charing Cross was ever hit, but without this precaution most of the Tube would have been forced to close once the raids began.

The onset of war brought with it immediate changes for the management and operation of London Transport, not least because the Board came under the direct control of a new government body, the Railway Executive Committee (REC). Day-to-day management remained in the hands of the LPTB, with the REC taking a strategic lead on matters affecting the coordination of the national rail network. Pick represented the interests of the Board on the Committee, but his tenure was to be short-lived. Senior colleagues at LT complained that Pick, often a difficult person to work with, had become even more distant and aloof during this time, unilaterally making decisions on the Board's behalf without proper consultation. Others, including Ashfield, were worried

6. The Railway Executive Committee met in the bomb-proofed safety of the converted Down Street Tube station, where offices were built in the passenger walkways and on the disused platforms. This photograph of the Committee, taken in April 1940, includes Frank Pick (fourth from the right) just days before his resignation from London Transport was announced.

about Pick's worsening mental and physical health, with the result that he was relieved of some of the more mundane aspects of his job, ostensibly to allow time for recuperation. But it seems that there was a deeper, and growing, rift between the two men who had built London Transport. Matters came to a head in early 1940, when Pick and Ashfield clashed over government terms for the financial management of LT during the war. Following a stormy meeting, Pick offered his resignation, which Ashfield accepted in April, informing the Board that his former deputy had resigned owing to 'ill heath'. There was clearly more to it than that, and in an uncharacteristic outburst Pick used a lecture at the Institute of Transport to deliver a stinging criticism of the way he had been treated:

> I have unfortunately been in the news these last days. I have learnt that I am older than I am, that my health is worse than I thought it was, that I am very tired, more tired than I thought I was, and also that the government are going to find me some other job, of which strange to say I know nothing.[10]

Whatever the exact cause of the rift may have been, Ashfield made little attempt to persuade Pick to stay. After leaving LT, Pick briefly worked for the Ministry of Transport before spending several unhappy months at the Ministry of Information. The man who had done so much to prepare LT for the coming conflict could now only watch the war unfold from the sidelines. His former post of chief executive was not filled, and London Transport entered a critical phase of the war without his guiding expertise. Access to this expertise was denied for ever in November 1941, when Pick died unexpectedly from a brain haemorrhage at his home in Hampstead Garden Suburb.

His legacy, though, lived on. Many of Pick's detailed plans had already been put into action by the time he left. Chief amongst these was the highly successful mass evacuation of children and vulnerable adults in September 1939, referred to at the start of this chapter. Most were taken by Tube to railway stations outside central London to continue their journey to reception centres around the country, thereby easing the pressure on mainline termini such as Paddington and Euston. Others were driven direct to their destination by London buses. It must have been a distressing time for both the parents left behind and the children embarking on an unknown adventure, although

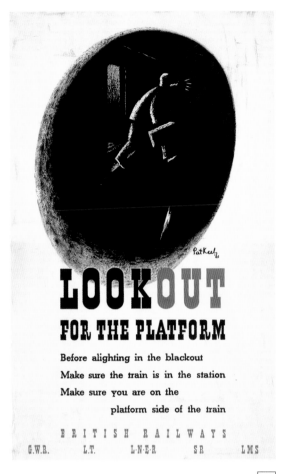

7

8

7. An early blackout poster issued by the Railway Executive Committee on behalf of the 'Big Four' mainline railway companies and London Transport. The design was by Pat Keely, who had previously done work for LT in peacetime.

8. Signs like this one were issued to every station on the Underground for display in the event of a gas attack.

some clearly enjoyed the novelty and excitement of it all. A harassed Underground guard recorded his memories of the evacuation for an article in the staff magazine:

> The alarm signal (five quid for improper use) meant nothing to the rascals on my train. They climbed on each other's backs and scrambled up hand-over-head in their efforts to reach the handle. Springing from seat to seat was another stunt. That journey added to my grey hairs, and that's putting it mildly.[11]

Blackout measures also came into force with the declaration of war, in the often misguided hope that enemy aircraft would be unable to navigate without brightly lit landmarks to guide them. The practical result was dimly lit stations and vehicles, leading to difficult travelling conditions for staff and passengers alike. Unnecessary luxuries, like first-class accommodation (still maintained on parts of the Metropolitan line) were quickly dispensed with and savings sought in all areas of the Board's operations.

By the beginning of 1940 London Transport had placed itself on a war footing in readiness for the situation ahead. But the feared air raids failed to materialize. Large numbers of evacuees began to drift back to London. Passengers complained about the seemingly pointless restrictions which hampered their journeys. Then, on 15 August 1940, the first bombs fell on London at Croydon airport, where coincidently several of the Board's staff were working. The Blitz had begun.

The shelter of the Tube

In 1917 Londoners had flocked to the safety of the Tube to escape the capital's first air raids. The Underground had put up no resistance, even encouraging shelterers with posters advising that it was 'bomb proof down below'. The memory of those days created an expectation that London Transport would fulfil a similar role in the next, more deadly, conflict.[12] But the attitude of those in charge had changed completely in the intervening twenty years.

As early as 1924, the Air Raid Precautions Sub-Committee of the Committee of Imperial Defence concluded that the Tube would be needed for transport purposes in any subsequent war and must not be used as an air raid shelter again. This remained the government's position throughout the 1930s, arguing that by far the greatest contribution that the Underground could make to public safety in the future would be by dispersing workers home each evening, rather than concentrating them in shelters which might receive a direct hit. Less publicly, the government was also concerned about the creation of a 'deep shelter mentality', whereby terrified Londoners would refuse to leave the protection of the Tube once the all clear was sounded. Such a scenario, it was feared, would quickly result in the collapse of essential services and could serve as a hotbed for civil unrest – although the experience of the First War provided no evidence to support this theory.

The government's views were shared by the planners at London Transport. The gloomy pre-war forecasts of air raid damage painted a picture of total destruction where roads would be impassable, leading to greater reliance on the Tube. This could hardly be achieved if the stations and platforms were full of shelterers. Besides, providing air raid cover for civilians just wasn't the Board's job. For Pick, in particular, any acceptance of the Tube as a possible shelter represented a failure of planning on the part of the responsible authorities, and he remained resolutely opposed to such a move. In June 1939 the Board formally rejected any possibility of adapting the Tube for shelter purposes, arguing that the costs of installing appropriate ventilation and sanitation equipment were prohibitively high, and the risks, from flooding and overcrowding, too great.[13]

With war declared, London Transport issued uncompromising posters warning passengers that Underground stations 'must not be used as air raid shelters'. In a message to the staff, Pick sought to explain the Board's reasoning: 'To keep London fit and convenient to live in at all times and in all circumstances, which means keeping London free to move, is a considerable contribution towards the conduct of the war.'[14] It was an important message to convey, as frontline staff were instructed to turn away non bona fide travellers once the bombs began to fall. In the event, this proved to be an impossible position to maintain.

On the evening of 7 September 1940 the East End took the full force of a heavy air attack which was to mark the start of a period of sustained night bombing lasting until May of the next year. Everywhere crowds rushed to use the Underground as a shelter. Staff were helpless to resist, and at Liverpool Street station opened the gates before things turned ugly. Many would-be shelterers avoided confrontation by simply buying a cheap penny travel ticket and then refusing to budge from the platforms. It was clear that the only way of preventing a repeat performance would be to post armed guards at station entrances. As this would mean turning away women and

9. Shelterers preparing to spend the night on a platform at Piccadilly Circus station, 25 September 1940.

10. Trains continued to run during the Blitz, resulting in crowded scenes on station platforms as here at Piccadilly Circus, 25 September 1940.

Daily Worker

No. 3329   REGISTERED AT THE G.P.O. AS A NEWSPAPER   **One Penny**

TUESDAY, SEPTEMBER 24, 1940   ✱ ✱ ✱ ✱

"People's Behaviour" Forces ARP Concessions

Admission By Ministry Of Home Security

" THE FACT THAT THE PEOPLE HAVE BEEN USING THE TUBE STATIONS HAS BEEN RECOGNISED," DECLARED THE MINISTRY OF HOME SECURITY YESTERDAY.

This "recognition" of the fact that the London workers have occupied the tubes despite all the orders and pleas of the Government, was delivered by Mr. William Mabane, Parliamentary Secretary to the Ministry yesterday.

The admission represents an important victory for the London people against the Government particularly as the Government is already using underhand means in some tube stations, to try to break up the decent organisation of people in the tubes and create disorder.

" The shelter policy," said Mr. Mabane, " has been guided largely by the behaviour of the people in London." This is the first outright confession by the Government that the people of London themselves have upset its " no tubes, no shelters " policy.

Mr. Mabane's remarks, obviously made under the severe pressure of opinion and action in London, were in the main directed towards trying to convince people that the Government—after refusing to do anything at all for the proper protection of the people —is now getting on with the job.

GUIDANCE : " The shelter policy has been guided largely by the people in London."—Mr. William Mabane, M.P., yesterday.

children during the full fury of a raid, LT was left with no alternative but to permit unofficial sheltering on its premises.

In the weeks that followed, growing demand was expressed from all sides of the political spectrum to overturn the 'no shelter' policy. The British Communist Party was one of the most vocal opponents, inevitably presenting the ban in terms of a class war whereby the government had failed to provide alternative deep-level shelters for working-class districts. There was some truth in this. The provision of official shelters was woefully behind schedule. Once the Blitz had begun, the Ministry of Information's Mass Observation investigators found that few Londoners had much faith in the hastily built street-level shelters, nicknamed 'concrete sandwiches' after the propensity of the brick walls to collapse from blast damage, leaving the inhabitants to be crushed by the concrete roof.[15] In contrast, almost mythical safety was ascribed to the deep Tube.[16] In response, the new Home Secretary, Herbert Morrison, announced a programme of deep-level shelter construction in October 1940 at sites adjacent to existing Tube stations, but these would take years to complete.[17] In the meantime, Londoners had little legitimate option but to install their own domestic shelters (providing they had the necessary outdoor space to put one up), or head off to the nearest communal street shelter. Not surprisingly, many took to the Underground.

In September 1940 the use of the latter was still, technically, an illegal act. But despite the posturing of the Communist Party, those engaged in this peaceful show of civil disobedience were not politically motivated. The press, initially discouraged from reporting the Underground invasion, referred to the nightly Tube dwellers as 'Tubites'.[18] London Transport called them squatters.[19] Soon, up to 177,000 shelterers were occupying seventy-nine of the Board's deep-level stations every night. 'From Earl's Court to Leicester Square,' reported the *Evening Standard* on 27 September, 'every platform was covered with people sitting on newspapers and leaning against the wall.'

At first conditions were pretty awful. Trains continued to run until 10.30 p.m.,

11. The newspaper of the British Communist Party, the *Daily Worker*, trumpeted the occupation of the Underground as a victory for 'people power' over bureaucracy. Shelterers, however, were lukewarm to the activities of Communist agitators, especially as Soviet Russia was allied with Nazi Germany at this time.

causing misery for all as passengers and shelterers jostled with each other on the overcrowded platforms. With the last train gone, people bedded down wherever they could: on platforms, in passageways, even on escalators. Drinking water was in very short supply and few stations offered toilet facilities beyond the occasional bucket separated from the sleepers by cloth partitions. Most shelterers stayed until the all clear was sounded in the early hours of the morning before trudging back home for a cursory wash and change of clothes. For those made homeless by the raids, even this luxury was denied. As one eyewitness remembered, 'Personal hygiene rather went out of the window, but you just got used to it.'[20]

Of course, there were far more serious things to worry about. At Belsize Park a Mass Observation investigator found that 'the people seem willing to put up with any discomfort and dirt and smells and heat in order to be safe'.[21] Some clearly enjoyed the camaraderie and feeling of shared security, expressed in the occasional communal sing-song or game of cards. For others LT issued free ear plugs – the company's sole concession to the comfort of its uninvited guests.

The same scene was repeated every day throughout September 1940, with long queues forming outside stations from early morning in an attempt to reserve the best places. Officially, no admission was allowed before 4 p.m., but 'droppers' (so called because of their practice of reserving spaces by dropping items of clothing against walls) would sometimes gain access earlier in the day and then sell the prime spots for up to half a crown each – a testimony to the value ordinary Londoners placed on getting a good night's sleep.

The shelterers themselves came from all parts of London and all walks of life, although the majority belonged to working-class districts. At Belsize Park, for example, a shelter survey in September found residents from Gospel Oak, Kentish Town, Camden Town, Euston, Hoxton and Shoreditch, but also Chelsea and Kensington.[22] Disused CSLR tunnels at Southwark were reportedly invaded by crowds from as far away as Finchley and Forest Gate – many of whom arrived by bus and private car – suggesting

12. The shelter policy U-turn in posters. The notice on the left was put up at the outset of the war in September 1939, while the example on the right was posted in November 1940.

that some were prepared to leave the relative safety of the suburbs for the perceived security of the Underground.[23] One reason why shelterers moved around town was the hope of reserving a pitch at a less-crowded station. The appearance of 'strangers', though, was often resented by local shelterers, who blamed the resulting overcrowding on Jews, foreign refugees or any other scapegoat they could think of.[24]

The government remained anxious that Tube sheltering should be seen as a concession, rather than a right, only to be used as a last resort. Police officers, who began patrolling stations from 22 September, were instructed to question would-be shelterers (especially young men) and turn them away if they were considered to have other options. LT staff were expected to assist with the evictions, and notices appeared urging men to leave the shelters to those who needed them most, i.e. women and children. Regular (and usually middle-class) Tube users tended to agree. The former *Daily Express* journalist and wartime political intelligence officer Sefton Delmer was disgusted to find 'able-bodied proletarians absenting themselves from their workshops while they lay on their mattresses in the Underground, publicly copulating on the platforms and blocking up the stations for those who had to go to work.'[25] The antipathy was often mutual. One shelterer complained that commuters returning from work 'found the sight of the people sheltering very funny and grinned at one as though one was a monkey or freak'.[26] Others resented the implication that they were cowards for seeking shelter in the first place. A young builder taking refuge at South Kensington told the American journalist Negley Farson that 'when a man's worked hard all day he's got a right to lie down. Hasn't he?'[27] Even so, the bullying campaign worked, and the number of single male shelterers dropped.

Along the line, some of the more enterprising shelterers began to set up committees and even published newsletters (such as the *Swiss Cottager* and the *Subway Companion*) to campaign for better facilities. The government, ever wary that conditions Underground might breed discontent, ordered an immediate investigation into the political motivation behind such periodicals.[28] One, *Searchlight Shelter*, was closed down because of its communist sympathies. The others were closely monitored, although most were short-lived. The shelterers' quite reasonable requests, though, couldn't be ignored any longer. In mid-September Lord Ashfield accompanied the Home Secretary and the newspaper magnate Lord Beaverbrook on an evening inspection of the Holborn Tube shelter. After listening to the shelterers' complaints it was clear that something had to be done, not least because the Board's own inspectors were receiving worrying reports about 'dangerous levels' of overcrowding on the platforms during operational hours. There was also considerable confusion amongst staff regarding their responsibilities during a raid, which threatened to endanger public safety.[29]

The matter was eventually settled by the personal intervention of the Prime Minister, who towards the end of September[30] called for an urgent review of the unenforceable ban on Tube sheltering. The resulting policy U-turn was announced on 8 October by the Home Secretary, who told the House of Commons that 'as far as is consistent with

public safety and with the overriding necessity of maintaining essential public transport facilities … The public are now allowed to use the Tube for shelter purposes.'

With the ban lifted, improvements quickly followed. The Board's initial reluctance evaporated in a remarkable about-face which saw the Tube's function as an air raid shelter transformed into a source of corporate and individual pride. With unconscious irony, LT's official history of the war later claimed that it had been 'sheer common sense on the part of the public' to seek protection 'obviously provided by the Tubes'.[31] The implication that it had been the government's decision, rather than the Board's, to ban sheltering was reinforced by the company's public relations officer, who assured the press that fellow staff had simply been 'too humane to turn the shelterers out'.[32] Even so, posters went up throughout October warning shelterers that they did so at their own risk – a concession that LT had insisted on before agreeing to the government's change of heart.[33]

The formidable ex-General Manager (Railways) John P. Thomas was coaxed out of retirement to spearhead the reforms. Within weeks a ticketing system had been introduced to reduce queuing and counteract the criminal activities of 'droppers' and others who sought to reserve platform space by nefarious means. Numbered metal bunk beds were installed at seventy-six stations from late November 1940, with over 22,000 erected by the end of the war. Most were allocated to regular ticket holders, but 10 per cent were left free for those caught in a raid. Many latecomers still had to pitch down

13. Tube refreshment staff distributing much-welcome snacks at Holland Park station, 9 December 1940.

14. Christmas underground, 1940. LT staff distributed over 11,000 toys presented by the America's Air Raid Relief Fund to children sheltering on the Tube. Platforms and booking office areas were festooned with Christmas trees and decorations, in scenes repeated each year until the end of the war.

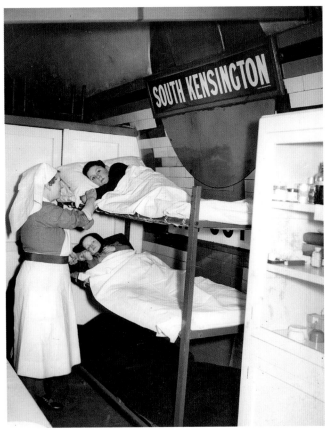

wherever they could, but at least now LT provided them with damp-proof sleeping bags and, most importantly of all, proper toilet facilities.

One of the most welcome initiatives was the introduction of the 'Tube Refreshment' service, which distributed seven tons of food to the shelters every night in six special trains. The massive operation showed just how far LT's attitude had changed. Over a thousand staff were needed to dispense the gallons of tea and mountains of pies and buns, all charged at less than a couple of pennies each. Other improvements included the establishment of first aid posts, attended by trained nurses, at every station, together with libraries and sometimes entertainment laid on by the Entertainment National Service Association (ENSA). At South Kensington, Negley Farson found morale high, with 'the majority of the people [feeling] that they were lucky to have such a decent place to spend the night'.[34] Little wonder that Mass Observation discovered some Tube dwellers reluctant to return home, especially as the living underground was cheap and relatively cheerful.

As the Tube continued to run during the Blitz, efforts were made to minimize rush-hour disruption by restricting the amount of space allocated to shelterers (carefully delineated by white lines painted on the platform). After 7.30 p.m. the available space was gradually increased until the whole station was transformed into a shelter after the last train had left.

Not all Tube shelters were managed by London Transport. Various redundant, partly built or little-used sections of the Underground were turned over to the local authorities for public shelters, such as the unfinished parts of the Central line extension beyond Liverpool Street. The most famous was at Aldwych, where LT transferred the whole of the short branch line from Holborn into the control of Westminster Council. Train services were suspended and the track boarded over to provide accommodation for 1,500.

Despite the huge improvements, the number of nightly shelterers actually fell from a September high of 177,500 to about 120,000 by Christmas 1940. This figure continued to fall during 1941, partly in response to the availability of alternative shelters and partly because of an increasing war-weariness that saw many Londoners taking their chances by staying at home. With the end of the first intensive period of Blitz in May 1941, the number of regular shelterers dropped sharply to a low of around 5,000 in 1942. Even so, the Tube's reputation as being the 'safest shelter of all' ensured that it continued to be used every night until the end of the war, with numbers again reaching over 150,000 during the V1 and V2 rocket attacks of 1944/5.

15. An improvised first aid post at South Kensington station, 6 February 1941. The availability of free medical services in the Tube shelters was an added bonus for some shelterers.

16. Shelterers at Bethnal Green station on the unfinished Central line extension, c.1941. Bethnal Green was one of several Tube shelters managed by the local authorities, rather than London Transport.

17

But safety was not guaranteed. Between September 1940 and May 1941, 198 people were killed when Tube shelters received direct hits. One of the worst incidents was at Balham on 14 October, when a bomb pierced the road surface, causing extensive damage to the platforms below. An off-duty Tube driver remembered what happened next:

> It was about 8.00pm I was standing on the platform talking to people when there was a terrific explosion above the station and, at the same time all the platform lamps 'arced', and that put the station into darkness. When the station went into darkness panic started; it was bad panic. I said to them 'it will be all right; we will have a light on in a few moments', but no light came and the tunnel gradually filled with water and sewage [from fractured mains].[35]

The driver did his best to get survivors out through an emergency exit. Others were not so lucky. Sixty-four shelterers died, together with four members of the station staff. Above ground a bus had fallen headlong into the bomb crater, providing one of the most famous and enduring images of the London Blitz. It took two months to repair the damage to the flooded tunnels. A memorial plaque to those who lost their lives can be seen today at the station entrance.

17. The bomb crater in Balham High Road, 15 October 1940, published in colour for the American *Life* magazine. The bus was returning empty to Vauxhall at the time. Amazingly, both the driver and conductor survived the impact unhurt.

Similar plaques can be seen at Bounds Green, where nineteen shelterers (mostly Belgian refugees) died on 13 October, and at Bank, where a huge bomb on the evening of 11 January caused a crater 120 feet across, blowing open the sub-surface booking hall and killing fifty-six people on the platforms below. Not all loss of life was due to enemy bombs, however. On 3 March 1943, 173 people were crushed to death in a stairwell at Bethnal Green Tube shelter after a mother carrying a baby tripped in the dark. The incident was especially tragic as many of those who died were children. An inquiry, published after the war, found that the lack of a crash barrier, poor lighting and inadequate supervision by either the police or ARP all contributed to the disaster, as did the use of a new type of anti-aircraft rocket being tested in nearby Victoria Park, which appears to have panicked the waiting crowd into believing that a raid was taking place. In fact, no bombs were dropped on London that night. The death toll was the worst single incident anywhere in wartime London and remains the greatest loss of life there has ever been on the Underground, although the station (part of the unfinished Central line) was under local authority control at the time.

Overall, though, there were remarkably few incidents involving civilians at Tube shelters, and little interruption to the Board's train services which had been such a cause for concern in the early days.

The Allied victory in Europe in May 1945 finally brought an end to the Underground's most famous wartime role. On the last night that sheltering was permitted (6 May) there were still 260 recorded Tube dwellers. Within three and half weeks all traces of the paraphernalia associated with sheltering had been removed.

Seeing it through

Seeing it Through was the title of a poster series commissioned from the war artist Eric Kennington in 1944 to commemorate the valuable contribution made by London Transport staff during the Blitz.[36] It could just as easily have referred to the wartime achievements of LT itself, which suffered bomb damage to vehicles and property on 9,000 occasions yet somehow managed to 'carry on'. There was a heavy price to pay, though. Almost 200 employees were killed on duty, with a further 1,867 wounded. Despite these appalling losses, and destruction to infrastructure on an unprecedented scale, the system was never fatally compromised. The Underground, together with the buses, trams and trolleybuses, continued to provide a vital service which, in the words of *The Times*, 'kept London alive'.[37]

This achievement is all the more remarkable given that over 22,500 experienced staff were called up for military service at the outset of the war. Women were recruited to fill some of the jobs formerly done by men, just as they had been in the First World War.

18. The *Daily Mirror*'s report on 13 January 1941 of the bomb damage at Bank station which left fifty-six people dead. In keeping with the strict censorship rules in force at the time, the station is referred to simply as 'a London subway' and all evidence of its actual location (such as the Royal Exchange and Bank of England) have been cropped from the photograph.

Pilot, all alone you ride
   Through the bowels of the town,
Up into the black outside
   Where the bombs are whistling down.

Bombs and blizzards, fogs and frights—
   "Dead man's handle" at your breast—
Lights—and lights—for ever lights—
   On you ride and never rest.

On to Barking, on to Kew!
   Master of a trying trade,
Seldom do we think of you,
   Never do we feel afraid.

A. P. Herbert

19

19. *Seeing it Through: 'Motorman'*, Eric Kennington, 1944. LT's Publicity Department selected six employees for the poster series (three men and three women) who had distinguished themselves in some way during the Blitz. This poster shows Frank Clarke, a train driver who kept his nerve during a raid in September 1940.

SHELTERING PROPAGANDA

Whatever its true significance may have been, Tube sheltering was elevated at the time into a symbol of civilian resilience and 'Blitz Spirit'. Independent journalists, artists and filmmakers, as well as those working for the government, all played a part in creating a positive image of the shelters that, while sometimes at odds with reality, was readily accepted by society at large. It remains London Transport's most famous contribution to the war effort, yet less than 4 per cent of Londoners sheltered in the Tube on any one night – far fewer than the estimated 27 per cent who took refuge in household shelters. [38]

The government's initial attempts to discourage Tube sheltering were quickly abandoned. Rather than suppressing news of the shelters, the Ministry of Information (MOI) came to recognize the propaganda value of cheery cockneys putting up with adversity in the shared struggle to defeat Hitler's Germany. The fact that secret Mass Observation reports often painted a less rosy picture of conditions underground hardly mattered. This was now the people's war. 'From the trousered, lipsticked Kensington girls to the Cockneys of Camden Town,' read a typical piece in the *Sunday Dispatch*, 'all were alike in their uncomplaining, patient cheerfulness.'[39] Journalists taking a different view would find their work heavily censored.

The success of the Tube Refreshments scheme offered the Ministry an obvious propaganda coup. Officially approved newsreel footage of defiant Londoners receiving tea and buns from LT staff played at cinemas throughout Britain, and also in the USA, where public opinion was still undecided about whether to join the war. A similarly up-beat portrayal of Tube sheltering featured in the MOI film *Christmas Under Fire*, narrated by the American journalist Quentin Reynolds and released in the States a week after its British debut on Boxing Day 1940.

The communal nature of Tube sheltering was considered

20

21

20. Detail from *Women and Children in the Tube* by Henry Moore, 1940

21. *The Tube Autumn 1940*, by Feliks Topolski. In common with several WAAC artists, Topolski had previously designed posters for London Transport in peacetime.

a suitable morale-boosting subject for official government war artists. Inspired by the shelter drawings of Henry Moore (which the artist had undertaken as a private study in September 1940), the War Artists Advisory Committee (WAAC) commissioned similar works for a touring exhibition from artists including Feliks Topolski, John Farleigh and Edward Ardizzone. The Committee's chairman, Kenneth Clark, director of the National Gallery, purchased several of Moore's drawings for inclusion in the show, which received very favourable reviews.[40] Moore's work went on to even greater fame and was eagerly purchased by American collectors following his 1943 solo exhibition in New York.

Others too, like the painter John Buckland-Wright,

and the photographer Bill Brandt, took their inspiration from the extraordinary scenes underground. Although different in style, the resulting body of work was united in presenting a stoic depiction of a people under attack and, inadvertently, a transport system rising to the challenge of the wartime situation.

An altogether more jolly vision of Tube sheltering was to be found in two popular British wartime comedies, *Gert and Daisy's Weekend* (Elsie and Doris Waters) and *I Thank You* starring Arthur Askey, both passed by the censor for release in 1941. Although the Underground doesn't feature extensively in either film it is, nevertheless, the location for much merriment and the inevitable cockney 'knees-up'.

22. In 1943 Henry Moore was persuaded to appear in the MOI film, *Out of Chaos*, a celebration of the WAAC's work. Moore is shown sketching shelterers on a station platform. Not only was the scene entirely recreated using actors, but Moore later confessed that he had based his sketches on hastily written notes rather than drawing from life in the Tube.

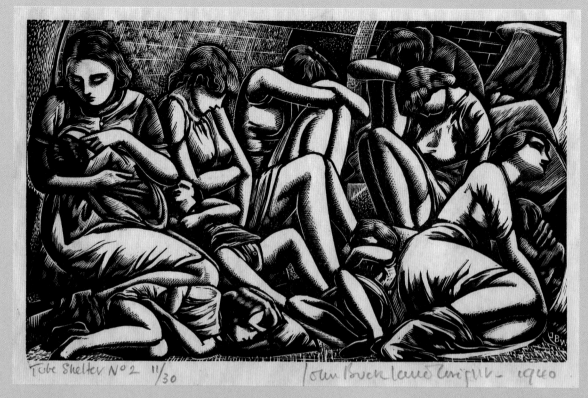

Tube Shelter Nº 2 11/30   John Buckland Wright – 1940.

A different approach was taken for *Confirm or Deny* (20th Century Fox, 1941), a traditional love story where the leading characters (ironically an American journalist and a British MOI employee) meet in a Tube shelter – accurately recreated with Ministry of Information collusion on a Hollywood film set.

Whereas civilian sheltering was often seen as a way of appealing to American sympathies, it could also be used to garner support for Britain's allies. The MOI film *A Tale of Two Cities* (1942), co-produced with the Soviet Film Agency, looked to Russia to emphasize the common experience of Londoners and Muscovites sheltering in their respective underground systems. But it was the example offered by the Tube dwellers for other UK cities that ultimately mattered most. In the language of the time, London could 'take it', and if London could take it so could Coventry, Liverpool and Manchester. The resolutely positive message, echoed in radio broadcasts and political cartoons,[41] meant that there was no place for bad new stories, such as the disasters at Balham, Bank or Bethnal Green, which would have handed the Nazis a dangerous propaganda victory.[42] Instead, Tube sheltering was used to tell a bigger, and more uplifting, narrative about national resolve. As the *Evening Standard* reported when the last bunk beds were removed from the platforms in 1945:

> So ended one of the most extraordinary chapters in all London's history. It is a strange story: a story of how a body of London citizens, ignoring flustered authority and obeying their own common sense, saved themselves and their children from the enemy assault.[43]

23. *Tube Shelter No. 2*, by John Buckland-Wright, 1940. His Tube shelter drawings were exhibited at the Leicester Galleries, London, at the end of 1940. Buckland-Wright also worked as a press censor for the Ministry of Information.

24. A production still from *I Thank You*, showing Arthur Askey (centre, with glasses) about to lead the Tube shelterers in a sing-song.

Most were employed as bus conductors, although nearly 5,000 worked on the Board's railways and in the engineering departments, often in physically demanding roles. Their immense contribution was singled out for praise at the time, as was LT's commitment to providing suitable facilities for its new female intake, including nurseries for working mothers.[44] Even so, powerful trade union interests and resilient social prejudices ensured that women were usually paid less than their male colleagues and barred from certain skilled jobs, such as driving.[45]

When the Blitz began all staff, irrespective of experience, were catapulted into the front line. Air raids affected every aspect of the Board's operation, with road vehicles especially vulnerable to bomb damage. On the Underground the nightly attacks left a wake of destruction that would have been difficult enough to repair in peacetime. As it was, exhausted teams worked round the clock in blackout conditions to clear debris from breached tunnels, shattered bridges and mangled railways, before they could begin to renew damaged track and replace broken power supplies. It was an unrelenting and demoralizing task. As London Transport's official history of the war put it, 'time and again the repairs were almost completed when another incident would occur and undo all the good work.'[46]

Photographs from the period give some idea of the scale of the physical destruction, but mask the real human cost. At Sloane Square, for example, a high-explosive bomb ripped through the station canopy at 10 p.m. on 12 November 1940, just as a crowded train was about to depart. Irene Haslewood, an ambulance driver based at Chelsea, recalled what happened:

> The utter carnage of the disaster beggared description. Some of the men who had been working on the job tried to tell me about it. They hardly got anyone out alive. Most of the poor bodies had been stripped of their clothing from the blast. Two stark naked and mutilated bodies of young girls hung high up in the twisted steel girders - trapped by their feet hanging head downwards. The men could not get them released for days and had to work under this ghastly spectacle.[47]

At least seventy-nine passengers were killed. Three more remained unaccounted for, presumably blown to pieces in the blast. Yet it could have been much worse if the Westbourne river, encased to this day in a pipe over the platforms, had burst. Ironically, the station had only recently been completely refurbished with escalators replacing the fifty-one steps to street level. It now lay in ruins.

Thankfully, many of the incidents took place after the last passenger trains had left or out on the open sections of railway. Such incidents presented their own problems, however, with repair crews searching for bomb craters and unexploded devices in the dark. Occasionally, the

25

25. 'A woman's job in war', 1941. This recruitment poster was based on a photograph of Miss Maylin, a station porter at Shepherd's Bush.

destruction was so great that it threatened to bring the Underground to a standstill. On the night of 29–30 December 1940, the Luftwaffe made a deliberate attempt to destroy the historic City of London. In what became known as the Second Fire of London, blazes raged throughout the district, completely gutting Moorgate Metropolitan line station and causing considerable damage to those at St Paul's, Farringdon, Mark Lane, Blackfriars, Whitechapel and Aldersgate. In a masterpiece of laconic understatement, the Board later informed the Railway Executive Committee that 'as a result of the intense attack last night, traffic conditions in the central London area this morning are bad'.[48] Incredibly, most train services were resumed within just twenty-four hours.

Worse was to come. On 10 May 1941 the Underground was hit in twenty different places in a night raid that left 1,500 Londoners dead. A train driver caught in the raid vividly recalled one incident from the many that befell the capital that night:

> We pulled into Aldgate. There was terrific gunfire and bombs bursting. Showers of incendiaries were coming down. I was about two coaches length away when the bomb fell … standing on the platform with my train beside me. The bomb smashed my cab in.[49]

The Board was quick to recognize individual acts of heroism, which, of course, reflected well on the organization as a whole. In February 1941 the first awards were made of a special London Transport medal to employees who had shown particular bravery, such as George Grimwood, a lengthman on the District line, who assisted with the removal of an unexploded bomb.[50] More formal public recognition followed, and by the end of the war over fifty decorations had been bestowed on London Transport staff, including two George Medals and twenty-nine British Empire Medals.

26. Air raid damage near Blackfriars station, 19 October 1940.

27. The carnage at Sloane Square station photographed after the bodies had been removed, November 1940.

Public honours also reflected the extent to which London Transport was regarded as part of the official war effort. It was a role that the Board was keen to exploit. Posters and press ads stressed LT's part in keeping the city moving and often contained morale-boosting messages for passengers and staff alike.[51] The high design values of peacetime were maintained, despite shortages of paper and ink. In fact, the Publicity Department produced almost 21,000 items of print during the war on subjects ranging from emergency procedures during air raids to the encouragement of thoughtful passenger behaviour.

Good communication was essential if the Underground was to work effectively. Passenger numbers, which had actually declined during the first year of the war, soared from 333 million in 1941 to 543 million by 1945, largely due to the influx of war workers and American servicemen. Many had never used the Tube before and had to be instructed in the lore of underground etiquette, such as where to stand on the escalator or the importance of 'moving down the car' to allow others to get on. Overcrowding in peak hours became such a serious problem that it threatened to disrupt normal services – something Hitler's bombers had failed to do. The result was a successful campaign to discourage 'unnecessary journeys' coupled with an appeal to businesses to stagger working hours, although passenger journeys remained uncomfortable.

Behind the scenes, several of the Board's properties had been placed on a war footing seldom guessed at by the travelling public. Disused stations and tunnels were taken over for secret military and government use, or used as safe stores for the nation's art treasures.[52] Two miles of unfinished Central line tunnel, from Wanstead to Ilford, were converted into an underground factory making aircraft electronic equipment and components for Plessey. Above ground Chiswick bus works and the part-built new Underground depot at Aldenham were given over to the manufacture of Halifax bombers as part of a London-wide production scheme. Key points on the network were protected by members of the Board's own Home Guard unit, and all sorts of precautions taken against the threat of German invasion or sabotage. Staff, for example, received stern

28. London Passenger Transport Medal for bravery, instituted in 1941.

29. A wrecked Underground train at Moorgate station, 31 December 1940. The heat of the fire was so great that aluminium panels and glass windows were reduced to molten pools.

30. Decorated by the King. Railwayman George Grimwood (left, wearing Home Guard uniform) and busman Ernest Price were awarded the George Medal for bravery at Buckingham Palace, 17 June 1941. George Grimwood had previously been awarded the LT Bravery Medal.

STILL IT BEATS REGULARLY

From home to work, from work to home — London's millions come and go as regularly as ever they did before the shock of war. There's a job to be done at a bench, at a desk, in a foundry: and it's done with the help of uninterrupted service by 59,000 men and 16,000 women of London Transport.

Some amenities of travel could not be maintained under war conditions. But they will return.

With you, and your workpeople, London Transport looks forward.

Please pass down the car?

—— SOMEDAY YOU MIGHT WANT TO GET IN, YOURSELF!

---

31. London Transport newspaper advertisement, 1943. This ad was designed for trade papers, where it was intended to be read by employers whose workforce used LT's services.

32. 'Please Pass Down the Car', 'Fougasse' (Cyril Kenneth Bird), 1944. This poster was one of several commissioned to explain Tube etiquette to unfamiliar users and remind others of the importance of considerate passenger behaviour.

33. 'Billy Brown of London Town' was created by the cartoonist David Langdon for passenger information posters and press ads. In this 1941 Tube poster Billy Brown is reminding a fellow commuter not to peel back the blast netting fitted to train, bus and tram windows. Not everyone appreciated Billy Brown's patronising tone, however, and the posters were sometimes completed with less enlightening rhyming graffiti couplets. A common addition to this poster, for example, ran 'I thank you for your information, but I can't see the bloody station!'

instructions to prevent uniforms from falling into enemy hands, and at one point the government banned the issue of geographic transport maps, although the diagrammatic Tube map was permitted – presumably because it wouldn't have been much help to Nazi paratroopers.[53]

As the war reached its closing stages, Acton railway works became a centre for the overhaul of landing-craft motors (used in the Allied invasion of Europe) and the conversion of tanks and Bren-gun carriers to drive through shallow water up the Normandy beaches on D-Day. Many of those employed at the London Transport factories (including a large proportion of female war workers) had little or no relevant experience of engineering work, but all played their part in the successful delivery of equipment urgently needed for the war effort.

34

Return to peace

The immediate post-war period was a time of transition and uncertainty for London Transport. When the war in Europe ended on 8 May 1945 many hoped for a rapid return to pre-war standards of service, encouraged by the ending of blackout restrictions and the steady removal of much of the physical apparatus of wartime operation. But there was to be no quick return to a perceived golden age of public transport for Londoners.

35

34. A section of the underground Plessey factory, housed in the Central line tunnels near Redbridge station. The secret factory had its own miniature railway (seen here on the left) to move aircraft electronic components along the two miles of tunnel.

35. American Sherman tanks photographed at Acton railway works on 30 November 1944, prior to deployment in France.

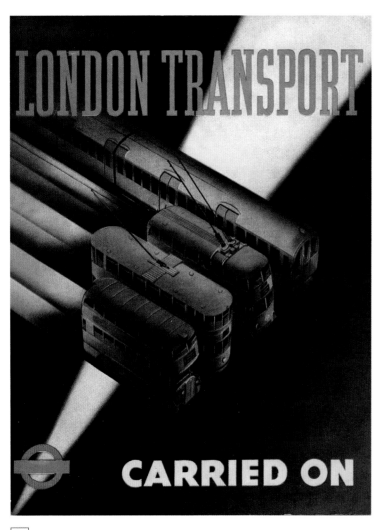

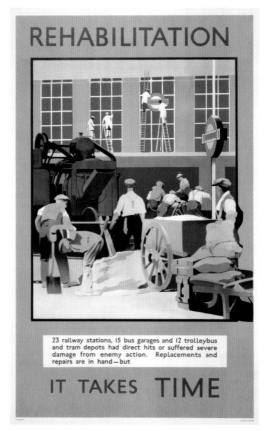

REHABILITATION

23 railway stations, 15 bus garages and 12 trolleybus and tram depots had direct hits or suffered severe damage from enemy action. Replacements and repairs are in hand—but

IT TAKES TIME

Almost six years of emergency working and extensive air raid damage had left the Board with a huge backlog of repairs and renewal. What was needed now was a programme of sustained investment to get the system back on its feet. London Transport, though, was to find itself low down the government's list of priorities as a near bankrupt nation struggled to rebuild. It was clear that the future funding and organization of the Board would require a radical rethink if it was to weather the challenges ahead.

The Labour Party's unexpected victory in the July 1945 general election gave a clear hint of the direction these changes might take. The new government lost little time in announcing its plans for the wholesale nationalization of the British transport industry, although it was initially assumed that London Transport, already under public control, would be exempt from the legislation. Or at least that's what the LPTB chose to believe.[54] Consequently, the Board drew up its own plans to tackle the immediate transport problems within the London area: principally the restoration of road and rail services to something like those existing in the 1930s and the development of new ones in outer areas to reflect shifting patterns of population. A key strand of this would be the completion of the New Works Programme, suspended in 1940, and the introduction of new buses and Underground trains.[55]

36. The cover of LT's official history of its wartime role written by Charles Graves (1947).

37. 'Rehabilitation', poster by Fred Taylor 1945. Ever conscious of the value of good communication, the Board published a flurry of posters and leaflets after the war explaining why improvements were sometimes slow to appear.

Such independent thinking, however, took little account of economic realities or the legacy of LT's wartime involvement with the government-controlled Railway Executive Committee which had resulted in the Board's fortunes being closely linked with those of the mainline railways. Complex negotiations regarding levels of compensation for war damage, for example, had tied LT into a national scheme with the private railways where it received only a proportion of the total money available, rather than full reimbursement. Moreover, the experience of wartime control had shown ministers the benefits of a single strategic planning authority to coordinate public transport policy. With the nationalization of the railways now on the cards, the prolonged independence of the Board looked increasingly anomalous.

Lack of funding and uncertainty about the future were not the only factors hampering the Board's aspirations to put its house in order. Post-war shortages of manpower, materials, equipment and fuel all played a part in delaying repairs and improvements. At the same time the number of passengers using LT's combined road and rail services continued to rise, reaching a high point of 4,259 million in 1946, compared with 3,782 million in 1938/9. Overcrowding, especially during peak hours, became endemic, with a predictable increase in complaints from travellers unwilling to accept poor service now the war was over. With no money to improve facilities, London Transport could do little more than appeal to customers to behave courteously towards each other and request businesses to stagger working hours in the hope of relieving the crush. Neither approach had much success, largely because the real problem lay in the decrepit nature of the bus and Underground fleet, as the Board's Annual Report made clear:

> This vast traffic has had to be carried not only without any commensurate addition to the vehicles available for service, but also with a fleet consisting to a large extent of over-age vehicles which are proving more and more difficult to maintain for service.[56]

To add to commuters' misery, fares rose steeply as the Board tried to raise money from the only source of revenue within its control. Even this didn't fully offset rising operational costs and union-negotiated pay awards which the company could ill afford.

There was some good news, though. Early in 1946 the government approved resumption of work on the eastern and western extensions of the Central line, suspended since 1940. Tube trains from Liverpool Street began running to Stratford by the end of the year and to Woodford and Newbury Park in December 1947. Most of the expensive tunnelling work on this stretch had, in fact, been completed before the war, while the overground sections east of Stratford shared existing rail infrastructure with the main line, making the whole venture relatively cheap to achieve.

38

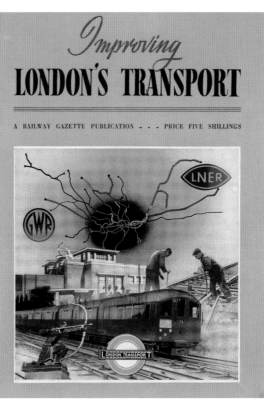

39

38. 'Courtesy aids service', by Bruce Angrave, 1946. One of a series of posters printed in 1945–7 'with the purpose of fostering a better understanding between passengers and staff and restoring that spirit of co-operation and good-humoured tolerance so characteristic in the past of the London travelling public and the transport workers who serve them' (LPTB Thirteenth Annual Report and Accounts, 1946).

39. A special edition of the *Railway Gazette* looking forward to the resumption of the pre-war building programme, published in 1946. The cover features the rebuilt East Finchley station completed in 1940 as part of the Northern line improvements.

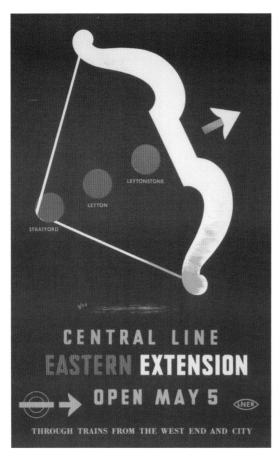

CENTRAL LINE
EASTERN **EXTENSION**
OPEN MAY 5

THROUGH TRAINS FROM THE WEST END AND CITY

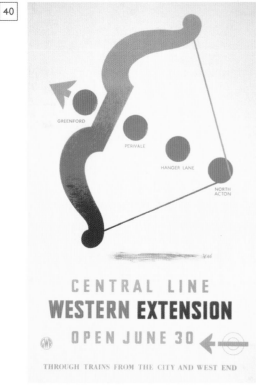

CENTRAL LINE
WESTERN EXTENSION
OPEN JUNE 30

THROUGH TRAINS FROM THE CITY AND WEST END

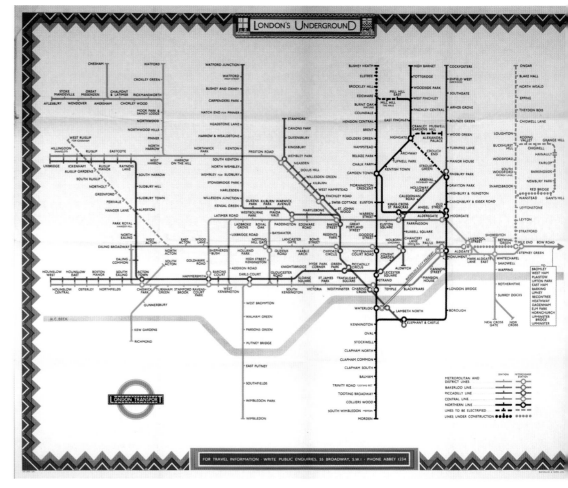

In West London, the Central line reached Greenford in June 1947 from a junction at North Acton station and was extended to West Ruislip a year later, though not on to Denham as originally planned. This whole section of the Tube was on the surface, built alongside the GWR main line.

In the meantime, the future governance of London Transport had become clear, following confirmation that it would, after all, come under the auspices of a new nationalized transport authority with effect from 1 January 1948. In seeking a structure for this new body, the government looked to the example of the LPTB, which had been effectively managing a diverse transport portfolio for fifteen years. In a further testimony to the influence of London Transport, Lord Ashfield was appointed a full-time member of the new Transport Commission from November 1947, an office which he held until his death a year later.

The Board's final Annual Report, published on 31 December 1947, devoted several pages to a retrospective celebration of London Transport's achievements since its formation in 1933. There could be no disguising, however, the Board's disappointment at its post-war record, despite its expressed optimism for the future:

40. A pair of posters by Hans Schleger ('Zero') advertising the western and eastern extension of the Central line in 1947. In both cases, extension was carried out in partnership with the mainline railways (GWR and LNER).

41. A poster version of the Tube map published in 1946 with the unbuilt sections of the New Works Programme marked as 'under construction'. The extensions to the Central line were finally completed in the 1950s, but plans to extend the Northern line were scrapped.

It is a matter of regret that a more rapid recovery from the effects of war has not been practicable. The Board have done all in their power to press on with new railway works and to obtain new supplies of rolling stock, but the progress made has been severely limited by the prevailing national restrictions. Nevertheless, plans for further development have already been prepared and, as soon as there is a relaxation in the present economic stringency, these plans will doubtless be put into effect.[57]

Nationalization

Nationalization proved to be a mixed blessing for London Transport. With its quasi-autonomous status removed, the Board's undertakings were transferred to the huge British Transport Commission (BTC), the new government body responsible for virtually all aspects of passenger and goods transport by rail and road on the British mainland as well as ferry services. From the outset it was clear that the Commission's energies and resources would be directed towards improving the run-down and antiquated nationalized rail network, BTC's biggest and most problematic asset, now renamed British Railways (BR) in public ownership. In comparison, the electrified Underground, with its modern stations recently upgraded as part of the New Works Programme, looked in pretty good shape. For the next fifteen years any further improvements to London's transport system would take second place to the main focus of the BTC, with a resulting decline in government investment.

Day-to-day management of the former LPTB was delegated to a London Transport Executive (LTE), whose members were appointed by the Minister of Transport in consultation with the BTC. Lord Latham, who had succeeded Lord Ashfield as head of London Transport in October 1947, became the Executive's first chairman, supported by a team of chief officers drawn from ex-London Transport staff. Others took the opportunity to advance their careers by transferring over to the BTC, while salary constraints imposed on LTE by the Commission made it difficult to recruit suitable replacements, and arguably the status of the new governing body declined accordingly. Certainly the Executive failed to attract leaders of the calibre of Pick and Ashfield and experienced a relatively high turnover of senior executives in the years that followed.

42

42. The so-called 'Moscow Concourse' at Gants Hill station, designed by Charles Holden and inspired by the original station designs of the Moscow Metro that the London Underground had recommended for the Soviet system in the 1930s. Gants Hill opened to passengers on 14 December 1947 as part of the Central line extension programme.

Nationalization did, however, afford an opportunity to tidy up some of the historic anomalies governing the management of railways in the London area. A number of formerly jointly owned lines now came under the control of the LTE, including the Metropolitan & Great Central Joint Railway (as far north as Amersham), the Watford Joint line, the Whitechapel & Bow Railway, the East London Railway, and the Hammersmith & City Railway. Sections of the former London & North Eastern, Great Western & Southern Railways, which shared passenger services with the Underground or were earmarked for Tube expansion, were also transferred to the Executive.[58]

These transfers helped to facilitate the completion of some aspects of the pre-war New Works Programme, especially on the Central line, which was extended westwards to West Ruislip in 1948 and eastwards to Loughton and Epping in 1948/9. Elsewhere, though, LTE's aspirations were stymied by lack of funds and planning restrictions imposed by central government. The imposition of the Green Belt around London, for example, effectively killed off existing plans to extend the Northern line beyond Edgware to Bushey Heath, while the scheme to link Finsbury Park with Alexandra Palace, via Highgate, was shelved due to costs. In both cases, preliminary building and electrification works were already well advanced and the £300,000 pre-war expenditure was simply written off. The dwindling and lightly used steam passenger service on the former LNER branch to Alexandra Palace was finally withdrawn by BR in 1954. Over twenty years later, much of the former railway line was turned into a pleasant public footpath called the Parkland Walk. Today it is almost certain that Crouch End and Muswell Hill will never be on the Tube.[59] At Aldenham, on the proposed line to Bushey, the unfinished railway depot was later transformed into a bus overhaul plant for London Transport, having previously been used to build aircraft during the war. Aldenham Works opened in 1956 but closed in the 1980s when LT's bus engineering operations were first reduced then privatized. Aldenham was demolished and can now only be seen on film, notably in a sequence at the start of Cliff Richard's musical *Summer Holiday*, made in 1963.

Part of the problem for the Executive was that improvements to the Underground could never be justified on purely economic grounds. Yet in the straitened financial circumstances of austerity Britain, and BTC's understandable priority to sort out the national rail network, there simply wasn't enough money to subsidize the Tube. This could result in seemingly quixotic decisions, as when the Commission agreed to extend the Bakerloo line from Elephant and Castle to Camberwell Green in 1949, only to backtrack the following year. In fact, there was no shortage of ideas about how public transport could be improved in the London area – just a lack of money to see them through. Members of the LTE and the nationalized British Railways Board spent years working on the government's London Railway Plan to rationalize the capital's rail infrastructure and cut journey times.

43. As an indication of LT's faith in the resumption of the New Works Programme, signage was pre-ordered showing the stops on the new routes. This Tube train destination plate was intended for Elstree services on the proposed Northern Line extension to Bushey Heath.

Their recommendations included the construction of several new Underground lines, a wildly optimistic conclusion given the government's financial position. One proposal, however, linking Euston and Victoria with north and south London (known as Route C), was selected for development. After much procrastination and delay, this route eventually opened as the Victoria line in 1968.

In the meantime, the dual problem of overcrowding and worn-out rail and road vehicles had not gone away. Passenger numbers reached a record high of 4,675 million in 1948, bumped up in part by London hosting the Olympic Games. Of this figure, the vast majority were carried on the Executive's buses, trams, coaches and trolleybuses.[60] Consequently, priority was given to upgrading these services at the expense of the Underground, most notably with the completion of the tram-replacement programme started before the war, but now using new diesel buses instead of electric trolleybuses.[61] Some advances were made, however, in the development of new rolling stock for the District line with a prototype ready for public inspection on the South Bank at the Festival of Britain in 1951.

At the start of the new decade, opinion about the experience of Underground travel was divided. Many regular commuters would have sympathized with Winston Smith, the hero of George Orwell's futuristic novel *Nineteen Eighty-Four* (published in 1949), whose journey to work in a dystopian London involves 'fighting for a place on the Tube' and putting up with the 'stench of the Tubes at rush hour'.[62] Certainly contemporary newspapers bristled with reports of overcrowding, delays and minor mishaps caused by out-of-date equipment.[63] For others the Underground retained much of its pre-war reputation for cleanliness and reliability, despite under-investment. As the journalist and broadcaster Maurice Gorham explained in *Londoners* (1951):

the Tubes remain the most efficient transport system in the world. Anybody who has experienced the Paris Metro and the New York subway will agree that the Tube is the most comfortable for the habitual traveller and much the easiest for the stranger who is trying to find his way.[64]

The international comparison with Paris and New York is revealing, reflecting a renewed confidence in London's place in the world and a feeling that the country as a whole was getting back on its feet, most notably expressed in the optimism of the Festival of Britain (promoted as 'a tonic for the nation') and the fanfare of the 1953 Coronation. Against this background, there were high hopes for a second 'golden age' of public transport in London. In reality, the Underground was about to enter a decade of chronic under-investment which was to cause long-term damage to the transport system.

44. Poster welcoming visitors to the Olympic Games, issued by London Transport and British Railways, 1948. The Games was the first major international event held in post-war London.

45. Travel information poster for the Festival of Britain designed by Abram Games. The Festival, which attracted huge crowds, ran from May to September 1951.

The lost decade

The unenviable task of steering the Executive through the troubled waters ahead fell to John Elliot, who replaced Lord Latham as the chairman of London Transport in 1953. Elliot was a career railwayman, although his early training as a journalist on the *Evening Standard* gave him an adroit understanding of media relations lacking in some of his senior LT colleagues.[65] As public relations officer for the Southern Railway (1925-37) he had helped transform the company's flagging image and was later promoted to deputy General Manager. Since the formation of British Railways in 1948 he had held a series of senior managerial roles, most recently as chairman of the Railway Executive (1951-3), where he was in direct contact with the British Transport Commission and the relevant government departments. With such an experienced, and sympathetic, high flyer at the helm the fortunes of London Underground might reasonably have been expected to take a sudden turn for the better. But Elliot knew better than most that funding for the Underground would always take second place to the demands of Britain's ailing rail industry. The point was tragically brought home by the Harrow and Wealdstone train crash in October 1952, where antiquated equipment and coaches contributed to the deaths of 112 people in the country's worst peacetime railway disaster. Against such an appalling death toll, requests to divert money from national rail upgrades to Tube improvements fell on deaf ears.

Investment continued to fall, reaching its lowest level in the history of the Underground. In 1953, for example, capital expenditure on railway works amounted to just £300,000 - a pitiful figure even then. In comparison, £5.9 million was spent that

46. Well-wishers camping out at Westminster Underground station to catch a glimpse of the Coronation procession the following day, 2 June 1953. Special trains ran until 1.30 a.m. on the eve of the ceremony, and from 3 a.m. the next morning.

47. John Elliot shortly after he had been appointed chairman of the London Transport Executive in 1953. He was knighted the following year.

year on modernizing London Transport's road services, which remained the focus for investment throughout the 1950s. In fact the only significant expenditure on the Underground during the period 1951–4 was the addition of two extra tracks through Wembley Park – hardly something to compare with the scale of the pre-war New Works Programme or the contemporaneous replacement of the London tram network. Not that things were much easier on the bus side. Declining ridership, caused in part by rising private car ownership and the lure of television as an alternative to off-peak leisure travel, meant that the previously profitable road services were no longer able to cross-subsidize the Tube. The wholesale modernization of the bus fleet, including the development of the new Routemaster bus (introduced from 1959 to replace the trolleybus fleet) was intended to halt this decline, but had little effect on either passenger numbers or the Underground's deteriorating financial position.

Lack of investment inevitably led to piecemeal service upgrades and one-off capital projects, such as the electrification of the little-used Epping and Ongar branch in 1957 and the £1 million construction of Upminster depot (on the District line) in 1959. The paucity of tangible improvements, however, belied the very considerable efforts on the part of Elliot and his team to secure government funding for more ambitious projects and shouldn't be taken as evidence of an absence of planning. Chief amongst these projects was the proposed deep-level Tube from Victoria to Walthamstow, estimated to cost in the region of £50 million and known from the mid-1950s as the Victoria line – apparently on the personal suggestion of Elliot, who instinctively understood the PR limitations of its official 'Route C' designation. First mooted in 1948, the new Tube was intended to cut cross-London journey times and relieve congestion on both the Underground and the buses. For several years the scheme had floundered on the grounds that it was unlikely to pay for itself from ticket revenue alone, despite the undoubted benefits for passengers. After much political manoeuvring and a government inquiry into the proposed financing of the line, London Transport was finally granted parliamentary approval in 1955 on the understanding that construction would go ahead only if national economic conditions improved. Undaunted, Elliot initiated a skilful press campaign, stressing the wider social benefits of the new route, which kept the debate firmly in the public eye.[66] His case was strengthened by the findings of the government's 1959 London Travel Committee, which reported that the new Tube was 'essential' in tackling the capital's growing traffic problems, although it was to take another three years to convince ministers to bankroll the scheme.

48. Prior to the electrification of the Epping and Ongar line, Underground trains terminated at Epping station (seen here in 1953), where passengers changed on to a steam-hauled shuttle service for the remainder of their journey.

SILVER TRAINS

The first generation of post-war Underground trains had their design roots in the New Works Programme of 1935. Under the original five-year plan new steel trains had been commissioned for the sub-surface lines, initially designated O, P and Q38 stock. When the District needed additional trains based on the same template after the Second World War, supplies of steel were very limited, so designers turned to a metal that had proven itself during the war in aircraft construction and was starting to be more widely accepted – aluminium. The 'new' metal had been used in tram and bus body panels in the 1930s, but never for a whole vehicle. It was easily available and, although it was more expensive than steel at this time, engineers calculated that the 16 per cent saving in weight would be an advantage in the long term. The new aluminium trains were called R49 stock.

A partially painted prototype was displayed at the Festival of Britain in 1951, with some panels left in bare aluminium alloy to highlight the new lightweight, rustproof material. While the exhibition car was subsequently resprayed in London Transport red before entering service, successful weathering trials on unpainted aluminium panels at the Board's research centre led to the introduction of an experimental eight-car 'silver' train in 1952. The performance of the unpainted train was then compared to painted steel

50

51

49

---

49. One of the first batch of post-war R49 silver trains, seen here headed by no. 22679 at West Kensington in 1982, just before withdrawal. This driving car is now preserved in the London Transport Museum collection.

50. The partially painted 'R stock' prototype arriving at the Festival of Britain site on the South Bank in 1951. The Dome of Discovery and Skylon (under construction) can be seen in the background.

51. Festival of Britain commemorative plaque from R49 stock car no. 23231 – London's first all-aluminium-bodied rail vehicle.

and painted aluminium trains before a final decision to go with unpainted for all new trains was made in 1953. The new silver trains were striking, modern and good for publicity, but they were in no sense a gimmick. The move to unpainted aluminium meant savings in weight and painting costs, while passengers benefited from improved rubber suspension and fluorescent lighting fitted throughout the cars.

The minimalist look continued with the 1959 and 1962 Tube Stock and the Metropolitan line 'A stock', and on through the 1960s and 1970s. By the 1980s, almost the entire Underground fleet had been replaced with unpainted aluminium-bodied cars. The rise of New York-inspired train graffiti, however, caused a rethink and from the 1990s painted liveries started to return.

Silver Trains

The Piccadilly and Central Lines are being re-equipped with 1,200 new cars. This is part of a £30 million plan to replace Underground rolling stock. The new trains are lighter in weight, with an unpainted aluminium finish to save maintenance costs.

Other features are:
Rubber suspension.
Fluorescent lighting throughout.
More room in every train.

There will be more comfort for travellers on the Underground

53

52. The 'A stock' was specially designed for the longer journeys experienced on the Metropolitan line, and included distinctive aluminium luggage racks, seen here in a 1961 publicity photograph.

53. The stripped-down simplicity of the new aluminium Tube trains earmarked for the Piccadilly and Central Lines is echoed in the design of Frank Overton's poster 'Silver Trains' (1960).

54

Of more immediate success was the planned modernization and refurbishment of the Metropolitan line, authorized in 1956 and completed in phases from 1960 to 1962. The £3½ million scheme was primarily designed to relieve congestion at Harrow-on-the-Hill and extend electrification from Rickmansworth to Amersham and Chesham, which were still served by ex-Metropolitan Railway steam-hauled trains. This time, funding proved easier to secure as the proposals were broadly in tune with government policy to stimulate the expansion of commuter towns in the outer London area through the development of existing services. The laying of additional tracks north of Harrow also improved the frequency of mainline railway services into Marylebone which shared part of the route with London Transport over the former Metropolitan & Great Central joint line, still used by Chiltern Railways today. As part of the project, the non-electrified section of the Metropolitan line from Amersham to Aylesbury was transferred to British Railways in September 1961, making Amersham station the northernmost terminus of the modern Underground and bringing to a close the last chapter of steam-hauled passenger services on London Transport.[67] From the passengers' perspective, the end of steam also meant the welcomed replacement of antiquated wooden-bodied carriages with the new aluminium A60 stock trains, thoughtfully fitted with luggage racks and umbrella hooks for the bowler-hatted commuters who filled the seats at rush hour.

New trains were also been promised to long-suffering commuters across the Tube network as part of a £30 million upgrade to replace a third of all Underground trains by 1962. Various improvements to stations, signalling and power supply were equally trumpeted in frequent press releases as evidence that London Transport was taking passenger complaints seriously and planning for a better future.

The problem was, of course, that such schemes took a long time to come to fruition. In the meantime, conditions on the Underground had worsened. After an initial fall in the early 1950s, passenger numbers stabilized at about 670 million a year, the majority of whom travelled in overcrowded trains during the peak hours. Questions were raised in the House of Commons as to why this was the case, with one MP comparing the treatment of commuters with the conditions endured by

54. A night-time view of Upminster depot photographed shortly after it opened in December 1959. This was the only major Underground project completed in the 1950s.

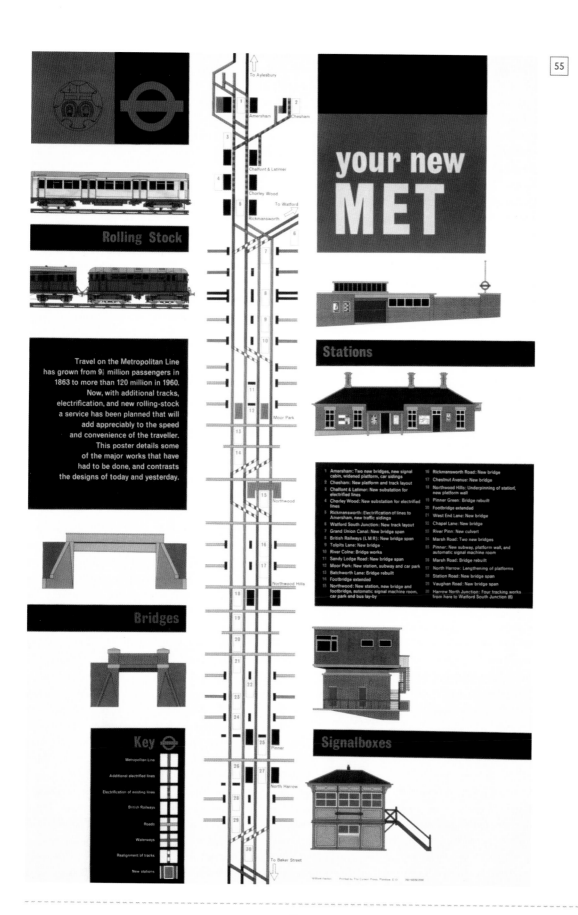

55. A teaser poster designed by William Fenton for London Underground in 1960 highlighting some of the improvements Metropolitan line passengers could expect over the next couple of years.

British prisoners of war a decade earlier.[68] Once again, London Transport executives invoked the perceived panacea of staggered working hours as the cure all for the current problem. Yet another government body, the Committee for Staggering Working Hours in Central London (1955), was established to look into the question. Unsurprisingly, its report recommended closer links between major employers and London Transport to coordinate adjustments to working hours and lay on extra services where necessary. The report went on to cite recent changes to the hours of 21,000 civil servants as evidence of how this could work, but without any legislative power to force a cultural shift in working patterns the Committee was doomed to failure. London Transport's rather testy response was to blame commuters for the problem:

> The Executive cannot over-emphasize the importance of staggered work hours as the first means of getting the public an easier ride morning and evening. Wide-scale action, however, will only come when the public itself realizes this, and insists on it. There is often complaint that the public is 'packed' into trains and buses. The fact is that the public packs itself in, to its own great discomfort and the Executive's heavy expense.[69]

Delays, caused by the not-infrequent breakdown of worn-out stock, only added to the misery. It was all very well to promise new trains and general improvements in five or ten years' time, but that was little comfort for stranded passengers trying to get to work.

More worrying was the spate of Underground fires caused by failing electrical equipment. Fifteen were reported between 1954 and 1959. On one occasion, a passenger was killed and sixty-three treated for smoke inhalation when a fire broke out on a Central line train.[70]

Matters came to a head in 1959 when frustrated passengers staged a series of sit-down strikes after being told to leave broken-down or delayed trains short of their destinations.[71] In an echo of wartime annoyance with civilian Tube shelterers, London Transport reacted aggressively to this show of defiance. Posters chastised unruly passengers for their 'thoughtless' behaviour. At Finchley Central station staff summoned the local police to evict commuters from a failed train, while at Stratford passengers who refused to leave a faulty service were taken on a 10-mile non-stop journey to Hainault depot, where they were eventually released to find their own way home.[72] Such bloody-mindedness was reflected in the Board's Annual Report, which blamed 'protesters' for making the situation worse, rather than acknowledging corporate responsibility for the cause of the unrest.[73]

56

56. A driver's-eye view of rush-hour crowds at Charing Cross (now Embankment) on the Northern Line, March 1959.

Passengers, of course, felt differently. In a letter to *The Times*, Ernest Lindgren, a commuter from north London, reasoned that the 'sudden, spontaneous demonstration [on the Northern line] was not provoked by one incident or one official, but by the accumulated resentment of rational people at being treated habitually and consistently as unreasoning cattle'.[74]

It was all a long way from the wistful vision of Underground travel evoked by John Betjeman in a trilogy of poems published in the 1950s. In one, 'Middlesex' (1954), the modern-day Central line links the carefree world of an office girl with her job in town and life in the suburbs:

Gaily into Ruislip Gardens
Runs the red electric train,
With a thousand Ta's and Pardon's
Daintily alights Elaine;
Hurries down the concrete station
With a frown of concentration,
Out into the outskirt's edges
Where a few surviving hedges
Keep alive our lost Elysium – rural Middlesex again.

'Harrow-on-the-Hill' and 'The Metropolitan Railway', Betjeman's other poems to feature the Underground, are more overtly nostalgic, harking back to a pre-war Metro-land heyday of panelled carriages with 'sepia views of leafy lanes in PINNER' and trips to Wembley Stadium. How far this portrayal was removed from the daily grind of commuting can easily be imagined. Such depictions also mask the changing nature of leisure and travel in 1950s Britain, where increasing prosperity was to have a direct effect on London Transport.

Many more people were choosing to stay at home and watch television than take an off-peak trip to the local cinema or sports ground. If they did decide to venture out at the weekend or in the evening, they were just as likely to use the car than hop on a bus or take the Tube. Between 1950 and 1965 the number of private cars licensed in the London Transport area leaped from 480,000 to nearly two million. The effect was most sharply felt on the Executive's road services, where passenger numbers continued to nose-dive. Young, upwardly mobile professionals no longer wanted to use public transport if they could help it. Neither did they want to live in central London, where the population fell by 190,000 in the ten years to 1962, compared with an increase of over half a million in the outer areas, prompted, in part, by the development of New Towns such as Crawley, Harlow and Stevenage. A rather telling outcome of shifting population and increasing prosperity was the greater

57

57. A sign of the times – the packed car park at Osterley station on the Piccadilly line, August 1957. The Underground had predicted the appeal of 'park and ride' facilities by providing car parks at new suburban Tube stations like this one in the 1930s, but by the late 1950s the demand was outstripping the available space.

demand for car parking spaces at suburban Underground stations. The total capacity rose by over 150 per cent during the late 1950s and early 1960s, with many former goods yards on the Metropolitan and Northern lines converted to this new use in testimony to the changing times.

At the same time, near full employment created a surfeit of well-paid semi-skilled jobs that made it difficult for LT to either retain staff or fill vacancies. Wages in the transport industry generally had fallen behind those of other sectors. Again, the impact was greater on the bus side, where there were more relatively low-paid grades, such as conductors and catering staff. At first, London Transport tried to bridge the gap by employing women in roles previously undertaken by men. A lasting solution was eventually found by mounting recruitment campaigns further afield, in Northern Ireland, Malta and, in particular, the West Indies. In 1956 LT began direct recruitment in Barbados, later extending the scheme to Jamaica. By 1969, when the programme ended, more than 4,000 staff had been recruited from the Caribbean islands.

Elliot retired from London Transport in March 1959, leaving his successor, Alexander Valentine, a legacy of authorized, but as yet unstarted, capital investment projects urgently needed to revive the Tube's battered reputation. Like Elliot, Valentine was an experienced railway operator, having worked for the Underground since the 1920s, and had been a serving member of the London Transport Executive since its formation in 1948. At this stage, the future of the Victoria line was still uncertain, although work could at least commence on the modernization of the Metropolitan line.

Fresh hope was given to the new Tube in 1959 with authority to construct a mile of experimental twin tunnel between Finsbury Park and Seven Sisters (later incorporated into the Victoria line) using newly developed methods of tunnel lining in concrete and cast iron. Successfully completed in 1961, the project gave London Transport a useful foot in the door when negotiating with the BTC and government ministers over funding for the entire scheme. Meanwhile, Valentine kept up the media campaign initiated by Elliot, which presented an irresistible case for the new Tube. He also commissioned an independent (and pioneering) cost/benefit analysis to prove the wider social and economic gains to be had from the scheme. The combined arguments proved effective, and in 1962 government authority was finally given to begin construction.

The decision was greeted with widespread support, and not a little relief in the boardroom of the London Transport Executive. Even the normally hostile *Evening News* joined in the celebrations: 'London leaps ahead again. The new Victoria cut-the-corners Tube line will be the most modern Underground railway in the world.'[75] The 'cut-the-corners' comment was a reference to the 'soft curves" and 'smoother riding' promised by the planners, rather than a slur on penny-pinching cost savings. In fact, press reporting (heavily briefed by LT's publicity men) was so positive that experienced heads must have worried that the Underground was setting up false expectations. Journey times in central London, it was claimed, would be halved, overcrowding eased

please avoid rush hour travel

and the whole passenger experience transformed by modern trains and stations 'finished in bright contemporary design'.[76]

This shining vision for the future was to be the Executive's swan song. The 1962 Transport Act reorganized the whole of the nationalized transport system into a number of separate boards corresponding to the previous divisions of the BTC. A new London Transport Board (headed by Valentine) was appointed in November 1962 to take over the responsibilities of the LTE with effect from 1 January 1963. The crucial difference between the LTB and its predecessor was that the new Board reported directly to the Minister of Transport and had its own budget similar to the days of Pick and Ashfield.

On the eve of the Underground's centenary year (1963) the management of London Transport had come full circle since the system was nationalized fifteen years before. The London Transport Board was, in theory, once more in control of its own destiny. It remained to be seen whether the 'lost decade' of underinvestment would be made good in the years ahead.

58. 'Please Avoid Rush Hour Travel', a Tube car poster designed by John Burningham in 1961 to discourage overcrowding. It was just this sort of problem that planners hoped would be alleviated by the new Victoria line.

WARNING
Doze off for 20 minutes and you'll end up in Walthamstow

Please try not to doze off on the Victoria Line. The new automatic trains are so quick that you're liable to miss your stop.

Of course if you're awake and in a hurry you're going to find this new rapid route across London a great blessing.

For example, it now takes a mere four minutes to get from Victoria to Oxford Circus. Remember how long it used to take?

London's new tube is designed to make the rush-hour more bearable by moving people more quickly and taking the load off other lines.

We only wish we could abolish the rush-hour altogether-but that would be difficult until they abolish work.

London's pride

CHAPTER 5

TRANSPORT IS POLITICS

Centenary

The Underground celebrated its centenary as the world's first underground railway in 1963 with a flurry of events and publications.[1] The public highlight was a grand parade of underground trains past and present at Neasden depot, led out by Met 23, the last survivor of the Beyer Peacock steam locos which provided the motive power for the Victorian Underground.[2] At the corporate celebration on 24 May, 300 invited guests joined the Centenary train, formed of eight cars of the Underground's most modern trains, the silver A62 stock, at a flag-decked Paddington platform 14 for departure to Moorgate. The train was driven by the Lord Mayor of London, Sir Ralph Perring (having apparently read the driver's manual and taken lessons on a trial journey), with driver James Stone in close attendance.[3] At Moorgate, in a theatrical moment, members of the London Transport Musical and Dramatic Society presented a tableau of Gladstone's trip in 1862.[4] The stage was provided by two wagons replicating the contractors' trucks used by Smith & Knight to build the line in the 1860s, headed by steam locomotive L48 and propelled by L44.[5] The part of Gladstone was played by the depot foreman at Hainault, Mrs Gladstone by a head office secretary, Lord Macclesfield by a toolmaker from Chiswick Works, and the Duke of Sutherland by a staff member from the Lost Property Office.

Guests were taken by new Routemaster buses for lunch at the Mansion House, where the Chairman of London Transport, Alec Valentine,[6] in proposing the health of the Lord Mayor and Corporation, mused on the centenary of the London Underground:

> We are today commemorating the completion of the hundredth year in public service of the first passenger underground railway ever to be opened anywhere in the world, and the presence here of distinguished visitors in the sphere of urban transport from overseas is both an honour in itself to London Transport and a recognition of London's primacy … They may feel inclined to think that their own underground railways … are as good as London's or better – though we may still surprise them even there – but, at any rate, no one has yet achieved a century in this business.

1. Poster emphasizing the speed of the new Victoria Line, part of the 'London's pride' campaign, 1969.

2. Commemorative headboard from the centenary train and poster for the Neasden centenary cavalcade.

3 4

5

The Chairman and Members of the London Transport Board
request the Pleasure of the Company of

TO RIDE WITH THE LORD MAYOR OF LONDON
ON A COMMEMORATIVE RUN FROM PADDINGTON (BISHOP'S ROAD) TO THE CITY
to celebrate **THE CENTENARY** of the London

UNDERGROUND

on Friday 24th May 1963 at 11.55 a m followed by
LUNCHEON at the **MANSION HOUSE**
at 12.45 for 1 p.m.
by kind permission of The Right Honourable the Lord Mayor, Sir Ralph Perring

R.S.V.P.: The Chief Public Relations Officer, London Transport, 55 Broadway, London, S.W.1

There was hope for the future as Valentine proudly described the rolling stock renewal programme: 'With the completion of these works, the Metropolitan is, at the end of one hundred years, as lively and well equipped as any underground railway in the world.'

Allowing for the self-congratulatory nature of the occasion, this assertion had some justification. Contracts had been placed for the first new underground line to be built under the capital since before the First World War, to be equipped with the world's first automatic train control and fare collection, and new aluminium-bodied 'silver' trains had been supplied for the Central, Piccadilly and Metropolitan lines. Valentine's speech concluded by anticipating two key issues which were to prove central to the story of the Underground's next fifty years: the political consequences of public subsidy of ticket revenues and London's relationship with the rest of the UK.

In 1963, high office costs and traffic congestion in the capital encouraged living and working away from London. The city's population had been in decline from 8.6 million in 1939 to 7.8 million in 1961 and was to reach a low point of 6.6 million in 1981. Post-war planning policy had sought to disperse people and jobs beyond London, through the building of New Towns beyond the Green Belt and encouragement of government and business relocation to the regions. The Location of Offices Bureau was set up by government in 1963 to disperse office jobs from central London. Indeed developers seeking to build new office space in London required a permit from the Bureau. Some 24,000 jobs were dispersed between 1963 and 1969.[7] Valentine questioned this, arguing for what is now known as agglomeration:

The City, with its close knit organisation of financial and commercial life, depends on personal contacts and swift operations which could not I believe be carried out with efficiency if, say, the Stock Exchange were at Hammersmith and Lloyd's

3. Former Met locomotive L52 with engineer's train at the Neasden centenary cavalcade, May 1963. This locomotive was scrapped in 1971.

4. Chairman Alec Valentine opens the LT centenary poster exhibition at the Royal Institute Galleries, Piccadilly in 1963.

5. Invitation for Centenary Train and Luncheon at the Mansion House, May 1963.

at Croydon; if the commodity exchanges and the big insurance companies were scattered around the New Towns; if the Big Five Bank headquarters were set up in some new stockade just beyond the Green Belt – leaving the Bank of England herself in solitary grandeur in Threadneedle Street. Must we not accept that concentration within the square mile is the right way to organise the City's vital work?[8]

In *The Times* Valentine wrote, 'if a centenary becomes merely an occasion for nostalgia, it loses most of its point. A centenary should help us to understand more clearly the nature of the problems that have been solved in the past ... we should be better able to make the right decisions for the future.'[9] The chairman referred to the severe congestion and parking issues caused by the growing dominance of the private car in London and pleaded not 'to destroy the character and efficiency of the city by motorways'. Car ownership in London quadrupled between 1950 and 1970; by the mid-1960s there were 1.5 million cars registered in the capital. Traffic congestion had made bus services increasingly unreliable and so reduced their patronage; a tenth or more of timetabled bus mileage was being lost by the early 1960s. This was compounded by staff shortages which had led to direct recruitment campaigns in Ireland, Malta and the Caribbean from the 1950s. Bus revenues had long sustained the financial independence of London Transport's operations, but as the service suffered, LT would be obliged to seek the public subsidy that was normal amongst other city metros worldwide.

However, consensus on the wider benefits of transport investment, let alone the primacy of London to the economic vitality of the whole country, did not exist in 1960s Britain. For transport in London, the next fifty years were to be a rollercoaster ride, fuelled by the partisan collision of national and local politics, and a mismatch between the short-term cycles of politics with the far longer wavelength of infrastructure investment. Since the earliest years of the Tube, investment in the Underground on purely commercial returns had never been enough; wider social or employment benefits had to be considered: 'Whether such additions and improvements, which will be costly, are properly to be provided solely by the passengers through their fares, or whether they should be considered as a civic improvement conferring benefits on a far larger number,

6

6. Colour lithograph by William Fenton commissioned to celebrate the Centenary, 1963.

is a question I do not raise now, though someone may have to do so in the future,' warned Valentine.[10] So, the stage was set for the funding of public transport in London to become a political football. Valentine concluded that 'the prosperity of London and the health of its public transport system are inseparable'.[11] This was to be tested by years of political dispute, start-stop funding, boom, bust and national and local political interference. The Underground and its chairman had good cause to celebrate the first hundred years of service to London, but good reason as well to fear for its future.

The grey heat of technology

The Underground's great triumph of the 1960s was the opening of the Victoria line. On 7 March 1969, Queen Elizabeth II officiated at the formal opening of the line from Walthamstow to Victoria.[12] The first reigning monarch to take the Tube, the Queen was received at 11 a.m. by the LT chairman, Maurice Holmes, on a blue carpet outside Green Park station. The civic party descended to the ticket hall, where Her Majesty was invited to purchase a 5d ticket from the new automatic machines and, after a momentary hitch, when the machine rejected both her equerry's sixpences, an alternative coin was found by Eric Wilkins, LT's chief public relations officer. The monarch was able to purchase a yellow pasteboard ticket with a brown magnetic coating, pass through the automatic gate and take the escalator to the platform.[13] Here, in her opening speech, she noted the pioneering role of Britain in building underground railways, praised the 'arduous work of the miners whose efforts made this project possible' and the role her great grandfather, King Edward VII, had played when, as Prince of Wales, he had opened the first electric Tube in 1890 and a section of the Central London Railway in 1900. She also recalled her 'vivid memory' of her only previous journey on the Tube in 1939. Finally, she congratulated all involved and declared the line open.[14]

7

7. Pre-opening publicity image for the new Victoria Line, emphasizing the spacious interior and modern technology.

The Queen took her place in the driving cab with driver Francis Fountain of Tottenham.[15] When official photographs had been taken, she pressed the two buttons to start the train, which was taken northbound by the world's first automatic train control system, breaking a blue ribbon with gold lettering saying 'Victoria line 7 March 1969' stretched across the tunnel mouth. At Oxford Circus the royal party inspected the station operations room, CCTV and the ticket office, returned by train to Victoria, with its cameos of Queen Victoria in the platform tiling, where the Queen unveiled a commemorative plaque in the ticket hall. Thus was the most technically advanced of Tube lines opened in a most traditional fashion.

8

Public service on the first new underground line to be built across London for sixty years commenced at 3 p.m. that day.[16] 'It will be the most highly automated and technically advanced underground railway in the world and in the peak hours its trains will be able to carry 25,000 passengers an hour in each direction – the equivalent of 11 motorway lanes.'[17] This proud boast was based on one-man-operated automatically driven trains, 20 per cent faster than those on older lines, and the automation of tickets and gates. The line provided interchange at all stations with other Underground or BR lines and was equipped with forty-two escalators, a closed circuit television system to monitor passenger flows and loudspeakers to make announcements. The line control centre was at the top of a new office block at Cobourg Street near Euston.

Construction had taken over six years and had set a world record for soft-ground tunnelling of 470 feet (140 metres) per week. Extensive use was made of new concrete tunnel-linings as well as traditional bolted iron sections. The first two sections of the line, from Walthamstow to Highbury & Islington and from the latter to Warren Street, had been opened without ceremony on 1 September and on 1 December 1968. The final section to Brixton was to open on 23 July 1971. An additional intermediate station at Pimlico had been approved only in 1968 when the Crown Estate, major landlords in the locality, offered a site for the station.

The Victoria line was designed in-house by chief architect Kenneth Seymour and LU engineers, with design consultancy from Misha Black and the Design Research Unit (DRU). As the line was wholly underground, architectural treatment was limited to ticket halls and platforms, the exception being Blackhorse Road, the only new surface station structure on the line. A common design was adopted of light-grey tiling, with darker grey tiles around the platform archways and dark blue, black or grey around the poster panels. The escalators were aluminium clad as were the ticket machines and gate housings, with padded gates which sprung aside when a magnetically backed ticket was placed in the slot.

9

10

8. Queen Elizabeth II in a Victoria Line car with, from left, LT chairman Maurice Holmes, Eric Wilkins, the chief public relations officer, deputy chairman Anthony Bull and the Transport Minister, Richard Marsh.

9. Commemorative train headboard from the Victoria Line opening ceremony.

10. Commemorative ticket for the opening of the Victoria Line, March 1969.

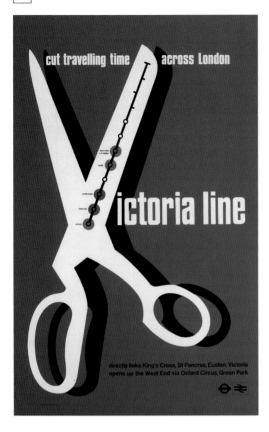

In the best tradition of the Underground, tiled panel designs for the platforms were commissioned from an eclectic selection of established graphic artists such as Hans Unger, Edward Bawden, Tom Eckersley and Abram Games, and rising stars, such as Alan Fletcher, later of Pentagram, George Smith of DRU and Julia Black. The designs were specific to each station, such as a black horse for Blackhorse Road and the demolished Doric portico for Euston. At Brixton, 'ton of bricks' was a pun on the place name, while local historical references were used at Walthamstow, birthplace of William Morris, and at Tottenham Hale, the ferry over the River Lea.

The line was not greeted publicly with quite the breathlessly triumphal quality of the Underground's own publicity. Anthony Sampson in the *Observer* described it as 'extraordinarily bleak', its 'late lavatorial style, with shiny grey tiles, harsh strip lighting … The long echoing passages with bare black ribs, seem to be leading to some mass underground grave.'[18] He went on to praise the Paris Metro's new Louvre station by contrasting it with the 'public squalor' of London Underground: 'surely the Victoria line needs something more than automatic tickets and coloured tiles if it is really to be (as its advertisements proclaim) "London's pride"'. Even the booklet provided for the public on opening was apologetic, suggesting that the tiled recess designs added a 'touch of interest and humanity to the rather severe platforms'.[19] The grey was defended by Black: 'The stations may be criticized for appearing visually unexciting, but we consider that preferable to a transient popularity without lasting qualities.'[20] The time taken to finance and build the line had led its design to feel dated by the time it opened - more Festival of Britain than Swinging Sixties.

11. 'Victoria Line', a poster by Tom Eckersley, 1969.

12. A Kinnear-Moody drum digger in a station tunnel at Green Park, being hauled through after completing the southbound tunnel from Victoria, 1965.

13. Railman Lloyd Manning and ticket-collector Lucille Richmond with the 'ton of bricks' tiling at Brixton, 1971. This was the first Tube extension south of the river since the 1920s.

14. Victoria line construction work. A 16-ft-diameter station tunnelling shield at Highbury & Islington, 1964.

15. Train and station platform at Seven Sisters, 1969.

16. Ticket hall at Oxford Circus with automatic ticket barriers, 1969.

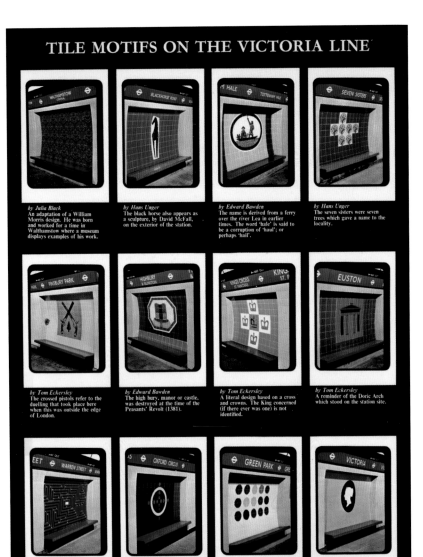

Despite intensive testing, innovative equipment took time to bed down under the pressure of daily use. On the first day of operation a power failure put the twelve automatic ticket machines out of action at Victoria and a queue of passengers stretched from the booking office to the BR platforms.[21] The phrase 'a dodgy solenoid' became an in-joke for booking clerks. Passengers took time to adjust to the four-door automatic gates – 'People must learn to use these barriers,' said the Oxford Circus station master, replying to complaints that the barriers tended to grip passengers' bags in the jaws. LT's public relations officer was obliged to reply to one passenger: 'These gates were carefully designed in consultation with our doctors to avoid any risk of injury ... in the unlikely event of the doors closing on a small child, the pressure is insufficient to cause him any harm.'[22] Severe budget restrictions meant that station infrastructure standards were lower than on older lines, with narrower platforms and undecorated ceilings at Walthamstow Central, Blackhorse Road and Tottenham Hale. To this day the concrete staircase, between the up and down escalators at most stations, is testament to the constrained regime under which the line was built, leading to severe congestion at peak hours.

17. 'Tile Motifs on the Victoria Line', 1969 poster.

18. A BR poster advertising the new Euston station, next to Tom Eckersley's tile design showing the recently demolished Euston Arch.

19 20

Nonetheless, the Victoria line was still the first application of automatic operation on a world metro. It chimed with the 'white heat' of technology promoted by the Wilson government and symbolized by the establishment of a Ministry of Technology to drag post-imperial Britain into the modern world. The Victoria line was one of the era's vaunted applications of cutting-edge technology, along with the GPO Tower, Concorde, the TSR2 fighter, the electrification of the west coast mainline and the rebuilding of Euston station. It was a remarkable achievement, built against the odds in competition with car-orientated transport thinking. It was developed largely in-house and stretched available technology to the limit on a very tight budget. Not everything worked; the automatic ticketing system failed, and the gates were removed in 1972. The benefits of automation would only be realized when installed across the whole system later in the 1980s.

21

The new line was to prove the last moment of outright world leadership for the London Underground; the Bay Area Rapid Transit in San Francisco opened in September 1972 with both automatic train control and ticketing. The Victoria line rapidly became a busy line; usage today stands at 183 million journeys a year and exceeds the original forecast by nearly three times. It is the fourth-busiest line in terms of passenger numbers and the most intensively used, carrying in excess of 13,000 passengers per mile.[23]

---

19. Ian Arthurton, future Passenger Services Director, with automatic train control electronics under development for the Victoria line, on the Hainault loop, 1966.

20. New technology in action, the Victoria line control centre at Cobourg Street, 1970, 'a strange drum-shaped room, green carpeted on floor and lower walls for noise absorption … in its silence two shirt-sleeved men [the train regulator and the line controller] sit at desks' (*The Times*, 6 March 1969).

21. New aluminium-clad escalators to the Victoria line at Victoria station, 1970.

THE SWINGING SIXTIES?

The swinging 1960s largely passed London Underground by. Along with RAF targets and flags, the symbolism of the Tube was adopted by artists and designers, but the Underground itself remained largely unmoved by the cultural changes taking place in London. The appearance of the map and roundel on record sleeves by the tongue-in-cheek New Vaudeville Band in 1967, the emergence of psychedelic pop act Picadilly (sic) Line and the blues-rock trio called Bakerloo all mirrored the popular spirit of the age. Similarly, Ray Davies' evocative reference to the crowds 'swarming like flies' around Waterloo Underground in The Kinks' 'Waterloo Sunset' reflected the perception of the Underground in popular imagination. At the same time the Underground itself commissioned only two Pop Art posters in the sixties (by Fred Millett and Hans Unger) and travellers on the network went about their daily business much as they had done before.

22. The album cover from the short-lived pop combo Picadilly Line, 1967.

23. Record cover of 'Finchley Centra'l, a single by the New Vaudeville Band, 1967.

24. Just another day for commuters, on the escalators at Piccadilly Circus station, 1966.

LONDON AFTER DARK

In the dusk, the West End comes to life. Street lamps brighten, and the twinkling lights turn Piccadilly Circus into a brashly magical fairyland. Floodlighting lends to St. Paul's, the National Gallery, Westminster Abbey, a silvery, sharp-etched clarity. Evening shopping (on Thursdays), theatres, cinemas, concerts, restaurants—London Transport takes you there, and home again. Buses run late, and the Underground until after midnight—23 30 on Sundays.

Travel Enquiries: telephone 01·222 1234 at any time, day or night.

ART TODAY The Tate, re-hung with taste and logic, offers the academically approved, the Whitechapel the young and middle-generation painters. The Greater London Council sets contemporary British sculpture against the simpler pleasures of Battersea Park. Complete your survey with the commercial galleries of deepest Mayfair and Chelsea, and the avant-garde extremes. For all these new frontiers, the explorer's kit is simple—an open mind, Underground and bus maps, and a sense of humour. For The Tate Gallery: Underground or bus to Westminster, then bus 77B. For The Whitechapel Art Gallery: Underground to Aldgate East. For Battersea Park: Underground to Sloane Square, then by bus 137.

25. Poster by Fred Millett, 'London After Dark', 1968.

26. 'Art Today', poster by Hans Unger, 1966.

The need to maintain the momentum of the Victoria line's opening into further new lines and renewal of the existing system was a feature of launch publicity and informed comment. *The Times* noted on the opening day:

the decision to build the Victoria line five years ago marked a turning point in the long history of under-investment in all forms of transport except one - road vehicles - which has produced the present malfunctioning in the city's transport system ... the decision rested on an appreciation for the first time of the fact that the value of such projects can be greater than the direct financial return.[24]

'How soon to the next Tube?' asked the *Evening News* on behalf of 'London's harassed travelling millions'.[25]

The difficulties encountered by public transport in the capital in this period have to be seen in relation to the dominant position of the car in transport policy. This was the era of the Beeching report,[26] which in 1963 proposed cutting the railway network by a third. There was a widely held belief that 'progress' would see an increasing dependency on private motor cars, and the real priority for transport investment was road building.

As far back as 1944, Lord Abercrombie's London Plan had proposed a series of ring roads around London with radial motorways leading into the city.[27] As traffic congestion grew, plans for four London 'Ringways' were published in 1966-7, proposing nearly thirty miles of mostly elevated motorway surrounding central London and at its core an inner ringway bringing the motorway right into the very heart of the capital. This tarmac policy became the cornerstone of transport planning for London in the 1960s.[28] The East Cross route to the Blackwall Tunnel and the Westway were both manifestations of this approach. The Westway was planned to link Paddington with the western arm of Ringway One. Work started in 1966 and involved the extensive demolition of property in North Kensington. At its opening in 1970, it was the largest continuous concrete structure in Britain and incorporated advanced features such as heating grids to prevent the formation of ice and a police operated traffic control and surveillance system. Rock band The Clash ironically referenced the Westway's exciting modernity in 'London's Burning' (1977), while for science fiction writer J. G. Ballard it represented a dystopian *Concrete Island* (1974).

The London Motorway Box

27. Rush-hour traffic at the Elephant & Castle, 1966.

28. London Motorway Box or Ringway One (marked in green) as proposed in the 1960s. Note the major interchanges, especially in north and west London. Only the sections in red were built.

The Greater London Council (GLC) had been created in 1965, with authority over an area twice the size of that covered by the old London County Council. The Conservatives won a landslide victory in the 1967 GLC elections. Their leader, Desmond Plummer, successfully negotiated the transfer of London Transport from the government to the GLC, with the added bonus of having all the debt for the Victoria line written off. In 1969, the GLC issued a draft Greater London Development Plan (GLDP), pursuing its motorway box policy. Even the proposed Fleet underground line, routed along Fleet Street from Charing Cross to Docklands, was to be subservient to the flagship policy by terminating with a park-and-ride scheme in Lewisham.

The Plan ran into serious public and political opposition, falling foul of both a sea change in thinking about cities, influenced by Jane Jacobs' *Death and Life of Great American Cities* (1961) and a growing public appetite for protest at the impact of planners' schemes on their communities.[29] Ringway One alone was expected to cost £480 million including £144 million for property purchases. It would have required 1,048 acres (4.24 km²) and affected 7,585 houses.[30] Fresh thinking suggested additional traffic would be generated purely as a result of new roads, while about 1 million Londoners would find their lives blighted by living within 200 yards of a motorway.[31] When the Plan was approved in 1973, *The Sunday Times* ran a two-page spread, despairing under the headline 'The Motor Car Wins Its Biggest Victory'. It revealed that the cost of the scheme had skyrocketed, with Ringway One now valued at £2 billion. The scheme was finally killed off by the Treasury: 'The Inner Motorway Box will never be implemented. We are no longer living in an environment when any Government can displace thousands of people from their homes.'[32]

Today's six-lane Archway Road, built between 1968 and 1971 from the Archway roundabout up the hill to the former LCC boundary at the Archway Bridge, is a relic of the ambitious Ringway plan. The road's further progress northwards through Hampstead Garden Suburb attracted huge local resistance. Four prolonged planning inquiries were severely disrupted by informed protest, and the scheme was abandoned first in 1978 and finally in 1990. At the inquiry a young, relatively unknown GLC councillor, Ken Livingstone, cut his transport teeth. The Archway Road protest was the first successful UK road protest. This, combined with the difficulties of the Heath government, led to Plummer and the Conservatives losing the 1973 GLC election to Labour.[33] The ebbing of the roads tide had been a tipping point for public opinion on transport in London. The new administration's emphasis on public transport fostered the Jubilee line and led to the watershed of Fares Fair.

29. Cover of London weekly listing magazine *Time Out*, 24 March 1972, with a special feature on the dire state of the city's public transport.

30. Electronic route indicator at Oxford Circus, 1974.

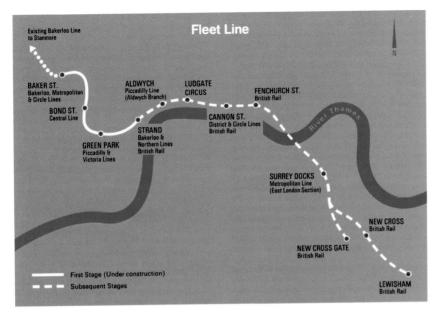

Fleet Line

Existing Bakerloo Line to Stanmore

BAKER ST. Bakerloo, Metropolitan & Circle Lines

BOND ST. Central Line

GREEN PARK Piccadilly & Victoria Lines

ALDWYCH Piccadilly Line (Aldwych Branch)

STRAND Bakerloo & Northern Lines British Rail

LUDGATE CIRCUS

CANNON ST. District & Circle Lines British Rail

FENCHURCH ST. British Rail

SURREY DOCKS Metropolitan Line (East London Section)

NEW CROSS British Rail

NEW CROSS GATE British Rail

LEWISHAM British Rail

River Thames

—— First Stage (Under construction)
- - - Subsequent Stages

N

31

32

Politics of transport

The 1970s were a difficult decade for public transport in London. The fourteen years of GLC control were to be characterized by stormy relations between the politicians and London Transport management, against the background of a depressed national economy. The 1974 Middle East oil crisis had stoked the flames of inflation, leading to steeply rising operating costs and difficult labour relations, as wages failed to keep up with the cost of living and there were deep cuts in public expenditure. In 1973, Labour, led by the moderate Sir Reg Goodwin, in its manifesto *A Socialist Strategy for London*, pledged a shift away from roads towards investment in public transport: 'Labour pledges itself to abandon the disastrous plans to build two motorways which threaten the environment of Central London.'[34] Once elected, Goodwin continued the distinctly green agenda set in the manifesto despite the many economic problems nationally that affected the GLC's finances.[35] A year later, Sir Richard Way's term as LT chairman was not renewed, and he was replaced – 'to make way for an older man' he commented acidly in his retirement speech – by Kenneth Robinson, a former minister in the Wilson government of 1964–8[36] and seen by County Hall as a Labour insider.

The GLC had sought to build on the opening of the Victoria line and the approval of the 'Fleet line' (the original name for the Jubilee line) by commissioning a far-reaching study of the capital's railways, the influential London Rail Study of 1973. This was led by a joint GLC and Department of Transport steering group to look at future transport needs and strategic plans for London and the south-east. This report contained options for new lines and extensions, including the Fleet line, a London orbital rail scheme (realized as the Overground in 2010), the first mention of Crossrail (only now under construction), and the Chelsea–Hackney line (now proposed as Crossrail 2). The Fleet line was named for its route from Baker Street via Charing Cross and Fleet Street, crossing the Fleet River, to Fenchurch Street and finally through the Surrey Docks to Lewisham. In the central area the line would act as a 'heart by-pass operation' for the highly congested Bakerloo line, whilst also bringing major benefits to the City and south-east London. Funding was secured in 1971, but only for the first phase to Charing Cross, as the future of Docklands was still unclear and the government reluctant to fund.

31. Proposed Fleet line route, from the LT *Annual Report*, 1971, running beneath Fleet Street to Fenchurch Street and then via Docklands to Lewisham.

32. LT retired its last surviving steam locos in 1971. A special day-time engineering train to Neasden depot was seen off by crowds of enthusiasts from Barbican station on 6 June.

London Transport had been typically upbeat in announcing the initiation of the Fleet line in 1971:

> With the completion of the Victoria line throughout from Walthamstow to Brixton, a start on work for the extension of the Piccadilly line from Hounslow to Heathrow Airport and now the green light for the first section of the Fleet line, London is forging ahead with Underground developments that will benefit millions of people.[37]

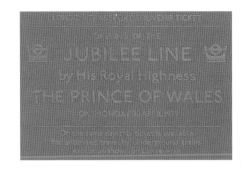

However, the investment of the Victoria line in new technology was not followed, and the Jubilee line seemed a backward step, built halfway to its destination, mostly using existing lines, without automatic train control, but with conventional signalling and two-man operated trains: 'a project bedevilled by piecemeal financial approval and lack of a consistent railway plan'.[38] The name change from 'Fleet' to 'Jubilee' was proposed in the Conservative manifesto for the 1977 GLC election. This was in honour of the Queen Elizabeth II's Silver Jubilee that year but also a hope that in this guise it would appeal more to those in charge of the government's coffers.[39] The first stage of the line was opened two years later on 30 April 1979 by Prince Charles.

LT chief architect Sydney Hardy and LU engineers designed the Jubilee line with the DRU, following the Design Panel method employed on the Victoria line. In reaction to criticism of that line's grey austerity, the four new sets of platforms, all part of existing stations, were tiled in flame red, with exit archways emphasized by grey tiles and yellow panels, which continued as a band around the tunnel barrels. Decorative graphic or tiled designs reflected the location and identity of each Jubilee line station: David Gentleman's Nelson's Column and pigeons for Charing Cross, Tom Eckersley's wrapped gift at Bond Street, June Fraser's leaves at Green Park and Robin Jacques' Sherlock Holmes illustrations at Baker Street.

The cynical Tube user was not much impressed by the television advertisements which launched the Jubilee line – 'in an almost Disneyland setting, pretend commuters ride down the escalators smiling and singing "Hi-ho, hi-ho, it's off to work we go."' 'What a bloody laugh,' said a real commuter, hurling himself into an overflowing carriage. Three weeks after opening, morning passengers used to a direct commute to Oxford Circus or Piccadilly, were obliged to change from the Jubilee line train at Baker Street. 'While that speeds near empty to the new Jubilee destinations, commuters try vainly to cram themselves into trains that will take them to where they want to go.' An LT spokesman commented wearily, 'People are a bit slow to change their travelling habits.'[40]

The other major project of the 1970s was the extension to Heathrow to replace the airport's dependence on the private car and coach services from airline terminals in west

33. Souvenir ticket for the Jubilee line opening, April 1979.

34. Prince Charles inaugurates the Jubilee line on 30 April 1979, with Bill Maxwell, MD Railways, in the cab at Green Park.

35. Even before the Jubilee line opened, LT chairman Ralph Bennett and GLC leader Horace Cutler 'started work' on the extension for a press call in 1978. Work did not actually start until fifteen years later.

London. Chosen in preference to a BR scheme from Victoria via Feltham, the extension of the Piccadilly from Hounslow West had been started in 1971 and was opened by the Queen on 16 December 1977. Proudly launched as the world's first direct link between the main airport and the centre of a capital city, the two new stations at Hatton Cross and Heathrow Central (now Terminals 1, 2, 3) were built by the cut and cover method. Hardy's designs at platform level were characterized by warm-coloured tiling and wide multi-coloured terrazzo platforms. Tom Eckersley's 'Concorde' tailfin motif and the Imperial Airways 'Speedbird' were the few decorative features beneath the DRU's crisp station name frieze.

Rampant inflation and loss of income from road congestion continued to erode LT's financial position. In 1975 two fare increases were necessary, well above the rate of inflation. In 1976 inflation had risen to 25 per cent while passenger numbers on the Tube dropped by 5 per cent and continued to decline every year until 1982. Car ownership in the capital was still increasing by 1 per cent a year, reaching 64 per cent. The Underground was in decline, staff morale was poor, the travelling environment was strewn with litter and cigarette ends, and crime on the system was rising: for many passengers, stations such as Camden Town, Stockwell and Tooting Bec had become no-go areas at night.

The Ashfield and Pick legacy had endured and helped carry the Underground through the lean post-war years. LT's brand and external communications had remained strong but this obscured an organizational culture that was increasingly inward-looking and self-regarding. The world had moved on and become much more demanding as the need for public subsidy had propelled LT into the political arena. The senior management were to come under fierce scrutiny from politicians of both hues as the need for subsidy became more evident. The Conservatives under the flamboyant, bow-tie-wearing Horace Cutler recaptured control of County Hall in 1977. Cutler's business background was with a family building firm. He was suspicious of big bureaucracies like the GLC and was above all suspicious of London Transport, 'the world's largest public transportation organisation and an albatross round the neck of the capital's ratepayers . . . Tradition and bureaucracy had conditioned too many attitudes, particularly at Board level, and this tended to frustrate change.'[41]

Cutler's concern was justified, supported as it was by a report commissioned under pressure by the LT Board themselves from PA Consulting in 1980. Despite the difficult context of staff shortages, the competition of the private car and declining patronage, the report suggested the executive board were defensive, reactive, focused on supply rather than market demand, demoralized by criticism and inward-looking.[42] Cutler's retrospective view in his memoir was that the performance of the LT board was weak;

36. Jubilee line platform at Baker Street, 1979.

37. Heathrow Central station, opened in 1977, with Tom Eckersley's Concorde decoration on the left.

38. Headboard from the opening-day train on the Heathrow extension, 16 December 1977. Only used for the ceremonial opening attended by the Queen, it featured the combined symbol of the aeroplane and the roundel.

it could not make up its mind whether it was a commercial undertaking or a social service, and it could not make decisions and was insufficiently aggressive in questioning the functional performance of colleagues. 'In all London Transport's thinking was static rather than dynamic.'[43]

Cutler was autocratic and inclined to intervene in executive affairs. Kenneth Robinson's association with Labour was deemed by Cutler unsuitable, so he was encouraged to leave in March 1978. Ralph Bennett, deputy chairman since the early 1970s, was appointed against (Cutler later stated)[44] his better judgement and was sacked in 1980. Strangely, it then proved difficult to find candidates willing to take on the role. The charismatic Freddie Laker had already turned Cutler down. Paul Garbutt, LT Chief Secretary at the time, judged that:

> Cutler would have liked a tough, youngish man from the private sector as the new chairman but such men were not tumbling over themselves to take on a job which three out of the previous four incumbents had had to quit before their time was up and which offered doubtful rewards for years of exposure to political pressures and, as often as not, public abuse.[45]

Nevertheless, the senior management was answerable to the elected politicians. Cutler shook up the executive by undermining them in the press. The publication of the PA Consulting report was greeted by the *Evening News* headline, '"Guilty"! Never has the management of a public service been so coldly exposed and condemned as the Board of London Transport is today.'[46] When Bennett was summarily dismissed, three other Board members followed suit. The *Evening Standard* commented: 'The impression is that LT is managed to some extent by bumbling idiots. It comes as a shock to recall that most of the idiots were actually appointed by Sir Horace.'[47]

Cutler's appointment of a whistle-blowing civil servant, Leslie Chapman,[48] to the Board in 1978 to investigate waste and inefficiency in the organization engulfed LT in a media frenzy that ultimately discredited both parties. Cutler described himself to Chapman as 'sitting on top of a £2 billion-a-year heap and not really knowing what to do next ... the service poor and getting worse.' Chapman's report in July 1979 went for the jugular, maintaining LT was failing to carry out its statutory functions by 'providing an expensive and inefficient service with scruffy vehicles and rolling stock and dirty stations'. His allegations of imminent bankruptcy, widespread waste, inaction on cost-cutting and declining operational performance, and reporting of non-salary benefits – chauffeured limousines, the subsidized officers' dining room at 55 Broadway – made great media copy despite the fact that the auditors investigating his complaints felt that this was quite normal for nationalized industries in the UK. All-out warfare at Board level ensued, with LT officials prepared to concede privately that there was some truth in what Chapman said but closing ranks publicly.

39. The award-winning 'Fly the Tube' poster by Geoff Senior of the FCB Agency, 1978.

40. In 1978 Hannah Dadds became the first woman Underground driver in 115 years of operation.

London: Thursday
November 2 1978
Price: Ten pence

Eventually an interim appointment to the chair was made in 1980. Sir Peter Masefield was already a part-time Board member, with a lifetime of aviation and marketing experience. Masefield was interviewed by the *Accountant*, who described his role as the hottest seat in world transportation in 'an authority that has had so much flak over the previous six months that a public hanging of the Board might have been less gruesome'.[49] Masefield's interim appointment as chairman and chief executive was to last nearly three years. 'Passengers are the purpose of our work,' he said, 'not a tiresome interruption.'[50] Masefield in his memoirs confirmed that 'LT's top management was floundering in a morass of positive disregard for tight financial control and a stubborn refusal to tackle the problems'.[51]

Masefield's corporate experience regrouped the Board and pushed back 'the ultra-right-wing and fearsomely autocratic' Cutler.[52] He lanced the Chapman boil at a dramatic Board meeting in November 1980. He began by saying that he had been 'particularly disappointed to hear on LBC Radio earlier in the day a hostile attack by Mr Chapman' and then played back a tape recording of the whole interview. 'Mr Chapman blames 99 per cent of London Transport's problems on management rather than the unions ... I don't think anything has been done ... been a lot of talk but hasn't been anything done.'[53] 'The chairman said he welcomed individual criticism at the board table but he was not prepared to accept that a member of his board should criticize the board in public, without forewarning, whilst a member. [Chapman] swept his papers into his bag and left the meeting, never to return. Peter had handled the situation with attention to detail, meticulous prior planning, and with his usual considerable style.'[54] The tactically inept messenger had been shot, but his message, nonetheless, contained a deal of truth. Masefield recalled the worsening state of LT's finances: 'In comparison with such cities as Paris or New York, London's transport was underfunded to an unbelievable degree ... LT had become a vast edifice cracking at the seams, propped up by ever rising fares and with the morale of its employees sinking rapidly.'[55]

Tony Ridley was appointed from Hong Kong as Managing Director (Railways). He recalled open warfare in the press between the GLC and LT: 'It was completely dysfunctional with the professionals and the politicians fighting like hell.' Ridley found LT to be 'inefficient and that's what got up [Cutler's] nose because he was going to have to increase fares in a way he didn't want because costs were out of control, that's why he put Leslie Chapman on the Board ... ridership on the Underground had been gradually declining from 720 million a year to 498 million in 1982.'[56]

The neglect of the Tube and low expectations of its long-suffering passengers in this period were even reflected in the bleakness of punk music and the angst of New Wave.

41. Publicity photograph highlighting the luggage space on the new Piccadilly line trains for the Heathrow extension, 1977.

42. This dramatic headline announcing the appointment of Leslie Chapman to the LT Board in 1978 hardly enhanced his prospects of success.

A diverse range of bands found inspiration in the darkness, mystery and menace of the scruffy Underground of the late 1970s. Vic Godard's Subway Sect used a photomontage of the band about to be run over by a train at Piccadilly Circus on the cover of their first single, based on an official Underground publicity photo. Press reports of violence against Underground staff were common in the late 1970s, and Godard remembers Camden Town station in particular as an unpredictable space patrolled by groups of violent skinheads. It is precisely this that is portrayed in the Jam's 1978 mini-epic song of aspiration and random violence 'Down In The Tube Station At Midnight'. Anton Corbijn's choice of a dark corner of Lancaster Gate station for Joy Division's first London photo session a year later references a similar view.[57] An apt illustration of the Tube's appearance at this time was in the film *An American Werewolf in London* (1981), where the central character rides a train full of punks and makes one of his first attacks as a werewolf prowling though Tottenham Court Road station after the last train. A more integrated approach to crime prevention was pursued in the wake of a working party report in 1986. This sought to get behind often sensationalized media reports and identify effective and targeted preventative measures: 'scruffy, run down, dimly lit, dirty and vandalised stations project an aura of criminality and provoke passenger fear, whether warranted or not'.[58]

Confidence in the Underground had been further eroded by the Moorgate disaster. At 8.46 a.m. on 28 February 1975, a six-car train from Drayton Park on the Northern City line approached the Moorgate terminus. Instead of braking, the train seemed to accelerate through the platform and into the 20-metre-long overrun tunnel. The train was travelling at about 40 mph as it ploughed through a sand-drag, demolished the

43. Picture sleeves featuring the Tube from singles by The Jam and Subway Sect, 1978.

44. Sir Peter Masefield with British Rail Chairman Sir Peter Parker at the opening of King's Cross Thameslink station, 1981.

buffers and hit the tunnel end wall. The driver was last seen standing upright, looking straight ahead with his hand on the controls. The first car, 52 feet long, was buckled into a v-shape just 20 feet long as the second car rode under it and the third car rode up over the second. Forty-three people were killed at the scene, either from impact or suffocation, the greatest loss of life on the Underground up to that time. The cause of the incident has never been satisfactorily explained. Driver Newsome had £300 in his pocket to buy his daughter a car after his shift and had asked his colleagues at Drayton Park to save him some sugar for his tea break on return. The jury at the coroner's inquest returned a verdict of 'accidental death'.[59]

At the time of the accident, speed-controlled train stops were being put into position on terminus sidings across the Underground, after six incidents (including two in which two drivers had lost their lives) since the Aldwych shuttle overran the sand-drag in 1955. Dead ends on the network had, before Moorgate, been highlighted as a potential risk, notably four years before following the death of a driver at Tooting Broadway. It still took nine years after the accident for all the 'Moorgate' protection measures to be installed.[60]

In terms of passenger numbers, the Underground had hit the bottom in 1982 with 498 million annual passenger journeys, a decline from 720 million in 1948. The policy of office relocation was reversed by the new Thatcher government. As deep-piled foundations for offices became the norm, the annual cost of safeguarding property through the City on the line of the unbuilt second phase of the Jubilee line extension had risen by 1980 to £10 million.[61] Dr Ridley remembered that 'with that decline there was not a cat in hell's chance of us getting any money out of the government and indeed we gave away the reserved rights of way for the [extension of] the Fleet line ... There was a Board decision to sell off the land.'[62]

'Fares Fair' and beyond

If the Cutler years had been difficult, the re-election of Labour to County Hall in the 1981 election, followed the day afterwards by Ken Livingstone's coup d'état to replace the moderate Andrew McIntosh as Labour leader, was the beginning of a fight to the death between Livingstone's municipal socialist GLC and Thatcher's free-marketeering Conservative government. London Transport was

45. Aftermath of the Moorgate crash, February 1975.

46. Original drawing for a Jak cartoon from 1981: 'Red Ken' famously always travelled by public transport, here with the communist star flying alongside the GLC coat of arms. Jak was the *Evening Standard*'s cartoonist from 1952 until his death in 1997.

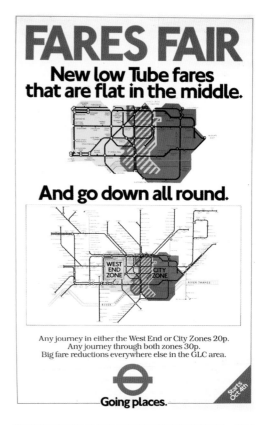

to be caught in the crossfire between County Hall and the Palace of Westminster, but it was also to benefit from having a stern advocate on its side. 'Red Ken's' more radical causes attracted a venomous opprobrium, the ferocity of which still surprises thirty years later, but he was a strong advocate for public transport's critical importance to the vitality and viability of the capital. The struggle over fares in 1981-2 was to prove a watershed for transport thinking in the capital. By the time Livingstone became London's first elected mayor in May 2000, politicians were being supported by consensus in the business community on the need to invest in public transport if London was to thrive. The origins of this, as well as the Oyster card and the GLA's strategic brief for all modes of transport, can be traced back to the 'Fares Fair' controversy and its aftermath.

'Fares Fair' had been a central plank of the Labour manifesto in 1981; indeed the municipal socialists around Livingstone had even flirted with making public transport free. In power, a reduction in bus and Tube fares by one-third, simplified by a zonal system rather than point-to-point fares, was implemented in October 1981. *City Limits*, a radical new listings magazine for London, was launched at the same time as 'Fares Fair': 'Since this is our first issue, we thought we'd launch with some local travel news and a brief guide to the socialization of London Transport on behalf of all who travel on her.' It described the new zonal fares and then the intent and context of the new policy:

> All of which is extremely good news if you've spent a lifetime waiting for London Transport, trying to decode its fare structures and fainting at the cost. Not only does it mean cheaper simpler fares, but with more people encouraged back on to public transport and therefore fewer private cars on the road, it should soon mean improved services.[63]

47. Dave Wetzel, GLC Transport Committee Chairman (left) and GLC Leader Ken Livingstone outside County Hall promoting 'Keep Fares Fair', February 1982.

48. London Transport 'Fares Fair' poster, 1981.

49. 'Keep Fares Fair' GLC campaign leaflet, 1982.

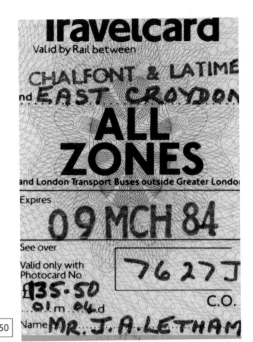

As a result, daily patronage of buses and the Tube jumped from 5.5 million to 6 million journeys. But 'Fares Fair' also attracted a storm of protest from domestic ratepayers who resented paying higher rates for a transport system used by non-payers such as commuters and tourists, and from businesses concerned at the high costs of rent and rates in London. The Conservative-controlled outer London Borough of Bromley was encouraged to contest the legality of such fare reductions under the terms of the Transport Act (1969). Undoubtedly though, behind this legal position, was a desire to cut 'Red Ken' down to size.[64] Bromley took their case to the High Court, where Lord Denning upheld their appeal. The GLC appealed to the House of Lords and controversially lost in December 1981. The Law Lords ruled that an average 32 per cent reduction in fares by London Transport and the supplementary rate levied to pay for it was illegal. Coverage of the case saw the two sides characterized as the forces of reaction lined up against the municipal socialists of Livingstone's GLC.

In the wake of the ruling, Ken Livingstone predicted 'a major and dramatic contraction of transport in London ... We have three months to save London Transport ... there could be a 200 per cent rise in fares, loss of 15,000 jobs [one-quarter] in London Transport, and the scrapping of whole bus and Underground routes.' The chairman, Sir Peter Masefield, suggested a 'loss of passengers of between 30 and 50 per cent'. By contrast, Margaret Thatcher welcomed the ruling and said the 'GLC's action was clearly a breach of its duty to London ratepayers and wrong in law', while the transport secretary said 'this crisis is entirely the fault of the GLC who have managed in seven months of folly to create financial chaos'.[65] Bromley councillors celebrated 'a wonderful Christmas present for London and Londoners, they should be dancing in the streets tonight'.[66] *The Economist*, not noted for socialist credentials, had commented after Denning's original judgement:

> What the GLC has been doing in London has been radical ... but it is by no means eccentric or unique. Fares have been cut similarly in Sweden and, in Britain, on British Rail and the nationalised bus company ... Ministers of the crown, and voters, should not cheer when they have had to rely on judges inadequately to do their work for them.[67]

The GLC mounted a media 'Campaign for London's Transport', pointing out that even with the reduction, at 46 per cent the subsidy level for public transport in London would have been well below that of New York, Berlin, Milan, Brussels and Paris, but following the Law Lords' decision it fell to 27 per cent; 'Other major cities in the world regard their public transport systems as much a social service as hospitals and education. They feel that high levels of subsidy are the only practical means of running a big city efficiently.' The advertisement included a cartoon, 'London Transport apologises for the Law Lords' decision – normal extortion will resume shortly'.[68] A 'Can't Pay, Won't Pay' protest on 21 March 1982 resulted in the GLC Transport Committee chairman,

50. Travelcards were first introduced in 1983.

51. Travelcard promotion 1986.

Dave Wetzel, being arrested for fare evasion as he and other protesters declared themselves unwilling to pay more than the old fare,[69] while Wetzel memorably described the Law Lords as 'vandals in ermine'.[70]

To comply with the Law Lords' ruling, London Transport was obliged to double fares, reduce services and introduce a severe economy drive from March 1982. In the following year, daily journeys on bus and the Underground declined from six million to five million. Even the Conservatives conceded that fares were now too high. The GLC successfully tested a 'balanced' plan in the High Court in January 1983. In March, a 25 per cent reduction brought fares back to roughly where they had been in 1981 before 'Fares Fair' and attracted 15 per cent more passengers back on to London Transport.

This switchback ride had seen three major fares changes within a year. Nevertheless, 'Fares Fair' had demonstrated that cheaper fares did indeed attract greater patronage and had excited significant debate about the wider social and economic role of public transport. It was an important moment in promoting a wider understanding that the state of public transport in the capital was linked closely to its economic viability and civic health. The doubling of fares had confirmed that subsidy was necessary to avoid fares reaching a level damaging to London's economy. A second legacy was the simplification of ticketing represented by zonal fares and the introduction of the Travelcard. Ticketing in London had long been based on 'point-to-point' or stage fares, where you paid a set amount for a trip from A to B, with separate tickets for bus and mainline rail journeys. Flat-rate fares within inner and outer zones were introduced in 1981 and then further simplified in 1982. Only the radical shake-up of 'Fares Fair' could have changed the Underground's long-term mind-set against zonal ticketing.

The political legacy of 'Fares Fair' was war between national and London government and the vindictive abolition of the GLC in 1984, leaving London as the only capital city without an elected authority. Looking back on the GLC years in 1998, Livingstone reflected:

> All the things we did with the GLC – making policy on gay rights, ethnic minorities, the environment, meeting Gerry Adams, they're all mainstream policies now ... It was too in-your-face, and a lot of people felt I wasn't interested in ordinary people, but the policies were right. We were ahead of our time.[71]

The Travelcard had come out of a fraternal visit to the Paris Metro in the mid-1970s led by the Board member for planning, David Quarmby, 'of which their Carte Orange[72] ticket system was one of the striking features'.[73] This series of ticketing innovations reduced the need to queue up to buy a ticket for each journey, encouraged unlimited Tube and bus travel, made transactions fewer and easier and, by putting a ceiling on daily travel costs, reduced the marginal cost of each journey, thereby promoting greater use of public transport. The Travelcard was a first innovative step in ticketing and payment which would eventually to lead to the Oyster card in 2003.

52. Keep London Transport Local – GLC campaign badge, c.1983.

THE LOWER DEPTHS

Photographer Wozzy Dias became fascinated with the unique environment of the Underground in 1980. He spent the next decade photographing enigmatic and atmospheric moments in the lives of strangers on the network, with its crumbling infrastructure as a backdrop. The photographs creatively capture a grim and low point for the Tube. At a time when passenger numbers were rising fast, the system felt almost overwhelmed by graffiti, neglect and underinvestment. Looking back more than twenty years later the oppressive, decaying environment is evocative but almost unrecognizable. In retrospect, Wozzy Dias' work gives a detached overview of the system in decline. His use of duotone processing in particular combined the aesthetics of film noir with a keen photojournalistic eye.

53. Tottenham Court Road, 1990

54. Litter-filled subway at Leytonstone, 1985.

55. Graffiti-covered train on the Central Line at Ongar, 1980s.

56. Buskers on the Piccadilly line in the mid-1980s.

57. Busker at Leicester Square station, 1987.

58. Commuters on the Piccadilly line on the day Margaret Thatcher resigned, 1990.

Symptomatic of the Underground's long-term neglect and growing political importance, the LT Board room continued to be a difficult arena in the Livingstone years. To outflank the executive members when necessary, the Board was packed with six non-executive members appointed by Livingstone. There were regular conflicts between the municipal socialists and the four executive Board members. Dr Keith Bright, previously chief executive of the Huntley & Palmers food group, was appointed Chairman when Sir Peter Masefield retired in 1982. 'Keith was a real scrapper,' recalls Tony Ridley, 'and he fought that Board, day in and day out, and wasn't going to let them get away with what he thought was interfering and politicizing.'[74] Bright's difficult brief was to reduce costs at a time when patronage of the system was rising steadily.

Attention switched from new lines to the suburbs to the backlog of maintenance in the central area. Against the background of tight funding, increasingly scruffy stations and an unreliable service, trains, escalators and lifts were an urgent priority. The new Labour administration at the GLC in 1981 approved a rolling programme to modernize 140 stations and work started with £65 million for sixteen major schemes on mostly central stations. Part of the argument for this expenditure was that it would attract patronage back to the Underground. London Transport Architects and their consultants placed their work in the tradition established by Frank Pick: 'In the station work of the 1980s, London

59. David Gentleman's 1979 design for the Northern line platforms at Charing Cross based on woodcuts depicting the building of the Eleanor Cross by Edward I in the 13th century.

60. Artist Eduardo Paolozzi and LT architect Duncan Lamb inspecting mosaic mural progress at Tottenham Court Road, 1983.

Underground sought to re-establish that tradition as part of a new design strategy.'[75] The resulting designs were exuberant and highly individual, designed by the LU architect in collaboration with external consultants and artists, an encouraging but limited facelift.

Later in the programme, there was a return to quieter, classic functional designs. The new station at Heathrow's Terminal 4 in 1986 took the brown terrazzo up the walls, set off by the Piccadilly line blue name band and station roundels. The Angel's precariously narrow island platforms, dating back to the City & South London Railway in the 1900s, were replaced in 1993 with a completely rebuilt station, served by the longest escalators yet on the system. In all, Mike Duffie, LT Architect, garnered twelve architectural and preservation awards between 1984 and 1992 for the stations programme.[76]

Tony Ridley was initially obliged to concentrate on refurbishment and efficiencies rather than new construction. Discredited by press exposure of wasteful practices, train maintenance was moved from the Acton Depot to line depots, and one-person operation was finally introduced, an agreement with the unions

61 Decaying platform area at Bond Street station in 1977.

62. Bond Street station platform decoration after refurbishment in 1983.

having been concluded ten years before but not implemented. This began the phasing-out of guards on trains, finally to be concluded in January 2000.[77] The growth of graffiti, a craze inherited from the New York Subway in the mid-1980s, was to lead to an unintentional change in the whole look of the network from the 1990s. The unfinished aluminium surface of the 'silver' trains was the perfect canvas for spray paint. The system seemed to be spiralling out of control, with many trains covered in 'tags'. In response, the Underground introduced a new red, white and blue corporate livery using baked-on tri-pack paint, designed to be resistant to spray cans, with enhanced security at train depots and stabling points. A long campaign to reduce fare evasion and increase revenue began with the installation of a new automatic fare-collection system. The Underground Ticketing System (UTS) swept away all previous machines and gates and installed new self-service ticket machines from 1987 onwards at every station, with entry and exit gates in the central area.

63. Cleaning graffiti at King's Cross station, 1987.

64. Graffiti removal on A60/62 stock at Neasden Depot, 1986.

65 66

Although the sharply contrasting political agendas of conservative and radical politicians made the GLC period highly contentious, the emergence of strategic polices for London was of great significance. 'Although it was in macro terms, a period of declining traffic, there was an energy and a vision really from the GLC at the time that was saying, "what are we going to do now with London Transport?" that the government never did.'[78] In the wake of the abolition of the GLC, the strategic vacuum created in London was filled by better inter-borough cooperation and, more significantly, by an increasingly effective lobby by business for investment in public transport in London. The influence of new bodies such as London First[79] did much to create consensus in the business community which lobbied for consistent government funding of the capital's transport and, ultimately successfully, for Crossrail.

67

Having hit the bottom, the Underground was to benefit from the remarkable and unpredicted turnaround in London's fortunes from the mid-1980s as the city's population and economy began to grow again. Fuelled by the Big Bang, the deregulation of London's financial markets on 27 October 1986, the Stock Exchange was transformed, letting 'the foreigner into what had been a largely closed shop of stuffed shirts'.[80] The Big Bang secured the City's status as a global centre for financial services and fostered a turnaround in London's fortunes, underpinning its renewed world city status – a focus for economic investment, the creative industries, tourism and ultimately the Olympics. Moreover, it also brought a political consensus on the primacy of London in the British economy and the vital need for a single strategic authority, under an elected mayor.

65 and 66. Angel station's original island platform still in use in 1988, and after rebuilding in 1992.

67. Dr Tony Ridley in 1985, when Managing Director (Railways).

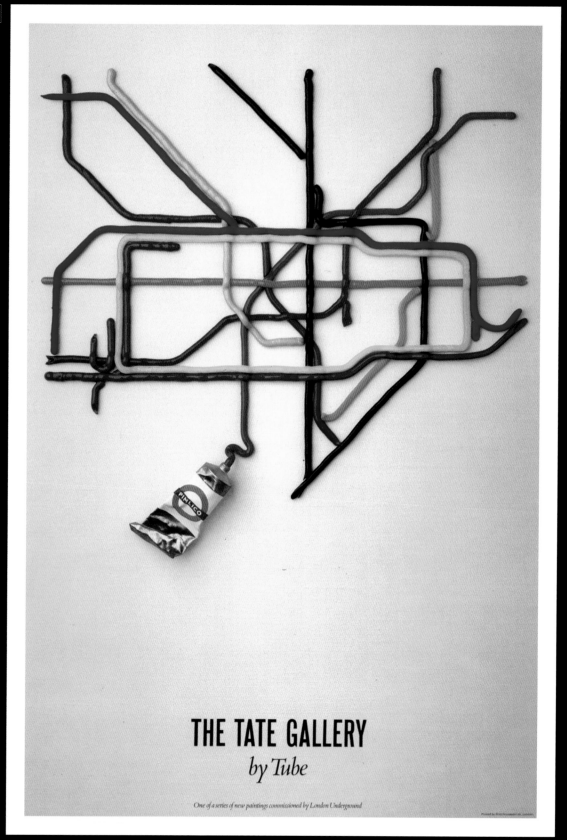

CHAPTER 6

OUT OF DISASTER

King's Cross fire

London Transport returned to central government control in 1984, a nationalization that ran counter to the Thatcher government's policy of privatization of state-owned industries. This was an indication of just how bitter her battle with Livingstone's GLC had become, but it also conceded that London Transport could not be readily privatized. London Regional Transport,[1] as it now became, found it had swapped GLC political accountability for Treasury micro-management. Change continued to be imposed upon LT by financial masters directed by politicians who instinctively challenged the public sector's monopoly and mistrusted the management's ability to change. In-house services such as catering and engineering as well as the bus services were scrutinized and reorganized to enable private-sector tendering. One-person operation was introduced on three lines, and income increased through the new ticketing system.

As Managing Director of London Underground from 1980, Tony Ridley found by the middle of the decade that his job had changed from 'Stop the decline' to 'How are we going to cope with this enormous growth in traffic?'[2] Congestion and passenger numbers had risen steadily with economic recovery and the benefits of the Travelcard.

> The guys I inherited, most of them, were wonderful people; very professional, hard-working, incredibly loyal, with only one basic failure. Anyone who had not worked thirty-five years for London Underground couldn't tell them anything, most particularly the new Managing Director who'd just come from the new Hong Kong metro. So I had a personal – I won't say battle – but I was looking for ways to open their eyes.[3]

The engineering-led culture of the Underground with which Tony Ridley was grappling found its nemesis at the King's Cross fire in 1987.[4] LT had been cautious about running ahead of public opinion on banning smoking and there was still an influential pro-smoking lobby.[5] On 21 June 1981, burning rubbish at Goodge Street

---

I. The best-selling Underground poster of the 1980s, 'Tate Gallery by Tube', by David Booth of Fine White Line, 1987.

station caused a major incident in which one man died and sixteen were taken to hospital. The inspector's report gave the probable cause as a burning cigarette end and recommended smoking be banned on trains. LT took their time, but on 9 July 1984 smoking on trains was banned for a twelve-month experimental period. There was little public opposition, and another major fire, at Oxford Circus on 23 November 1984, overtook the experiment. The fire started in contractors' materials in a cross-passage store and spread to the northbound Victoria line station tunnel; 700 passengers were escorted from smoke-filled tunnels and stopped trains, fourteen were taken to hospital, £2.5 million worth of damage was caused, and the Victoria line platforms were closed for over three weeks.[6] A full ban on smoking was implemented on all stations below ground level, the ban on smoking on trains indefinitely extended, and a hurried clearance of contractors' rubbish implemented across the system.[7]

A Fire Safety Task Force was set up, but by late 1987 its impetus had ebbed. Significantly, the recommendations of the London Fire Brigade (LFB) after Oxford Circus had not been followed, most notably the need to call the Brigade immediately on the report of any fire. Following an incident at Baker Street in August 1985, the chief fire officer had again requested the Brigade be called immediately fire or smoke was reported.[8] However, the Underground staff handbook still required staff to tackle the blaze themselves before calling the fire service.

This instruction was to have a disastrous consequence at King's Cross station on 18 November 1987. At about 7.15 p.m., just as the evening rush began to subside, a member of staff extinguished a burning tissue using a rolled-up magazine at the bottom of the Victoria line escalator.[9] If the Fire Brigade had been called for this 'false alarm' they would have been on site for what was to come next. At about 7.25 p.m., an unknown smoker made his or her way up escalator 4 from the Piccadilly line, lit up on the way out and discarded the match. This fell between the steps and the wooden skirting board on the right-hand side of the escalator, lodging in the running track on which the maple wood steps ran. The track was well greased and had not been cleaned for many years. It incorporated readily combustible

2

2. Smoking was both an issue of safety and cleanliness across the Underground. A Northern line smoking car before cleaning at the end of a working day, 1978.

material left by thousands of passengers: matches, paper, sweet wrappers, hair. A small fire started in this greasy, flammable cocktail. It was noticed by a passenger halfway up the escalator and reported to the ticket office. Station staff investigated the Northern line escalators in error. A second passenger reported smoke but, nothing being visible, the booking clerk returned to the ticket office. The fire spread and was carried upwards by the moving escalator. Another passenger saw flames beneath the escalator, pushed the diamond stop button and shouted down for people to get off.

Two British Transport policemen descended the escalator and saw smoke and a four-inch flame about a third of the way down. One returned to the surface to call the LFB, as his radio did not work below ground. The other stopped escalators 5 and 6. The LFB dispatched four appliances to King's Cross at 7.36 p.m. Staff blocked the foot of the Piccadilly escalators with builders' materials and redirected passengers to the surface by the Victoria line escalators. A staff member investigating the fire in the escalator machine room passed but failed to operate the water-fogging controls which would have doused or controlled the fire. The Piccadilly line controller learned of the blaze from the Transport Police while on the phone about another issue. Ten minutes after it had started, the blaze was already too fierce to tackle with a CO_2 extinguisher. The booking office staff were evacuated as the first appliance from the Soho fire station arrived. Firemen saw a blaze on the escalator, with four-foot flames licking up the handrail, and breathing apparatus and a jet were called for. On the lower concourse a passenger saw flames rapidly spreading up the escalator. As the timber steps, the rubber handrail and the varnished plywood sides heated up, the fire was reaching a critical point. Unaware, passengers were still coming up the halted Victoria line escalators from the last Piccadilly line train to stop in the station at 7.43 p.m.

At 7.45 p.m., sixteen minutes after the first reports, still not a drop of water had been applied to the fire. Suddenly it flashed over, erupting up the escalator and engulfing the ticket hall like a tornado, with intense heat and dense black smoke billowing across the concourse and surrounding passages. One passenger at the top of a Victoria line escalator heard a 'whoosh' and saw flames shoot across from the top of the Piccadilly line escalators to where he was standing, followed instantly by thick black smoke. A policeman near the top of the Victoria line escalators directing passengers saw a jet of flames shoot up from the Piccadilly line escalator shaft, hit the ceiling of the ticket hall and travel along the ceiling towards him, knocking him off balance. He crawled back to the Victoria line escalators under the thick black smoke and shouted to passengers to keep low and get out by the nearest ticket hall exit. Fire crews, police officers, staff and passengers retreated rapidly back down the Victoria escalator or to the exits. Smoke and fumes overcame a fireman evacuating passengers from the ticket hall;

DEPARTMENT OF TRANSPORT

Investigation into the King's Cross Underground Fire

Desmond Fennell OBE QC

HER MAJESTY'S STATIONERY OFFICE

3. The Fennell Report into the fire was produced with unusual speed in November 1988, less than a year after the incident. It had a huge impact on safety across the network.

4

5

4. The emergency services above ground at King's Cross on the night of the fire, 18 November 1987.

5. King's Cross ticket hall the day after the fire: ITN *News at Ten* reported that 'in the main ticket hall, the intense heat cracked concrete. Survivors said it was like an oven, floor, walls and ceiling were alight, and hours after the fire was out the metal ticket machines were still too hot to touch ... the inferno stripped tiles from the walls and dripped molten plastic from the ceilings.'

his body was found later by the exit. Most of the thirty-one casualties died around this moment of flashover. Those who escaped dived under the flames and somehow found their way out through the black smoke, many with severe burns. At street level screaming passengers began to emerge from the station entrances, accompanied by thick black smoke.

Firefighters attempting to re-enter the ticketing hall likened the conditions to climbing down into a volcano.[10] Television news showed firemen in the dark November evening peering into the dense smoke as it poured up the steps of an exit. It was not until 1.46 a.m. that the fire was confirmed as out. In all there were thirty-one deaths and more than sixty injuries ranging from severe burns to smoke inhalation. It was the worst incident on the Underground since the Moorgate disaster in 1975.

Chairman and Managing Director of the Underground, Tony Ridley, faced a barrage of media scrutiny in the aftermath. This was to be a hellish period of incessant public and media criticism and then the damning evidence of the Fennell Inquiry. 'After King's Cross … every fireman, every policeman was a hero and even the most humble LU employee … was regarded almost as though they were a murderer.'[11] It was to end with Ridley and Bright being told to resign. The real anger of Londoners was expressed by Frank Dobson, MP for Holborn and St Pancras, in the Commons the next day. He blamed staff cuts and totally inadequate fire and evacuation training and called on the government to 'change to a management who would take safety seriously'.[12] The effect on the Underground in the following years was to be profound. The fire at King's Cross brought a pace and depth to organizational change inconceivable without the impetus of disaster. It also proved to be a watershed moment in reversing the corrosive lack of investment in repairs and renewals of the previous two decades.

The Fennell Report, published in November 1988, provided a forensic insight into both the fire and the management ethos and organizational culture of London Underground itself. The Report noted Ridley's eloquent account of the changes and restructuring already undertaken in the wake of the fire but demanded that, 'a much more searching and outward-looking approach to safety management is required, which will demand a willingness to embrace new ideas'. The report asserted that the old idea of the engineers running a railway must be replaced with recognition at all levels of the responsibility of providing a mass passenger transport service for the public.[13]

The crux of the Fennell Inquiry was the testing of the Underground's whole approach to fire safety. Ridley concedes that he failed to convince the Inquiry of the Underground's judgement that the primary risk to public safety was the rapidly increasing overcrowding, rather than escalator fire, and reckoned without the adversarial nature of the Inquiry.[14] When questioned, Ridley did not agree with the court's assertion that 'fire should be regarded as an unacceptable hazard to be eliminated … In effect he was advocating fire precaution rather than fire prevention … A mass passenger transport service cannot tolerate the concept of an acceptable level of fire hazard.' Fennell's conclusions noted that London Underground had a good safety record – 'considerably safer than ... almost every other form of transport' – but had a blind spot about fire on escalators not being a potential danger to passengers.[15]

The most damaging symptom of the lack of a management culture, let alone a safety culture, across the Underground was the unpreparedness of the station staff at King's Cross for a fire. There was no evacuation plan for the station, ticket office staff had no fire training, and the training of the two gateline staff on duty in the use of fire extinguishers was 'inadequate and likely to have been stale'.[16] The manual water-fogging system under the escalators that might have put out or delayed the fire in its early stages was not operated.[17] Safety officers, who found the same problems with poor housekeeping and electrical wiring in machine rooms year after year, were unable to get their message across to senior management and thought of themselves as 'voices in the wilderness'.[18] These failings were compounded by poor communication and control across all the emergency services, which tended to arrive and work independently. An overstretched organization, the Underground simply did not give fire the priority it demanded and did not believe fires on escalators were sufficient risk or a priority as

6

they wrestled with underfunding, overcrowding and an unreliable train service. It was not as if fires were unknown on the Underground. There had been forty-six escalator fires on the Underground between 1956 and 1988, the majority of which had been attributed to smokers' materials. The MH-type escalators installed at King's Cross in 1940 were noted as particularly prone to fire. Indeed the detailed examination of escalator number 4 evidenced many previous small-scale fires that had burned themselves out.

Denis Tunnicliffe had been appointed by Ridley as MD of London Underground to share the burden of changing the Underground and started work in August 1988, after the fire but before the publication of the Fennell Report. With the sudden departures of Ridley and Bright in November 1988, it fell to Tunnicliffe to effect the profound cultural change called for by Fennell and, in the short term, to handle the press; 'These thirty-one people will not have died in vain ... We got across contrition, we got across commitment to change, we got

6. Wooden MH-type escalator at Holborn, about 1980. A fire on one of these escalators had closed the station for four hours in 1985.

across apology and that we will pay compensation as if we were liable.'[19] Coming from the aviation industry – 'if it can happen, it will happen' – the primacy of safety was second nature to Tunnicliffe.[20] He was also untainted by being new to the railway industry and able to deploy what he describes as 'heroic naivety': 'Why do we need to change it? Because we've killed thirty-one people.'[21]

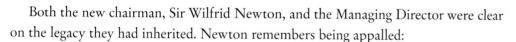

> The (Fennell) Report cut through that in a way nobody or nothing else could. And you could face old-timers and say, 'You're really serious about that question?' It allowed a total discontinuity as to how people thought about safety. People were saying, 'You can't do that, you know,' and I said, 'Sorry, the world has changed.' We had lost our licence to operate, the informal licence that society gives you. That needed regaining at all costs, and money was thrown at the problem.[22]

Both the new chairman, Sir Wilfrid Newton, and the Managing Director were clear on the legacy they had inherited. Newton remembers being appalled:

> It was worse than I expected: the state of the kit was bad, the electrical installation was dangerous, it had landslips. It was an organization that was criticized by the press every day; the morale in the managers and the station staff was bad. When I came to London and went round the Underground, it was a shambles, it really was. And we found some appalling inefficiency.[23]

Alongside this, Tunnicliffe recognized the strong legacy of the Underground: 'I had a great respect for the areas of professionalism where they were good, but on the operational side there was a happening: people happened to turn up and the railway happened to run. It was a management desert.'[24] The customer and safety now replaced engineering as the organization's priorities. The pace of change was fast, and the restructuring of the Underground into business units based on each line and 'centurions' – station and train crew managers responsible for around one hundred staff – unlocked the qualities of loyalty and dedication long recognized in Underground staff.

> Somebody worked out we needed one hundred managers, one hundred centurions. They said, 'There aren't one hundred centurions,' and I said, 'We'll find them.' I think the youngest was twenty-three and the oldest was sixty-two; people who it had never crossed their mind they'd have a proper management role became centurions. They weren't appointed by seniority, and the world was going to stop. At a stroke we destroyed the seniority system for middle management.[26]

The public sector as a whole was going through major cultural change at this time. Privatization and compulsory competitive tendering (CCT) were driving efficiencies, cutting costs and demanding better definition of public services. Above all, this had

7. MD Denis Tunnicliffe in a publicity photograph for the Jubilee line extension, after opening in 1999.

SOMETHING FOR EVERYONE

at Clapham. Part of this became the London Transport Collection displayed at Syon Park from 1972. Eventually in 1980 the fully fledged London Transport Museum opened at Covent Garden. Enthusiasm for the Tube, though, was essentially a sub-set of the world of the railway enthusiast, with its connotations of anoraks and spotters' handbooks.

The picture today is very different. The introduction of the internet in the 1980s has allowed a broad cross-section of people to develop an interest in Underground poster design, or the Tube map, or seek out Tube-themed souvenirs and reproduction prints. The emergence of a host of social media platforms in the last decade has enabled

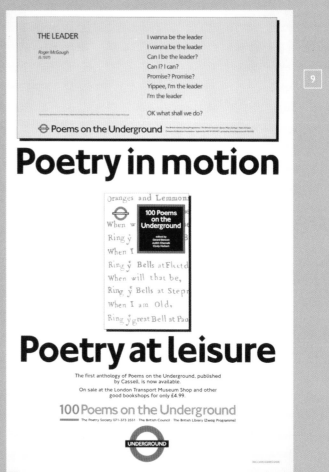

In the early 1960s there were relatively few avenues open to someone with more than a passing interest in the London Underground. You could join the London Underground Railway Society, formed in 1961, and receive their typed newsletter *Underground News*, and you would probably have visited London Transport's open day at Neasden Depot for the Metropolitan Railway centenary celebrations in 1963. You might have seen the British Transport Films documentary *One Hundred Years Underground* or caught a newsreel or two at your local cinema about the start of work on the new Victoria line. From 1962 you could visit the Museum of British Transport

8. Ian Allan's *ABC of London Transport Railways*, 1950. An essential guide for trainspotters.

9. Poster advertising the *100 Poems on the Underground* anthology in 1991. This initiative was launched by American writer Judith Chernaik in 1986 to bring poetry to a wider audience.

Tube-ophiles from around the world to discuss and share interests in design and architecture, disused and haunted stations, tiling patterns and moquette, along with the best route for visiting all 270 stations in one day.

Transport for London has developed powerful information tools such as the online Journey Planner (averaging 6 million visit a month in 2012), which smooth the journeys of millions of passengers each day. A myriad of third-party applications based on live TfL data, global positioning and the ability to share with online friends has moved enthusiasm for the way London and its transport works firmly into the mainstream.

The Tube itself has become a superbrand. The red and blue roundel symbol and Harry Beck's diagrammatic map are recognized throughout the world. London Transport Museum has undoubtedly contributed to the higher profile of the network's design heritage, while TfL works hard licensing images inspired by the Underground for clothing, furniture, housewares, stationery and other products, broadening the reach of the brand. London Underground itself has actively conserved the historic features of the Tube's environment whilst modernizing it. English Heritage added another 16 Tube stations to their Listed Buildings register in 2011, bring the total to 72. Art on the Underground provides a programme of contemporary art that enriches the Tube environment, while poems displayed in Tube carriages have engaged the minds of passengers for over 25 years.

10

12

11

10. TfL Home page featuring the Journey Planner, 2012.

11. British Design Classics stamp series included the Underground map in 2009.

12. Sofa covered in a patchwork of Underground moquette, manufactured by Squint in 2010.

brought in private-sector management models and the awareness that the customer was now king. From his time at British Airways (BA, privatized in 1987) Tunnicliffe brought convictions about not only safety but also customer-led services, heroic leadership and teamwork with shared values and goals to the radical restructuring of the Underground. Such was the impetus of change, his team was selected with minimal process. He just asked chosen individuals to get on with the job: 'The line general managers were a copy of what we'd done in BA. We'd created market-centre managers, and each had a chunk of the world, and I moderated their demands and then managed the whole thing.'[27]

Meanwhile, a huge programme of work was carried out to make the system safer. Wood was removed from escalators; trains were refurbished to remove flammable materials and painted with fire-resistant paint. A 'Dads' Army' of retired staff was recruited to inspect all rooms underground every hour until the automatic alarms required by the Fire Brigade could be fitted. Every nook and cranny of the system was cleared of rubbish to reduce its flammability. The cleaning regime was doubled to tackle the fire hazard of uncontrolled litter and to demonstrate ownership of the stations by cleaning floors, walls, ceilings and ventilation shafts. Help points for passengers, better lighting, closed-circuit cameras with video recording, a new intolerance of busking and an increased British Transport Police presence asserted that the Underground was now an owned and managed environment. Crime on the network was as a result declining by the early 1990s.[28]

In the 1980s and 1990s, however, the Underground was not just simply associated with tragedy. Through the medium of the pop video it gained a new kind of media exposure, the first signs of the 'new coolness' which the Underground has acquired in the early twenty-first century. The process started inconspicuously with The Chills, big stars in their native New Zealand, and continued with established artists such as Boy George, the Eurythmics, Kate Bush, The Prodigy, Suede and, more recently, Duffy. Notable visual nods to the Tube on album cover art include Madness outside Chalk Farm station,[29] a painting of the band Blur inside a District line train and a modified roundel by the cult indie band The Times.

As the end of 1990 approached, the Underground was facing a financial crisis once more. Ticket revenues and property development had been hit by the national economic recession, but the main cause was the huge cost of safety work after King's Cross. Tunnicliffe took around 180 selected managers out of their day-to-day jobs to form thirty value analysis teams (VATs), which scrutinized every aspect of the business and pulled the results into

13. Organizational change at the Underground extended to all aspects of the business. Westminster station staff in new uniforms, January 2000.

14. Night worker on the cleaning team in the tunnel at Piccadilly Circus station, 1998.

15   16

the Company Plan: 'a programme for radical change in pursuit of higher safety and performance standards, lower operating costs and better planned capital expenditure'. This unleashed energy, commitment, talent and operational experience from all corners of a siloed institution to radically rethink every aspect of the organization in the interests of safety, economy and efficiency.

An endorsement of the progress made by 1991 came from an unexpected quarter: the Monopolies and Mergers Commission. While it confirmed the public perception of 'an erratic, overcrowded and poorly maintained service', it stated that this was the result of 'chronic underinvestment' both in new capacity and in the renewal of existing assets. Their report also confirmed that a huge organizational change was underway and achieving results. There had been significant change in the senior management, the major programme of safety works and the implementation of a comprehensive fire safety management system. There was greater efficiency and better investment project management, notably in the new ticketing system (UTS) and one-person operation of trains on eight out of ten lines. All this had been achieved against the background of a 50 per cent growth in passenger demand in a decade. It endorsed the Underground's view that at least £750 million needed to be spent annually for the next ten years on the existing assets and regretted that in the past five years an average of only £290 million had been achieved.[30]

On the front line, there was still some way to go, as Molly Dineen's 1989 documentary *Heart of the Angel* suggested. Dineen's film painted a Dickensian picture

15. Cult Indie band The Times appropriate a newspaper masthead and the Underground roundel for their album in 1983.

16. Paul Stephen's painting of Blur on a District line train was used on the back cover of their 1993 album, *Modern Life Is Rubbish*.

of the run-down 90-year-old Angel station: demoralized, scruffy station staff, dismissive of customers, waiting to retire.[31] The tag 'Misery Line' was reapplied by the *Evening Standard* to the Northern line, as its once proud silver trains groaned and creaked up and down the line, unreliable and defaced by graffiti, until replaced by new rolling stock in 1998. Alexei Sayle's graphic 1987 novel *Geoffrey the Tube Train* depicting a vicious Tube train was entirely in tune with the times. The benign 'Underground Ernie' character introduced in 2006 was a reflection of the vastly improved perception of the Underground.

In November 1991, Newton and Tunnicliffe launched the Company Plan, setting out a programme of radical changes to improve safety, quality and efficiency. Three years later, the Underground reported[32] that the Plan had delivered a reduction in staff from nearly 22,000 to just over 17,000 with a complete overhaul of the original arcane pay and grading system. Furthermore, customer satisfaction had improved from 79 per cent to 91 per cent by March 1994, while internationally recognized safety standards were achieved across all operational areas of the company. The modernization of the Central line had commenced in 1988, while the Jubilee line extension (JLE) had reappeared on the radar. Tunnicliffe's pragmatic vision for a 'Decently Modern Metro' would take years to achieve, but they were heading in the right direction. For the first time since the 1960s, the Underground was on an upward curve.

17. Alexei Sayle with Geoffrey the Tube train, 1987. Illustration by Oscar Zarate.

18. Circle, the chilled-out new age Tube train character, with Underground Ernie, 2006

19. Edgware Road Bakerloo line station after complete refurbishment in 1992. Restored heritage features were combined with new ticket gates and safety signage as part of an improvement programme across the system.

From Jubilee line to Public Private Partnership

As the Docks declined and container traffic moved downstream, London was left by the 1970s with eight square miles of redundant industrial land just to the east of the City. Transport provision was crucial to the successful regeneration of Docklands, even in the early 1980s, when regeneration was envisaged as low-rise residential, commercial and light-industrial usage. A 'Minitram' proposal of 1973 linking with the Jubilee line at Fenchurch Street had been based on an assumption of just 9,000 journeys a day. Despite Horace Cutler staging a 'start' on construction in the Strand in April 1978, government approval for the second stage of the Jubilee line was not forthcoming. Forecasts of only 25,000 jobs still did not justify an Underground extension, so the new London Docklands Development Corporation (LDDC) asked London Transport to bring forward a light railway scheme within a total budget for road and rail improvement of £100 million. In 1984 Canary Wharf, far from being a household name, was an undistinguished, empty two-storey former banana warehouse on the Isle of Dogs. It had been leased to Fruit Lines Limited for their Canary Islands and Mediterranean fruit trade and named Canary Wharf at their request.

Anticipating the need for space for large dealing floors in the wake of the 'Big Bang' of 1986 – the deregulation of the City – the Canary Wharf scheme far outstripped any existing plans for the regeneration of Docklands. Conceived in 1984 by property developer G. Ware Travelstead and banker Michael von Clemm on a visit to Docklands searching for food preparation space for Roux Restaurants, the scheme developed over

20

20. Canary Wharf warehouse, demolished in 1986 in one of the first stages of the massive redevelopment project, which retained its historical name.

lunch into the biggest commercial development in Europe, a financial services district of one million square metres, built around One Canada Square, which would be the highest building in the UK, and housing 50,000 jobs. It was taken over by Canadian developers Olympia & York, then the biggest property company in the world, owned by the Reichmann brothers. Development of this scale could not be sustained without a significant expansion of transport capacity.

It had seemed like a leap of faith in 1982 to even authorize £77 million of investment for a new light railway as the transport spine for Docklands. Many had argued at the time that a new network of buses would be all that was needed.[33] In fact the pace of the regeneration of the area was to rapidly outgrow the first lines; '£77 million and not

21. First day of passenger operation, Docklands Light Railway, August 1987.

22. Toy train in a new financial district. A Docklands Light Railway train passing South Quay Plaza, March 1989.

23. Canary Wharf with Jubilee line station under construction, 1994.

a penny more … it was a disastrous little system because it was done on the cheap, and when LDDC took it over in 1992 it had to be completely re-engineered,' remembers David Quarmby, then an LT board member.[34] Between 1982 and 1990, employment forecasts for Docklands were to rise eightfold on the back of Canary Wharf.[35] The original two lines – Island Gardens to Stratford and to Tower Hill – were being replanned even before they opened in August 1987. The original DLR station at Canary Wharf was never completed and was dismantled before the line officially opened. Passenger demand on the 'Legoland' railway exceeded expectations from the start, rose steadily and outran the technology of driverless trains.[36]

The Canary Wharf development revived a proposed extension of the Jubilee line eastwards from Charing Cross to Ilford. Passenger numbers had risen dramatically in the 1980s as employment and residence in central London grew, while overcrowding on the Central line was a particular concern. A range of options was presented by British Rail Network SouthEast,[37] the Department for Transport and London Transport in the Central London Rail Study of 1988: the cross-London line, later to emerge as Crossrail, and the Chelsea–Hackney route. A subsequent proposal for the Jubilee line extension (JLE) to Stratford via Docklands was approved in 1992 by a government keen to secure the Canary Wharf development.

The Canary Wharf development depended on transport capacity if investors and tenants were to be convinced to make the seismic move out of the City to Docklands. The developers had proposed a dedicated railway from Canary Wharf to the Bank or an express line from Waterloo to Greenwich ('Canaryloo') the Docklands equivalent of the Waterloo & City line. The Reichmanns opened an exhibition of their scheme within a stone's throw of parliament in 1988 to lobby the Thatcher government, who were believers in private-sector solutions to providing public services. Tony Ridley remembers being asked by Paul Reichmann:

> 'What do you think I need to do to persuade Mrs Thatcher to push the Jubilee line up the decision-making ladder?' I said, 'It's very simple: put some money on the table.' And of course it didn't turn out to be as much money as he'd hinted at.

Ridley was accused by colleagues of selling out to the enemy, 'But I think it was right, because you couldn't miss that opportunity to develop at Canary Wharf.'[38] Eager to facilitate the developers of its 'pet major project',[39] and encouraged by the offer of private funds, the government commissioned the East London Rail Study, which recommended the extension of the Jubilee line from Green Park to Stratford via Canary Wharf. As one insider put it, 'The Reichmanns were very influential; eventually we were told to develop the railway,'[40] and a bill was deposited for the JLE jointly by London Underground and Olympia & York in 1992.

Of the final cost of £3.5 billion, the much-trumpeted developers' contribution of one-third of the cost (£400 million) was only ever paid in part, about 5 per cent.[41] In

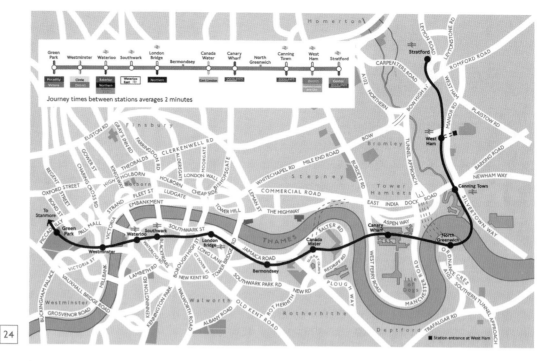

May 1992, in response to the London commercial property collapse, O&Y went into administration, and the Canary Wharf development came to an abrupt halt. Having been dragged reluctantly into building the Reichmanns' railway, the Underground then found itself rescuing it, as Denis Tunnicliffe remembers:

> David Bayliss [LT Director for Planning] and I were in his office. I'm sure this project should go ahead. There should be the political momentum and a vision to see London in the future. It will shake up the City of London, and I can see this whole south-east corner will be revitalized. That's what we need, and we need the politician who is responsible for London to grasp this, see it and do it, but there isn't one ... 'Well, David, there's you and me and I think we should build it.'[42]

With cancellation by government imminent – Treasury minister Michael Portillo even bragged about it at the Conservative Party conference – Tunnicliffe and his team became the Jubilee line extension's, and by implication Canary Wharf's, saviours. The administrators faced two scenarios for the development: 'Cinderella' – placing barbed wire around it for ten years – or 'Sylvester' – building out of it. 'We took every opportunity to tell the JLE story ... we would hammer on about it, how the south-east would be left derelict.'[43] It took eighteen months through the deep recession of 1992 to revive the project, it becoming clearer than ever that the completion of the Canary Wharf development depended on the Underground: 'Never before had an Underground line been such a key issue in maintaining confidence in economic regeneration.'[44] Endless discussion with government over funding ensued alongside the press and lobbying campaign. Tunnicliffe remembers a meeting with the then Transport minister, Roger Freeman:

24. Jubilee line extension route map, 1997.

Roger came briefed by his civil servants to take cost out of the project. Eventually, I said, 'Somebody like you came to somebody like me at the same point in the Victoria line and they took a brilliant design, nice big station tunnels, plenty of redundancy in the escalator system, space for it to grow, and the person like me let them take the money out, let them take the sets of escalators out, made the tunnels smaller, and I live with it every day, Roger, and I'm not going to do that to my successors. We're either going to build this railway big enough or not at all'. [It was a] ridiculous gamble. At the end of the meeting he left with £90 million of station finishes. Roger, you want to spend £2.1 billion on a railway and not paint it, I don't care, we'll paint it afterwards. Roland (Paoletti) just rolled that into the design philosophy. He said, 'You'll have natural light wherever we can. We'll have lovely shapes. We'll make sure it's for purpose. We'll have a heroic scale where it needs to have a heroic scale, has simplicity, and we have wonderful public architecture but we won't paint it.'[45]

Canary Wharf Limited came out of administration in October 1993, releasing £98 million for the JLE project, and the Prime Minister, John Major, formally initiated construction at the site of Canary Wharf station in December 1993. The 10-mile Jubilee line extension from south of Green Park with eleven stations was an Underground project which set out to learn from the experiences of the Victoria and Jubilee lines, and the King's Cross fire, and from metros worldwide, notably that of Hong Kong. For the first time a line was designed to be future-proof, by recognizing the need to design not only for traffic forecasts but also for the growth in traffic it would create. While the stations at Waterloo, Southwark and London Bridge would meet the major challenge of being threaded through existing rail and underground infrastructure, new spacious stations at Bermondsey, Canada Water, Canary Wharf and North Greenwich were placed within massive concrete boxes. There was step-free access, dual exits at both ends of the stations for safety evacuation, smoke ventilation systems, fireproof lifts and at least three escalators at each station, a total of 116 on the extension out of a total of only 243 escalators across the whole Underground system in 1999. Platform-edge doors separated the track from the platform for the first time in London, making stations quieter, safer and less draughty. New six-car trains incorporated regenerative braking[46] and car-end windows.

25. Section of the tunnel boring machine 'Sharon' (the other was 'Tracy') being lowered into the station box at Canary Wharf to begin tunnelling, August 1994

With Keith Bright sacked after the King's Cross fire, a new LT chairman, Sir Wilfrid Newton, had been recruited in 1988 from Hong Kong, then the newest and best metro in the world. As an experienced and successful operator, Newton inspired confidence in the corridors of power and worked them very effectively. As executive chairman of the Underground, his railway experience channelled and supported Tunnicliffe to effect far-reaching change in the Underground. Together they formed the most effective team

26. Construction at Westminster was on a huge scale – the 'station box' is seen here under construction in close proximity to the Palace of Westminster, 1997.

27. The New Austrian Tunnelling Method (NATM), using sprayed concrete, was used for much of the extension; seen here at Waterloo in 1994.

at the head of the Underground since Ashfield and Pick and were ably supported by a newly selected and talented executive team. Newton introduced architect Roland Paoletti, who was to be the creative influence over the whole Jubilee line extension: 'Quite an unusual sort of chap … but he's very good.'[47] Early on, Paoletti set out his method to Tunnicliffe:

> Roland said, 'Denis, this programme is going to have a design committee of two, you and me.' And I said, 'What are you talking about, Roland? We've got LT Standing Orders and we've got a design committee with the great and the good on it.' He said, 'I know, Denis, that's exactly what your job is: to keep them off my back while I build the railway.'[48]

Having engaged the managing director with his vision, he commissioned eight new subterranean and three surface stations and a stunning train depot at Stratford from the best of young British architects. 'I knew that they'd give the job their full attention,' said Paoletti. 'I didn't particularly want the big boys.' All but three of the stations would be subterranean – 'even Holden didn't get below ground,' said Paoletti. 'The architecture ran out in the ticket-hall – get on the escalator and you're in the realm of the civil engineers.'[49]

28. Watercolour of Canary Wharf station construction, by Robert Soden, 1998. One of a series of twenty-four commissioned by London Transport.

29. Roland Paoletti (JLE Project Architect), Richard Rogers (architect of the Millennium Dome), Stephen Norris (Minister of Transport) and Sir Wilfrid Newton (Chairman of London Transport), October 1992.

30

Michael Hopkins was already building Portcullis House over Westminster station, so he was commissioned for the station below, while Norman Foster was also keen to be involved and turned out to be a powerful ally in keeping the project on course. His station at Canary Wharf proved to be one of the most spectacular of all, a cathedral of the urban metro, with entrances redolent of his Bilbao metro. At North Greenwich, Paoletti was determined to have his way:

He'd come and see me every three months and tell me where we were design-wise and he brought a model of North Greenwich made of balsa wood and a shoe box painted very blue – 'I must have my blue station' –

30. London Bridge station under construction, October 1996.

31. A craftsman applies cobalt blue glass mosaic tiles to the top of a support column in the station concourse at North Greenwich, 1996.

32

and when they built it the blue is a beautiful lapis lazuli blue. The decoration is the advertising and the people, who will always be contemporary.[50]

The extension opened in stages from May 1999 but by then had become a byword for cost overrun and delay. This was by no means of the Underground's making as the complexity of tunnelling beneath London threw up continual challenges. Tunnicliffe reflected on 'how little we knew about the first two metres of London. At London Bridge we stopped for eighteen months. We found things built to withstand nuclear explosions.'[51] Beneath the Houses of Parliament, a new method of compensation grouting had to be applied to prevent possible settlement of St Stephen's Tower and Big

32. Underground cathedral: Canary Wharf station in 1999, designed by Norman Foster.

33

Ben. At Westminster station, the District and Circle lines operated as normal while the largest hole in Europe was dug beneath them. At London Bridge, threading tunnels around three existing Tube lines was a design and construction nightmare, compensation grouting and reinforced jointing on tunnel segments being needed to stabilize the access tunnels: 'These holes were awesome before we filled them in: problem after problem after that, and the moment you get things out of phase then you have delay. The moment you have delay, you have money, and that's really where our twenty-one months and seventy per cent came from.'[52] On 21 October 1994, a spectacular collapse occurred during the building of a rail tunnel for the Heathrow Express Rail Link. A huge crater opened up between two runways, structural damage was caused to buildings and car parks, and tunnelling was delayed for six months while the Health and Safety Executive undertook investigations into the New Austrian Tunnelling Method (NATM). The JLE was also using this shotcrete method for two tunnel contracts, and so it too was delayed. Despite such challenges, the civil engineering phase of the project ran broadly to programme.

It was to be the fitting-out phase that brought the project to its knees.[53] The JLE was conceived as technologically innovative in the use of moving-block signalling. Specified by the Underground and designed by Westinghouse, this was to achieve thirty-six trains per hour by computerized control of the headway between moving trains rather than using traditional fixed signals. Design of the moving-block system over-ran, and Westinghouse admitted in February 1998 that they could not make the software work. It was abandoned and replaced in a crash programme by a traditional fixed-block signalling system. This caused considerable delays, labour difficulties and additional cost at the back end of the project. 'You cannot change horses late in the day on a sophisticated thing like a signalling system,' rued project director Hugh Docherty, who would have preferred to start with a traditional system and move to moving-block when it was ready.[54]

A £25 million contribution from British Gas had encouraged the JLE to be routed through the North Greenwich peninsular to serve a proposed housing development on the poisoned site of a disued gasworks. This barren site was chosen by the government in 1996 as the site for the Millennium Dome. Designed by architect Richard Rogers, from 1997 it became a pet project of the prime minister, Tony Blair, who envisaged the experience within as 'a triumph of confidence over cynicism, boldness over blandness, excellence over mediocrity'.[55] Few, however, had his confidence. The Dome was to act as the centrepiece of the Millennium celebrations, when the prime minister and VIPs, having arrived by train from Westminster, would cut the ribbon on New Year's Eve 1999. This immovable deadline focused the mind mightily, and in September 1998 the leading American company Bechtel was brought in at great expense to throw project management

33. Platform level at Westminster station. Platform-edge doors were introduced in London in 1999 on the JLE for safety reasons, and to improve the passenger environment.

34

resources at its completion. The deadline also put the project over a financial barrel as electrical contractors fitting out the line and its delayed signalling system pushed for pay increases and inflated overtime rates; 'Their only game in town is to screw us for every penny they can before they become redundant.'[56]

When the line opened, its legacy was initially eclipsed by cost overrun, delay, a less frequent train service than planned, the politics of the Millennium Dome and the teething problems it experienced in its first few months. Tunnicliffe's

34. Newly completed tunnel section near Canary Wharf in Docklands, January 1996.

Simply Nightlife by Tube and bus

Collage commissioned by London Transport from Dan Fern.
This poster is available from the London Transport Museum, Covent Garden Piazza.

Supported by
TDI

35

36

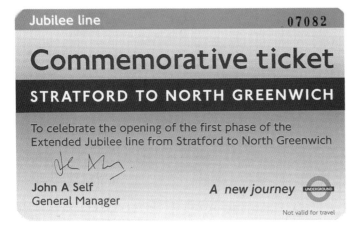

Jubilee line   07082

Commemorative ticket

STRATFORD TO NORTH GREENWICH

To celebrate the opening of the first phase of the
Extended Jubilee line from Stratford to North Greenwich

John A Self   *A new journey*
General Manager

Not valid for travel

retrospective view was that 'it was worth all the pain – it has changed London for ever'.[57] Its quality as the best new public architecture in London for decades was recognized immediately, and it has since attracted more than thirty architectural and engineering awards.[58] The extension raised the experience of travelling on the Underground – a Westminster passenger was overheard saying, 'I wish I could live in this station, it's blindingly fab.'[59] Automatic train operation on moving-block signalling was finally introduced in the summer of 2011 to realize thirty-three trains per hour. Now the extended Jubilee line soaks up passengers in the peak and has enabled subsequent phases of development at Canary Wharf, helped secure the Olympics at Stratford and been key to the regeneration of Docklands and east London. Tunnicliffe remembers saying prophetically to the beleaguered project team: 'Delay is only a concept in prospect. It is not a concept in retrospect. When they're using the railway, nobody will remember the delay.'[60]

The JLE had been the product of national and London politics from the outset: the name change by Cutler, the support of Docklands regeneration by the Thatcher government, the rescuing of the Canary Wharf development and the site of New Labour's Millennium Experience. The JLE opened twenty-one months late, and the final cost of £3.5 billion was 70 per cent more than the stated Treasury approval figure of £2.1 billion. The disused stub of the original line to Charing Cross stands as testament to its prolonged gestation. Although based on false assumptions, the Jubilee line convinced the Labour government and in particular the Treasury that London Underground was incapable of delivering major projects. Arup's concluding report suggested a 'more realistic assumption of the "estimated final costs" would have been £2.5 billion rather than the budget of £2.14 billion (let alone the £1.9 billion figure for the cost used by the government) announced at the go-ahead'.[61] This would suggest the JLE was responsible for the 40 per cent over-spend typical of transport infrastructure projects.

'A new public-private partnership' was in the Labour manifesto for the 1997 General Election, as opposed to the Conservatives' plan for outright privatization of the Tube. No detailed proposals existed for either party's commitment. Looking to address the considerable task of modernizing public infrastructure such as hospitals, schools and transport, without adding to the public-sector borrowing requirement (PSBR), Labour in 1997 were anxious to avoid their predecessors' mantra of privatization while still deploying the allegedly superior project management and delivery skills of the private sector though public finance initiatives (PFIs). For the Underground, private investment now and repayment from income over the life of the asset created offered to provide the long-term investment needed for railway infrastructure. 'When the Labour government came in, I was

35. 'Simply Nightlife' by Dan Fern, 1998; one of a series of new artworks commissioned as part of the long-running 'Simply' campaign in the 1990s to promote use of the system and return to the design values of an earlier age.

36. Commemorative ticket for 'a new journey'. The JLE opened in stages during 1999.

running out of money in a big way,' remembered Tunnicliffe, 'and John Prescott said, "You've got to find me a solution." I saw PPP as the solution, and everybody was very gung-ho about the private sector in those days. Its attraction to me was getting rid of annuality, because governments are unwilling to commit to long-term programmes.'[62]

John Prescott as Minister for the Environment, Transport and the Regions and Deputy Prime Minister, was responsible for taking forward the public–private partnership as well as the creation of the Greater London assembly and an elected mayor. With the need for investment in the refurbishment of the Underground agreed, the issue became how, rather if, to fund this. To maintain momentum, London Underground commissioned Big Four auditors KPMG and investment bankers Lazards to evaluate the options for funding long-term investment in the Tube, from no change to outright privatization. Famously, a public–private partnership model ranked fifteenth of sixteen options. This report was to prove prescient, as it argued against splitting up the integrated management of the Tube on grounds of high set-up and legal costs, more difficult coordination between engineering and operations and the need to maintain a seamless service for customers. 'The Underground is too important to experiment with … It is convention which excludes the possibility of committed grant, direct borrowing or hypothecated revenue. The assumption that the private sector will be more effective needs challenging.'[63] The wise men and women of the Treasury dismissed this contribution from a management whose reputation for them was sullied by their recent record in delivering major projects.

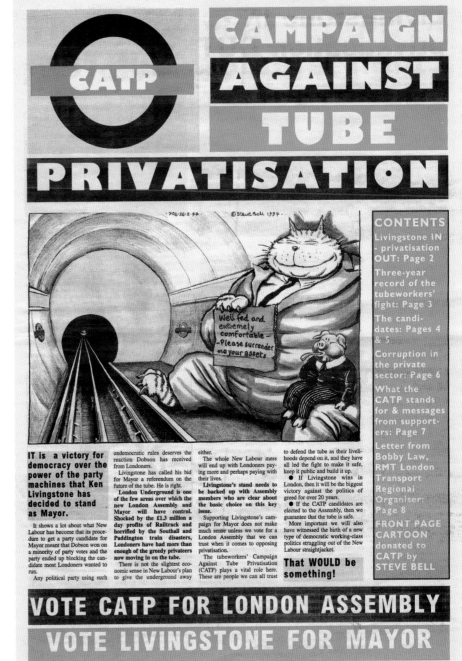

37

In March 1998, John Prescott announced a PPP for the Underground. The contracts were to be for fifteen years, starting in 2000, to cost LU nothing and be worth £7 billion. By contrast, the final contracts signed with Metronet and Tube Lines in January 2003 were worth £13 billion over thirty years and cost LU £1 billion a year, reflecting the tortuous path taken by government in the interim. There were more than two years of

37. At the General Election in 1997, the Conservative manifesto included a commitment to privatizing the Underground which was opposed by the Campaign Against Tube Privatization who published this newspaper in 1997, using Steve Bell's 'Fat Cat', originally published in the *Guardian*.

wrangling that eventually delivered a fatally diluted and distorted PPP. Through 1999, as the Greater London Assembly (GLA) bill went through the House, opposition to the PPP began to gather pace. In March, the Greater London Group at the London School of Economics published a critique, describing the PPP as 'flawed in principle and impracticable', and arguing for the GLA to be allowed to raise finance by issuing bonds as LT had done in the 1930s, the transit authority had in New York in the 1980s, and indeed Prescott himself had when bailing out the Channel Tunnel Rail Link only the previous year.[64] The Conservative candidate for the mayoralty, Lord Archer, told the party conference he would dismantle the 'half-baked' PPP and go for outright privatization. Simon Jenkins, former editor of *The Times*, found it 'absurd to have to argue the virtue of public-sector values with a Labour government. I am an enthusiast for most forms of privatization but this one makes no sense. Further fragmenting ownership and investment in mass transit is stupid.'[65] Ken Livingstone used opposition to the PPP as the main plank of his own campaign for the mayoralty, losing him the Labour nomination and leading him to stand as an independent. As the advent of the GLA loomed in 2000, transport journalist Christian Wolmar noted, 'the public was treated to the bizarre spectacle of the right-wing press attacking a supposedly left of centre government in alliance with Ken Livingstone, an avowed old-fashioned socialist, on a scheme that seemed on the face of it to fit with the Conservative agenda of privatizing as many public services as possible'.[66]

Such a rainbow coalition in opposition perversely seemed only to strengthen government resolve. The senior management of the Underground was also in favour of the PPP. It was the only game in town for a system badly in need of investment and under pressure from rising passenger numbers. Rail disasters at Ladbroke Grove in October 1999 and the Hatfield rail crash in October 2000 had profound effects on the reputation of Railtrack (the privatized infrastructure company carved out of the former British Rail) and its private-sector contractors. Both could have been the occasion for a volte-face, but the government ploughed on, seeking through 1999 to attract and then retain bidders, despite the growing tide of opposition. In the process the externalization of risk to the private sector was lost, and the taxpayer picked up the bill later when the contracts failed. At the judicial review in 2002, the value of the PPP to consultants and lawyers alone was estimated at £400 million.

The creation of a new city-wide authority for London had been Labour Party policy since the abolition of the GLC in 1986. Following Tony Blair's 1997 election victory, a White Paper was produced proposing, along the lines of many American cities, a directly elected executive mayor and a scrutinizing assembly for London. A referendum held with council elections across the capital in May 1998 resulted in 72 per cent approval by Londoners, and the Greater London Authority Act went through parliament in 1999, with the first election to the GLA to be held in May 2000. Enabling legislation for the Underground PPP was included within the GLA Act but attracted little immediate attention. The timetable for PPP was initially intended to deliver the scheme to coincide with the vesting of the new government for London in July 2000. As the timetable for instituting the PPP slipped and opposition mounted, the chancellor, Gordon Brown, and his Treasury advisors were determined to face down opposition of whatever hue by setting the PPP in stone before transfer to the mayor. The contracts were to be designed and negotiated by the national government but handed over for implementation to the GLA, who had no part in, influence over or ownership of this arrangement.

Ken Livingstone won the first mayoral election in May 2000, as an independent, and appointed Bob Kiley as transport commissioner. Kiley had been a CIA officer, deputy mayor of Boston and then chairman and CEO of the Metropolitan Transit Authority of New York from 1983 until 1990. He was credited as being the architect of the revival of Boston's and New York's ailing public transport systems. Having been a deputy mayor, Kiley was not a traditional British transport operator: he understood the political interface and he knew about bond finance. The former CIA man and the municipal socialist mayor were not an obvious match, but they made a powerful team in the creation of the new transport executive, Transport for London, adding the strategic road network, taxis and private hire, cycling, walking, the DLR, Victoria Coach Station and the river services to bus, and after PPP was concluded, the Underground. The Tube was about to join the world's biggest integrated transport authority.

For a time from the autumn of 2000, it seemed as if Kiley's opposition to the PPP and his advocacy of raising money on the bond market might succeed. He was a persuasive and charismatic operator, deeply knowledgeable and seemingly prepared to talk. He was backed by a sharp team of Americans, all with experience of running and funding city metros. Cross-table negotiations continued with government into early 2001, 'not an operator among them', said Kiley.[67] Livingstone similarly sniped that the PPP had been thought up by 'two Treasury civil servants. One has a degree in theoretical economics, and the other in classics. Only in Britain could this weigh more heavily in the balance than the opinions of the men who have run the second- and third-oldest Underground systems in the world.'[68] There were false dawns – an *Evening Standard* headline on 2 February 'Kiley Victory in Tube Plan' – but at the end of March the talks finally collapsed amid accusations on both sides of bad faith. Kiley was to leave in 2006, ironically after initiating a successful bond finance deal for TfL.

38. Mayor Ken Livingstone with TfL Commissioner Bob Kiley at St. James's Park station, November 2000.

39

A 'civil war' ensued between the new Transport for London (TfL) and government. On the day Prescott announced the delivery timetable for the PPP in April 2001 – £13 billion over fifteen years, fifty-six stations refurbished by 2006, new trains on most lines by 2019 – TfL won permission in the High Court for a judicial review of the PPP. The government pressed on, in May announcing the preferred bidders for the three contracts: sub-surface lines (SSL) and two Tube line contracts, Jubilee, Northern and Piccadilly (JNP), and Bakerloo, Central and Victoria (BCV). The Underground had restructured its engineers into three companies and had been shadow-running the new arrangements since September 1999. As the negotiations dragged on, the Underground's senior managers, now led by Derek Smith, were caught in the increasingly adversarial crossfire, having infamously been described by Livingstone as 'dullards' and 'knuckleheads', causing Smith to resign, protesting 'a disruptive and unsettling effect on morale in the company'.[69] In September 2001, the successful consortia were announced: Metronet (WS Atkins, Seeboard, Adtranz, later Bombardier, Thames Water, Balfour Beatty) won both the sub-surface and BCV contracts, while Tube Lines (Jarvis, Amey and Bechtel) were awarded the JNP contract. Tony Blair became briefly involved in the run-up to the 2002 election, inviting Kiley to Chequers and asking him to chair London Transport for the final negotiations with the bidders. Kiley's account suggested that Blair could see the PPP contracts were over-complex but also wanted to avoid the PPP becoming an election issue. His appointment to LRT before and sacking after the election suggests this had been a blatant political fix.

Brown and the Treasury remained adamant that the bidders were to be kept onside at any cost, including being indemnified against London Underground being 'unreasonable' in its management of the contract, eventually underwriting 95 per cent of the bank loans taken out by the infrastructure companies (infracos) and agreeing to a reduced scope and higher costs. The final contracts were signed in May, when it was revealed that the infracos would receive in the order of £500 million to cover success fees and the costs of bidding. What had been described in 2002 as a 'massive gamble' which could only be tested in practice was up and running. The scale was huge: the Underground PPP equalled in value all the other PFIs signed up to 2001. In January 2003 the Underground began operating as a public–private partnership, with the infrastructure and rolling stock maintained by two private companies under thirty-year contracts, while London Underground Limited remained publicly owned and operated by TfL.

Six months before this, Ken Livingstone had recruited a new MD for the Underground. Tim O'Toole was another American but not one of Kiley's set. His career in the US had been in freight railroads with ConRail ('a public sector basket-case which had been turned around into this fabulous success story')[70] but his legal and financial

40

39. 'Faster Service', one of a series of LU posters promoting the PPP in 2003

40. Licensed busker at Liverpool Street station, 2011.

knowledge was significant for operating within the PPP framework. His arrival in London had been delayed as the negotiations swayed backwards and forwards. O'Toole was finally called over in February 2003, but closing the deal with Metronet was delayed until July: 'So for five months, I was here but I didn't really have a proper job. I was taught you have to go out in the field and meet people. So I spent all my time just riding [the railway] every day and meeting people, and that proved invaluable later.'[71] 'Rainbow' boards telling passengers the state of each line were a simple and highly visible outcome of his operational induction.

O'Toole found Kiley and his team anxious to do battle with the PPP contractors:

41

> Terrible structure but I am here to make it work. I very quickly decided that the legal and finance side of this, fighting the PPP battles and the stuff that got the headlines, was all a side show. The real job was running the railway and rebuilding it and bringing the employees back into the story.[72]

O'Toole instituted a new direct style of internal communications based on a strong narrative linking pride in the history of the Tube with the contemporary challenges faced by upgrading the Underground. A series of mass events for staff were fronted initially by O'Toole himself and his managers. He later used a hologram of himself to personally present his persuasive vision.

The licensing of busking on thirty-nine sponsored pitches in twenty-five central stations in 2003 suggested that the Underground was now sufficiently confident in the management of its estate to reverse its long-held aversion to busking as a semi-criminal activity, a symbol of its inability to control and own its own system. Now auditions are held, and 300 buskers selected to hold a year-long licence. Celebrity appearances in these most demanding of venues have included the Libertines, Julian Lloyd Webber, Seasick Steve and Katherine Jenkins, who, dressed in torn jeans and holey jumper, brought tears to the eyes of seasoned commuters: 'It's got a great acoustic down there,' said the Welsh mezzo-soprano.[73]

The proponents of PPP had been adamant that the private sector was needed to eliminate the inefficiencies of public-sector enterprises and take on the risks associated with maintaining the network. Opponents of the PPP had maintained the need to make profits and the cost of

41. Tim O'Toole's simple but effective innovation, the 'Rainbow boards' and the associated positive message of the announcement, 'The Underground is running a good service on all lines this morning'.

42. Positive messages on the covers of Tube Lines and Metronet house magazines in 2003.

borrowing would add to the price and would reduce public benefit. Work on this scale took time to shake down, but construction started across the system in 2003, and Londoners began to experience regular weekend closures for an unprecedented programme of upgrade work. The National Audit Office's retrospective verdict on the Metronet consortium was that the main cause of its failure was poor corporate governance and leadership. The shareholders' differing priorities and positions as beneficiaries of supply contracts meant that they did not tackle problems effectively. The executive management was unable to manage the work of its shareholder-dominated supply chain effectively. These suppliers had power over some of the scope of work and expected to be paid for extra work undertaken. The poor quality of information available to management, particularly on the station and track programmes, meant that Metronet was unable to monitor costs and could not obtain adequate evidence to support claims to have performed work economically and efficiently.[74] If the consortium itself was unclear on this, how could the Underground be expected to monitor or partner their contractor's performance? Metronet were unable to convince the PPP Arbiter of the need for more money and went into administration in July 2007.

Tube Lines tendered work out rather than using the shareholders as suppliers and exercised better cost control. One commentator has suggested that future archaeologists will be able to distinguish between a Metronet and a Tube Lines station upgrade: 'Metronet did things slowly, with no cost control to a very high standard, whereas Tube Lines are much tighter on cost control and did them to a basic acceptable standard.'[75] Tube Lines' record on refurbishment work was undermined by severe difficulties with the Jubilee line upgrade, which was delayed by nine months, while prolonged closures requested for the Northern line upgrade were politically unacceptable. As negotiations started for the second seven-and-a-half years of the contract, TfL was asked to provide an additional £1.75 billion to cover the shortfall, refused and referred the matter to the PPP Arbiter, who stated that only £400 million could be justified. In May 2010 TfL agreed to buy the shares of Bechtel and Amey from Tube Lines for £310 million, a figure which was recovered in two years by cheaper debt refinancing.

The last rites of the PPP saw Tube Lines shareholders depart, according to O'Toole,

happily singing a tune because they were paid a lot of money. The banks were all paid off, and yet TfL was thrilled it had saved money. That goes to show you how bad the system was. The equity payments were so outrageous there was enough money in that stream of payments to make everybody happy.[76]

43. A holographic projection of Tim O'Toole prepares to address staff at one of a series of over thirty staff communication events called 'Valuing Time' in 2008.

44. New station at Wembley Park to accompany the new stadium, 2008.

Even if you accept the Jubilee line extension and the Central line as projects that failed on time and efficiency, 'the Tube PPP has proved a cure worse than the disease'.[77] Meanwhile, while the PPP unwound, London Underground undertook several successful major projects that suggested to O'Toole that, 'if they had given us this [work], I think we would have delivered'.[78] The Connect PFI for train radios was turned round, while a major station upgrade at Wembley Park alongside the new stadium used Tube Lines as contractors.

This Whitehall farce in several acts had many twists and turns and more than one opportunity to turn back. It was bedevilled with personal vendettas and generated huge fees for consultants. The Underground was turned inside out by privatization and renationalization.[79] In the long run, PPP proved to be a significant watershed for the Underground. The case for capital investment of around £1 billion a year was made, stations were refurbished and new trains were delivered, however procured and at what cost. The years of under-investment could be rolled back, albeit at the expense of many years of service disruption from weekend working. As O'Toole put it:

> There is no panacea. The record of large, urban civil projects is spotty at best under any structure, and success is highly dependent on good people. Yet, when resources are dear and government must sort priorities, one is best advised to adopt a structure that is transparent and simple. That should be the North Star for the rebuilding of the Tube and Crossrail.[80]

Mike Brown came from BAA as MD of the Underground in April 2010, 'knowing it is always better to have a conventional contractual relationship ... it is critical to have a good direct conversation between contractor and the end user and that wasn't proving possible in the complexities of the PPP structures'.[81] Meanwhile, demand continued to rise, with nearly 1.2 billion Tube journeys in 2011. Upgrades such as the Victoria line, completed with new trains in 2011, were picked up in more difficult funding circumstances after the onset of recession in 2008 and the consequent constraints on public expenditure. The enhanced reputation of public transport to deliver for London and the powerful influence of Boris Johnson, elected as mayor in 2008, secured a financial settlement with government in 2010 which maintained the Crossrail project (albeit to open a year later in 2018) and kept both the ongoing Tube upgrade programme and the bus network intact.

45

45. A growing cross-party consensus on transport policy. Conservative Mayor Boris Johnson (left) with Labour Prime Minister Gordon Brown and Transport Minister Lord Adonis, study the route map at the Crossrail launch, March 2010.

Terrorist attack, 7/7

July 2005 was to prove a month of terrible contrast for Londoners and the Underground. On 6 July, the International Olympic Committee announced their choice of London for the 2012 Olympics at a meeting in Singapore. As the head of the IOC, Jacques Rogge, made the announcement – 'The Games of the thirtieth Olympiad are awarded to the city of ... London' – British Olympians on the base of Nelson's Column and the crowd in the Trafalgar Square jumped for joy and hugged each other tearfully. Relayed simultaneously, Parisians slumped in hubristic disbelief at their non-selection, having considered themselves clear favourites. London's joy and self-esteem knew no bounds. The mayor of London, Ken Livingstone, in Singapore with Lord Coe and Tessa Jowell supporting the bid team, declared 6 July 'one of the best days London has ever had – and it is one of the proudest days for Britain and for British sport'.[82] Commuters went home feeling good about their city and its future, with the day's Olympic Special copy of the *Evening Standard* under their arms, headlined 'We've Won' across a photo of celebration and tickertape in Trafalgar Square. London was back as a world city.

The following morning started badly on the Underground as three lines experienced serious delays. The service was well on the way to recovery at 8.49 a.m. as some 250,000 people travelled into central London, standing or sitting – relieved to find a seat – reading a book or newspaper, listening to music on their iPods, doing their make-up, worrying about being late for work, seeing but trying not

46. *Evening Standard* covers, 6 and 7 July 2005.

to look at each other – a normal day on the Underground network.[83]

The Underground's Network Control Centre (NCC) at 55 Broadway had been coordinating recovery of the service throughout the morning peak. From 8.50 the NCC and the Metropolitan Police began to receive a stream of calls from six sites. The first impression was that there had been a major power outage. The Underground network was halted and 250,000 passengers brought to the surface. The loss of power was accompanied by loud bangs and smoke and then injured passengers struggling on to platforms. As Underground staff rushed into darkened tunnels and on to halted trains, the reality of London's first multi-site terrorist bombings began to emerge. For three trains and their passengers, the routine of the morning commute had been torn apart. At 8.50 a.m. three young British Muslims had detonated explosive devices carried in backpacks on to the Underground earlier that morning. Bombs had exploded in three trains between stations – on the Circle line between Aldgate and Liverpool Street and between Edgware Road and Paddington, and on a Piccadilly line train which had just left Kings Cross for Russell Square. A fourth on the Northern Line had failed to explode, and the suicide bomber had backtracked, later exploding his bomb on a number 30 bus in Tavistock Square at 9.47 a.m.

47

Below ground for a few moments all was eerily quiet; the trains had stopped and lost all power, the air was thick with smoke and brake dust, and the blasted cars were in darkness, the emergency lights flickering into life. The train operators found themselves in scenes of unprecedented devastation; trying to establish what had happened, evacuate their trains, bring in the emergency services and offer help to the injured. Station staff and off-duty drivers sensed 'something's not right' and rushed down the tunnels to assist the stricken passengers; at Russell Square, the station supervisor 'jumped down on to the track. The smoke was very, very heavy. At one point, it was difficult to see that far in front of me. I went towards the train, and there was quite a few walking wounded.'[84]

Above ground well-rehearsed emergency plans were activated, and London came to a halt as ambulances and emergency vehicles rushed to the

48

47. Camera phone image of passengers being evacuated through the tunnel to Russell Square, taken by Piccadilly line passenger Alexander Chadwick, 7 July 2005.

48. Floral tributes at Russell Square, in the days after 7 July.

scenes, and the bus service was halted. Walking wounded emerged at Aldgate, Edgware Road, Russell Square and King's Cross, where platforms and ticket halls became casualty clearing stations with more serious cases were carried in by staff and police.

The Piccadilly line train was packed tight due to earlier delays, and the close fit in the Tube tunnel constrained rescue work. When the drivers opened the cab door into the bombed car 'what confronted us was a sea of faces, blackened, bloodied', recalled train operators Tom Nairn and Raymond Wright, 'in a state of panic, naturally, and we tried to communicate with them. Because we had to make ourselves heard, I started shouting. I was aware that there was a problem, that I was going to sort it out.' They deployed the ladder down on to the track. 'As those passengers came out, it got progressively worse. The kind of state of the people that were leaving the train: burns, splattered with blood, hair standing on end, clothes blackened, that sort of thing.'[85] Passengers walked or were carried along the 700 yards of tunnel to Russell Square station.

The senior team of the Underground were meeting at Canary Wharf that morning when news reached them. It took a police boat to get the top team back to the NCC at 55 Broadway as central London was gridlocked. O'Toole was already there: 'So we went to Code Amber, and, over the next hour or so, that's when we made our reputation, because all the people did such a magnificent job of moving about a quarter of a million people off this railway without a single injury.'[86] Once back at HQ, the team faced three tasks: continuing to deal with the incidents, restoring the three sites and bringing back the service across the network. From the earliest moments, O'Toole recalled knowing

49 50

49. Newspaper stand at King's Cross, 14 July 2005.

50. Pictures of the missing posted outside King's Cross station, 14 July 2005. An eerie echo of New York after the 9/11 attack on the World Trade Center in 2001.

that 'we must bring this place back as soon as possible, because it's going to be important to the country. We actually said things like that because we thought we are the show and what we do will determine how people feel about this day.'[87] As *The Economist* put it:

> Cities will always bounce back quickly after the initial shock. They are resilient organisms, with powerful social and economic reasons to shrug off terrorism … Being attacked will make Londoners more determined to resume their normal lives not less. That would be true even if Londoners had not previously endured decades of attacks from Irish terrorists, but that history makes resilience an even safer bet.[88]

There were 129 passengers packed into the front car of the Piccadilly line train as it left King's Cross, of whom twenty-six were killed, including the suicide bomber. Six died at Edgware Road, and seven passengers were killed at Aldgate. The fourth bomb, which exploded in Tavistock Square, killed a further thirteen. In all, fifty-two passengers were killed and over 700 wounded, more than a hundred of whom required an overnight in hospital. The Piccadilly line was the last to return to service, on 3 August 2005.

The coroner's inquest reported in May 2011. The exhaustive gathering of evidence and testimony offered a detailed narrative of the Underground's worst ever day. The inquest filled the gap occupied since 2005 by conspiracy theories and individual accounts and offered closure both organizationally and individually for those who had been involved. What emerged were many individual acts of heroism on the part of staff, passengers, policemen, firemen and medics. The inquest vividly related how Underground staff were first on the scene, first to experience the carnage and for twenty minutes or more did their best to make sense of what they saw and to bring comfort to the victims. Lady Justice Hallett was reminded of this: 'We've heard much evidence over the course of the last few months about how superbly well individual members of your staff performed on that day, and, if there was insufficient credit given to them at the time, I hope very much that that's been corrected.'[89] Her thanks to the Edgware Road train operator, Dave Matthews, must stand for all: 'For those of us who travel by Tube, it's very reassuring to know there are people like you prepared to go down into a tunnel, not knowing what to expect, but to do your best to help, and you obviously did do your best to help, and you stayed to the bitter end until there was nothing more you could do. I'm sorry we've had to ask you to relive it and I hope you haven't found it too distressing.'[90]

The 7/7 inquest demonstrated just how far the Underground had come since the King's Cross fire in 1987 and the damning conclusions of Fennell. The management of safety had created ownership, with clear roles and responsibilities. Integrated plans

51. *The Economist* adapted the Underground roundel for its edition of 9th July 2005. This issue referred to the eleven previous but failed attacks on London: 'We have to be lucky all the time, they have to be lucky only once,' 9 July 2005.

51

OVERGROUND AND CROSSRAIL

The creation of Transport for London (TfL) in 2000 and Mayoral governance led to a far more strategic approach to transport planning in the city than was ever possible under London Transport. Two major twenty-first-century rail development projects linked to the Underground, but not actually part of it, demonstrate this improvement. When complete they will both help meet new travel needs and increase capacity on London's public transport.

London Overground was created by TfL in 2007 to manage some suburban rail services transferred from the national network. Some had been run down and neglected for many years. For the first time since the nineteenth century the benefits of running orbital passenger services around London's suburbs, linked to radial routes through

52. Installing the new railway bridge over Shoreditch High Street for the extended East London Line link, 2008.

53. New London Overground train on the extended East London Line near Hoxton in 2010, with the towers of the City of London in the background.

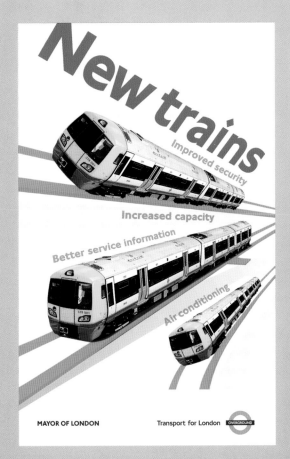

New trains
Improved security
Increased capacity
Better service information
Air conditioning

MAYOR OF LONDON   Transport for London OVERGROUND

the centre, was recognised. By reinstating and upgrading old routes and creating new links at both ends of the fully refurbished and extended East London line, a complete orbital metro network with new trains and much improved services was created by 2012. It runs through twenty of London's thirty-three boroughs, and 30 per cent of Londoners now live less than 15 minutes' walk from an Overground station.

Crossrail is a joint venture between TfL and the Department of Transport to build a new railway under London linking Maidenhead and Heathrow in the west with Shenfield and Abbey Wood in the east. New tunnels will take high-frequency mainline-size trains deep below central London, with Tube interchange at seven new stations between Paddington and Canary Wharf. This huge and costly project was first proposed over twenty years ago but only finally authorized and started in 2010. Tunnel boring began in 2012, and construction is due for completion in 2018. Crossrail will be, in effect, London's next Tube, but on a mainline scale.

54. New trains for the Overground 2007.

55. Mayor Boris Johnson and Transport Secretary Justine Greening unveiling the tunnel boring machines at Westbourne Park, 13 March 2012. The first machine was named Phyllis after Phyllis Pearsall, the woman who mapped the original London A-Z in 1935.

56. Artist's impression of the huge new Crossrail station at Tottenham Court Road, which, combined with the existing station, will stretch from Soho to Centre Point.

put in place for major incidents had been tested and exercised and worked well. 'People who were there did the right things, and the right help came.'[91] The emergency services collaborated effectively. The inquest concluded none of the dead could have been saved by more rapid response. London and its public transport proved to be remarkably resilient: the bus service was back in place from around 5 p.m. that afternoon to take Londoners home, and the Tube was in operation the next morning, albeit with three crime scenes under investigation. 'The staff were magnificent because they were all frightened out of their skins from top to the bottom,' reflected TfL commissioner, Peter Hendy.[92] Six weeks later passenger numbers had recovered to normal levels.

The London bombings were the biggest terrorist attack in the UK since Lockerbie in 1988. A severely injured passenger summed it up: 'London is my home, and I continue to use the Tube every day.'[93] 'I have tremendous respect for what they did. They could have gone off and saved themselves, but they acted in the best interests of everyone,' recalled another survivor.[94] London was to face a copycat attack just two weeks after 7/7, but the four bombs failed to explode.[95]

The Underground emerged from 7/7 with the reputation of both its senior management and its frontline staff enhanced: 'Recognized as making a real contribution to the way we live in the city, they went in there and sorted it out.'[96] As O'Toole left the control room to face the press at the Queen Elizabeth II conference centre opposite Westminster Abbey, someone shouted not to forget the staff.[97] That stayed with him throughout an intense day. He just stuck to the story about the pride and professionalism of his staff, and this chimed closely with Londoners' reawakened esteem for their Underground. In the weeks that followed, customer satisfaction scores peaked, Underground staff were regarded with a renewed respect, and the reputation of the organization achieved a new high. Peter Hendy reflected that what really boosted morale was the 'public feeling that these ordinary people had actually performed quite extraordinary things'.[98] O'Toole and Hendy, then MD for Surface Transport, both received public honours in recognition of their organization's achievement in July 2005.

A railway revived

Twenty years after its lowest moments, public transport in London has experienced a remarkable revival. The successful winding-up of the PPP contracts with Metronet and Tube Lines, record patronage of the system at 1.2 billion journeys a year, a £5 million reduction of costs following the 2010 Comprehensive Spending Review, high levels of customer satisfaction ratings, the delivery of DLR extensions, the opening of the Overground and the Barclays Bike Hire Scheme, allied to earlier successes with the Congestion Charge and the renewal of the bus service, have done much to dispel the view that the public sector cannot be relied upon. Since 2000 London's transport has benefitted from the powerful advocacy of two highly effective and charismatic elected mayors within the corridors of power.

57

57. TfL leaflet explaining the advantages of the Oyster card, which can be used on all forms of transport in London, 2012.

Despite the financial crash of 2008 and the onset of recession, passenger numbers on the Underground are at record levels; TfL has a long-term funding deal with government in place until 2014/15 with clear funding intentions for Tube upgrades beyond that. Crossrail construction has begun and new trains are in service on the Victoria and Metropolitan lines, the latter air-conditioned for the first time. Stations are cleaner and better-maintained than at any time in living memory. Oyster cards have revolutionized ticket transactions by moving payment away from cash to automated top-up and pay as you go. The Overground[99] has revived the principle of the Victorian Outer Circle by drawing together and upgrading neglected lines into an orbital network. This has brought a strong regenerative effect to parts of London hitherto off the Underground map and has extended the reach of the Tube, effectively pulling the focus of the capital eastwards.

December 2011 saw the highest ridership ever on the Tube, with 4.17 million passenger journeys made on Friday 9 December. That was almost 7 per cent higher than the corresponding day in 2010. That week ending on Saturday 10 December was also a record-breaker, with a new weekly high of nearly 25 million people using the Tube as the festive season got into full swing. Over the previous year over 1.1 billion journeys had been made, more than the total for the entire national rail network. London Underground trains ran nearly 70 million train kilometres, the equivalent of 1,750 laps of the world or 90 trips to the moon and back.

A system under such pressure from record patronage inevitably falls over from time to time under the strain of both overcrowded services and prolonged renewal programmes being pursued relentlessly in the same tight spaces. A huge transformation

58. New trains for the Metropolitan line.
Air-conditioned 'S stock' units at North Harrow,
2011.

is now under way. Upgrading the Underground after years of underinvestment is an enormous and ongoing challenge for everyone involved, probably the biggest in the organization's history. This is requiring a change in people's behaviour as well as major physical alterations to the system. 'It's like trying to run your first marathon while having open heart surgery,' is the colourful analogy that Howard Collins, LU's chief operating officer in 2012, used to describe it. Transforming the Tube while keeping London moving is incredibly complex and difficult. It will require years of sustained work by builders, engineers and operators, but there is no alternative. 'If we don't create 30 per cent more capacity it will eventually gridlock,' is Collins' assessment.

As a fundamental part of London's fabric, the demands made on the Underground and its staff are immense and always growing. Lines have been upgraded to create greater capacity and reliability, with a seventh car adding 17 per cent capacity to Jubilee line trains in 2006. Wembley Park station has been rebuilt and expanded to cope with the large football crowds attending the FA's new stadium. Key interchange stations like Blackfriars, Victoria, and Tottenham Court Road are being rebuilt to reduce congestion and extend step-free access. The £800 million redevelopment of King's Cross/St.Pancras has quadrupled the size of the station, which already sees more passengers than Heathrow Airport.

January 2008 saw the completion of the Heathrow Terminal 5 link on the Piccadilly line – the first extension of the Tube since the opening of the full Jubilee line in 1999.

59. Canary Wharf station, 2009.

Stratford regional station was extensively redeveloped by 2011 ready for the Olympics and in time for the opening of the giant Westfield shopping centre alongside the station. The Victoria line has a new control centre, track and signalling, and a fleet of spacious new walk-through trains. The first fully air-conditioned trains on the Underground are now running on the Metropolitan line. These new units will eventually replace all existing trains on the Met, Circle and District lines. The arrival of Crossrail in 2018, interlinking mainline services with the Underground right across London from west to east, will be the biggest single new development in the next decade.

The journey over 150 years since 1863 offers an insight into the dynamic and complex history of one of the world's great cities. As London grew, so the need for mobility grew. This in turn promoted further growth, which demanded that transport provision keep pace. The Underground is the essence and the enabler of this remarkable city. London was the first city in the world to boast an underground. Now in the twenty-first century it must have one that is world-class if it is to sustain itself.

From just six stations on the original 3¾ mile line, the Underground today, with its 250 miles and 270 stations, is much more than an incredible people mover. It is iconic of London, classless, used by everyone, a worldwide brand, a landlord of civic spaces which are beacons of place and identity. The last word goes to the current Underground MD, Mike Brown:

> The numbers wanting to use the Tube will keep rising and the expectations of our great city will rise too. That simple truth must continue to drive everything we do … The ultimate prize will be a world class Tube that makes the capital a better place to live, work, visit and do business. All the work is designed to ensure Tube passengers can travel more quickly and easily around the city. In short, it's to get the Tube fit for now and the future.[100]

60

60. 'Upgrade Under Way' logo, 2012.

TIMELINE

1863
Metropolitan Railway opens the first passenger-carrying underground railway in the world between Paddington (Bishop's Road) and Farringdon Street (now part of the Circle line).

1868
Metropolitan District Railway opens between South Kensington and Westminster (now part of the District and Circle lines).

1869
East London Railway starts running steam trains through the pioneer Thames Tunnel, built under the river between Rotherhithe and Wapping by Marc Brunel.

1870
Tower Subway opens under the river near the Tower of London, the first Tube tunnel built using a shield.

1880
Metropolitan 'Extension line' running out of London through open countryside reaches Harrow-on-the-Hill.

1884
Eventual completion of the Inner Circle (now part of the Circle line) through linking up the Metropolitan and District lines at both ends. It was then jointly operated by the two original underground companies.

1890
City & South London Railway (C&SLR) opens the world's first deep-level electric Tube railway between Stockwell and King William Street (now mostly part of the Northern line). Access to the station platforms was by hydraulic lift.

1892
Metropolitan Railway extension line reaches Amersham and Aylesbury.

1898
Waterloo & City Railway opens (operated by London Underground since 1994 with standard Tube trains but still separate from the rest of the network).

1900
Central London Railway ('Twopenny Tube') opens between Shepherd's Bush and Bank (now part of the Central line).

1902
Formation of the Underground Electric Railways of London (UERL) Ltd, a holding company known as the Underground Group.

1904
Great Northern & City Railway opens between Finsbury Park and Moorgate (now part of Network Rail).

1905
District, Circle and part of the Metropolitan Railway electrified.

1906
Baker Street & Waterloo Railway opens between Baker Street and Elephant and Castle (now part of the Bakerloo line). Great Northern, Piccadilly & Brompton Railway opens between Hammersmith and Finsbury Park (now part of the Piccadilly line).

1907
Charing Cross, Euston & Hampstead Railway (known as the Hampstead Tube) opens from Charing Cross to Golders Green and Highgate (Archway). Now part of the Northern line.

Albert Stanley (later Lord Ashfield) appointed general manager of the UERL.

1908
Start of coordinated marketing across the separate underground railway companies through distinctive UNDERGROUND

lettering, free pocket maps, posters and signage, all promoted by Frank Pick. First version of the bar and disc on station platform nameboards, later developed into the Underground's famous bar and circle logo (now known as the roundel).

1911
First escalators on the Underground installed at Earl's Court station.

1912–13
UERL takes over two other Tube lines (Central London and C&SLR) and the main bus company (LGOC).

Metropolitan Railway takes over the Great Northern & City Tube and acquires the East London Railway, which it electrifies.

1914–18
First World War.

1915
Women first employed extensively by UERL and Metropolitan Railway in formerly male roles as 'wartime substitutes'.

Metro-land guide and publicity campaign launched by Metropolitan Railway.

1916
Edward Johnston completes design of a unique sans serif letter face commissioned by Frank Pick for Underground signage and publicity.

1917
First Tube extension into London's countryside with projection of Bakerloo line services through to Watford Junction (now London Overground beyond Harrow & Wealdstone).

1924-6
Underground extensions north to Edgware and south to Morden, combined with reconstruction and link to the City & South London completed (all now part of the Northern line).

1925
Metropolitan mainline electrification extended from Harrow to Rickmansworth, with new electric branch line to Watford.

1928
Reconstruction of Piccadilly Circus completed, the Underground's showpiece station in the heart of London.

1929
New Underground headquarters at 55 Broadway, designed by Charles Holden, opens. This was then the tallest building in London.

1932-3
Piccadilly line extensions opened north of Finsbury Park to Cockfosters and west of Hammersmith, including Holden's finest modern station designs in the Underground's new house style (nearly all now listed for protection as heritage buildings).

Metropolitan Railway branch opened from Wembley Park to Stanmore (now part of the Jubilee line).

1933
First printing of Harry Beck's iconic Underground diagram, an instant popular classic.

London Passenger Transport Board (LPTB) created as a single public corporation to run all bus, tram and underground railway services in London, including the privately run UERL and Metropolitan Railway and council-

run tramways. Lord Ashfield becomes chairman and Frank Pick chief executive of London Transport.

1935–40
London Transport's New Works Programme includes new Bakerloo line extension from Baker Street to Stanmore (opened 1939, part of the Jubilee line since 1979) and Northern line extension beyond Archway to link up with and electrify the LNER's surface branch lines at East Finchley (through Tube services opened to High Barnet and Mill Hill East 1940/41, but work suspended because of the war).

1938
Introduction of 1938 stock, the classic London Tube train, a benchmark design by W. S. Graff-Baker, the Underground's chief rolling stock engineer.

1939–45
Second World War. Thousands of Londoners take shelter in Tube stations during wartime bombing.

1946–9
Opening of Central line extensions east and west, started in 1930s but suspended because of war.

1948
London Transport nationalized along with the four mainline railway companies, becoming the London Transport Executive, part of the British Transport Commission.

1952
First unpainted silver aluminium alloy train introduced on the District line.

1957
Electrification of Epping-Ongar branch, which becomes the furthest outpost of the Central line (closed by London Underground 1994).

1961
Electrification of Metropolitan line from Rickmansworth to Amersham and Chesham, ending use of steam and electric locomotives on London Transport passenger trains.

1963
London Transport Executive becomes the London Transport Board, reporting directly to the Minister of Transport.

1968–9
Victoria line opens between Walthamstow Central and Victoria, the first computer-controlled underground railway in the world, with automatic trains and ticket gates.

1970
London Transport transferred to Greater London Council (GLC) control.

1971
Victoria line extension opens to Brixton, the first new Tube built south of the river since the Northern line in 1926.

1977
First airport link for the Tube as Piccadilly line extension opens to Heathrow Central (Terminals 1, 2 and 3). It was later extended to Heathrow T4 (1986) and T5 (2008).

1978
First woman driver on the London Underground, Hannah Dadds, starts work on the District line.

1979
First stage of Jubilee line opens between Charing Cross and Baker Street, where it took over the former Bakerloo line branch to Stanmore.

1980
London Transport Museum opens in the former Covent Garden Flower Market.

1983
Introduction of zonal fares and the Travelcard on the Underground following the legal battles over 'Fares Fair' between the Labour GLC and Conservative government in 1981/2.

1984
Government removes London Transport from GLC control, renaming it London Regional Transport, reporting to the Secretary of State for Transport. The GLC was then abolished completely in 1986.

1985
London Underground Ltd formed as a subsidiary company of LRT but still in public ownership.

1987
Serious escalator fire at King's Cross Underground station kills thirty-one people.

1999
Jubilee line extension (JLE) opens from Green Park to Stratford and original spur to Charing Cross closes.

2000
Transport for London (TfL) established as a new transport authority for the Capital.

2002-3
Public/private partnership (PPP) contracts drawn up for maintenance and upgrading of Underground lines on behalf of London Underground with two private infrastructure companies (infracos), Tube Lines and Metronet.

Oyster card touch ticketing system, smartcards with embedded computer chips, introduced.

2003-4
LU signs PPP contracts with Tube Lines and Metronet.

2005
7/7 coordinated suicide bomb attacks on three Underground trains and a bus kill fifty-two people, London's worst terrorist incident.

2007
London Overground created as part of TfL to manage some suburban rail services.

London Underground carries one billion passengers in a year for the first time.

East London line closes for rebuilding, extension and transfer from LU to London Overground management.

2010
Extended East London line reopens.

2011
Start of Crossrail construction.

2012
Completion of orbital rail links all round London as part of the growing London Overground network.

2013
London Underground 150th anniversary celebrations.

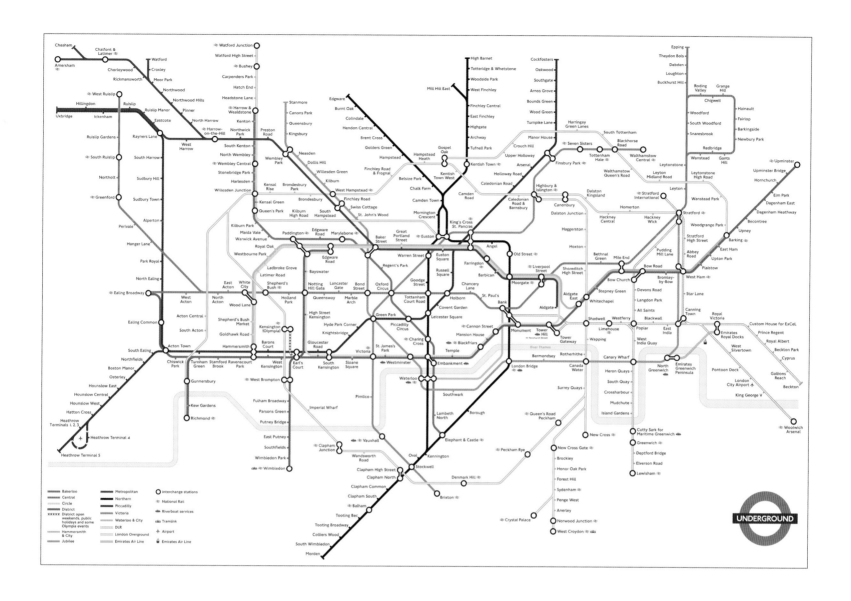

London Underground map, 2012. Includes the
completed London Overground orbital network
and the cable car across the Thames.

NOTES

INTRODUCTION

1. William Hosking to Select Committee on Metropolitan Termini, 1846 [91] XVII, qq. 2585-7, Samuel Laing to Select Committee on Metropolitan Bridges, 1854, [370] XIV, qq. 14-15, both quoted in T. C. Barker and Michael Robbins, *A History of London Transport: Passenger Travel and Development of the Metropolis*, vol. 1: *The Nineteenth Century*, George Allen & Unwin, 1963, p. 65.

2. Tony Travers, quoted in Matthew Engel, 'The Tube is more confident now than at any time in memory. What is going on?', *FT Weekend Magazine*, 14 January 2012.

3. Ibid.

4. The author is very grateful to Ian Pring and Emily Price of TfL for guiding me through the research for this paragraph: Ian Pring, interview with author, September 2011 and in 'Going Underground: How Ethnography Helped the Tube Tunnel to the Heart of Its Brand', *International Journal of Market Research*, vol.49, no. 6 (2007), pp. 693-705.

CHAPTER I
THE VICTORIAN UNDERGROUND

1. 'Opening of the Metropolitan Railway', *Daily News*, 10 January 1863.

2. 'Opening of the Metropolitan Railway', *Morning Post*, 10 January 1863.

3. Christian Wolmar, *The Subterranean Railway: How the London Underground Was Built and How It Changed the City Forever*, Atlantic Books, 2004, p. 16.

4. Quoted by Benjamin Baker, 'The Metropolitan Railways. The Metropolitan and Metropolitan District Railways', paper presented to the Institution of Civil Engineers, 17 February 1885.

5. 'Half yearly meeting of the Metropolitan Railway', *Standard*, 18 August 1858.

6. *Daily News*, 8 February 1860.

7. George Godwin, *Another Blow for Life, 1864*, quoted in Wolmar, *op. cit.*, p. 29.

8. John Hollingshead, *Underground London*, Groombridge & Son, 1862, pp. 205-12.

9. Henry Mayhew, *The Shops and Companies of London and the Trades and Manufactories of Great Britain*, 1865, pp. 142-53.

10. *Daily News*, 23 June 1862.

11. *Morning Chronicle*, 28 March 1861.

12. *Reynold's Newspaper*, 27 September 1863. For reports of similar cases, see: *Standard*, 4 September 1863; *Lloyd's Weekly Newspaper*, 25 October 1863; *Standard*, 8 and 28 January 1864.

13. Hollingshead, *op. cit.*

14. See, for example: 'Police News', *Daily News*, 20 August 1861; and 'The murder of a labourer at King's Cross', *Standard*, 29 May 1862.

15. See, for example: 'Fatal occurrence on the Metropolitan Underground Railway', *Morning Chronicle*, 18 May 1860; and 'Alarming accident at the Metropolitan Railway Works', *Daily News*, 25 May 1861.

16. 'The first trip on the Metropolitan Railway', *Morning Chronicle*, 30 November 1861.

17. 'The Metropolitan Railway', *Daily News*, 1 September 1862.

18. *Illustrated London News*, 13 September 1862.

19. Quoted in Barker and Robbins, *op. cit.*, vol. 1, p. 117.

20. See, for example, *Building News*, 10 October 1862 and 12 December 1862.

21. *Standard*, 4 August 1862, p. 2.

22. 'The Metropolitan Railway', *Daily News*, 12 January 1863.

23. Interviewed by Oliver Green for London Transport Museum, 16 May 1984.

24. The locomotives were advertised at between £500 and £700 each. Among the buyers were the Cambrian Railway and the South Hetton Coal Company (*Railway Press*, 27 October 1905).

25. Mayhew, *op. cit.*; 'New carriages for the Metropolitan Railway', *Morning Post*, 1 October 1863.

26. 'Destruction of London', *Morning Post*, 5 March 1863.

27. Report from the Joint Select Committee on Railway Schemes (Metropolis), 1864, quoted in Barker and Robbins, *op. cit.*, vol. 1, p. 148.

28. David Hodgkins, *The Second Railway King, The Life and Times of Sir Edward Watkin 1819-1901*, Merton Priory Press, 2002.

29. Ibid., p. 353.

30. 'Overcrowding on the Underground Railway', *Morning Post*, 20 October 1884.

31. 'The Overcrowding of Carriages on the Metropolitan Railway', *Pall Mall Gazette*, 21 February 1877.

32. 'Dangers of the Metropolitan Railway', *Globe*, republished in *Cheshire Observer* and *Chester, Birkenhead, Crewe and North Wales Times*, 31 August 1867.

33. A company bye-law of 1884 laid down a maximum fine of forty shillings for both the driver and the fireman of locomotives found to have breached this rule ('Bye-law in operation

from 5th November 1884 respecting the exhausting of Steam unto the Tunnels of this Railway', Metropolitan Railway).

34. 'The atmosphere of the Metropolitan Railway', *Daily News*, 31 October 1867.

35. Quoted in 'The Jubilee of the Metropolitan Railway', *Railway Gazette*, 10 January 1913.

36. *New York Times*, 12 February 1869.

37. *The Times*, 14 June 1879.

38. 'By Rail through Tartarus', *Pall Mall Gazette*, republished in the *New York Times*, 18 March 1883.

39. H. B. Sheridan, 'The Metropolitan Railway and smoking carriages', *Standard*, 17 January 1871.

40. *Newcastle Courant*, 9 June 1882. For similar views, see *Belfast News Letter*, 30 July 1888.

41. *Railway News*, 10 November 1888.

42. William Morris, *Commonweal*, vol. 2, no. 17, 8 May 1886.

43. 'London Locomotion', series of articles published in the *Lady*, 1891. For a similar article aimed at a general readership, see G. E. Mitton and Wilfrid Klickmann, 'Underground London: A Chat about Its Railways', *Windsor Magazine*, vol. 6, 1897.

44. R. D. Blumenthal, *Diary 1887-1914*, Heinemann, 1930.

45. *New York Times*, 25 October 1887.

46. Angus Evan Abbott, *The Spawn of Fortune* (1896), quoted in David Welsh, *Underground Writing*, Liverpool University Press, 2010, pp. 65-6.

47. 'Accident on the Metropolitan Railway', *Daily News*, 28 February 1863; 'Accident on the Underground Railway', *Lloyd's Weekly Newspaper*, 1 March 1863.

48. The story appeared in almost every national and regional UK newspaper. For an overview, see 'The Fatal Accident on the Metropolitan Railway', *Daily News*, 29 December 1866.

49. 'The Dangers of Underground Railway Travelling', *Huddersfield Daily Chronicle*, 30 April 1873.

50. 'Railway Accident at Earl's Court Station', *Illustrated London News*, 29 August 1885.

51. 'Shocking death on the Metropolitan Railway', *Lloyd's Weekly Newspaper*, 18 September 1864.

52. 'Strange shooting affair on the Underground Railway', *Illustrated Police News*, 6 August 1887.

53. 'Outrage on the Metropolitan Railway', *Illustrated Police News*, 4 September 1880.

54. 'Supposed murder on the Metropolitan Railway', *Sheffield and Rotherham Independent*, 20 October 1880.

55. See, for example: 'Dreadful suicide on the Metropolitan District Railway, *Standard*, 7 April 1871; 'Suicide on the Metropolitan Railway', *Daily News*, 18 September 1889; 'Determined suicide on the Metropolitan Railway', *Morning Post*, 28 January 1891.

56. 'Romantic suicide at the Charing-Cross station of the Metropolitan Railway', *Penny Illustrated News*, 15 October 1887.

57. For details see: 'Extraordinary suicide on the Metropolitan Railway', *Daily News*, 24 October 1868; and 'Suicide on the Metropolitan Railway', *Illustrated Police News*, 31 October 1868.

58. Welsh, *op. cit.*, especially chapters 1 and 2.

59. Ibid., p. 48.

60. *The Adventure of the Bruce-Partington Plans* was first published in the *Strand Magazine* in December 1908 with illustrations by Arthur Twidle and in *Collier's* in December, 1908 with illustrations by Frederic Dorr Steele.

61. Comic songs often had references to topical personalities and events, including public transport (see, for example, *Orpheus and Eurydice* (1891) by Edward Rose and Captain Coe, discussed in Welsh, *op. cit.*

62. *Baedeker's London and Its Environs*, 12th edn, 1900, p. 62.

63. Arthur H. Beavan, *Tube, Train, Tram, and Car or Up-to-date Locomotion,* introduction by Llewellyn Pearce, Geo. Routledge & Sons Ltd, 1903, pp. 103-4.

64. Andrew White Tuer, *Old London Street Cries*, Field and Tuer, 1885.

65. See, for example, a short story set on the District Railway entitled 'The More Haste the Worse Speed', c.1895, reproduced in *Mr. Punch's Railway Book*, c.1900. The basic premise was also used for cartoons, and in a syndicated newspaper article 'Spending a holiday on the Underground Railway', August 1889. 'London visited in July', *New York Times*, 29 July 1883.

66. Barker and Robbins, *op. cit.*, vol. 1, pp. 207-8.

67. Alan A Jackson, *London's Metropolitan Railway*, David & Charles, 1986, pp. 128-9: Ladies-only carriages were not reintroduced on the Metropolitan Railway until 1931.

68. See, for example: 'Dreadful outrage on the Underground Railway, *Illustrated Police News*, 28 August 1880; 'Dangers of the Metropolitan Railway', *Penny Illustrated Paper and Illustrated Times*, 1 January 1887; 'Charge of assault on the Underground', *Pall Mall Gazette*, 26 September 1894.

69. For an excellent overview of the transport-led development of suburbia see Jackson, *Semi-detached London: Suburban Development, Life and Transport 1900-39*, Wild Swan Publications, 1973 and 1991.

70. Watkin's principal motivation was the connection of the two largest companies under his control: the Manchester Sheffield & Lincolnshire Railway (MSLR), in the north, and the South Eastern Railway, in the south. His complex, and changing, strategy included deals with rival companies and the takeover of smaller railways (such as the East London Railway) which could provide a through-link. His mainline ambitions later resulted in the Metropolitan entering a joint working relationship with the Great Central Railway (as the MSLR became) in 1906 to provide access over the Metropolitan 'Main Line' to the Great Central's new terminus at Marylebone (see Hodgkins, *op. cit.*)

71. For a detailed description of the Metropolitan's northern expansion and discussion of Watkin's aims see Jackson, *London's Metropolitan Railway*, especially chapter 6.

72. *Yorkshire Herald*, 3 February 1896.

73. Quoted in Barker and Robins, *op. cit.*, vol. 1, p. 102.

74. Board of Trade report into collision on the District Railway, reported in the *Huddersfield Daily Chronicle*, 30 April 1873.

75. 'The Metropolitan Railway Tunnels', *Standard*, 8 October 1897.

CHAPTER 2
DOWN THE TUBE

1. *Pall Mall Gazette*, 6 March 1890.

2. See James Hodge, Richard Trevithick, *Lifelines 6*, Shire Publications, 1973, pp. 24-7.

3. For a detailed but very readable description of Brunel's inspiration for shield tunnelling and the dramatic history of the Thames Tunnel project see Paul Clements, *Marc Isambard Brunel*, Phillimore, 2006.

4. See Charles E. Lee, *The East London Line and the Thames Tunnel: A Brief History*, London Transport, 1976, for an account of its conversion into the first railway tunnel under the Thames.

5. In the twenty-first century the East London line has been rebuilt and extended to reopen as part of the London Overground network in 2010. For the story of this major project see

John Glover, *London's Overground*, Ian Allan, 2012.

6. For a detailed description of the Tower Subway see Barker and Robbins, *op. cit.*, vol. 1, pp. 300–303.

7. Quoted in Richard Trench and Ellis Hillman, *London Under London, A Subterranean Guide*, John Murray, 1993. The Post Office pneumatic tube railway operated until 1880, when it was abandoned. Mail cars from it are preserved in the collections of the Science Museum and Museum of London. In the early twentieth century the Post Office built a new electric tube railway to carry mail under central London between sorting offices and mainline railway stations. London's only 'goods tube' opened in 1927 and was finally closed down by the Royal Mail in 2003.

8. For details of Rammell's pneumatic underground railway projects see Anthony Badsey-Ellis, *London's Lost Tube Schemes*, Capital Transport, 2005.

9. The best account of the railway's development is in Printz p. Holman, *The Amazing Electric Tube*, London Transport Museum, 1990. The publication accompanied a centenary exhibition at the museum, where the only surviving original C&SLR electric locomotive and 'padded cell' passenger car are now on display.

10. See Barker and Robbins, *op. cit.*, vol. 1, pp. 295-6.

11. See T. H. Beare, 'John Hopkinson', Oxford Dictionary of National Biography; and 'A Great Engineer, Mr Edward Hopkinson', obituary, *The Times*, 17 June 1922, p. 12.

12. Holman suggests that Figgis may have mistakenly provided these lofty enclosed spaces to house what he thought would be bulky lift winding equipment. In fact the space required at the upper level for the original Armstrong hydraulic lifts was minimal. See Holman, *op. cit.*, p. 24.

13. Quoted in a long report and description on the front page of the *South London Press*, 8 November 1890.

14. *Railway Times*, 8 November 1890.

15. C. G. Mott to Commons committee on City & South London Railway Bill, House of Lords Record Office, 16 March 1891.

16. 'The Lord of the Dynamos' first appeared in the weekly *Pall Mall Budget*, 6 September 1894. It is now available in John Hammond (ed.), *The Complete Short Stories of H. G. Wells*, Phoenix Press, 1998.

17. The original tunnels under the river from Borough to King William Street carried trains for only ten years. They have been disused since the diverted extension opened as far as Moorgate Street in 1900, although the station tunnel at King William Street was converted into an air raid shelter during the Second World War. The derelict space is still there, hidden below an office block at the north end of London Bridge.

18. The complex business and funding issues surrounding Tube projects are very well explained in non-financial language by Stephen Halliday in *Underground to Everywhere: London's Underground Railway in the Life of the Capital*, Sutton Publishing, 2001.

19. For details of more than forty proposals for new Tube railways in London considered by parliament between the 1880s and 1914, most of which came to nothing, see Badsey-Ellis, *op. cit.*

20. The size of the tunnel is the major factor which determines the cost of building a tube railway. Even the modest increase recommended in 1892 meant that the Central London Railway had to excavate 20 per cent more earth than the City & South London. A full-size mainline-diameter tunnel would have required 133 per cent more earth removal, and consequently more than doubled the construction costs. See ibid., p. 55.

21. For more details of the GN&C see J. Graeme Bruce, *The Big Tube*, London Transport, 1976.

22. Barker and Robbins quote these figures from the evidence of Richard Thomas Kingham to the Commons Committee on the Central London Railway Bill, 30 April 1890.

23. Halliday quotes as his source for this opinion the *Railway News, Finance and Joint Stock Companies Journal*, 30 June 1900.

24. This resulted in three of the stations, Post Office (now St Paul's), Chancery Lane and Notting Hill Gate, having eastbound and westbound platforms at different levels, an oddity that survives today.

25. See Greg Borzo, *The Chicago 'L'*, Arcadia Publishing, 2007.

26. O. S. Nock, *Underground Railways of the World*, A&C Black, 1973.

27. Quoted by Halliday, *op. cit.*

28. Central London Railway Board Minutes, 3 October 1900.

29. See David E. Nye, *Electrifying America*, MIT, 1990, for a fascinating account of the 'social meanings of a new technology'. The impact of electrification was much faster in the US, both in urban transport and other areas.

30. The Kingsway tram subway opened in 1908, was enlarged to take double-deck trams in 1931 and finally closed in 1952, when London's trams were replaced. Most of the tunnel survives intact, and the northern access ramp in Southampton Row is now the only place in central London where tram tracks can still be seen.

31. For a detailed look at the first century of the Subway, see John Wright and Ian Maclean, *Circles under the Clyde: A History of the Glasgow Underground*, Capital Transport, 1997. The system was completely modernized in the late 1970s, and another major refurbishment is now under way. Early Subway cars can be seen in a reconstructed station display in Glasgow's new Riverside Museum, opened in 2011.

32. Royal Commission on London Traffic, 1903-5, London Transport Museum Library.

33. Melmotte is the dishonest central character in Trollope's great novel of business life and speculation in Victorian London, *The Way We Live Now*, published in 1873. After his death, Yerkes' notorious life and career was thinly disguised through the fictional character Frank Algernon Cowperwood in American writer Theodore Dreiser's trilogy of novels *The Financier* (1912), *The Titan* (1914) and *The Stoic* (1947).

34. From Yerkes' entry in the *Dictionary of American Biography*, which also notes that the urban transit empire he had built up in the US was known as the 'Chicago Traction Tangle, a network of construction companies, operating companies and holding companies, of interlocking directorships and friendly contracts, of financial manipulation and political corruption'.

35. For a comprehensive history of the New York subways and their impact on the city see Peter Derrick, *Tunneling to the Future*, New York University Press, 2001. The New York Transit Museum has a cache of superb archive photographs recording the construction of the city's subways in the early 1900s, published as a centenary volume in *The City Beneath Us: Building the New York Subways*, with text by Vivian Heller, W. W. Norton & Company, New York 2004.

36. See Paul Bolger, *The Dockers' Umbrella: A History of the Liverpool Overhead Railway*, Bluecoat Press, 1992. An original 1892 LOR car is on display in the new Museum of Liverpool, opened in 2011.

37. For a brief history of metro development worldwide in the twentieth century, see Paul Garbutt, *World Metro Systems*, Capital Transport, 1997.

38. From a court report in *The Times*, 27 January 1904.

39. *Railway Times*, 28 October 1905.

40. *Westminster Gazette*, 31 December 1905.

41. See chapter 8, 'The Dodgy American', in Wolmar, *op. cit.*, for an entertaining summary of Yerkes' brief but critical impact on the London Underground.

42. Reno's spiral escalator was simply dismantled and left at the bottom of the shaft, only to be rediscovered during renovation work at Holloway Road station some ninety years later. The remains survive in the care of the London Transport Museum and can be seen at the Museum Depot in Acton Town. A short section has recently been reconstructed, but the project was a bit like having an old Meccano set with some missing parts and no instructions. Appropriately enough, the construction toy originally sold as 'Mechanics Made Easy' was rebranded with its snappy new name Meccano in 1907, just as Reno's spiral escalator was abandoned.

43. The well-known story of Bumper Harris, the one-legged man supposedly employed to ride up and down the Earl's Court escalator all day to show that it was safe to use, turns out to be largely untrue. Harris was a clerk of works employed on many Tube tunnelling projects, including the escalator shaft at Earl's Court. He had lost a leg in an accident and was present at the press opening of the first escalator, where he apparently showed how simple it was to use, but then returned to his supervisory job in the tunnels. The press then created an urban myth which was sustained for many decades by London Underground's own press office. The true story was only established a few years ago when members of Harris's family contacted the London Transport Museum.

44. For the detailed story of lifts and escalators on the London Underground, see Ray Orton, *Moving People from Street to Platform: 100 Years Underground*, Elevator World, 2000.

45. For a description of the London Underground's unique early signalling arrangements see Nock, *op. cit.*, chapter 11.

46. For Underground rolling stock development see J. Graeme Bruce, *Steam to Silver*, Capital Transport 1983, and *The London Underground Tube Stock*, Ian Allan, 1988. See also a series of articles from 2007 onwards by Piers Connor published in Underground News, the monthly magazine of the London Underground Railway Society (LURS).

47. A bas-relief memorial to Lord Ashfield, unveiled by Lady Ashfield in 1950, now stands on the ground floor of the London Underground Head Office at 55 Broadway, over St James's Park station.

48. For a description of Chapman's background and working methods see John Franch, *Robber Baron: The Life of Charles Tyson Yerkes*, University of Illinois Press, 2006, pp. 176, 314–16.

49. The original C&SLR power station at Stockwell no longer exists but the former CLR power house at Wood Lane, now a listed building, has been converted into a bus garage in the twenty-first century and stands midway between the giant modern Westfield shopping centre and the new Wood Lane Underground station.

50. 'Very much in control, as general manager he was almost always the sole source of new initiatives and policy changes, treating his senior officers very much as second fiddles.' For a perceptive assessment of Selbie's key influence on the Met between 1908 and his death in 1930, see Jackson, *London's Metropolitan Railway*, p. 194ff.

51. *The Jubilee of the Metropolitan Railway*, a special publication for the Met by the Railway Gazette, 10 January 1913. This is a complete history of the company, giving a suitably rose-tinted account of the first fifty years.

52. See T. C. Barker and Michael Robbins, *A History of London Transport*, vol. 2: *The Twentieth Century to 1970*, George Allen & Unwin, 1975, chapter 1, for statistics and trends.

53. Quoted in Charles E. Lee, *The Bakerloo Line*, London Transport, 1973, p. 11.

54. R. D. Blumenfeld, *RDB's Diary 1887-1914*, Heinemann, 1930, p. 77.

55. For the best account of Golders Green's boom years see Jackson, *Semi-Detached London*, pp. 42–55.

56. H. G. Wells, *Anticipations of the Reaction of Mechanical and Scientific Progress upon Human Life and Thought*, rev. edn 1914, p. 46.

57. UERL Traffic Notice No. 31, 24 January 1908, quoted in *Underground News*, no. 590, February 2011.

58. Nock, *op. cit.*, p. 60.

59. Unreferenced comment made in September 1915 quoted by Desmond Croome and Alan A. Jackson, *Rails Beneath the Clay: A History of London's Tube Railways*, Capital Transport, 2nd edn, 1993, p. 10.

60. Christian Barman, *The Man Who Built London Transport: A Biography of Frank Pick*, David & Charles, 1979.

61. Unreferenced comment by Pick c.1928, quoted by Barman, op. cit., p. 36.

62. The expression was coined by Michael Saler in his book *The Avant-Garde in Inter-war England: Medieval Modernism and the London Underground*, Oxford University Press, 1999.

63. Johnston's book *Writing and Illuminating and Lettering*, first published in 1906, became the benchmark for all future calligraphers and typographers and was immensely influential.

64. Unreferenced quote in Barman, op. cit., p. 43.

65. See Justin Howes, *Johnston's Underground Lettering*, Capital Transport, 2000.

66. Figures quoted Barker and Robbins, *op. cit.*, vol. 2, p. 195.

67. Figures from Jackson, *London's Metropolitan Railway*, p. 229. For a forthright analysis of the vital role played by female transport workers during the war, often underplayed by male historians, see Helen Wojtkczak, Railway Women: Exploitation, Betrayal and Triumph in the Workplace, Hastings Press, 2005.

68. This information is taken from the remarkably detailed reconstruction of the First World War bombing raids on London by Ian Castle in *London 1914-17: The Zeppelin Menace*, and *London 1917-18: The Bomber Blitz*, Osprey Publishing, 2008 and 2010.

69. *Railway Gazette*, 5 October 1917.

70. This was the awful incident at Bethnal Green on 3 March 1943, described on page 163, when 173 people were crushed to death on a stairway to the Tube station.

71. This was the first appearance of the name, apparently thought up by James Garland, a Met copywriter, who was at home with the flu when the word occurred to him. He leaped out of bed with excitement at his inspiration. See Alan Jackson, *London's Metro-land, Capital Transport*, 2006, chapter 3.

72. Information from ibid., p. 233. The Baker Street memorial has recently been cleaned and restored by London Underground after ninety years. It was rededicated with a short service on Remembrance Day, 11 November 2010.

CHAPTER 3
THE UNDERGROUND GOES OVERGROUND

1. For a full description of the reconstructed Piccadilly Circus, see Croome and Jackson, *op. cit.*, pp. 195–7, and David Lawrence, *Bright Underground Spaces: The London Tube Station*

Architecture of Charles Holden, Capital Transport, 2008, pp. 86–9.

2. Steen Eiler Rasmussen, *London: The Unique City*, Jonathan Cape, 1937.

3. See *Krushchev Remembers*, Andre Deutsch, 1971, pp. 52–6, for the Soviet Premier's highly selective reminiscences in later life of the Moscow Metro construction in the 1930s. He does not mention the consultancy report prepared by Frank Pick and three London Underground engineers in 1932.

4. For the best account of London's phenomenal suburban growth between the wars see Jackson, *Semi-Detached London*.

5. Hansard, 1921, quoted by Croome and Jackson, *op. cit.*

6. The 'Big Four' companies that became responsible for most of Britain's railways from 1923 were the Great Western (GWR), London Midland & Scottish (LMS), London & North Eastern (LNER) and Southern Railway (SR). In the London area each of them ran both mainline and suburban passenger services. The SR also took over one underground line, the Waterloo & City, but the UERL and the Metropolitan were excluded from the Grouping.

7. The local lines between Queen's Park and Watford Junction used by Bakerloo Tube trains were electrified during the war by the LNWR for its own suburban services. The Ealing & Shepherds Bush Railway was built by the GWR to carry steam freight services, but was then electrified and connected to the Central line to take Tube trains. Neither began as an Underground project. See Croome and Jackson, *op. cit.*, for details.

8. Lord Ashfield's speech at the AGM of the Underground Group companies, 21 February 1924, quoted by Charles E. Lee in a press article on the Underground's centenary, *The Times*, 24 May 1963.

9. Ashfield confidently predicted that the Underground's extension projects would provide work for 20,000 men for about two years, as reported in *The Times*, 10 March 1922.

10. For an account of the intricate creation of the modern Northern line in the 1920s see Antony Badsey-Ellis, *The Hampstead Tube*, Capital Transport, 2007, pp. 57–85.

11. See Alan A. Jackson, *The Middle Classes 1900-1950*, David St John Thomas, 1991, for an astute analysis of the suburban market and middle-class lifestyle that blossomed in the inter-war years.

12. The UERL recorded every stage of the Edgware extension's progress; the record includes aerial photographs, many of which were used in UERL's advertising. This detailed pictorial record of suburbia in the making is now in the London Transport Museum's archives. Over 200 of the photographs appear in Simon Murphy's book *Northern Line Extensions*, Tempus Publishing, 2005.

13. See David Bownes, 'Selling the Underground Suburbs', in D. Bownes and O. Green (eds.), *London Transport Posters*, Lund Humphries, 2008.

14. For a case study of 'Edgware, the Underground Suburb' see Jackson, *Semi-Detached London*, pp. 205–22.

15. Figures from J. p. Thomas, *Handling London's Underground Traffic*, London Underground, 1928. This remarkable book by the Underground's operating manager had originally been planned as a staff manual. As Frank Pick explains in the foreword, the Underground decided to publish it to show a wider audience what the organization did and why they did it: 'I hope that it may serve as a groundwork for study and thought so that the next twenty years may show as great a measure of progress as the past twenty years.'

16. On relations between the Underground and SR see C. F. Klapper, *Sir Herbert Walker's Southern Railway*, Ian Allan, 1973.

17. Pick followed international design developments with great interest, visiting the seminal Paris 1925 show twice, and later presented a copy of the official exhibition poster by Robert Bonfils to the Victoria and Albert Museum. A substantial part of the V&A's poster collection was acquired through donations by Pick at this time, both of Underground posters and others he had collected.

18. From an internal memo dated 8 August 1925, Frank Pick archive, London Transport Museum Library.

19. See Lawrence, *op. cit.*

20. Harry Peach (1874-1936) set up the Dryad cane and metal furniture company in Leicester. He was another founder and leading light of the DIA. See Pat Kirkham, *Harry Peach*, Design Council, 1986.

21. Unreferenced quote from a letter to Peach c.1925 quoted by Barman, *op. cit.*, p. 118.

22. *Opening of the Morden Extension and Kennington Loop*, London Underground, 1926, p. 20.

23. Eric L. Bird, 'The New London Tube Stations', *Architect's Journal*, 23 February 1927, p. 288.

24. Eitan Karol, *Charles Holden*, Shaun Tyas, 2007, p. 287. Karol's carefully researched account of the Pick–Holden collaboration (pp. 259-383) complements Lawrence's excellent *Bright Underground Spaces*.

25. Saler, *op. cit.*, p. 27.

26. Pick told the House of Commons Select Committee considering the Morden extension proposal in 1923 that the journey from Charing Cross to Tooting Broadway by tram took forty-one minutes. By the new Tube it would be halved to twenty-two minutes. *The Times*, 27 April 1923.

27. This very early silent promotional film, now in the London Transport Museum's archives, was presumably shown in cinemas. Part of it appears in John Betjeman's *Metro-land* film made for the BBC in 1974.

28. Clark, whose assistant status was elevated to company architect in 1921, designed about twenty-five new or rebuilt stations for the Met between 1911 and 1933, as well as houses on Metro-land estates and Chiltern Court, the huge block of mansion flats over Baker Street station which eventually replaced the abandoned hotel project in 1929-30. Lord Aberconway, the Met chairman, always referred to him as 'our clarkitect'. Information from Jackson, *London's Metropolitan Railway*.

29. *Metro-land*, 1915, 1916 and 1920 editions.

30. R. H. Selbie, Railways and Land Development, Modern Transport, 11 June 1921, quoted by Jackson, whose research into the MRCE funding arrangements for Metro-land suggest that it bordered on illegal business practice. Ashfield and Pick often complained that the UERL made no money out of its suburban development, but others did. Selbie's accounting arrangement was never challenged, but neither did any other railway company adopt this financial mechanism, perhaps because they doubted its legality. Most railway companies built some housing as accommodation for their own staff, but only the Met went on to do it for purely commercial reasons.

31. *Metro-land*, 1932 edition, p. 38.

32. Evelyn Waugh was the first writer to refer to it through his fictional character Margot Metro-land, who makes her first appearance in his novel *Decline and Fall*, published in 1928

33. 'Place selling' was an American concept, possibly brought to England by C. T. Yerkes, who had used similar methods to sell real estate in Chicago. See John R. Gold and Stephen V. Ward, *Place Promotion: The Use of Publicity and Marketing to Sell Towns and Regions*, John Wiley & Sons, 1994.

34. Cited by Jackson, *London's Metro-land*, Capital Transport, 2006, p. 123.

35. Figures taken from selected official Metropolitan Railway statistics listed in ibid., Appendix 6.

36. Bolton Wanderers beat West Ham 2-0. The match nearly had to be abandoned before kick-off when the over-capacity crowd spilled on to the pitch. A potentially dangerous situation was skilfully averted in the famous 'white horse incident', a successfully improvised crowd control manoeuvre led by a single mounted policeman, who slowly circled the touch line, easing the fans back until the pitch was clear. Metro-land's copywriter boasted in the 1924 edition that the Met carried 152,000 passengers to the match that day, depositing them 'at the amazing rate of a thousand a minute'. If this is correct, the Met alone brought in thousands more fans than the stadium could accommodate and contributed directly to the chaotic situation. See *Metro-land British Empire Exhibition Number* (1924 edition, reprinted as facsimile by Southbank Publishing with an introduction by Oliver Green 2004).

37. Described and illustrated in *Metro-land BEE Number*.

38. Even the less successful second season at Wembley looks impressive when compared with the ill-fated Millennium Dome exhibition at North Greenwich in 2000, which was served by a brand new station on the Jubilee line extension. Only 6.5 million people visited the Dome in twelve months, just over half the projected target figure.

39. Both the LNER pacifics and the Metro-Vicks were in passenger service until the 1960s. Flying Scotsman is now preserved at the National Railway Museum, York. Two of the Met electrics also survive: no. 5 John Hampden is on display in the London Transport Museum at Covent Garden; no. 12 Sarah Siddons has been restored to working order by London Underground to work occasional specials. For full details of these unusual engines, see K. R. Benest, *Metropolitan Electric Locomotives*, London Underground Railway Society, 1984.

40. Lord Aberconway to Metropolitan Railway Annual Meeting, 20 February 1930.

41. *Metro-land*, 1932 edition, p. 39.

42. 'Design in Relation to London of the Future', DIA Dinner, 1926, in the Pick archive, LTM Library, quoted by Saler, *op. cit.*, p. 109.

43. C. Holden, 'The Aesthetic Aspects of Civil Engineering Design', lecture at the Institute of Civil Engineers, London, 1944, quoted by Karol, *op. cit.*, p. 299.

44. For a contemporary review of Broadway see Walter Bayes, 'Sense and Sensibility: The New Head Offices of the Underground Railway', *Architectural Review*, November 1929, pp. 225–41.

45. For a full account of the controversy over Epstein's sculptures see Richard Cork, *Art Beyond the Gallery in Early 20th Century England*, Yale University Press, 1985.

46. Quoted by Croome and Jackson, *op. cit.*, p. 173.

47. Down Street and York Road were closed in 1932, and Brompton Road in 1934. The distinctive ox-blood street-level façades of all three can still be seen today. For full details and images of all closed stations, see J. E. Connor, *London's Disused Underground Stations*, Capital Transport, 2001.

48. For a comprehensive account of the new works in the 1930s see Mike Horne, *The Piccadilly Tube*, Capital Transport, 2007.

49. Taken from General Manager's Personal Letter no. 18, 30 April 1934. This document is a detailed explanation of the Underground's planning and implementation of the western extensions to the Piccadilly line. Thomas describes the 'drift of business westwards from the City' reported by the Post Office since 1930 and suggests that 'the enormous drawing power of the West End at the present time, both for shopping, business and pleasure purposes, is probably without equal anywhere'. Even so, he was clear that 'several years must elapse before the extension is at all likely to be self-supporting'.

50. Internal Underground memo from F. Pick to Operating Manager J. p. Thomas.

51. *Architects' Journal*, 96, 26 March 1942, p. 233.

52. Beck was not entirely original. Diagrammatic maps had been used before inside some suburban train compartments but these were not complete colour-coded system maps or available to passengers in pocket format. For comparison with other systems see Mark Ovenden, *Transit Maps of the World*, Penguin Books, 2nd edn, 2007, esp. pp. 20–23.

53. It appears that Harold Hutchison, LT's publicity officer, decided to cut Beck out and design his own map. Hutchison was not a graphic designer and he came up with a disastrous spidery design for 1960. It was clearly inferior, but LT did not want to go back to Beck. Instead Paul Garbutt, LT's assistant secretary, who hated the Hutchison design, decided to have a go himself. He did this over the Christmas break in 1962, working at his kitchen table, and offered it to LT on his return. Garbutt was no more a graphic designer than Hutchison, but his map followed Beck's principles and was officially adopted by LT from 1964.

54. The winner was Concorde, certainly a design classic but of use to far fewer people over a much shorter period of time.

55. F. Pick, paper to the Royal Institute of British Architects, 3 March 1930.

56. C. Holden, 'Designing a Passenger Station', in *Design for Today*, August 1933.

57. See Barker and Robbins, *op. cit.*, vol. 2, ch. 10, for a useful but tedious summary of what the authors rightly describe as 'the whole repetitive and apparently hopeless public debate about London's transport in the twenties'.

58. Quoted by B. Donogue and G. W. Jones in *Herbert Morrison, Portrait of a Politician*, Phoenix Press, 2001, p. 121. See pp. 114–88 for an account of Morrison's crucial role in the creation of London Transport.

59. See J. Graeme Bruce and Piers Connor, *Underground Train Overhaul: The Story of Acton Works*, Capital Transport, 1991.

60. A total of 1,121 cars were built by Metropolitan-Cammell and the Birmingham Railway Carriage & Wagon Company to London Transport's specifications.

61. From W. S. Graff-Baker, 'Design in Engineering', Presidential Address to the Locomotive and Carriage Institution, October 1938. See also his talk to London Transport's Third Annual Staff Conference on 'Some Factors in the Life of Rolling Stock', LPTB, November 1938, LTM Library.

62. For a comprehensive look at the evolution of London Underground train design in the twentieth century, see Paul Moss, *Underground Movement*, Capital Transport, 2000. See also Piers Connor, *The 1938 Tube Stock*, Capital Transport, 1989, for a detailed history of this classic Tube train.

63. Former UERL and Metropolitan Railway mileage combined.

64. For comparison London Underground now covers 402 route km (205 miles), making it the second-largest metro system after Shanghai. LU serves 270 stations, also one of the largest totals in the world. Passenger numbers have more than doubled. In 2006/7 one billion passenger journeys in a twelve-month period were recorded for the first time.

65. Vice Chairman's Address to LPTB Second Annual Conference, 1937, LTM Library.

66. These were engines used on the original underground services in central London in the 1860s. Only one, no. 23, was kept operational

and used on engineering trains until 1948. It was eventually restored for the Underground centenary celebrations in 1963 and is now on display in the London Transport Museum.

67. Pick was furious that Holden's small architectural practice could not keep up with the demand for new station designs from the LPTB. Many now had to be carried out by other architects in the Holden style but without his supervision. See Lawrence, *op. cit.*

68. The Ovaltine incident was recalled by Charles Hutton, an architect in Holden's office who worked on Arnos Grove and other new stations in the 1930s, in a letter to Oliver Green, 8 August 1987, LTM files. Sadly Stephen Bone's painted Piccadilly panels have apparently not survived.

69. See Barker and Robbins, *op. cit.*, vol. 2, ch. 16, for details of the LPTB's history from 1933 to 1947.

70. Forty years later, in 1979, this branch of the Bakerloo became part of the new Jubilee line.

71. See Tony Beard, *By Tube Beyond Edgware*, Capital Transport, 2002, for a meticulous study of the Northern line's furthest extension, which was planned in some detail but never built and abandoned completely after the war. On the parts of the New Works Programme which were stopped in 1940 and never resumed see Brian Hardy, *The Northern Line Extensions*, London Underground Railway Society, 2011.

CHAPTER 4
FROM WAR TO AUSTERITY

1. Subsequently renamed Oakwood station in 1947.

2. Barman, *op. cit.*, p. 254. Pick had been working on evacuation plans since at least June 1938 (*LPTB War Diary*, 1941, LTM 2000/86).

3. There have been several accounts of London Transport's role during the war, but the best (despite the occasional error) remains *London Transport Carried On*, written by Charles Graves and first published by the London Passenger Transport Board in 1947.

4. London Transport Notice No. ARP 1, *Instructions for the Working of the Board's Railways during War*, LPTB, September 1938.

5. Croome and Jackson, *op. cit.*, pp. 267–72.

6. See Connor, *London's Disused Underground Stations*, pp. 44–51.

7. For a more detailed discussion of Pick's views at this time and his involvement with the government's Air Raid Precautions (organization) Committee, see Barman, *op. cit.*, pp. 251–60.

8. Letter from Frank Pick to E. L. Burgin, 27 September 1938.

9. Ibid.

10. Barman, *op. cit.*, p. 259.

11. *Pennyfare*, October 1939, p. 2.

12. This widely held expectation was reflected in popular literature, such as *The Poison War* (L. Black, 1933), which depicted the Tube being used as a shelter during future wars (quoted in Welsh, *op. cit.*, p. 236).

13. 'Tube Station: Use as Shelters and Prevention of Flooding by Sewage. 1936–1940' (PRO HO 45/18540), quoted in John Gregg, *The Shelter of the Tubes: Tube Sheltering in Wartime London*, Capital Transport Publishing, 2001, pp. 14–15.

14. *Pennyfare*, November 1939.

15. MO Archive FR A14.

16. MO Archive FR 436.

17. The Home Secretary's plans for new deep-level shelters finally got off the drawing board in January 1941, with authorization for eight new tube-like shelters to be built next at Clapham North, Clapham Common, Clapham South, Stockwell, Goodge Street, Camden Town, Belsize Park and Chancery Lane. The first opened in 1942, with the remainder following two years later. There were plans at the time to use the shelters as the basis for new express Tube lines in the post-war period, but the idea was dropped, and today some of the tunnels are used for archival storage.

18. For background on the Home Office's attempts to control press reporting see J. G. Gardiner, *The Blitz. The British under Attack*, Harper Press, 2010, pp. 88–9.

19. See, for example, the report of the District Inspector (Arnos Grove) into the Bound's Green disaster, 13 October 1940 (LTM archive) and Graves, *op. cit.*, p. 31.

20. Gardiner, *op. cit.*, p. 90.

21. Gregg, *op. cit.*, p. 38.

22. MO Report, 23 September 1940 (MO Archive Air Raids 5/E).

23. Graves, *op. cit.*, pp. 30–31. Other contemporary accounts also refer to 'suburbanites' using the Tube during air raids (e.g. N. Farson, *Bomber's Moon*, Victor Gollancz, 1941, p. 73).

24. Anti-Semitism was especially virulent among a minority of Tube shelterers (MO Archive FR 466)

25. S. Delmer, quoted in p. Ziegler, *London at War, 1939-1945*, Sinclair-Stevenson, 1995, p. 136.

26. MO report (Belsize Park), 23 September 1940 (MO Archive Air Raids 5/E).

27. Farson, *op .cit.*, p. 66.

28. MO Archive Air Raids 5/J. Other titles included: *The Piccadilly Gazette* and the *St James' Lyre*.

29. When a baby in a pram was left in the street during a raid at Old Street, for example, station staff refused to unlock the station gates which had been closed according to procedure. After much deliberation, the distraught mother, who had made it into the shelter, was eventually allowed out though an emergency exit, as the senior booking clerk felt powerless to contravene company rules (report from the Senior Booking Clerk, Old Street, to the Station Master, St James's Park, 20 September 1940, LTM archive).

30. 24 September 1940, National Archives.

31. Graves, *op. cit.*, p. 30.

32. Quoted in Gregg, *op. cit.*, p. 22.

33. 'Use of the Tubes as shelter', National Archives, 28 October 1940.

34. Farson, *op .cit.*, p. 72.

35. Graves, *op. cit.*, p. 50.

36. For more information about this series, see J. Black, *The Face of Courage, Eric Kennington, Portraiture and the Second World War*, Philip Wilson Publishers, 2011.

37. 'Transport in Air Raids. How L.P.T.B. Carried On', *The Times*, 4 April 1945.

38. This figure is based on a Mass Observation survey for November 1940 of the total number of Londoners sheltering on a given night. Taken as a percentage of all Londoners (whether sheltering or not) the figure would drop further to about 2 per cent. However, an earlier MO report estimated that up to 25 per cent of Londoners had experienced Tube sheltering on one or more occasions [MO FR 466, 24/10/1940].

39. *Sunday Dispatch*, 22 September 1940.

40. The *Picture Post* thought that Topolski, in particular, was comparable with Doré, Hogarth and Daumier as a 'portrayer of the London scene'.

41. See, for example, the radio broadcasts of George Orwell (BBC) and the cartoons of David Low (*Evening Standard*) and Joseph Lee (*Evening News*)

42. Disasters were reported in the press, but under government restrictions the exact location, and sometimes the number of casualties, would

be omitted. See, for example, *The Times* report of the Bethnal Green tragedy (5 March 1943), which suppressed the location but not the number of dead.

43. 'Down the Tube', *Evening Standard*, May 1945.

44. See, for example, *The Times*, ibid. and various wartime issues of the LPTB staff magazine *Pennyfare*. Writing for an American paper, the London-born author and journalist Ethel Mannin painted a particularly rosy picture of the harmonious working environment to be found in the Board's workshops with men and women working side by side as equals (reported in *Pennyfare*, October 1941).

45. For an excellent, and revealing, account of the history of female railway workers in Britain see Helen Wojtczak, *Railway Women: Exploitation, Betrayal and Triumph in the Workplace*, Hastings Press, 2005.

46. Graves, *op. cit.*, p. 61.

47. Quoted in Gardiner, *op. cit.*, pp. 186–7.

48. Graves, *op. cit.*, p. 63.

49. Ibid., p. 77.

50. *The Times*, 22 February 1941, p. 2.

51. See B. Lewis and D. Bownes, 'Underground Posters in Wartime', in Bownes and Green, *op. cit.*

52. The Elgin Marbles, for example, were stored in a disused tunnel at Aldwych station. For a comprehensive overview of the 'hidden' use of the Underground during and after the war see A. Emmerson, T. Beard and members of Subterranea Britannica, *London's Secret Tubes: London's Wartime Citadels, Subways and Shelters Uncovered*, Capital Transport, 2007.

53. *The Publicity Office* (since 1939), LT Publicity Department (n.d. c.1946), typed manuscript, LTM archives.

54. London Passenger Transport Board Twelfth Annual Report and Accounts, 1945, p. 37.

55. Ibid., p. 38. The completion of the New Works Programme, in partnership with the Great Western and the London & North Eastern railways, was seen as being especially important in improving London's transport network. This pre-war scheme included extensions to the western and eastern ends of the Central line, and improvements to the Northern line including an extension to Bushey Heath. For a detailed summary of the work completed by 1940 and the aspirations for post-war expansion see: *Improving London's Transport*, a special Railway Gazette publication, 1946.

56. London Passenger Transport Board Fourteenth Annual Report and Accounts, 1947, p.11.

57. Ibid., p. 19.

58. For a full list of the lines transferred to the London Transport Executive see Barker and Robbins, *op. cit.*, p. 341.

59. See Alan A. Jackson, *London's Local Railways*, Capital Transport, 2nd edn, 1999, pp. 314–27.

60. 3,955 million passengers were carried by the Executive's combined road services, compared with 720 million by Underground.

61. The replacement of the tram network was completed in July 1952.

62. Quoted in Welsh, *op. cit.*, p. 265.

63. See, for example: 'Fumes in Underground Trains', *The Times*, 28 April 1951; 'Underground train derailed', *The Times*, 17 May 1951; 'Rush Hour', *Evening Standard*, 17–21 December 1951; 'Underground train breaks down. Second big delay in two days', *The Times*, 20 December 1951.

64. Maurice Gorham, *Londoners*, illustrated by Edward Ardizzone, Percival Marshall, 1951, pp. 12–13.

65. Elliot's career had begun as a journalist on the Evening Standard. His father, R. D. Blumenfeld, was the *Daily Mail* news editor and later managing editor of the *Daily Express*.

66. Elliot had, in fact, been briefing the press on the issue since taking office in 1953 (see, for example, 'Mr John Elliot addresses London suburban newspaper editors', *London Passengers' Association News Letter*, no. 4, January 1954). The briefing became more regular after 1955 (for example, 'Benefits of new Tube line'. *The Times*, 6 December 1955)

67. LT used a small fleet of steam locomotives for engineering and works trains for another ten years. The last of these was decommissioned in June 1971.

68. *The Times*, 20 July 1957.

69. *London Transport in 1955*, LTE (1956), pp. 29–30.

70. *The Times*, 6 February 1959.

71. The protests took place during January and September 1959 on several parts of the Underground network, and were widely reported in the press at the time. Similar protests had occurred in the 1920s and 30s.

72. *The Times*, 7 January 1959 and 29 September 1959.

73. *London Transport in 1959*, LTE (1960), p. 21.

74. *The Times*, 7 January 1959.

75. *Evening News*, 20 August 1962.

76. Ibid.

CHAPTER 5
TRANSPORT IS POLITICS

1. Including a bronze commemorative plaque facing the Marylebone Road at Baker Street, a five-month exhibition of posters from 1908 to 1963 at the Royal Institute Galleries, Piccadilly, the publication of volume 1 of Theo Barker and Michael Robbins' *A History of London Transport*, a steam-hauled enthusiasts' run from Baker Street to Aylesbury, cinema shows featuring LT films at Charing Cross station and a BBC TV documentary – *One Hundred Years Underground* – broadcast in December 1963.

2. Much of the heritage rolling stock on display was to be scrapped shortly afterwards – including the 'John Lyons' Metrovick loco, 'F' and 'T' Standard stock underground cars and some of the Dreadnought coaches. Met No. 1 (formerly L44), the last locomotive built by the Metropolitan at Neasden in 1898 and which hauled the ceremonial opening train on the Uxbridge branch in 1904, played a part in the Neasden cavalcade and was sold to the Quainton Railway Society in 1964. It has been restored by LTM for the Underground's 150th anniversary celebrations in 2013.

3. *Evening Standard*, 24 May 1963.

4. See chapter 1, p. 28. Liberal statesman William Ewart Gladstone was Chancellor of the Exchequer in 1862 and served four times as prime minister.

5. Met No. 1 was built in 1892 as a replacement for 'A Class' 4-4-0T No.1 *Jupiter*, which was broken up after an accident at Baker Street in 1897 at the junction with the Circle line. It was later renumbered as L.44 after the creation of London Transport in 1933.

6. Chairman 1959-65; Valentine had joined London Underground in 1928 as an assistant to the managing director, Frank Pick.

7. R. K.; Hall, Location of Offices Bureau (1972), 'The movement of offices from Central London', *Regional Studies* 6(4), pp. 385-92.

8. A. B. B. Valentine, speech at the Mansion House, May 1963.

9. *The Times Supplement*, on the Centenary of the London Underground, 2 May 1963, p. viii.

10. Valentine, speech at the Mansion House.

11. *The Times Supplement*, 2 May 1963, p. viii.

12. This was her second Tube trip; the first time was on 15 May 1939, aged thirteen, when with her governess Marion Crawford and

sister Princess Margaret she travelled from St James's Park to Tottenham Court Road and back. She sat next to Mrs Simmons, a presumably surprised charwoman from Muswell Hill. The third time was to be in 1977 for the opening of the Heathrow extension of the Piccadilly line, when she travelled in the driver's cab from Hatton Cross to Heathrow Central. The Queen visited Aldgate station 24 February 2010 for the unveiling of a plaque to commemorate the bombing of 7 July 2005, but travelled by car. She was presented with a 'Buckingham Palace' roundel. She has also been known to use the train to King's Lynn when visiting her country home at Sandringham.

13. 'Queen opens new line – then ticket trouble', *The Times*, 8 March 1969.

14. *London Transport Magazine*, April 1969, p. 15.

15. 'This great effort which will mean so much', *London Transport Staff News*, no. 903, 12 March 1969, p. 1.

16. Services had been running on the northern half of the new line since September 1968.

17. LT press information, 26 February 1969.

18. Anthony Sampson, 'Journey into Limbo', *Observer*, 9 March 1969, p. 11.

19. Victoria line, London Underground pamphlet for opening, 1969.

20. From *Notes on the Design of Stations on the Victoria line*, Kenneth Seymour and Misha Black, March 1969, quoted in David Lawrence, *Underground Architecture*, Capital Transport, 1994, p. 168.

21. Press cutting, 8 March 1969; and *The Times*, 8 March 1969, p. 3.

22. Letter by F. E Wilkins, LT Chief Public Relations Officer, 21 March 1969.

23. By number of passengers carried, the busiest lines are the Northern (207 million), Central (199 million) and District (188 million), while the Victoria carries 13,132 passengers per mile, followed by Bakerloo (7,172), Waterloo & City (6,410) and the Northern (5,743).

24. 'The Victoria Line – a special report', *The Times*, 7 March 1969.

25. Leonard Vigars, *Evening News*, 7 March 1969.

26. The report *The Reshaping of British Railways* (or 'Beeching I' report) of 27 March 1963 proposed that of Britain's 18,000 miles (29,000 km) of railway, 6,000 miles (9,700 km) of mostly rural branch and cross-country lines should close. Further, many other rail lines should be kept open for freight only, and many lesser-used stations should close on lines that were to be kept open. Implementation of this radical reshaping of the railways was characterized in the press as the 'Beeching Axe'.

27. Orbital roads for London were first proposed by Sir Charles Bressey and Sir Edwin Lutyens in a Ministry of Transport report, *The Highway Development Survey*, 1937.

28. For this and other abandoned motorway schemes around the capital try the chatty and informative 'Pathetic Motorways' website, http://pathetic.org.uk, and Chris's British Road Directory, www.cbrd.co.uk/histories/ringways.

29. Jacobs had been hugely influential. Her observations about the organic ways in which cities function revolutionized the urban planning profession and discredited many of the accepted planning models that had dominated mid-century planning. Jacobs was also known for her participation in grass-roots activism to block projects that would have destroyed local communities. She was instrumental in the eventual cancellation of the Lower Manhattan Expressway, a monster ten-lane $100 million highway projected across New York in 1962.

30. Michael Bailey, 'Road programme cost estimated at £1,700m', *The Times*, 19 August 1970.

31. Michael Bailey, 'Experts condemn London Ringway scheme', *The Times*, 23 October 1969.

32. Quoted in the excellent online resource *Chris's British Roads Directory*, http://www.cbrd.co.uk/histories/ringways/background/epilogue.shtml: 'Writing from the Treasury on 20 February 1973, a letter to Mr Howard simply ran: "The Minister of State has been following these papers and has commented: 'The Inner Motorway Box will never be implemented. We are no longer living in an environment when any Government can displace thousands of people from their homes. I am sorry that RE and Cabinet should have endorsed another project which is socially and financially out of the question.'"' (This refers to the proposed third London airport at Maplin in Essex on land reclaimed from the sea, abandoned due to its high cost in favour of Stansted in 1974.)

33. Parts of Ringways 3 and 4 were opened in 1975-6 and were eventually combined as the single circular M25.

34. Quoted in *A Socialist Strategy for London* (1973), p. 10

35. http://en.wikipedia.org/wiki/Reg_Goodwin.

36. Chairman LT 1975-8; chairman of the Arts Council of Great Britain, 1977-82.

37. LT press information, 18 August 1971.

38. Croome and Jackson, *op. cit.*, p. 375.

39. David Bayliss, Director of Planning, LT, in his foreword to John Willis, *Extending the Jubilee Line*, London Transport, 1997, p. 5.

40. Georgina Walsh, 'Commuter fury over the Jubilee jam-up', *Evening Standard*, 16 May 1979.

41. Horace Cutler, *The Cutler Files*, Weidenfeld & Nicolson, 1982, pp. 141-3.

42. Report to the Board, PA International Management Consultants Ltd, 1980, paragraph 2.2.3.

43. Cutler, *op. cit.*, pp. 142-3.

44. Ibid., p. 148.

45. Paul E. Garbutt, *London Transport and the Politicians*, Ian Allan, 1985, p. 62.

46. Quoted in ibid., p. 61.

47. Richard Hope, in the *Evening Standard*, quoted in ibid., p. 61.

48. A former civil servant from the Ministry of Public Works (later the PSA), and author of *Your Disobedient Servant*, published in 1978. He had achieved economies of the order of 30 per cent in annual expenditure without reduction of service, simply by eliminating waste. Cutler read Chapman's book, 'a devastating exposure of bureaucratic extravagance', and, up to his eyebrows in dispute with Ralph Bennett over the 1980 LT budget, sent Chapman a telegram: 'Must see you urgently about a matter of great importance.'

49. Sir Peter Masefield with Bill Gunston, *Flight Path*, Airlife Publishing, 2002, p. 300.

50. Obituary, *The Times*, 16 February 2006.

51. 'Masefield, *op. cit.*, p. 299.

52. Ibid.

53. Transcript of Interview with Mr Leslie Chapman broadcast on LBC's *AM* programme on 4 November 1980, signed appendix to confidential minute 2498A.

54. Ian Phillips, LT Finance Director, quoted in Sir Peter Masefield, Obituary, *Independent*, 23 February 2006.

55. Masefield, *op. cit.*, p. 299.

56. Tony Ridley, interview with the author, 5 July 2011, p. 2.

57. I'm grateful to my colleague Simon Murphy and his encyclopedic knowledge of London popular culture for this information

58. *Crime on the Underground*, report of a study by the Department of Transport, HMSO, 1986.

59. For a full account see Sally Holloway, *Moorgate: Anatomy of a Railway Disaster*, David and Charles, 1988.

60. Croome and Jackson, *op. cit.*, pp. 400–401.

61. Willis, *op. cit.*, p. 14.

62. Professor Tony Ridley, interview, 5 July 2011, pp. 4–5.

63. *City Limits*, issue no. 1.

64. Led by a maverick group of Bromley councillors and applauded by the Conservative government. Councillor Dennis Barkway was offered a tour of the Houses of Commons by the environment secretary, Michael Heseltine, while a taxi driver recognized him: 'You're the bloke who done Ken Livingstone, aren't you? Well, all London is cheering for you.' Quoted in Andrew Hosken, *Ken: The Ups and Downs of Ken Livingstone*, 2008, p. 118.

65. 'Fares will Jump GLC warns', *The Times*, 18 December 1981.

66. Quoted in Peter Gerrard Pearse and Nigel Matheson, *Ken Livingstone or the 'End of Civilization as We Know It?'*, Proteus Books, 1982, p. 62.

67. 'Denning's law?', *The Economist*, 14 November 1981.

68. 'Keep Fares Fair', GLC press advertisement, published in the *Evening Standard*, 16 February, illustrated in Pearse and Matheson, *op. cit.*, p. 67.

69. Aileen Ballantyne, 'LT fair warriors ride into battle', *Guardian*, 22 March 1982.

70. Quoted in the *Guardian*, 19 January 2000; www.independent.co.uk/news/business/ten-years-after-big-bang-little-has-change.

71. Decca Aitkenhead, 'London Pride', *Guardian*, 14 November 1998.

72. Launched in 1975, the Carte Orange was valid on mainline rail (SNCF), buses and metro, the first ticket that gave the passenger unlimited use on a zonal basis to all of the Paris region's public transport and during a specific period of time.

73. Quarmby, interview 28 April 2011.

74. Tony Ridley, interview with author, 5 July 2011, p. 12.

75. *Changing Stations*, LUL Architectural Services, 1993.

76. The station's programme is well illustrated in ibid.

77. On 24 January 2000 the Northern line saw the last service train using 1959 stock and the services of a guard after 137 years of the practice.

78. David Quarmby, interview with the author, 28 April 2011.

79. London First's transport mission in 2011: 'London's transport capacity is full. 25 million journeys are made in London every day, 8 million of these on public transport. A safe, comfortable and efficient transport system is essential to support London's growth and maintain London's competitiveness as a global city. With our members, we develop innovative solutions to London's transport problems, helping to make London a better place to live, visit, work and do business. We ensure Transport for London's (TfL) plans reflect business' concerns and are cost effective.'

80. Jeremy Warner, *Independent*, 26 October 1996: www.independent.co.uk/news/business/ten-years-after-big-bang-little-has-changed.

CHAPTER 6
OUT OF DISASTER

1. LT's formal name during central government control from 1984 until 2000 when TfL was created as the transport executive of the mayor and GLA.

2. Wolmar, *op.cit.*, pp. 49–53.

3. Tony Ridley, interview with the author, 5 July 2011, p. 10.

4. This account of the fire is derived from the report of the investigation into the fire led by Desmond Fennell OBE QC. Desmond Fennell, *Investigation into the King's Cross Underground Fire*, HMSO, 1988. I have given page references for specific judgemental statements.

5. The Metropolitan Railway had tried unsuccessfully to ban smoking altogether in the 1870s (see chapter 1). Smoking compartments were introduced on the Metropolitan and the District Railway after favourable public pressure in 1874, while facilities were provided at each end of the Central London Railway's trains from its opening in 1900. From November 1926, smoking on the Underground was extended to four cars in a seven-car train. Many complaints were received from the libertarian pro-smoking lobby, with whom the Secretary of State, Nicholas Ridley was known to sympathise.

6. *London Transport Annual Report*, 1985, p. 17.

7. Smoking on the Underground, see Croome and Jackson, *op. cit.*, pp. 65, 205, 419, 459, 533–4.

8. Letter to John Cope, Operations Director (Railways) from Deputy Chief Officer Kennedy LFB, 23 August 1985, quoted in full in Fennell, *op. cit.*, p. 76.

9. Ibid., p. 61.

10. Paul Grimwood, a fire investigator with the London Fire Brigade, report to the website 'Fire Tactics', quoted in *London Fire Journal*, 13 July 2005. http://londonfirejournal.blogspot.com/2005/07/kings-cross-fire-1987.

11. Tony Ridley, interview with the author, 5 July 2011, p. 19, and letter to author 22 November 2011.

12. *Hansard*, 19 November, 1987, p. 3.

13. Fennell, *op. cit.*, p. 31.

14. Professor Ridley in letter to the author, 22 December 2011.

15. Fennell, *op. cit.*, pp. 31–2 , 183.

16. Ibid., p. 119.

17. Ibid., p. 44.

18. Ibid., p. 127. The equipment had been installed in 1948 after a fire at Paddington, it had originally been intended to use for a short time every night, but because its operation caused excessive corrosion of the machinery, testing was reduced to fortnightly and had then fallen into irregularity.

19. Denis Tunnicliffe, interview with the author, 25 May 2011 (hererafter 'Tunnicliffe 1').

20. Ibid., p. 7.

21. Ibid., p. 9.

22. Denis Tunnicliffe , interview with the author, 14 July 2011 (hereafter 'Tunnicliffe 2'), and Tunnicliffe 1.

23. Sir Wilfrid Newton, interview with author, 12 July 2011. p. 5–6.

24. Tunnicliffe 2, p. 5.

25. Tunnicliffe 1, p. 13.

26. Ibid.

27. Tunnicliffe 1, p.17.

28. Croome and Jackson, *op. cit.*, p. 497.

29. The inner sleeve features a London Underground-style roundel for a railway station called 'Cairo East' on one side, which later reappeared in the video for '(Waiting For) The Ghost Train'.

30. Monopolies and Mergers Commission, *London Underground Ltd. A Report on Passengers and Other Services Supplied by the Company*, HMSO, June 1991.

31. *Heart of the Angel*, a forty-minute documentary made by director/producer Molly Dineen in 1989, before the renovation of the Angel station. The film follows forty-eight hours in the lives of the people who worked in the station. The Royal Television Society gave her film its Documentary Award.

32. London Underground Ltd, *Final Response to the Recommendations of the Monopolies and Mergers Commission Report*, July 1994.

33. http://www.lddc-history.org.uk/transport – a useful official website telling the story of LDDC and Docklands.

34. Quarmby, interview 28 April 2011.

35. Willis, *op. cit.*, p. 38.

36. The line was plagued with reliability and performance issues in its early years, and DLR was transferred from LT to the LDDC in 1992 and back to TfL in 2000. The UK's first light rail network has proved flexible, with its original network extended successively, from 8 miles and 15 stations carrying 17 million journeys a year in two-car trains, to 19 miles and 45 stations carrying 70 million journeys in three-car trains.

37. Network SouthEast was one of three passenger sectors of British Rail created in 1982. NSE principally operated commuter trains in the London area and inter-urban services in densely populated south-east England.

38. Professor Tony Ridley, interview with the author, 5 July 2011, p. 29.

39. Wolmar, *op. cit.*, p. 81.

40. Prof Ridley, quoted in ibid., p. 81.

41. Ibid., p. 83.

42. Tunnicliffe 1, p. 43.

43. Tunnicliffe 2., p. 26.

44. Willis, *op. cit.*, p. 87.

45. Tunnicliffe 1, pp. 45-6.

46. Braking is used to generate electricity and add the resulting by-product power back down the rails.

47. Tunnicliffe 1, p. 45.

48. Tunnicliffe 1, p. 44.

49. Paoletti quotations are all from Kenneth Powell, 'Lights at the End of the Tunnel', *Daily Telegraph*, 9 April 1998.

50. Tunnicliffe 1, pp. 44-5.

51. Tunnicliffe 1, p. 48.

52. Tunnicliffe 1, p. 49.

53. Ove Arup Partnership Ltd, *The Jubilee Line Extension: End of Commission Report by the Secretary of State's Agent*, July 2007.

54. Quoted in Bob Mitchell, *The Jubilee Line Extension from Concept to Completion*, Thomas Telford, 2003, pp. 235-6.

55. Blair's speech on visit to Dome, 13 December 1999. By October 2000 Blair was quoted thus: 'Hindsight is a wonderful thing, and if I had my time again I would have listened to those who said governments shouldn't try to run tourist attractions.'

56. Tunnicliffe 1, p. 50.

57. Quoted in Mitchell, *op. cit.*, p. 364, recommended as a detailed account of the JLE by a senior member of the Underground's JLE team.

58. Listed in ibid., pp. 355-6.

59. Quoted in ibid., p. 358.

60. Tunnicliffe 1, p. 49.

61. Ove Arup Partnership Ltd, *The Jubilee Line Extension*, p. 55.

62. Tunnicliffe 1, p. 50.

63. London Underground, *The Future for London Underground: Evaluation of Options*, September 1997, p. 22.

64. Stephen Glaister, Rosemary Scanlon and Tony Travers, *The Way Out: An Alternative Approach to the Future of the Underground*, London School of Economics, 1999, p. 15.

65. Simon Jenkins, 'Blair's troubles could be good for London', *Evening Standard*, 28 September 2000.

66. Wolmar, *op. cit.*, p. 144.

67. Quoted in ibid., p. 172.

68. Ken Livingstone, quoted by John Kampfner, 'Duel for the Tube', *New Statesman*, 2 April 2001.

69. Quoted in Wolmar, *op. cit.*, p. 179.

70. Tim O'Toole, interview with the author, 20 April 2009 (hereafter O'Toole 2), p. 2.

71. Tim O'Toole, interview with the author, 14 April 2011 (hereafter O'Toole 1), and O'Toole 2.

72. O'Toole 1, p. 3, O'Toole 2, p. 2.

73. Annabel Rivkin, 'From riches to rags: Katherine Jenkins' 60-minute make-under', *Evening Standard* Magazine, 9 December 2011.

74. National Audit Office, 'The Department for Transport: The Failure of Metronet, 05 June 2009', http://www.nao.org.uk/publications/0809/the_failure_of_metronet.aspx.

75. Tony Travers, interview with author, 27 April 2011, p. 23.

76. O'Toole 2, p. 4.

77. Tim O'Toole, 'A Well-Intentioned Mess', *New Statesman*, 17 September 2009.

78. O'Toole 2, p. 5.

79. Those twists and turns as well as the labyrinthine structure of the PPP contracts are well documented in Christian Wolmar's *Down the Tube*, Aurum Press, 2002, originally written before both contracts were wound up but predicting their inherent difficulties.

80. O'Toole, 'A Well-Intentioned Mess'.

81. Mike Brown, quoted in the *Independent*, 1 July 2010.

82. *Evening Standard*, 6 July 2005.

83. All these activities were described by survivors in their evidence to the coroner's inquiry.

84. David Boyce MBE, evidence given to coroner's inquiry, 1 December 2010, 104 (http://www.independent.gov.uk/7julyinquests/).

85. Tom Nairn, driver of Piccadilly line train and Raymond Wright, driver riding in the cab, evidence to coroner's inquiry.

86. O'Toole 1, p. 9.

87. Ibid, p. 9.

88. *The Economist*, 7 July 2005.

89. Lady Justice Hallett to senior manager Andrew Barr at the end of his evidence, quoted from coroner's inquest.

90. Lady Justice Hallett to train operator David Matthews at the end of his evidence, quoted from coroner's inquest.

91. Peter Hendy, MD surface transport 2001-6, TfL Commissioner 2006–present, interview with the author, 6 September 2011.

92. Ibid.

93. Davinia Douglass, née Turrell, the 'lady in the mask' in the iconic image from 7/7.

94. Mr Henning, survivor.

95. On 21 July 2005, four attempted bomb attacks were made in London, three on the Underground (Shepherd's Bush, Warren Street, Oval) and one on a bus at Shoreditch, apparently emulating 7/7. A fifth bomber dumped his device without attempting to set it off. By the end of the month the principal suspects had been arrested together with accomplices. The four bombers were found guilty of conspiracy to murder in July 2007.

96. Hendy, interview 6 September 2011.

97. O'Toole 1, p. 9.

98. Hendy, interview 6 September 2011.

99. 'Overground' is the brand for the network of London orbital rail services specified and procured by TfL. By late 2012, this will provide an orbital service around London, comprising the former East, West, North and South London lines, Gospel Oak to Barking and the Watford DC lines.

100. Mike Brown, Foreword to *London Underground PPP & Performance Report, 2010/11*.

FURTHER READING

This list is by no means exhaustive, but rather a series of pointers for those wishing to investigate further the story of London Underground and its place in the broader history of the Capital.

ARCHIVAL SOURCES

London Transport Museum holds the most comprehensive collection of objects, publications and ephemera documenting the history and development of London's transport, including: posters, photographs, drawings, maps, guides, staff magazines and the Frank Pick collection of personal papers.

The business records of London Underground are held in the Corporate Archives at Transport for London. Other collections with significant material relating to the history of the Underground include: The National Archives, London Metropolitan Archives, The Institution of Civil Engineers and the Parliamentary Archives. Consult the relevant websites to find out more about these collections and how to access them.

LONDON SOCIAL AND ECONOMIC HISTORY

Peter Ackroyd, *London: the Biography*, Vintage, Random House, London, 2001.

Sir John Betjeman, *London's Historic Railway Stations*, Capital Transport, Harrow Weald, 2nd edn, 2002.

Hugh Clout (ed.), *The Times History of London*, Times Books/HarperCollins, London, 4th edn, 2004.

Edwin Course, *London's Railways*, Batsford, London, 1962.

Susan Fainstein, *The City Builders: Property Development in New York and London, 1980-2000*, University of Kansas Press, Kansas, 2001.

Jonathan Glancey, *London: Bread and Circuses*, Verso, London, 2001.

Peter Hall, *Cities in Civilisation: Culture, Innovation and Urban Order*, Weidenfeld & Nicholson, London, 1998.

Richard Trench and Ellis Hillman, *London Under London: A Subterranean Guide*, John Murray, London, new edn, 1985.

Stephen Halliday, *Making the Metropolis: Creators of Victoria's London*, Breedon Books, Derby, 2003.

Keith Hoggart and David R. Green (eds.), *London: A New Metropolitan Geography*, Edward Arnold, London, 1991.

Stephen Inwood, *A History of London*, Macmillan, London, 1998.

Stephen Inwood, *City of Cities: The Birth of Modern London*, Macmillan, London, 2005.

Alan A. Jackson, *Semi-detached London: Suburban Development, Life and Transport 1900-39*, Wild Swan Publications, Didcot, 2nd edn, 1991.

Simon Jenkins, *Landlords to London: The Story of a Capital and Its Growth*, Constable, London, 1975.

Joe Kerr and Andrew Gibson (eds.), *London from Punk to Blair*, Reaktion Books, London 2003.

David Kynaston, *The City of London: A Club No More, 1945-2000*, London, 2001.

Liza Picard, *Victorian London: The Life of a City*, Weidenfeld & Nicolson, London, 2005.

Roy Porter, *London: A Social History*, Hamish Hamilton, London, 1994.

Steen Eiler Rasmussen, *London: The Unique City*, Jonathan Cape, London, 1937.

Cathy Ross, *Twenties London: A City in the Jazz Age*, Museum of London/Philip Wilson, London, 2003.

Cathy Ross and John Clark, *London: The Illustrated History*, Museum of London/Allen Lane, London, 2008.

Andrew Saint (intro), *London Suburbs*, Merrell Holberton/English Heritage, London, 1999.

Alastair Service, *London 1900*, Granada Publishing, St Albans, 1979.

Francis Sheppard, *London: A History*, Book Club Associates/Oxford University Press, Oxford, 1999.

Gavin Weightman and Steve Humphries, *The Making of Modern London*, Ebury Press, London, 2007.

Ben Weinreb and Christopher Hibbert (eds.), *The London Encyclopedia*, Macmillan, London, revised edn, 1995.

Jerry White, *London in the 19th Century*, Jonathan Cape, London, 2007.

Jerry White, *London in the 20th Century*, Penguin Books, London, 2002.

Peter Whitfield, *London: A Life in Maps*, British Library, London, 2006.

Philip Ziegler, *London at War 1939-45*, Pimlico, Random House, London, 2002.

LONDON UNDERGROUND HISTORY AND OPERATION

Anthony Badsey-Ellis, *The Hampstead Tube: A History of the First 100 Years*, Capital Transport, Harrow, 2007.

T. C. Barker and Michael Robbins, *A History of London Transport, vol. 1: The Nineteenth Century*, Allen & Unwin, London, 1963.

T. C. Barker and Michael Robbins, *A History of London Transport, vol. 2: The Twentieth Century to 1970*, Allen & Unwin, London, 1974.

Theo Barker, *Moving Millions: A Pictorial History of London Transport*, London Transport Museum, London, 1990.

Bob Bayman, *Underground Official Handbook*, Capital Transport, Harrow, 6th edn, 2008.

Tony Beard, *By Tube Beyond Edgware*, Capital Transport, Harrow Weald, 2002.

David Bownes, *The Metropolitan Railway*, Tempus Publishing, Stroud, 2004.

J. Graeme Bruce, *The Big Tube: A Short Illustrated History of London's Great Northern & City Railway*, London Transport, London, 1976.

J. Graeme Bruce and Desmond F. Croome, *The Twopenny Tube: The Story of the Central Line*, Capital Transport, Harrow Weald, 1996.

J. E. Connor, *London's Disused Underground Stations*, Capital Transport, Harrow Weald, 2nd edn, 2001.

Desmond F. Croome, *The Circle Line: An Illustrated History*, Capital Transport, Harrow Weald, 2003.

Desmond F. Croome and Alan A. Jackson, *Rails through the Clay: A History of London's Tube Railways*, Capital Transport, Harrow Weald, 1993.

John R. Day and John Reed, *The Story of London's Underground*, Capital Transport, Harrow Weald, 11th edn, 2010.

Dennis Edwards, *London's Underground Suburbs*, Capital Transport, Harrow Weald, 2nd edn, 2003.

Andrew Emmerson, *The Underground Pioneers: Victorian London and Its First Underground Railways*, Capital Transport, Harrow Weald, 2000.

H. G. Follenfant, *Reconstructing London's Underground*, London Transport, London, 1975.

Paul Garbutt, *How The Underground Works*, London Transport, London, 1963.

Paul Garbutt, *London Transport and the Politicians*, Ian Allan, Shepperton, 1985.

Paul Garbutt, *World Metro Systems*, Capital Transport, Harrow Weald, 2nd edn, 1997.

John Glover, *London's Underground*, Ian Allan, London, 11th edn, 2011.

John Glover, *London's Overground*, Ian Allan, London, 2012.

Charles Graves, *London Transport at War*, Oldcastle Books/London Transport Museum, Harpenden, 1989 (facsimile edn of original published as *London Transport Carried On*, London Transport, 1947).

Oliver Green, *The London Underground: An Illustrated History*, Ian Allan, Shepperton, 1987.

Oliver Green and John Reed, *The London Transport Golden Jubilee Book 1933-1983*, The Daily Telegraph, London, 1983.

John Gregg, *The Shelter of the Tubes: Tube Sheltering in Wartime London*, Capital Transport, Harrow Weald, 2001.

Stephen Halliday, *Underground to Everywhere: London's Underground Railway in the Life of the Capital*, Sutton Publishing, Stroud, 2001.

Sir Harold Harding, *Tunnelling History and My Own Involvement*, Golder Associates, Toronto, Canada, 1981.

Brian Hardy, *The Northern Line Extensions*, London Underground Railway Society, London, 2011.

Printz P. Holman, *The Amazing Electric Tube: A History of the City & South London Railway*, London Transport Museum, 1990.

Mike Horne, *The Jubilee Line: An Illustrated History*, Capital Transport, Harrow Weald, 2000.

Mike Horne, *The Bakerloo Line: An Illustrated History*, Capital Transport, Harrow Weald, 2001.

Mike Horne, *The Metropolitan Line: An Illustrated History*, Capital Transport, Harrow Weald, 2003.

Mike Horne, *The Victoria Line An Illustrated History*, Capital Transport, Harrow Weald, 2004.

Mike Horne, *The District Line: An Illustrated History*, Capital Transport, Harrow Weald, 2005.

Mike Horne, *The Piccadilly Tube: A History of the first 100 years*, Capital Transport, Harrow, 2007.

Alan A. Jackson, *London's Metropolitan Railway*, David & Charles, Newton Abbot, 1986.

Alan A. Jackson, *London's Local Railways*, Capital Transport, Harrow Weald, 2nd edn, 1999.

Alan A. Jackson, *London's Metro-land: A Unique British Railway Enterprise*, Capital Transport, Harrow, 2006.

Charles E. Lee, *The East London Line and the Thames Tunnel: A Brief History*, London Transport, London 1976.

Bob Mitchell, *The Jubilee Line Extension from Concept to Completion*, Thomas Telford, London, 2003.

Simon Murphy, *The Northern Line Extension to Edgware*, Tempus Publishing, Stroud, 2004.

O. S. Nock, *Underground Railways of the World*, A&C Black, London, 1973.

Ray Orton, *Moving People from Street to Platform: 100 years Underground*, Elevator World Inc., Mobile, Alabama, 2000.

W. J. Passingham, *Romance of London's Underground*, Sampson Low, London, 1932.

Alan Pearce, Brian Hardy and Colin Stannard, *DLR Official Handbook*, Capital Transport, Harrow, 6th edn, 2006.

Douglas Rose, *A Diagrammatic History of the London Underground*, Capital Transport, Harrow, 8th edn, 2010.

Anna Rotondaro, *Women at Work on London's Transport 1905-1978*, Tempus Publishing, Stroud, 2004.

Sheila Taylor (ed.), *The Moving Metropolis: A History of London's Transport since 1800*, Laurence King, London, 2001.

J. P. Thomas, *Handling London's Underground Traffic*, London Underground, London, 1928.

David Welsh, *London Underground Writing: The London Tube from George Gissing to Virginia Woolf*, Liverpool University Press, Liverpool, 2010.

H. P. White, *A Regional History of the Railways of Great Britain, vol. 3: Greater London*, David & Charles, Newton Abbot, 2nd edn, 1971.

Jon Willis, *Extending the Jubilee Line: The Planning Story*, London Transport, London, revised edn, 1999.

Christian Wolmar, *Down the Tube: The Battle for London's Underground*, Aurum Press, London, 2002.

Christian Wolmar, *The Subterranean Railway: How the London Underground was Built and How It Changed the City Forever*, Atlantic Books, London, 2004.

UNDERGROUND ARCHITECTURE AND DESIGN

Christian Barman, *The Man Who Built London Transport: A Biography of Frank Pick*, David & Charles, Newton Abbot, 1979.

David Bownes and Oliver Green (eds.), *London Transport Posters: A Century of Art and Design*, Lund Humphries/London Transport Museum, London, 2008.

Tamsin Dillon (ed.), *Platform for Art: Art on the Underground*, Black Dog Publishing, London, 2007.

Claire Dobbin, *London Underground Maps: Art, Design and Cartography*, Lund Humphries/London Transport Museum, London, 2012.

Ken Garland, *Mr Beck's Underground Map: A History*, Capital Transport, Harrow Weald, 1994.

Oliver Green, *Underground Art: London Transport Posters 1908 to the Present Day*, Laurence King, London, 2nd edn, 2001.

Oliver Green and Jeremy Rewse-Davies, *Designed for London: 150 Years of Transport Design*, Laurence King, London, 1995.

Justin Howes, *Johnston's Underground Type*, Capital Transport, Harrow Weald, 2000.

David Lawrence, *Underground Architecture*, Capital Transport, Harrow Weald, 1994.

David Lawrence, *A Logo for London*, Capital Transport, Harrow Weald, 2000.

David Lawrence, *Bright Underground Spaces: The London Tube Station Architecture of Charles Holden*, Harrow Weald, 2008.

David Leboff, *The Underground Stations of Leslie Green*, Capital Transport, Harrow Weald, 2002.

David Leboff and Tim Demuth, *No Need to Ask: Early Maps of London's Underground Railways*, Capital Transport, Harrow Weald, 1999.

Mark Ovenden, *Transit Maps of the World*, Penguin Books, London and New York, 2007.

Kenneth Powell, *The Jubilee Line Extension*, Laurence King, London, 2000.

Jonathan Riddell, *Pleasure Trips by Underground*, Capital Transport, Harrow Weald, 1998.

Douglas Rose, *Tiles of the Unexpected Underground: A Study of Six Miles of Geometric Tile Patterns on the London Underground*, Douglas Rose, London, 2007.

Michael Saler, *The Avant-Garde in Interwar England: Medieval Modernism and the London Underground*, Oxford University Press, Oxford, 1999.

UNDERGROUND ROLLING STOCK

K. R. Benest, *Metropolitan Electric Locomotives*, London Underground Railway Society, Hemel Hempstead, 2nd edn 1983.

J. Graeme Bruce, *Steam to Silver: A History of London Transport Surface Rolling Stock*, Capital Transport, Harrow Weald, revised edn, 1983.

J. Graeme Bruce, *The London Underground: Tube Stock*, Ian Allan, Shepperton, 1988.

J. Graeme Bruce and Piers Connor, *Underground Train Overhaul: The Story of Acton Works*, Capital Transport, Harrow Weald, 1991.

Piers Connor *The 1938 Tube Stock*, Capital Transport, Harrow Weald, 1989.

John Day and William Fenton, *The Last Drop: The Steam Age on the Underground 1863-1971*, London Transport, London, 1971.

Brian Hardy, *Underground Train File: Tube Stock 1933-59*, Capital Transport, Harrow Weald, 2001.

Brian Hardy, *London Underground Rolling Stock*, Capital Transport, Harrow Weald, 15th edn, 2002.

Brian Hardy, *Underground Train File: Surface Stock 1933-59*, Capital Transport, Harrow Weald, 2002.

Paul Moss, *Underground Movement*, Capital Transport, Harrow Weald, 2000.

John Scott-Morgan and Kirk Martin, *Red Panniers: Last Steam on the Underground*, Lightmoor Press, Lydney, 2008.

Martin Smith, *Steam on the Underground*, Ian Allan, Shepperton, 1994.

ACKNOWLEDGEMENTS

We would like to thank the many people who have helped and contributed in some way to this book, sometimes without knowing it. We have cited our information sources in the notes wherever possible, but we must also acknowledge the value of conversations and interviews, both on and off the record, with many people who have played a part in the Underground's recent or more distant past.

In an enterprise with the longevity of the Underground, one is always acutely aware of standing on the shoulders of giants. Senior figures from LT/TfL, past and present, have been interviewed and readily shared their experiences of the recent history of the organization, with our thanks especially to Nick Agnew, Ian Arthurton, Andrew Barr, David Bayliss, Mike Brown, Howard Collins, Leon Daniels, Peter Day, Peter Hendy, Barry Le Jeune, Richard Meades, Sir Wilfrid Newton, Tim O'Toole, David Quarmby, Professor Tony Ridley, John Self and Denis (Lord) Tunnicliffe. Professor Stephen Glaister and Tony Travers have generously shared their long-term experience as academics and commentators on London and its transport, while Stephen Joseph opened up the story of the roads protest. All significantly helped the authors to write a new narrative and avoid the bear traps. We are very grateful for the contribution of volunteer research assistants Niall Devitt and Alex Joseph. Special thanks also go to our colleagues Simon Murphy for picture research and additional text and Caroline Warhurst in the LTM library for editing. We have received huge encouragement from the TfL Commissioner, Peter Hendy, the MD Marketing and Communications, Vernon Everitt, and the Chairman of LTM, Sir David Bell, and of course from each other. Any mistakes remain the responsibility of the authors.

Despite the boom in studies of all kinds on modern London, the centrality of transport's role, and the Tube in particular, is still remarkably under-recognized for its vital contribution to urban life. Most histories of London gloss over in a few pages the perennial importance of the Tube to the capital. To quote Frank Pick, explaining his vision in 1935 for the new urban transport authority he had just helped to create; 'London Transport is, or will be, a work of art.' We agree, and would like to dedicate our book to all those who have contributed to the remarkable work of art which is London Underground, by keeping a great city perpetually on the move.

David Bownes, Oliver Green, Sam Mullins

PICTURE CREDITS

While every effort has been made to locate copyright holders, it has not always been possible to establish ownership. Any queries should be addressed to London Transport Museum.

The majority of images reproduced in this book are from the London Transport Museum collection. We would like to thank the following institutions and individuals for providing additional material as follows:

INTRODUCTION
Image 8 (Metropolitan Police), image 12 (Crossrail)

CHAPTER 1
Image 8 (National Portrait Gallery), images 12, 25, 32, 41 (British Library), image 43 (Special Collections, Templeman Library, University of Kent, Canterbury), image 50 (Derek Hayward), image 54 (Mary Evans Picture Library)

CHAPTER 2
Image 31 (The National Archives), image 32 (Strathclyde Partnership for Transport), image 66 (Imperial War Museum, London)

CHAPTER 3
Image 2 (Getty images), images 39 and 62 (Oliver Green)

CHAPTER 4
Images 2, 17 and 24 (Getty images), image 11 (Daily Worker), image 20 (Imperial War Museum, London), image 21 (Estate of Feliks Topolski), image 22 (Lee Miller Archives), image 23 (The Estate of John Buckland-Wright), image 45 (Estate of Abram Games)

CHAPTER 5
Image 29 (Time Out), image 42 (Evening Standard), image 46 (Solo Syndication), images 53 – 57 (Wozzy Dias)

CHAPTER 6
Images 4, 5, 38, 47 (PA images), image 8 (Ian Allan Publishing), image 10 (Royal Mail), image 16 (Paul Stephen), image 17 (Joella Productions), image 18 (Oscar Zarate), image 20 (English Heritage), images 23, 30, 31, 34 (QA Photos), image 33 (Simon Murphy), images 39, 53, 58, 59 (Oliver Green), image 43 (Dillon Bryden), image 44 (Sunil Prasannan), image 45, 56 (Crossrail), image 51 (The Economist)

INDEX

UNDERGROUND

METROPOLITAN DISTRICT RAILWAY.
(FIRST CLASS.)
LONDON ELECTRIC RAILWAY.
CITY & SOUTH LONDON RAILWAY.
CENTRAL LONDON RAILWAY.

1925

LONDON

1925

THE METROPOLITAN RAILWAY COMPANY
FREE PASS

LONDON PASSENGER TRANSPORT BOARD
G. ADKINS
FREE PASS—RAILWAYS
Between BARKING, SHOREDITCH, NEW X, ADDISON RD.
PUTNEY B'DGE, EALING B'WAY (via
And Westminster) PICCADILLY LINE EDGWARE,
HIGHGATE & MORDEN, ELEPHANT & CASTLE
AND WILLESDEN JUNC. WOOD LANE &
UNTIL LIVERPOOL ST. (via Bond St.)
No. B 521 31 DEC 1943
Secretary

CHEA
THREE MONTHS—RATE £

E.C.E. DISTRICT RY. CHILD
Available for day of issue only
CHILD ONE SHILLING DAY
MANSION HOUSE
000 TO 000
EARLS COURT Series 1
WEST BROMPTON (DR) or WEST KENSINGTON
VIA TEMPLE
INCLUDING ENTRANCE TO
EARLS COURT EXHIBITION
1/0 THIRD CLASS 1/0 (See over

PASS
Rt. Hon.
LORD ASHFIELD

METROPOLITAN RAILWAY.
First Class [No. 314] Free Pass
AVAILABLE DURING THE YEAR 1926
Between
ALL STATIONS

UNDERGROUND
London Electric Ry.
Issued subject to the Cos' Bye-laws, Regulations and
advertised conditions.
Available day of issue only
KNIGHTSBRIDGE
(1) TO
MOORGATE (C.&S.L)
VIA KING'S CROSS
FARE 3d.
12914

LONDON TRANSPORT in conjunc
with The LOCAL AUTHORITY
Admit one Person for Shelt
(if available) at
COVENT GARDEN Stati
Persons permitted to use
Station as, or as a means of access to,
Air Raid Shelter do so at their own
in all respects,
FOR FURTHER CONDITIONS SEE BACK

3rd CLASS QUARTERLY SEASON TICKET BETWEEN
27 APR 1955
PINNER
and MOOR PARK
Term Half Rate £1 14 10
15 JUL 55
Mr J. M. LEACH
FOR CONDITIONS SEE BACK
Holder's Name
Pinner

Metropolitan Ry
WORKMAN'S TICKET
Edgware Rd.
2 V 8.5A
KING'S CROSS
Via Portland Road
Third Class 2d
Available only for
return after 12 noon
and for the day of issue
9665

Mr. J. H. B. JENKINS,
London & North Eastern Railway.
This Pass is granted on the following conditions: (1). It is
personal to the holder and is not transferable. (2). The holder is
subject to the same Rules and Regulations as other passengers.
(3). The Company shall not be liable for any loss, injury, damage or
delay, however caused, to the person or property of the holder.
Exd.
General Manager.

LONDON TRANSPORT SOUVEN
OPENING OF THE
EXTENSION OF THE PICCADILL
HEATHROW AI
by Her Majesty
THE QUEE
ON FRIDAY 16 DECEMBER
On the same day, this ticket is a
for unlimited travel by Undergro
except as shown on the rev

THIRD CLASS
METROPOLITAN RAILWAY
HARROW ON THE HILL
&
LIVERPOOL STREET
VIA BAKER STREET

C. & S. L. R. (See Back)
WORKMAN.
Not available after 8 a.m.
EUSTON (Joint)
TO S.I.
CITY R'D or OLD STREET
Fare 1d.
1718

2 JANUARY 1958   SERIAL No. 0052
THE SILVER TRAIN
special round trip between
ACTON TOWN and HOUNSLOW WEST
BOYS or GIRLS FARE 6d.
Issued subject to the bye-laws, regulations and conditions
of the London Transport Executive.

2nd Guaranteed Exc
"THE JOHN MILTON
(C.M.12670) 3rd,
ALDGATE EAST or MO
CHALFONT & L
or CHESHAM &
(S) FOR CONDITIONS

Jubilee line   07082
Commemorative ticket
STRATFORD TO NORTH GREENWICH
To celebrate the opening of the first phase of the
Extended Jubilee line from Stratford to North Greenwich
John A Self
General Manager   A new journey
Not valid for travel

LONDON TRANSPORT 4
16 DE
80p
HEATHROW CENTRAL
00335

7/3   3rd CLAS
SU
FOR CONDITIONS SEE BACK
and
COV
via
UNTIL SATURDA
NOT TRANSFERABLE
Not available unless sig